Narratives of Disenchantment and Secularization

Also Available from Bloomsbury

An Unnatural History of Religions, Leonardo Ambasciano
Beyond Tradition and Modernity, R. J. Werblowsky
Semiotics of Religion, Robert A. Yelle

Narratives of Disenchantment and Secularization

Critiquing Max Weber's Idea of Modernity

Edited by Robert A. Yelle and Lorenz Trein

BLOOMSBURY ACADEMIC
LONDON • NEW YORK • OXFORD • NEW DELHI • SYDNEY

BLOOMSBURY ACADEMIC
Bloomsbury Publishing Plc
50 Bedford Square, London, WC1B 3DP, UK
1385 Broadway, New York, NY 10018, USA
29 Earlsfort Terrace, Dublin 2, Ireland

BLOOMSBURY, BLOOMSBURY ACADEMIC and the Diana logo
are trademarks of Bloomsbury Publishing Plc

First published in Great Britain 2021
This paperback edition published in 2022

Copyright © Robert A. Yelle, Lorenz Trein and contributors, 2021

Robert A. Yelle, Lorenz Trein and contributors have asserted their right under the Copyright,
Designs and Patents Act, 1988, to be identified as Author of this work.

For legal purposes the Acknowledgments on p. viii constitute
an extension of this copyright page.

All rights reserved. No part of this publication may be reproduced or transmitted
in any form or by any means, electronic or mechanical, including photocopying,
recording, or any information storage or retrieval system, without
prior permission in writing from the publishers.

Bloomsbury Publishing Plc does not have any control over, or responsibility for,
any third-party websites referred to or in this book. All internet addresses given
in this book were correct at the time of going to press. The author and publisher
regret any inconvenience caused if addresses have changed or sites have
ceased to exist, but can accept no responsibility for any such changes.

A catalogue record for this book is available from the British Library.

Library of Congress Control Number: 2020940526

ISBN:	HB:	978-1-3501-4564-1
	PB:	978-1-3503-2775-7
	ePDF:	978-1-3501-4565-8
	eBook:	978-1-3501-4566-5

Typeset by Integra Software Services Pvt. Ltd.

To find out more about our authors and books visit www.bloomsbury.com
and sign up for our newsletters

Contents

List of Contributors	vi
Acknowledgments	viii
Introduction *Robert A. Yelle and Lorenz Trein*	1
1 Dialectics of Disenchantment: The Devaluation of the Objective World and the Revaluation of Subjective Religiosity *Hans G. Kippenberg*	9
2 Max Weber and the Rationalization of Magic *Jason Ā. Josephson-Storm*	31
3 Science as a Commodity: Disenchantment and Conspicuous Consumption *Egil Asprem*	51
4 Multiple Times of Disenchantment and Secularization *Lorenz Trein*	71
5 The Disenchanted Enchantments of the Modern Imagination and "Fictionalism" *Michael Saler*	87
6 Narratives of Disenchantment, Narratives of Secularization: Radical Enlightenment and the Rise of the Illiberal Secular *Jonathan Israel*	111
7 "An Age of Miracles": Disenchantment as a Secularized Theological Narrative *Robert A. Yelle*	129
8 Counter-Narratives to Secularization: Merits and Limits of Genealogy Critique *Monika Wohlrab-Sahr*	149
Notes	172
Bibliography	220
Index	250

Contributors

Egil Asprem is Senior Lecturer in the History of Religions at Stockholm University. His research interests focus on the history of esotericism, ritual magic, and natural science in Europe, and on social scientific and behavioral research methods in the study of religion. He is the author of *The Problem of Disenchantment: Scientific Naturalism and Esoteric Discourse, 1900–1939* (2014), which was awarded the 2014 Max-Weber-Preis für Nachwuchsforschung.

Jonathan Israel is emeritus faculty at the Institute for Advanced Study in Princeton, NJ. He was born in London and earned his BA at Cambridge in 1967 and his PhD at Oxford in 1972. His university teaching career was at Hull (1972–3), in Yorkshire, and then at University College London (1974–2000), where he was appointed to the chair in Dutch History and Institutions in 1985. His series of volumes on the Enlightenment, beginning with *Radical Enlightenment* (2001), was completed with the publication of *The Enlightenment That Failed* (2019).

Jason Ā. Josephson-Storm is Professor of Religion and Chair of Science & Technology Studies at Williams College. He received his PhD from Stanford University in 2006 and has held visiting positions at Princeton University, École Française d'Extrême-Orient, Ruhr University, Bochum, and the University of Leipzig. Storm is the author of *The Invention of Religion in Japan* (2012), *The Myth of Disenchantment: Magic, Modernity and the Birth of the Human Sciences* (2017), and *Metamodernism: The Future of Theory after Postmodernism* (forthcoming).

Hans G. Kippenberg is Professor Emeritus of the Theory and History of Religions at the University of Bremen. His research areas are the ancient and modern Mediterranean and European religions, the emergence of Religious Studies as a discipline, religion and violence in the contemporary world, Max Weber's sociology of religion and the legal regulations of UNDHR Article 18, which grant the "freedom of thought, conscience and religion." His books include *Violence as Worship: Religious Wars in the Age of Globalization* (2011) and *Regulierungen* *der Religionsfreiheit: Von der Allgemeinen Erklärung der Menschenrechte zu den Urteilen des Europäischen Gerichtshofs für Menschenrechte* (2019).

Michael Saler is Professor of History at the University of California, Davis. He is the author of *The Avant-Garde in Interwar England* (2000) and *As If: Modern Enchantment and the Literary Prehistory of Virtual Reality* (2012); editor of *The Fin-de-Siècle World* (2015); and coeditor, with Joshua Landy, of *The Re-Enchantment of the World* (2009).

Lorenz Trein is a postdoctoral scholar in the study of religion at Ludwig Maximilian University, Munich. He specializes in modern European history of religions, Muslim subjectivities, the temporal culture of religion in modernity, ideas of secular time, and theories of the historical. His most recent publication is "'Weil das Christentum nie eine Geschichte hat haben wollen': Theologische Voraussetzungen und eschatologische Ambiguität der Säkularisierung in religionswissenschaftlicher Sicht," in: *Theologische Zeitschrift* 76/1 (2020).

Monika Wohlrab-Sahr is Professor of Cultural Sociology at Leipzig University. Presently she is one of the directors (with Christoph Kleine) of the Humanities Centre of Advanced Studies on "Multiple Secularities: Beyond the West, Beyond Modernities" (funded by the German Research Foundation since 2016). Her research focus is on conversion to Islam, Islam in Europe, secularity in East Germany, and Multiple Secularities.

Robert A. Yelle is Professor of Religious Studies at Ludwig Maximilian University, Munich. He was educated at Harvard, Berkeley, and Chicago. A former Guggenheim Fellow, Yelle is the author of several books, including *Explaining Mantras* (2003), *The Language of Disenchantment* (2013), *Semiotics of Religion* (2013), and *Sovereignty and the Sacred* (2019).

Acknowledgments

This volume emerged from a conference held in October 2017 at Ludwig Maximilian University in Munich, as well as from many conversations between the two coeditors over the past several years. We would like to thank all participants in the conference, including those who presented but did not contribute to this volume: Joydeep Bagchee, Gustavo Benavides, Wolfgang Eßbach, and Ernst van den Hemel. Maria Kaldewey, David Demmel, and Elke Dünisch assisted with the organization and advertising of the conference. Funding for the conference was provided by the LMU Munich Interfaculty Program in Religious Studies. Wenzel Braunfels assisted with compiling the bibliographies, checking the references, and copyediting and formatting the manuscript. Lara Löhr helped locate several references. We are grateful to our editors at Bloomsbury, including Camilla Erskine, who commissioned the volume, and Lalle Pursglove, who saw it through to completion. Robert would like to thank additionally his wife, Lynda Sagrestano, for bearing with his weekend work habits, partly acquired from a version of the Protestant Ethic. Lorenz would like to thank Judith, Felix, and Noah for the precious moments.

Introduction

Robert A. Yelle and Lorenz Trein

What does it really mean to be modern? And, are we in fact "disenchanted"? In 1917, the German sociologist Max Weber gave in Munich a lecture that was to become famous as a diagnosis of our age. "Science as a Vocation" (*Wissenschaft als Beruf*) announced the "disenchantment" (*Entzauberung*) and rationalization of the modern world.[1] On the centenary of this event, in October 2017, we convened at Ludwig Maximilian University in Munich a conference to explore the fraught question of the nature of secular modernity. This volume is the fruit of that conference. It addresses not only the idea of disenchantment as understood by Weber and others but also, and more broadly, the manner in which we narrate our relationship to a religious past within competing accounts of modernization. Moving beyond the question of Weber's own ideas and direct influences, this volume sharpens his diagnosis of what modernity represents, particularly vis-à-vis religion. Taking Weber's diagnosis as a point of departure, it is possible to frame competing narratives: for example, of a genealogical connection in which religion persists as the root of the present, or of a "new beginning" marked by rupture with a superstitious past. The chapters in this volume examine such narratives of continuity and discontinuity, and of disenchantment and Enlightenment, in order to evaluate the function that these play in an overall philosophy of history.

In recent decades, Weber's thesis that the world has been disenchanted has come under attack from various directions. Some scholars, including Wouter Hanegraaff, Egil Asprem, and Jason Ā. Josephson-Storm, have provided rich intellectual histories detailing the many ways in which modernity, even in some of its most scientific and critical dimensions, has been nourished by currents of esotericism and in fact remains enchanted.[2] Others, such as Talal Asad and Michael Saler, have argued that the very idea of disenchantment represents a retrospective construction of an enchanted past, one that is possibly no older than Romanticism.[3] Both of these critiques pose significant challenges to still-dominant accounts that trace the origins of modernity to a break with a religious past, as forcefully articulated by Jonathan Israel in *Radical Enlightenment* (2001) and other works.[4]

Our conference converged also with the 500th anniversary of the Reformation, which is often dated to Martin Luther's nailing of his *Ninety-Five Theses* to the door of the church at Wittenberg in October 1517. This was another inspiration for the timing. Weber himself traced the process of disenchantment to the Protestant reformers, who supposedly resuscitated certain theological ideas inherent in biblical monotheism.[5] In so doing, he followed earlier thinkers, such as Friedrich Nietzsche and Georg Jellinek, in tracing a genealogical connection between an ostensibly secular modernity and its Christian past.[6] We wanted to test this thesis and also to apply it to Weber's own work. As various scholars have noted, Weber drew extensively upon the German Protestant theological scholarship of his time,[7] and in so doing could hardly avoid echoing certain of the presuppositions of this scholarship. Although the question of which historical sources may have shaped Weber's understanding of disenchantment remains open,[8] some recent arguments suggest that his sociology of religion repeated themes in Christian theology that were significantly older than such immediate and well-known influences as Rudolph Sohm's thesis that charisma had declined in the early Christian church.[9] Revisiting the influence of Protestantism, not only on Weber but also on historical narratives of modernization and periodization more broadly, therefore seemed especially appropriate in the "Year of Luther" (*Luther-Jahr*). While scrutinizing Weber's claim regarding the influence of the Reformation on modernity, we aimed to revivify the debate over the "legitimacy" of modernity, in which Hans Blumenberg defended the idea that our contemporary age represented something new, rather than a simple continuity with its religious past.[10]

Weber's claim that Western modernity is, in some manner, indebted to its Christian past appears more timely than ever. The recent rise of "post-secular" thinking implies, once again, the dubiousness of the claim that we have broken irreparably with religion.[11] Weber showed already the indeterminacy of such periodizations as "modernity" since despite tracing disenchantment to the Reformation, he also stated that disenchantment has progressed for "thousands of years" in Western culture and can be traced to the monotheistic religion of the Hebrew Bible.[12] It appears that we have a choice regarding the starting point of modernity, a starting point that is determined, presumably, by the nature of the story we wish to tell about our present moment.

To discuss these issues, we brought together a group of distinguished and emerging scholars deliberately selected, not only for their contributions to the literature on disenchantment and secularization but also for their ability to represent a diverse range of perspectives on what these events might have entailed. The participants came from religious studies, history, and sociology, among other disciplines. We invited well-known critics of the idea that a general disenchantment of the world, such as Weber described, had occurred; equally strong proponents of such an event; and experts on Weber's oeuvre and its interpretation. Our confidence that this would produce a robust and fruitful conversation was not disappointed.

The resulting volume is distinguished by a focus on disenchantment and related transformations in religion as key to understanding those aspects of modern society and culture that Weber diagnosed. We do not ignore the task of evaluating his diagnosis of modernity in light of a broader range of evidence drawn from the scholarship on secularization.[13] However, as Hans Kippenberg notes in his chapter in this volume, "secularization" was scarcely a central concept for Weber, who deployed this concept mainly in his accounts of the rationalization of law and its separation from theology—something that he believed happened already in medieval Catholic canon law. Nor did Weber believe in an overall decline of religion, which many have regarded as the hallmark of the secular.

Another novel contribution of the volume is its sustained discussions of temporality, meaning the genealogical sense of time or of historical change that posits a separation and/or continuity between an ostensibly secular modernity and its religious past. The narratives through which such a sense of time is constructed and disseminated often themselves resemble religious myths. We explore the possibilities that disenchantment may be a narrative with either Enlightenment, Romantic, or earlier Christian theological roots, thereby developing a conversation between critical studies in the field of secularism (such as those of Talal Asad and Gil Anidjar) and approaches to historical ideas and conceptual histories of secularization and modernity (such as those of Karl Löwith and Reinhart Koselleck).[14]

Accordingly, we debate the following questions:

1. What did Weber actually mean by the "disenchantment of the world"?
2. Is Weber's formulation of the problem of modernity still relevant; and if so, in what sense?

3. Which alternative accounts of modernization (secularization, disenchantment) have emerged; and how do these relate to, interact, or compete with each other?
4. What mode of relation do we observe between modernity and its past, or between secularism and the religion that preceded it? Is this relation one of rupture, one of continuity, or both?
5. Is disenchantment only a "myth" or narrative, as some have claimed, rather than a historical event? What would the consequences be for our understanding of modernity, and of history, if such proved to be the case?
6. To what extent is genealogy, understood as a scholarly practice that uncovers origins and their transformations, relevant for understanding the place of religion in modernity today? Are such genealogical readings deconstructive, rather than productive?

In *A Secular Age* (2007), Charles Taylor criticized "'subtraction stories'" that characterized secular modernity as a lack or loss of religion, rather than as a new form of religiosity, indeed as a legacy of Christianity.[15] In response, Jonathan Sheehan posed the rhetorical question, "When was disenchantment?" Sheehan implied the fundamentally ahistorical nature of romanticizing narratives of secularization and classified Taylor's account as a mode of Catholic apologetic that "ensures that the (religious) past might always exert its claim over the secular age ... [and] that Christianity is preserved as a history whose presence the present can ignore only at the price of its own inauthenticity."[16] Similarly, in a recent volume on *Narratives of Secularization* (2017), Peter Harrison and his colleagues grappled with the implications of the view that "histories of secularization turn out to be expressions of competing theological and philosophical programmes that seek to use history as a means of advancing various factional cultural-political agendas."[17]

However, the term "narrative" does not necessarily imply falsity. Any historical account must choose its topical focus, starting point, and whether to emphasize continuity or change. Moreover, any such account should be viewed in relation to others, as part of a dialogue among scholars. For example, an emphasis on the continuities between secular modernity and its Christian past may constitute an appropriate response to older accounts that exaggerated the degree to which a secular Enlightenment broke decisively with religion.[18]

Accordingly, the chapters in this volume offer critical attempts both to reread Weber's narrative of disenchantment as a historical process and to develop further his understanding of what the contested relationship between modernity and religion represents.

Hans Kippenberg is an eminent German historian of religion as well as a leading Weber scholar. His chapter revisits, in light of recent scholarship on the question, what Weber meant by disenchantment. Disenchantment did not mean the decline or even disappearance of religion, an aspect of the standard account of secularization that, as pointed out already several decades ago by José Casanova,[19] has been widely rejected. Instead, as Kippenberg shows, for Weber disenchantment implied the transformation of religion into new forms. Although events in the natural order had indeed lost any inherent meaning, through a kind of demystification that accompanied the rise of mechanistic philosophies, this transformation was correlated, through a "dialectics of disenchantment," with the generation of new forms of religious meaning in the subjective world and in communities. In this way, Weber anticipated recent developments such as the rise of individualism and charismatic movements in the form of New Age and esoteric religions.

Jason Ā. Josephson-Storm published an important study called *The Myth of Disenchantment* (2017), in which he argued, against the standard interpretation of the disenchantment thesis, that the belief in magic and spirits remains robust.[20] He showed already that various enlightened scholars, including Weber himself, were aware of the persistence of magic and even actively participated in the esoteric currents of their times. In his contribution to this volume, Josephson-Storm extends his argument to show that given Weber's own proximity to the Stefan George Circle and to Ludwig Klages, inter alia, he could not have meant that magic had vanished in modernity; and that he in fact did not say this. Instead, Weber believed that magic had been rationalized, partly by being separated from science and developed as an independent technique. Focusing on an ongoing process of "disenchanting" as the differentiation of spheres of value in which magic achieves its own independence, Josephson-Storm sketches what such a rationalized magic might look like in terms of Weber's overall account of modernity.

Following up on his celebrated book, *The Problem of Disenchantment* (2014),[21] Egil Asprem argues for the continuing relevance of Weber's "Science as a Vocation" lecture as a critique of the contemporary academy and as an expression of scientific ideals. Weber insisted on the need for scientists to eschew charisma in order to attain these ideals. However, the very rationale for his message was the persistence of charismatic modes of self-presentation on the part of scientists in a world in which their knowledge had been transformed into a prestige commodity, made more prestigious given its increasing lack of accessibility. Drawing on Thorstein Veblen's analysis of "conspicuous consumption" among the "leisure class," Asprem shows how religious scientists deliberately flouted Weber's injunctions and perpetuated the role of science as a vehicle for (re-)enchantment. He proposes, as a model for understanding this economy, the "Mirror Funnel," a circuit of communication and consumption that converts esoteric science into consumer goods for the general public, goods that generate in turn new modes of religiosity that attempt to bridge, rather than reinforce, the gap between science, on the one hand, and magic and religion, on the other.

Narratives of disenchantment and secularization tend to appear at once as historical self-descriptions and as possible modes of theorizing modern religious history. The chapter by Lorenz Trein interrogates this circularity by reading Weber's idea of disenchantment and Karl Löwith's genealogy critique of secularization through a multiple temporalities approach. Building on the work of historian Reinhart Koselleck and on more recent attempts to theorize historical time as multi-layered, Trein suggests that we should historicize the "presence" of the religious past in our genealogical accounts of secularization and a disenchanting world. His chapter offers both a theoretical critique of "genealogical time" and a historical contribution to the ongoing excavation of the temporal implications and theological currents in narratives of secular modernity. Trein thereby invites scholars of religion and neighboring disciplines to engage more thoroughly in a sustained discussion of temporality. Sharpening the temporal implications of the ideas of disenchantment and secularization may also help us to recognize the positions that scholars assign to religion in their historical imaginings of modernity.

Michael Saler is an historian who has contributed significant studies on secularization and disenchantment.[22] Rather than trying to reinterpret what Weber meant in order to bring his thinking more in line with contemporary opinion, Saler highlights the manner in which Weber's claim in "Science as a Vocation" that now "everything is calculable" has been falsified by events. Weber's claim that reason now dominates the imagination is incorrect. Even in Weber's own day, quantum physics and Werner Heisenberg's "uncertainty principle" had falsified this idea. However, it is above all in the domain of the imagination, as reflected in literature and art, that we have witnessed the increasing awareness of and, indeed, deliberate adaptation to what Saler calls "fictionalism," borrowing Hans Vaihinger's provocative phrase. We inhabit a "disenchanted enchantment," in which "the ideal is to balance reason with imagination, to be delighted without being deluded." The limitations of Weber's paradigm may have been exposed; however, the good news is that we are not nearly so tightly confined in the "iron cage" (*stahlhartes Gehäuse*) as he feared.

Jonathan Israel may be the most famous exponent of the thesis that a "radical Enlightenment" made a clean break with the past though its skepticism regarding traditional modes of religion.[23] Reaffirming this thesis in normative as well as historical terms, Israel here points to another limitation of Weber's account of modernization. Weber linked disenchantment with the routinization of charisma as a more or less irrevocable process. However, the persistence of charisma in the political domain represents a danger for which Weber may have prepared us inadequately. Israel contrasts Spinoza, the author of the *Tractatus Theologico-Politicus* (1670) and a staunch critic of traditional religion, with Carl Schmitt, the author of *Political Theology* (1922), who developed further some of Weber's claims of continuity between Christian theology and secular politics and called for a kind of re-enchantment and re-theologization of politics. Identifying different and contradictory forms, including illiberal ones, within secularism, Israel argues strongly for caution when not only narrating but also applying the lessons of the past.

Robert Yelle's chapter builds from his earlier work that showed how Weber's ideas of disenchantment and the routinization of charisma echoed earlier Christian supersessionist narratives, according to which the Gospel revelation witnessed the cessation of miracles and the silencing of the oracles. Each of these tropes was taken up by Protestants early in the Reformation, well before their adaptation by the radical or skeptical Enlightenment. The idea that miracles ceased after the Church was established was normative doctrine in English Protestantism already by 1600. Weber took this idea over from Rudolph Sohm's theory of the decline from charismatic to legal organization in the early Christian church. A major difficulty for our understanding of history, as well as for the contemporary sociology of religion, is that, in principle, such narratives can never be made scientific. The cessation of miracles is every bit as miraculous as the miracle; neither can be reconciled with the canons of secular reason and historical thought. Yet the trope that modernity represents a rupture with enchantment haunts us still, as the figure or trace that connects us to a theological past. Much of what Weber reported as scientific history now appears deeply indebted to such theological polemics. However, other aspects of Weber's account—such as his emphasis on the Protestant origins of disenchantment and on the importance of the Reformers' polemics against ritual—have held up quite well and in fact establish him also as a pioneer of theological genealogies of secularism, if not precisely a post-secular thinker.

In the concluding chapter, sociologist and scholar of religion Monika Wohlrab-Sahr offers a powerful as well as balanced and nuanced defense of a renewed account of secularization as a historical reality against certain arguments that secularization is a narrative. She describes such skeptical approaches as Talal Asad's as "counter-narratives" that abdicate the responsibility to say what, precisely, occurred en route to the modern world. Agreeing with Casanova's argument that secularization entailed not the disappearance of religion but its differentiation from other spheres, Wohlrab-Sahr points out that counter-narratives often depict, as an antipode to such differentiation, an undifferentiated wholeness that existed in some mythical past, whether in precolonial Islam or in the medieval Catholic Church. In this way, these counter-narratives ignore that something like the secular-religious divide has existed in other places and historical eras and is not merely an invention of the modern West.

Collectively, these chapters chart different pathways to modernity and mediate the inherently contested relation between the secular present and its religious past. The variety of approaches represented by this volume certainly reinforces the conclusion that our ability to know the past is conditioned by our competing and multiple perspectives. The contestation of historical narratives may never be finally resolved. Our recognition of this fact requires, at the same time, that we acknowledge the fragility and contingency of our understanding of the present.

At the same time, we need not embrace a complete skepticism regarding our ability to know the past, particularly once we admit that this past itself is not uniform, but multiform, and that our choice to highlight certain events such as disenchantment, or to emphasize continuity over change, is provisional and subject to correction, rather than definitive. The objection that history has been drafted into the service of the present does not appear fatal in this case, given that we seek precisely a better understanding of our current moment. We wish to render more precisely the mode of relation between past and present, not to deny their connection. Finally, the imperative to consider critically the role played by narratives in the construction of modernity, especially as focused on a fresh appraisal, both of what Weber meant and of what he might still mean for us today, turns out to be fruitful. To call something a "narrative" does not mean to dismiss its potency. Haven't Weber's own narratives proved to be generative for more than a century? Moreover, what alternative is there to telling stories about the past?

1

Dialectics of Disenchantment

The Devaluation of the Objective World and the Revaluation of Subjective Religiosity

Hans G. Kippenberg

Introduction: Disenchantment Does not Mean the Disappearance of Religion

Max Weber was interested in the fate of religion precisely in the modern period, but he did not apply the concept of secularization for this. Richard Swedberg did not include "secularization" in the lexicon of Weber's key words, but he did include "disenchantment."[1] For Weber, "secularizing" and "secularization" are concepts from the history of law that had been employed since classical antiquity to denote the transfer of land, institutions, and persons from ecclesiastical to secular law. When we inquire into Weber's understanding of religious history in the modern period, it is "disenchantment" that occupies the central position.[2] As the debate about whether the legal concept of "secularization" is an appropriate key to grasp the decisive transformation of religions in the modern period has intensified in recent decades, an increasing number of studies on the theme of disenchantment, in connection with intellectualization and rationalization, have appeared. The list is impressive.[3] Highly pithy remarks by Weber have favored this thematic concentration. For example, in his celebrated lecture "Science as a Vocation" (*Wissenschaft als Beruf*) in 1917 in Munich, he observed:

This chapter was presented first on the centenary of the publication of Weber's study on Hinduism and Buddhism at a conference held October 8–10, 2016, in London, and was published subsequently as "Dialectics of Disenchantment: Devaluation of the Objective World—Revaluation of Subjective Religiosity," *Max Weber Studies* 17, no. 2 (2017): 254–81. It has been revised for this volume and is reprinted here by permission of the journal.

Translated by Dr. Brian McNeil, Munich.

> The increasing intellectualization and rationalization do *not* indicate an increased and general knowledge of the conditions under which one lives. It means something else, namely, the knowledge or belief that if one but wished one *could* learn it at any time. Hence, it means that principally there are no mysterious incalculable forces that come into play, but rather that one can, in principle, master all things by calculation. This means that the world is disenchanted. One need no longer have recourse to magical means in order to master or implore the spirits, as did the savage, for whom such mysterious powers existed. Technical means and calculations perform the service. That is all that intellectualization means.[4]

The advantage of this way of looking at things is that there is an interaction between social processes, particularly progress in scientific knowledge, and the history of religions, driven by disenchantment. Not every scholar admits this. Hans Joas, in his book *Die Macht des Heiligen: Eine Alternative zur Geschichte der Entzauberung*,[5] argues that Weber's concept of "disenchantment" is so ambiguous that it needs to be translated by three notions indicating three different historical processes at different times: *Entmagisierung, Entsakralisierung, Enttranszendentalisierung* (demagicalization, desacralization, detranscendentalization). For Joas the notion of disenchantment is unable to cover contemporary religious renewal. It indicates the rise of an immanent frame, crucial for modern science and denying any transcendence; the world is transformed into a causal mechanism, devoid of any meaning.[6] Instead he proposes to conceive of sacralization in modern societies in Émile Durkheim's terms, as a process of articulating experiences. Since Joas excludes a renewal of religions in the modern world due to their disenchantment, typically modern religious phenomena such as fundamentalism, evangelicalism, New Age movements, and esotericism are mentioned only in passing.[7] However, as I will show, the concept of disenchantment indicates a liberation of religion from the shackles of magic and establishes, in the long run, a religion independent from natural constraints.[8] Disenchantment generates a specific form of religion and does not cancel religion altogether. In his chapter "Religious Communities," Weber maps an independent history of religion, which is shaped by various forces: by persons gifted with extraordinary powers (called "charisma") such as magicians, priests, prophets, mystagogues, and intellectuals who teach a cult, an ethics, mysticism, or asceticism as different means of salvation, in a variety of forms, in agreement with different social classes and political situations. Disenchantment is part of this history.

We have learned from José Casanova and Jürgen Habermas that the removal of religion from the official public sphere that we commonly identify with secularization does not entail a disappearance of religion in public altogether.[9] When religious believers experience a world governed by autonomous laws that are inimical to their religious values, these values can be articulated as an oppositional force in the public realm of their society. In this process the view of the world changes as the meaning of religion does. Likewise, the notion of a disenchantment of the world generates a different view of the world and has an impact on religions as well.[10] This dialectic of disenchantment was crucial for Max Weber when he turned to comparative religious studies. Hence my chapter addresses:

1. the inherent connection between the section on religion in Max Weber's *Economy and Society* (titled "Religious Communities" or "Sociology of Religion") and his studies of *The Economic Ethic of the World Religions*;
2. Weber's concept of the consequences of disenchantment and its ensuing processes in his "Religious Communities" and other contemporary texts;
3. dialectics of disenchantment of religion in recent approaches to history, nature, and society.

The Link between the Section on Religion in Max Weber's *Economy and Society* and His Studies of *The Economic Ethic of the World Religions*

Economy and Society has a prehistory that surfaced with the critical edition of Max Weber's works.[11] In her preface to the second part of the work, published in 1921–22, Marianne Weber pointed out that, with the exception of some later additions, the manuscripts originated in the years 1911–13.[12] The reconstruction of the composition of *Economy and Society* confirms that date for the section on religion. The studies cited by Weber in this text include no publications after 1913.[13]

A closer look at the genesis of the section reveals that Weber's first outline of the *Handbook* in 1910—the work that was finally published posthumously as *Economy and Society* after Weber's death in 1920—lacked a separate treatment of religion; at this point, Weber merely planned a section "Economy and Culture (Critique of Historical Materialism)."[14] This was to change in the years to come. A clear indication of this appears in a letter dated July 3, 1913, in which Weber thanks his longtime friend Heinrich Rickert for an off-print and adds that he would soon return the favor by sending him the manuscript of "*my* systematic of religion." In late November of the same year, Weber repeated this, telling Rickert that he would like to send his "(*empirical*) casuistry of contemplation and active religion," but adding that the manuscript was only three-quarters typed. Then, on December 30, 1913, Weber informed his publisher Paul Siebeck that he had finished an exposition relating all major forms of community to economy: the family, the domestic community, the commercial enterprise, the clan, the ethnic community, and religion. In brackets, Weber explained what could be expected from the segment on religion: "comprising all great religions of the earth: a sociology of the doctrines of salvation and of the various religious ethics—similar to Troeltsch, however now for all religions, only much more concise." In an outline of the content of the entire series that appeared in 1914,[15] Weber projected as a contribution of his own the part "The Economy and the Social Orders and Powers," consisting of sections on communities. After "Household, Oikos, Enterprise" came "Neighbourhood, Kinship Group, Local Community," then "Ethnic Communities," and finally "Religious Communities." Weber clarified the last item with the further title "The Class Basis of the Religions; Cultural Religions and Economic Orientation."[16] Weber's topics and sequence in this announcement correspond roughly to the manuscript he described to Siebeck in December 1913 and to the text published in 1921–22.

The changes, evident in Weber's 1914 outline when compared with that of 1910, reflected his growing interest in the history of world religions. According to Weber, his thesis about the Puritan origins of a methodical pattern of life conduct, enabling the development of Western capitalism, had withstood all objections in the heated scholarly debate that followed the publication of *The Protestant Ethic and the "Spirit" of Capitalism* (1904–05).[17] Now he wanted "to correct the isolation of this study and to place it in relation to the whole of cultural development," he explained in the second edition of his essay in 1920/21.[18] In her biography, Marianne Weber gives some valuable particulars about this shift in her husband's thought and work.

> When around 1911 he resumed his studies on the sociology of religion, he was attracted to the Orient—to China, Japan, and India, then to Judaism and Islam. He now wanted to investigate the relationship of the five great world religions to economic ethics. His study was to come full circle with an analysis of early Christianity.[19]

The segment "Religious Communities" was an outcome of this scholarly work. When composing it in 1913, Weber drew (as his direct and indirect quotations reveal) on a profound study of comparative religion, Buddhism, Christianity, Hinduism, Islam, Judaism, Confucianism, Taoism, Zoroastrianism, tribal, ancient, and Hellenic religions.[20]

Although Weber published his studies of *The Economic Ethic of the World Religions* separately in 1915 and 1916, he did not see them as standing alone; he conceived of them, rather, as "preliminary studies and annotations to the *systematic* sociology of religions."[21] When the first of these studies appeared in 1915 (*The Religion of China*), Weber pointed out in a footnote to his introduction to both articles that he had written them and read them aloud to friends two years earlier, that is, in 1913.[22] And he added in the same footnote that "they were designed to be published simultaneously with" his treatise "Economy and Society," his contribution to the manual *Outline of Social Economics* (*Grundriss der Sozialökonomik*), and were intended to "interpret and complement the section on the sociology of religion (and, however, to be interpreted by it in many points)."[23]

Likewise, in 1919, when Weber reviewed the text of *The Protestant Ethic and the "Spirit" of Capitalism* for inclusion, along with the studies that constituted *The Economic Ethic of the World Religions*, in his *Gesammelte Aufsätze zur Religionssoziologie* (Collected Papers on the Sociology of Religions), he added that he hoped to treat ethnographic material when systematically revising "the sociology of religion."[24] Even at this late date, Weber viewed this section (now in its projected revised form) as a bridge between *The Protestant Ethic* and his subsequent historical studies of the ethics of the world religions, emphasizing again that systematic issues were crucial for its function.

The concepts and sources Weber relied on were derived from German scholars of religious history. Weber adopted a German Orientalist perspective that differed from the "Orientalism" famously described by Edward Said.[25] It was not tied to politics of colonialism but grappled with religious meanings and their subjective appropriation.[26] An early public forum for the German Orientalists was a series edited by Paul Hinneberg under the title *Die Kultur der Gegenwart* (Contemporary Culture). In 1906, two important volumes were issued, one on so-called Oriental religions, another on Christianity as well as Israel and Judaism. Some of the most eminent scholars who established the historical-critical method in their fields contributed to these volumes and became key sources for Weber's "Religious Communities": Julius Wellhausen on Israel and Judaism, Ignaz Goldziher on Islam, and Hermann Oldenberg on Hinduism and Buddhism.

According to Hermann Oldenberg (1854–1920) and his *Indian Religion* (1906),[27] the gods in early India were personified powers of nature. This primordial view ceased, however, when the necessities of social life required gods who would protect law and morals. Moreover, these gods were approachable not only by sacrifice and prayer but also by magic—a force that was expected to intervene directly in the course of events. From cosmological speculation about the efficacy of both sacrifice and magic there then arose the notion of Brahman, understood as the unchanging essence of the universe, an essence that is also present in the individual (as Atman). Combined with the belief that the transmigration of the soul is dependent upon its karma, these notions formed the matrix on which Jainism and Buddhism emerged as religions of world rejection. Oldenberg's contribution to Hinneberg's manual retrieved from the Indian sources worldviews and ethics that were constitutive of human subjects and their social practices.

Similar considerations informed philosophers. Hermann Siebeck, in a textbook published in 1893, divided historical religions into three categories: natural religions, which considered gods as rescuers from external evil; moral religions, which viewed gods as guarantors of social norms and upheld a positive attitude toward the world; and salvation religions, which postulated a contradiction between the existence of God and the reality of evil in the world, and fostered an attitude of rejecting the world.[28] Siebeck's entire concept depended on an understanding of religion in terms of "world-denial" (*Weltverneinung*).

Another important document for the German branch of comparative religious studies was an encyclopedia edited by the Protestant theologians Friedrich Michael Schiele and Leopold Zscharnack: *Religion in Geschichte und Gegenwart* (*RGG*). From its first edition (1909–13) onward, this encyclopedia regarded it as its task to look at popular religious notions independently of their theological or philosophical interpretation and to trace the worldview on which they were based. Religious phenomena must be more than purely external. One of the main entries in the dictionary explains this. In the entry "Erscheinungswelt der Religion" (Phenomenology of Religion), Edvard Lehmann wrote in 1910:

> Phenomenology should study religion as this emerges into the world of phenomena and can be observed as an empirical and historical reality.... These external phenomena presuppose an internal life.... In general, it can be said that the external emerges especially on the lower levels, and the internal on the higher levels.[29]

An alleged "inner life" turned historical religious facts into circulating intellectual goods. This approach established a new category of entries. Current religious notions derived from popular communication and not specifically from theology became part of it. Entries conceived of the future not in secular terms of progress but in terms of meaning for the believer: "millenarianism," "eschatology," and "apocalyptic"; entries related to nature showed the same kind of approach: "magic," "mysticism," and "contemplation" articulated noninstrumental relations to nature; those related to society were "sect," "acosmism of love," and "brotherliness." If one compares the notions of the first edition of the encyclopedia (1909–13) with the second (1927–32), the third (1957–65), and the fourth editions (1998–2002), one notices that some of these concepts were replaced by others more popular at their time. "Fundamentalism" and "cult" took the place of "sect"; "esotericism" and "New Age" took the place of "new mysticism."[30] The hermeneutics elaborated by Wilhelm Dilthey and Rudolf Otto had made an important contribution to the autonomous status of popular concepts as independent points of orientation or contents of consciousness. The validity of these notions was dependent on their ability to articulate the subjective experience of the laity, and they could be replaced in later times by other equally popular, roughly equivalent concepts.

Weber's Concept of a Dialectics of Disenchantment

The notion of "disenchantment" emerged in Weber's writing for the first time in 1913, in an essay in which he explained the fundamentals of his theory of action: "Some Categories of Interpretive Sociology."[31] Here Weber introduced a crucial distinction. An action may be called instrumentally correct when relating to external natural laws, but it may also be called rational when it is based on an intelligible subjective meaning that consistently informs the practical attitudes of actors to the world. Even an action oriented toward magical conceptions may be called rational in this sense. Weber sketches a process turning the rational attitude into an irrational one: "In a world increasingly divested of magic [*mit zunehmender Entzauberung der Welt*], religiosity must take on increasingly (subjective) irrational meaning relationships (ethical or mystical, for instance)."[32] Weber introduces the notion of disenchantment of the world as a *process* that is open-ended, not as an irreversible development. Two types of subjective religiosity emerge (ethics of commitment [*Gesinnungsethik*] and mysticism), and these are independent of any instrumental relations to nature, history, and society.

In the chapter "Religious Communities" in *Economy and Society*, Weber sketches the typology of the bearers of charisma who answer the expectation of salvation. Weber constructed the whole section ("Religious Communities") around the *process* of disenchantment. Symmetrical constructions at the beginning and at the end of his sketch elucidate it. In the beginning, "only the things or events that actually exist or take place played a role in life." This changed with the rise of the magician. "Now certain experiences of a different order, in that they only signify something, also play a role. Thus magic is transformed from a direct manipulation of forces into a *symbolic activity*."[33] Weber maps a history of religion, liberated from natural constraints and shaped by various forces: by charismatics as magicians, priests, prophets, intellectuals—teaching cult, ethics, mysticism, and asceticism as means of salvation, in a variety of communities in agreement with different social classes and political situations. The charisma of the magician is represented by ecstasy. "For the laymen, this psychological state is accessible only in occasional actions…. [It] occurs in a social form, the orgy, which is the primordial form of religious association [*Vergemeinschaftung*]."[34]

In Weber's understanding, this occasional form of association was usually replaced by more regular forms, urged on by political necessities. In this context, he points to the interdependence of community and society: "There is no concerted communal action [*Gemeinschaftshandeln*], as there is no individual action, without its special god. Indeed, if a social association [*Vergesellschaftung*] is to be permanently guaranteed, it must have such a god."[35] By this route, the gods of religious communities became "guardians of the legal order," a transformation accompanied by the emergence of priests and stable cults that, together, ensured the permanence of a social association. At the same time adherents, in their practical lives, began conceiving of the entire world as an "enduringly and meaningfully ordered cosmos" (*dauernd sinnvoll geordneter Kosmos*).[36] Historically, acceptance of this postulate of a meaningful world stimulated the spread of legal orders and ethical requirements[37] while simultaneously eliciting an awareness of the rift between this expectation and the inevitable experience of a reality devoid of meaning. In this circumstance, according to Weber, prophets arose to furnish explanations for this experience and to address the increasing ethical demands that the gods seemed unable to answer. To differentiate types of prophecy, Weber drew from contemporary religious scholarship the distinction between a strict, transcendent God who demands loyalty and obedience to His commandments and a divine being that is immanent in man and can be approached by contemplation.[38] In his essay on categories of interpretive sociology, he described them as two different kinds of subjective relation to the world: either ethical or mystical.[39] While the former conception dominated Near Eastern religions and was at the origin of Western patterns of rational life-conduct, the latter conception prevailed in India and China.[40] The two prophetic types correspond, respectively, to Weber's "ethical" and "exemplary" forms of prophecy. Finally, turning to intellectuals, Weber presented this group as driven by "metaphysical needs," by the urge to reflect on ethical and religious questions and to "understand the world as a meaningful cosmos and to take up a position toward it."[41] Driven by such needs, intellectuals played a crucial part in suppressing beliefs in magic and promoting the process of world disenchantment. Weber is reconstructing a process that is responsible for the rise of a rational disenchanted vision of the world: the notion of a meaningful world order, an experience of a world devoid of meaning, various kinds of subjective religiosity coping with that experience, and, finally, communal activity assuring salvation.[42] In his introduction to the first of the essays on *The Economic Ethic of the World Religions*, which was composed in 1913 and published in 1915, Weber recapitulates his conception of the history of worldviews:

> The unity of the primitive image of the world, in which everything was concrete magic, has tended to split into rational cognition and mastery of nature, on the one hand, and into "mystic" experiences on the other. The inexpressible contents of such experiences remain the only possible "beyond," added to the mechanism of a world robbed of gods.[43]

The shift of religion into the realm of the irrational corresponds to a rational conception of the external world.[44] Only the religious ascetic virtuosos succeeded in blocking the path to salvation by a "flight from the world." The path to salvation is turned from a contemplative "flight from the world" toward an active ascetic "work in this world."[45] This is not a thesis of a necessary evolution but a narrative abbreviation for a complex process, viewed retrospectively.[46] Comparing Confucianism and Puritanism, Weber attributed a "magical religiosity" to Asian religions such as Confucianism, preserving life in a "great enchanted garden" (*Zaubergarten*),[47] while Puritanism was able to get rid of magic and expected salvation instead from ethics.[48] In this comparison, "magical religiosity" replaced Weber's former notion of "traditionalism," the counter-notion he had previously applied in his study of the economic rationalism of Puritanism, as shown by Stefan Breuer.[49]

Weber sketches the *social consequences* of a fully developed disenchantment for the first time in chapter 11 of the section on religion in *Economy and Society*. He opens with the words: "The more a religion of salvation has been systematized and internalized in the direction of an 'ethic of ultimate ends' [*Gesinnungsethik*], the greater becomes its tension in relation to the world."[50] Weber makes a distinction between an ethic of compliance (*Gesetzesethik*) with existing rules of responsibility and a subjective ethic of conviction or ethic of ultimate ends (*Gesinnungsethik*).[51] The first one sanctifies an existing order; the latter, in conjunction with a religion of world-denial, is able to establish new values and practices. If the actor takes into account the consequences of his action, Weber calls it an ethic of responsibility.[52] In 1915, he revised and expanded his argument in the "Intermediate Reflection" (*Zwischenbetrachtung*).[53] Religious communities that require brotherly love as a pure ethics of conviction generate tensions with respect to the spheres of economics, politics, sexuality, science, and art. The believers experience these orders as autonomous and hostile, and resolve the tensions either by "fleeing" the world or by "mastering" it—the former pathway constituting what Weber calls "mysticism," the latter "asceticism." In either case, new religious practices arise. For Weber, "disenchantment" was not the rise of a godless culture, as Marianne Weber in her biography about her husband assumed.[54] An increasingly rational and unethical culture of the dominant social orders corresponds to the emergence of a variety of new forms of subjective religiosity defying those orders. Religion becomes independent of society. Weber's exposition abounds in examples of this process. With regard to the sphere of politics, congregational religiosity did not merely oppose military violence; it favored either a world-fleeing pacifism or measures to fight the power of sin. With regard to the spheres of sexuality and art, he noticed a rise of practices that opened "a gate into the most irrational and thereby real kernel of life, as compared with the mechanisms of rationalization.... The lover realizes himself to be rooted in the kernel of the true living, which is eternally inaccessible to any rational endeavor. He knows himself to be freed from the old skeleton hands of rational orders, just as completely as from the banality of everyday routine."[55] Likewise art is for Weber "a carrier of magical affects."[56] Weber doesn't use the notion of "re-enchantment" as modern authors are doing.[57] In Weber's understanding even transmitted types of religiosity are transformed by the subjective experience of modern rationality.

Weber, who studied religious world-denial much more intensely than anybody else, recognized that the otherworldly values are by no means exclusively values of the beyond. "Psychologically considered, man in quest of salvation has been primarily preoccupied by attitudes of the here and now."[58] The one who renounces the world experiences his deed as a victory over the temptations of this world. "The ascetic who rejects the world sustains at least the negative inner relationship with it which is presupposed in the struggle against it."[59]

In his "Intermediate Reflection" he explains the link between the devaluation of the world based on experiencing injustice, suffering, sin, and futility, and a certain kind of religiosity:

> The need for "salvation" responds to the devaluation by becoming more other-worldly, more alienated from all structured forms of life and in exact parallel, by confining itself to the specific religious essence. This reaction is stronger the more systematic the thinking about the "meaning" of the universe becomes, the more the external organization of the world is rationalized, and the more the conscious experience of the world's irrational content is sublimated.[60]

Weber resists conceiving of religion in terms of a definition of its essence. Instead, he conceives of religion as a process, generating a rift between worldly values and confining itself to the articulation of transcendental mystical or ethical claims. He states in his "Religious Communities":

> To define "religion," to say what it is, is not possible at the start of a presentation such as this. Definition can be attempted, if at all, only at the conclusion of the study. The essence of religion is not even our concern, as we make it our task to study the conditions and effects of a particular type of social action. The external courses of religious behavior are so diverse that an understanding of this behavior can only be achieved from the viewpoint of the subjective experiences, ideas, and purposes of the individual concerned—in short, from the viewpoint of the religious behavior's "meaning" [*Sinn*]. The most elementary forms of behavior motivated by religious or magical factors are oriented to *this* world. "That it may go well with thee ... and that thou mayest prolong thy days upon the earth" (Ephesians 6:2–3) expresses the reason for the performance of actions enjoined by religion or magic.[61]

Weber called this approach in *The Protestant Ethic* a "historical concept-formation" (*historische Begriffsbildung*).[62]

Marianne Weber reported in her biography of her husband that Weber, while researching the world religions, had made a most exciting discovery:

> The process of rationalization dissolves magical notions and increasingly "disenchants" the world and renders it godless. Religion changes from magic to doctrine. And now, after the disintegration of the primitive image of the world, there appear two tendencies: a tendency towards the rational mastery

of the world on the one hand and one towards mystical experience on the other. But not only the religions receive their stamp from the increasing development of thought; the process of rationalization moves on several tracks, and its autonomous development encompasses all creations of civilization—the economy, the state, law, science, and art. All forms of Western culture in particular are decisively determined by a methodical way of thinking that was first developed by the Greeks, and this way of thinking was joined in the Age of Reformation by a methodical conduct of life that was oriented to certain purposes. It was this union of a theoretical and a practical rationalism that separated modern culture from ancient culture, and the special character of both separated modern Western culture from Asiatic culture. To be sure, there were processes of rationalization in the Orient as well, but neither the scientific, the political, the economic, nor the artistic kind took the course that is peculiar to the Occident. … Weber regarded this recognition of the special character of occidental rationalism and the role it was given to play for Western culture as one of his most important discoveries. As a result, his original inquiry into the relationship between religion and economics expanded into an even more comprehensive inquiry into the special nature of all of Western culture.[63]

The significance of this discovery for her husband was tremendous, according to her biography. From this point onward, the process of "disenchantment" figured centrally in Weber's thinking about religion. Different types of ethics (of compliance, of responsibility, or of commitment) and different interests of social and political classes were at the root of diverse types of subjective religiosities.

Dialectics of Disenchantment of Modern Religions: Recent Approaches to Nature, History, and Society

Weber refers to two processes: a first disenchantment of the world by religion and then a second by science, and it is at this point that he notices a disenchantment of religion itself occurring.[64] "Disenchantment" denotes a denial of the inherent meaning of objects of experience and is a precondition for generating independent worldviews and ethics that are able to cope with the experience of a world devoid of meaning. Wolfgang Schluchter describes the process as follows:

> The process of disenchantment intervenes in the basic constellation of the spheres of value, manners of life, and lifestyles. Weber's view of the modern world is guided by a theory of the growing conflicts between the spheres of value and the orders of life and lifestyles that correspond to these.[65]

The types of religion and the secularity of the world are mutually dependent on each other. The notion of disenchantment provides the link: the more the world is regarded as rational, the more religion shifts to the subjective realm of irrationality. An indication that Weber avoids any evolutionary assumption can be seen in the contemporary examples and cases he adduces, when illustrating the activity of the bearers of charisma—the magician, the priest, the prophet, the intellectual, and their supporters—in his section "Religious Communities" or when dealing with ecstasy, orgy, magic, and mysticism by choosing contemporary cases. "The disenchantment of the world does not mean there is no magic. We understand Weber better if we read him as also theorizing the persistence of magic into modernity."[66] This persistence has shaped the interpretation of Indian religion, as Robert Yelle shows in his examination of the matter.[67]

When Weber speaks of a religious development by which the world becomes disenchanted, he envisages a transformation of religion itself. The objects and occurrences in the world lose their significance as a divine sign—as prodigy or miracle[68]—and become simple facts that no longer signify anything in religious terms. On the one hand, the world is conceived as governed by an autonomous rational causal mechanism.[69] On the other hand, religion reflects an independence from that kind of causal rationality.[70] Religion, confronted with a growing demand that the world and the total pattern of life be subject to an order, provides significance and meaning. According to Weber, in the beginning, "only the things or events that actually exist or take place played a role in life." This changed with the rise of the magician. "Now certain experiences of a different order, in that they only signify something, also play a role. Thus magic is transformed from a direct manipulation of forces into a *symbolic activity.*"[71]

What Weber sets out here is discussed today from the standpoint of the study of science. The rational scientific comprehension of history, of nature, and of society generated both: secularity and religiosity. This result is echoed by contemporary attempts to rethink the theory of secularization. Craig Calhoun, Mark Juergensmeyer, and Jonathan VanAntwerpen made the following point in their volume *Rethinking Secularism*:

> Until quite recently, it was assumed that public life [in the West: HGK] was basically secular. ... Scholars could write with authority about politics, economics, and social behavior as though religion did not exist at all. Secularism, on the other hand, appeared to have no ideological significance of its own.[72]

Our authors are not alone in doubting this assumption. The Canadian Charles Taylor has given an impressive account of the rise of secularism. In *A Secular*

Age (2007) he reconstructs the path that made it possible in Western history for secularism to emerge. Today, secularism is taken for granted, in much the same way that, for centuries, faith in God, in the soul, and in immortality was taken for granted. In Taylor's account, the powers that once were located in the outside world were transposed into objects of scientific observation, on the one hand, and relocated within the human being, in his or her thoughts and feelings, on the other;[73] they were placed in an "immanent frame." Two cross-pressures define our culture today: an ordered, impersonal universe and a search for spiritual meaning. These cross-pressures are experienced in two different ways: as an objective universe that functions impersonally in accordance with laws and as a subjective universe that is seen as a source of spiritual meaning. Taylor quotes Czeslaw Miłosz with approval when he speaks of the "dichotomy between the world of scientific laws—cold, indifferent to human values—and man's inner world."[74] This means that neither religion nor secularism is self-evident. For Taylor—as for Weber—it would be a mistake to see the relentless process of disenchantment as proof of the decline of religion.[75] Here we recall again Weber's words:

> Intellectualism suppresses belief in magic, the world's processes become disenchanted, lose their magical significance, and henceforth simply "are" and "happen" but no longer signify anything. As a consequence, there is a growing demand that the world and the total pattern of life be subject to an order that is significant and meaningful.[76]

Disenchantment of Nature: Distinguishing Rational Scientific Operations from Subjective Meanings

Weber described in 1907 a process of the disenchantment of nature without using the notion. Nature becomes a rational scientific object without any meaning, whether metaphysical, religious, or symbolic.

> Suppose that for conceptual purposes we distinguish the "meaning" which we find "expressed" in an object or process from all the other components of the object or process which remain after this "meaning" is abstracted from it. And suppose that we define the sort of inquiry that is exclusively concerned with this last set of components as "naturalistic." The result is still another concept of "nature." It can be differentiated from the concepts of "nature" identified in our earlier discussion. In this sense of "nature"[,] nature is the domain of

"meaninglessness." Or more precisely, an item becomes a part of nature if we cannot raise the question: What is its "meaning"?[77]

But there is another side of this operation. Meaning loses its dependence on its original mooring. Later, in "Religious Communities," he construed how symbolic action became separate from magic actions and, vice versa, how actions became independent of magic. The process of the disenchantment of actions established, on the one hand, a calculable/rational understanding of natural processes and, on the other hand, a separate level of magical/religious meanings.

Kocku von Stuckrad has investigated the history of the scientification of the study of religion from 1800 to 2000. His conclusion is that religion was framed as a scientific concept against the background of the distinction between what is rational, reasonable, and secular (on the one hand) and what is irrational, unreasonable, and religious (on the other hand). These mutually exclusive categories were so firmly established in the academic discourse from the nineteenth century onward that they permeated the entire terminology of the academic rhetoric of ethnographic and religious-historical descriptions: astrology as opposed to astronomy, alchemy as opposed to chemistry, magic as opposed to science, and so on. The one was now regarded as religious but scientifically wrong or irrational, the other as secular and correct from a scientific point of view.[78] The consequence of this scientific operation was that the link was broken between phenomenon and meaning, sign and symbol, semantics and pragmatics. On the one hand, an object fell victim to a naturalistic isolation. On the other hand, an independent realm of religious meaning was generated. This dialectic is the subject of his impressive study.

Egil Asprem in *The Problem of Disenchantment: Scientific Naturalism and Esoteric Discourse*[79] examines the paradigm of "scientific naturalism." Between 1900 and 1939, scientists took this paradigm for granted when describing and explaining natural phenomena. But what happened, Asprem asks, when scientists encountered in the world of natural phenomena notions that could not be derived from empirical observation and were neither verifiable nor falsifiable by observation, but were nevertheless necessary in order to understand natural processes? His answer is that "the processes of rationalization have created the conditions for the problem of disenchantment to emerge."[80] The rational approach generates an unreasonable, incalculable, irrational realm distinct from the reasonable, calculable, rational realm that the scholar inhabits. As von Stuckrad has shown, this pattern was dominant since the very beginning of the scientification of religious history, as the profane/rational versus the sacred/irrational.[81] Applying this distinction to natural data yields likewise an exclusion of nonempirical metaphysical meanings from the natural world that by exclusion became a field of their own.

In his investigation of this process in the fields of physics, biology, psychology, and other disciplines, Asprem brings to light debates among well-known scientists that revealed that they could not completely avoid concepts that eluded the status of empirical observation but were nevertheless necessary for understanding nature. Here he refers to *Angels Fear* by Gregory Bateson (1904–80) and his daughter Mary Catherine Bateson, which attacks the two rival "superstitions" that feed each other: the supernatural and the mechanical models of reality. The second believes that quantity can determine natural pattern. The first claims the power of mind over matter. Both are untenable according to Bateson's view. Analyzing natural processes requires a paradigm that integrates matter and mind. Take, for example, chemical elements. They are objects that contain some kind of "communication" in and between things. The entire conceptual separation between mind and matter is odd, Asprem argues.[82] "Holism" or "system" or "mind" became watchwords for attempts to reintegrate immaterial elements into the observation of natural processes. According to Asprem, a field of natural theologies emerged. Academic scientists and philosophers had to find "alternative solutions to the problem of disenchantment." This field emerged not merely because of unsolved problems in the natural sciences but also through the transmission of an ancient Mediterranean worldview that celebrated the visible cosmos as a place where divine powers reveal themselves to the human mind: "cosmotheism" or "panentheism."

> Post-Enlightenment establishments may not have been all "that" disenchanted …
> It was not only the attempt to get rid of cosmotheism that was unsuccessful; the attempt to create a stable disenchanted identity for the Western academy was not completed either.[83]

Asprem sees the natural sciences as the driving force behind the disenchantment of the human attitude to the natural world. But this force did not succeed fully. The falsified and rejected knowledge turned into a stable and enduring Western tradition, today known as "esotericism."[84] In the discussion of this remarkable study in the *Journal of Religion in Europe* 8 (2015), I pointed out that the impact of religion, as Weber assumed it, should not be ignored altogether. The disenchantment of nature created a rift between the objective scientific observation of natural objects and the subjective experience of the same objects by means of philosophical or religious concepts.[85] The great variety of subjective experiences of nature has generated a host of different contemporary topics. Von Stuckrad starts from a common principle of various worldviews called "esoteric," an idea authored by Antoine Faivre, who called esotericism a "pattern of thought" (*forme de pensée*).[86] Its characteristics are thinking in correspondences between visible and invisible parts of the universe; comprehending the cosmos as living, ensouled nature; and believing that imagination mediates and reveals esoteric knowledge and provides an experience that transforms human beings.[87] Von Stuckrad conceives of Western Esotericism as a mode of thought operating in Gnosticism, Hermeticism, Kabbalah, Mysticism, Alchemy, Astrology, Theosophy, Shamanism, and New Age. The advantage of these approaches is that they do not conceive of even strictly rational science as a simple rejection of religion but rather as the background against which a religious field of its own emerged.

The Doubling of the Concept of the Future: Human Progress and Divine Salvation History

Dealing with meaning in relation to nature, Weber, after the passage from his *Critique of Stammler* quoted above, follows the proposition that "nature is the domain of the 'meaningless'" with the words: "It is self-evident that the polar antithesis of 'nature' as the 'meaningless' is not 'social life,' but rather the 'meaningful': that is, the meaning ascribed to a process or object, the 'meaning' which *can* 'be found in it.'"[88] According to Weber there is no progress in the history of nations and states. Their internal social life is dependent on religious worldviews, carried by social classes and strata. The social fabric is shaped by a plurality of religious values and views of history.[89] The current of occurrences doesn't reveal a clear direction; the meaning of it must be produced by the people.

The historian Lucian Hölscher has made a detailed description of a case of simultaneity and competition, in nineteenth-century industrializing Germany, between religious expectations about a final judgment in the future and secular expectations about future progress through a socialist revolution. He argued that, alongside the long-established religious belief, a political expectation of a man-made revolution spread in the nineteenth century, inspired by the experience of the French Revolution. The context for this spread was an increased belief in the possibility of predicting the future and controlling it. This prediction seemed to bring the future into the sphere of the manageable, but it did not thereby entail the abandonment of hope in the coming of the kingdom of God in society. Alongside the prediction of a man-made future, the religious faith in divine providence persevered. The social conditions in the new industrial sector generated ambivalent feelings toward the future; some people lost confidence in social progress. Hölscher registers a "doubling of the concept of the future."[90]

Both conceptions presuppose an open future, dependent on human action. The nature of this relationship is a matter of dispute, as we see from the debate between Karl Löwith and Hans Blumenberg. Löwith (1897–1973) argued that a secular faith in progress had displaced the Christian expectation about the last judgment; the modern philosophy of history articulated in the Communist Manifesto originated in the biblical faith in a fulfilment of time and "secularized" this eschatological model.[91] Blumenberg (1920–96) objected that the faith in progress was based on the extension of the domination of nature—while the biblical expectation of salvation had its roots in a general lack of meaning in human existence and had not been diminished in the course of history. The two positions are autonomous, and neither can replace the other.[92] The disenchantment of history enabled the rise of contradictory views of history.[93]

The Fundamentalism Project at the University of Chicago showed a quarter century ago that all major modern religions display this doubling of the understanding of the future.[94] This is why considerable attention has been paid in recent decades to "fundamentalism," which exemplifies the complex relationship between religion and modern culture.[95] Originally, fundamentalism designated a collective movement in American Protestantism that began before the First World War and actively criticized the modernistic milieu of the growing industrial society. Bruce Lawrence made a distinction that is essential for understanding this movement:

> *Modernity* is the emergence of a new index of human life shaped, above all, by increasing bureaucratization and rationalization as well as technical capacities and global exchange unthinkable in the premodern era. *Modernism* is the search for individual autonomy driven by a set of socially encoded values emphasizing change over continuity; quantity over quality; efficient production, power, and profit over sympathy for traditional values or vocations, in both the public and private spheres. At its utopian extreme, it enthrones one economic strategy, consumer-oriented capitalism, as the surest means to technological progress that will also eliminate social unrest and physical discomfort.[96]

The program of the Protestant fundamentalists was the defense of basic biblical truths ("fundamentals") against enlightened liberal theologians who distanced themselves from particularly offensive teachings such as the infallibility of the Bible, the virgin birth, the resurrection of the body, the vicarious expiatory sacrifice of Christ, and his bodily return at the end of time. The heart of the fundamentalist movement was a rigorous rejection of modern liberal culture and an acute expectation of the imminence of the Last Judgment. It rejected especially the liberal Protestant belief that Christ would return at the end of the millennium (postmillenarianism), only after a gradual transition to the perfect society.[97] This was the basis on which liberals taught the Social Gospel: social reform was a task enjoined on Christians to bring about the millennium. Fundamentalists took a different position: they awaited the return of Jesus before the beginning of the Thousand Years' Reign and believed that true Christians would be caught up in the "rapture" before the terror of the last days (*premillenarianism*). It seemed to them impossible that the world, as it existed, could be saved, with the exception of the community of the elect. They were disappointed with the alleged progress of industrialized society. Sexual promiscuity, prostitution, and alcoholism belonged to an order of things on which the Lord would pronounce his annihilating verdict. Nevertheless, this expectation did not necessarily lead to a withdrawal from politics. Fundamentalists speak out in the public arena to demand moral reform. They make use of the technical advances of the modern period, find support in the experience of communal faith, and oppose the further spread of individual autonomy. Global studies of the messianic expectation of salvation confirm these findings.[98] The doubling of the concept of the future presupposes the distinction between the experience of autonomous social orders and subjective expectations of salvation—in other words, the dialectic that Weber linked to disenchantment.

The Ethic of Brotherliness in a Society Devoid of Solidarity

In "Religious Communities," Weber addressed the specific logic of congregational religion. He pointed out:

> Congregational religion added the fellow worshipper and the comrade in faith to the roster of those to whom the religiously founded obligation of assistance applied which already included the blood-brother and the fellow member of clan and tribe. Stated more correctly, congregational religion set the coreligionist in the place of the fellow clansman. ... Out of all this grows the injunction of

brotherly love, which is especially characteristic of congregational religion, in most cases because it contributes very effectively to the emancipation from political organization.⁹⁹

In his plan of relating the great forms of community to the economy, Weber kept to a particular sequence. Before he discussed the faith community, he dealt with the neighborhood of household communities. Here, too, he followed his strategy of turning a static state of affairs into a type of communal action.¹⁰⁰ His reflections centered on help in need: when households get into difficulties, they must call on their neighbors for help.¹⁰¹ According to Weber, neighborliness, as a mutual support in times of need and therefore bearer of brotherliness, exists not only in the forms of life that are found in villages but also in the tenements in the big city slums, where it is also the neighbor who is the typical helper in need.¹⁰²

The ethic of religious communities which had their origin in prophets took over the obligation of neighbors and clans to help in emergencies and turned this into the commandment of brotherliness, rejecting requirements of politics and economy. Hence the religious congregation constitutes the "second category of congregation," alongside the "neighborhood that has been associated for economic or for fiscal or other political purposes."¹⁰³ Assistance and help in need are detached from neighborly reciprocity or clan obligation and become demands made by a prophetic religious ethic. This renders the faith community independent both of politics and of the laws of the market: "The more the world of the modern capitalist economy follows its own immanent laws, the less accessible it is in any imaginable relationship with a religious ethic of brotherliness."¹⁰⁴ When this commandment is radicalized in a further step to become a specifically religious "attitude of love," a "communism of love,"¹⁰⁵ the autonomy of the ethic of brotherliness comes into a fundamental tension vis-à-vis societal reality and becomes an element in a religiosity rejecting the social orders of the world.¹⁰⁶

Weber regarded the transformation from neighborly help in need into an ethic of brotherliness as highly consequential:

> The religiosity of the congregation transferred the ancient economic ethic of neighborliness to the relations among brethren of faith. … The more imperatives that issued from the ethic of reciprocity among neighbors were raised, the more rational the conception of salvation became, and the more it was sublimated into an ethic of absolute ends [*Gesinnungsethik*]. … The religion of brotherliness has always clashed with the orders and values of the world, and the more consistently its demands have been carried through, the sharper the clash has

been. The split has usually become wider the more the values of the world have been rationalized and sublimated in terms of their own laws.[107]

The religiosity of salvation transposes the old ethics of neighborhood onto the brotherhood in faith. The obligation to help widows, orphans, the poor, and the sick in their need becomes a fundamental ethical obligation, and salvation depends on its fulfillment.[108] When reality is seen as incomprehensible suffering, the societally limited reciprocal obligation gives way to a universalistic ethic of brotherliness and transcends all societal barriers.[109] The more consistently it is practiced, the more harshly will it clash with the structures and values of the world. The more its own inner logic unfolds, the more irreconcilable will the rift be. A disenchantment of the world opens a space for an antagonistic ethic. The religions of Judaism and Christianity, as well as of Islam, which see themselves as bearers of the promise made to Abraham (Genesis 12:1–3), are in this sense community religions par excellence. The faith community is the addressee of the assurance of salvation and thus is itself the object of its members' faith. This communal religiosity is linked to the idea that the individual local faith communities are a part of a transcendent community of all the redeemed ("people of God," "church," "umma"). The community demands that its members help and assist fellow believers or all human beings globally when they are in need ("ethic of brotherliness").

With their praxis of an ethic of solidarity in times of globalization, faith communities can spread independently of the powers of state and finance, thereby unfolding a power of their own. We should note here that even Pentecostal communities, which are attractive to many because of their individualized spiritual good things such as ecstasy, healing, and prosperity, have made societal commitment their trademark.[110] Social activism has taken hold of faith communities of other orientations and religions too, and has formed the basis of their power in contemporary civil society. The deprivatization of their ethic of brotherliness has allowed them to become activists in the public arena.

According to Jürgen Habermas, the religious neutrality of the secular state does not exclude religious convictions from the public arena, provided they are translated for the unbelievers. The separation enables citizens to express their position on present-day public issues (e.g., abortion; asylum for refugees; solidarity with needy people) in terms of a religious conviction. Habermas called this the "dialectics of secularization":

> When secularized citizens act in their role as citizens of the state, they must not deny in principle that religious images of the world have the potential to

express truth. Nor must they refuse their believing fellow citizens the right to make contributions in a religious language to public debates.[111]

According to Habermas, the duties of citizens of a state are largely fixed by law, but this does not apply to their role as members of society. This is particularly relevant when one considers that the powers of the markets and bureaucracy no longer bring about the social integration of the citizens by means of a mutual solidarity. Under such conditions, Habermas argues, we must be ready to extend reason beyond its own borders and promote "a solidarity with those who are oppressed and insulted, hastening the coming of the messianic salvation."[112] Citizens in a democratic state who are interested in maintaining this mode of social integration have good reason to establish, with the help of religion, a social bond that is independent of the rules of the market and the law, and to claim public recognition for it. With these ideas in mind, Habermas gave an affirmative answer in the discussion of whether there were "pre-political foundations [for] the democratic constitutional state."[113]

The concept of disenchantment must be distinguished from the concept of secularization. Whereas the concept of secularization postulates religion as something private that can acquire a new relevance in the public arena (José Casanova's "deprivatization"[114]) the concept of disenchantment focuses on a different process that favors the rise of antagonistic world views, ethics, and communities. Both are typical for religion in modern culture.[115] Studies that investigate modern scientific representations of natural processes have demonstrated how the elimination of religious interpretations from the analysis has helped to make possible the development of modern esotericism. Modern constructions of history likewise show that, alongside faith in man-made progress, the expectation of a sudden irruption of salvation has left its mark on modern ways of looking at history. And the understanding of society as marked exclusively by rational conduct opens areas of freedom for an irrational ethics of brotherliness. Thanks to the disenchantment of our world, as conceived by Max Weber, we recognize that secular orderings operate according to principles that are independent of religion and that, vice versa, religious communities operate according to meanings that resist social constraints.

2

Max Weber and the Rationalization of Magic

Jason Ā. Josephson-Storm

"Magic, for example, has been just as systematically 'rationalized' as physics."
—Max Weber, *Der Sinn der "Wertfreiheit,"* 1917

To state my thesis bluntly at the outset: the standard account of Max Weber's notion of "disenchantment" is wrong. There are a few bright exceptions, but most of what scholars have been saying for decades about Weber's poetical phrase "die Entzauberung der Welt" (usually translated as "the disenchantment of the world" but more literally "the de-magic-ing of the world") is based on a mistaken reading of his project. The error originates in a very reasonable interpretation of Weber's most famous lecture "Science as a Vocation" (*Wissenschaft als Beruf*) (1917). The problem is that for many nonspecialists, disenchantment is understood as a poetical synonym for secularization and even most Weber scholars take the phrase at face value and assume that a disenchanted world has absolutely no magic in it.

As illustrative of the standard view, one of the world's leading Weber scholars, Peter Ghosh has argued that "for Weber, by contrast, the defining feature of 'magic' (if such a thing existed at all) was that it formed a conceptual antithesis to rational conduct …. Weber had no developed idea of magic as such, except as the miscellany of non-rational behavior."[1] Ghosh's claim is far from unique and instead reflects the general opinion of most scholarship on Weber.

Yet, the epigraph above should already begin to put pressure on the standard account, because scholars accustomed to thinking of rationality and enchantment as opposites will have trouble reckoning with how magic can itself be rationalized. This quote is no aberration in Weber's corpus, for his own published writings and letters provide plenty of evidence that Weber thought that magic persisted in modernity, albeit in rationalized forms.[2]

Building off of some of my previous work in *The Myth of Disenchantment: Magic, Modernity and the Birth of the Human Sciences* (2017), this chapter demonstrates both that the belief in spirits and magic persists in the contemporary world and that Weber himself was no stranger to the occult milieu. After laying out this background in Part I, Part II provides a close reading of Weber's writings about disenchantment to show the textual evidence for undoing the standard account of disenchantment. There are two main myths about Weber I would like to dispel: that Weber saw magic and rationality as incompatible, and that he thought that magic had vanished in modernity. Both of these statements prove to be false. Indeed, as I interpret Weber, we live in a *disenchanting* world where magic is besieged and intermittently contained within its own cultural sphere, but not in a *disenchanted* world in which magic is gone. The difference is significant. A brief third part of this chapter is a thought experiment gesturing at how Weber might have conceived of the rationalization of the magic sphere in different cultures.

Part I: In the Realm of Enchantment

From indescribable transformation hails
such creations—Feel! and believe!
We suffer often: flames become ash; but, in art: flames come from dust.
Here is magic. In the realm of enchantment [*das Bereich des Zaubers*].
—Rainer Marie Rilke, *Magie*, 1924[3]

Munich, 1917. A group of artists, poets, students, and other bohemians gathered at the home of Gustav Willibald Freytag (1876–1943), a professor of ophthalmology and son of a famous novelist. They were assembled on that particular cold December night to listen to a lecture by a man named Alfred Schuler (1865–1923), a charismatic local eccentric who lived with his mother but who claimed that he was the reincarnation of a pre-Christian Roman leader and that he received clairvoyant visions and direct communications from pagan gods.[4] By way of explanation, Schuler maintained that he had a mystical experience whenever he came into contact with an artifact from classical antiquity.[5] Hence, he claimed that archaeological objects were condensed figures of a distant time that he could decode through a kind of oracular psychometry as his fingertips unlocked new revelations and visions from ancient eons.[6]

With Freytag's home as his headquarters, Schuler delivered a series of seven lectures under the title *Vom Wesen der ewigen Stadt* (On the Essence of the Eternal City), which he advertised as evoking "telesmatic" energies and intended to "develop their listener's inner light."[7] But Schuler's grand narrative was about the gradual alienation of humanity from the sacred cosmos and Great Mother Goddess (Magna Mater) initiated by the Jewish rejection of idolatry and exacerbated by the Christian banishment of the pagan gods. As the lectures unfolded, Schuler went on to share not only his idiosyncratic recovery of "esoteric" paganism but also his insights into an eternal realm of the dead (*Totenreich*) beyond the veil of ordinary space and time. This was Schuler's twist on a claim common to Swedenborg and later spiritualists that there was a timeless spirit world parallel to our own.

Although Max Weber was in Munich giving lectures in almost the same period as Schuler's series of talks, the two men still might seem to have come from different circles. Indeed, perhaps the single most quoted sentence from Weber's parallel 1917 lecture is: "The fate of our times is characterized by rationalization and intellectualization and, above all, by the disenchantment of the world." But Schuler and Weber were much closer than one might think.

Indeed, at least one person—the poet Rainer Maria Rilke (quoted in the epigraph above)—attended both Max Weber's *Politik als Beruf* (Politics as a Vocation, 1919) and Alfred Schuler's *Vom Wesen der ewigen Stadt*. We do not know what Rilke thought of the content, but it might surprise you that he seems to have found Schuler to be the more enthralling figure.[8] But Rilke was not the main connection between the two theorists.

Schuler was the leader of a Munich-based group of poets and neo-pagans known as the Cosmic Circle (*Kosmikerkreis*, *Kosmische Runde*, or *Kosmiker*). Beyond Schuler, the Cosmic Circle included the German-Jewish poet and translator Karl Wolfskehl (1869–1948), the neo-pagan philosopher Ludwig Klages (1872–1956), and for a time the famous mystical poet Stefan George (1868–1933). I discuss this group and their beliefs in greater detail in *The Myth of Disenchantment*, but in many respects the Cosmic Circle resembled many other *fin-de-siècle* occult movements. One thing that made them distinctive—but not unique—was that they shared a reverence for Friedrich Nietzsche, whom they described as one of the great "pagan martyrs: whose soul fought and died for the ardor of Life."[9]

Like many of their contemporaries, the Cosmic Circle also believed in magic. Their particular philosophy of magic was described by the German author and translator Franziska zu Reventlow (1871–1918), who had a relationship with Klages and who was for a time an unofficial member of the group. In her account:

> They claim to have discovered secrets of immeasurable importance and thereby have gone so far as to achieve mastery of certain inner powers. Hence sooner or later they will be in a position to work magic [*zaubern*] …. They explained it to me like this: one succeeds by means of a mystical procedure—I believe by absolute self-absorption in the primordial cosmic principle …. When this is successful, one's essence is completely permeated by the primordial cosmic substance, which is in itself all-powerful. Then one is made just as powerful, and those who are all-powerful can work magic [*zaubern*].[10]

Paraphrased, the Kosmikers had a theory about the source of a-causal supernatural power. Elsewhere in her work, Reventlow also discussed how the Kosmikers had an account of how the enchantments of a primordial matriarchy had been lost.[11]

The beliefs of the Cosmic Circle are relevant for two reasons—first, based on archival evidence I discuss in *The Myth of Disenchantment*, we know that Weber read this paragraph describing the Kosmikers' magical beliefs in 1913 while he was vacationing at the Monte Verità neo-pagan commune in Switzerland. The dating is significant because this is before Weber began publishing about disenchantment, and there is some reason to think that he came to his notion of *Entzauberung* after visiting with neo-pagans and reading Reventlow's account of the Munich Cosmic Circle.[12] Moreover, he knew that Reventlow's account referred to real people.

Second, while it is unclear if Weber ever met Schuler, Weber definitely knew Wolfskehl, George, and Klages.[13] Wolfskehl's contact with Weber was fairly limited, but Weber met with George on multiple occasions and there is evidence that George had a significant impact on Weber's notion of mysticism and his sense of how the history of religion centered on charismatic leadership.[14] Indeed, the sociologist's first reference to "charisma" was in a letter about George to his student Dora Jellinek.[15]

It was Weber's interactions with Klages, however, that were likely the most important on his later formation of a notion of enchantment. Again, I devote a chapter to Klages in *The Myth of Disenchantment*, but two significant takeaways are relevant here—first, Klages articulated a further philosophy of magic and, second, more importantly, it was enmeshed in a later disenchantment narrative.

At times Klages referred to his project as "magical philosophy" (*magische Philosophie*), which he explained as follows:

Magic is the practice of our philosophy and our philosophy is the theory of magic. The philosophy of the academy is mechanistic theory and their practice is mechanical. Magical philosophy rejects the [Aristotelian] Law of Identity [in favor of flux], hence, it denies unity, objects, duration, reoccurrence, and mathematics; it denies concepts and causality, because causality is the functional parallel to the logical correlation [*Verknüpfung*]. Magical philosophy works with images and symbols, and its method is the method of analogy. The most important terms it uses are: element, substance, principle, demon, cosmos, microcosm, macrocosm, essence, image, primal image, vortex, tangle, and fire. Its final formulas are spells [*Zaubersprüche*] that have magical power.[16]

In this passage, we can see Klages working out in greater detail the philosophy of magic associated with the Cosmic Circle as a whole. One of Klages's contributions, however, was to ground it in a Heraclitean (or Nietzschean) ontology of becoming.

In a set of essays and lectures beginning with the 1913 work, *Mensch und Erde* (Man and Earth), Klages also gave an account of how humanity became alienated from the flowing flux of existence. This was his disenchantment or rationalization narrative. In his version of this narrative, the ancients knew the earth to be a "living being" and that "forest and spring, boulder and grotto were filled with sacred life; from the summits of their lofty mountains blew the storm-winds of the gods."[17] Primitive humans were in closer harmony with nature, which they sought to propitiate or protect by way of ritual and various prohibitions.[18] Nevertheless, Christianity suppressed the old gods and nature was stripped bare of animating forces. Modern Europeans, he went on to argue, see the earth instead as nothing but "an unfeeling lump of 'dead matter.'"[19]

As Klages further elaborated, "The will to rational truth is the will to the deactualization of the world."[20] In its fully articulated form, Klages's master narrative is that a progressively hyper-potentiated mind (*Geist*) or quantifying reason became yoked to the domination of nature, leading to the domination of humanity and potentially, if unchecked, to the annihilation of all life on earth. Klages argued:

We have counted, weighed, and measured, that which could be counted, weighed, and measured. We have quantified the world in width, height, and depth. We have become accustomed to speaking of "mechanisms" and even living and psychological processes, just as we got used to seeing the microscopic and macroscopic universe in the light of supremely functional furnished laboratories. We have by means of these things obtained the famous "dominion over nature."[21]

Accordingly, Klages describes the transformation from the magical or phenomenal world of flux into the static world of objects. As he argued, rational thinking renders the world lifeless and comprehensible, a taxidermied butterfly. His words: "Whatever is touched by the ray of mentality [*Geist*] is instantly changed into a mere thing, a quantifiable object that is afterwards connected to other objects only 'mechanically.'"[22] This is Klages's version of something Marxists have long critiqued, namely the process of reification, which, after all, literally means "thing-ification." But even more importantly, he provides a philosophical narrative about the displacement of magic and humanity's alienation from nature. Klages and Weber had very different accounts, but my main point is that some notion of loss of magic (or at least its marginalization) was being worked out within an occult milieu, and Weber knew about this.

Although it is unclear if Weber and Klages were acquainted by 1913, Weber began reading Klages's works sometime in that period. It is possible that Weber knew Klages through his brother Alfred Weber, because in 1913 Alfred and Klages both participated in the Free German Youth Movement.[23] But Max Weber and Klages shared multiple friends, so the connection could have come through multiple venues.[24] Later, Weber had his handwriting analyzed by Klages, whose readings he thought were accurate.[25] More importantly, however, they read each other's work.

In his own writings, Klages adopted Weber's famous phrase "Entzauberung der Welt" to describe the gradual distancing of humanity from the "cosmic Eros."[26] But the conversation went both ways, for Weber cited Klages on several occasions.[27] Weber observed, for example, that Klages's writings contained "very good remarks" on "the peculiar contraction and repression of natural life-impulses" brought about by rationalization.[28]

All this is to say, Max Weber must have known that many of his contemporaries believed in magic. Even if he had never encountered the Munich Circle, read Reventlow's account of them, or visited a neo-pagan commune, Weber would have only to open a German newspaper to see evidence for popular belief in witches, magic, spiritualism, and angels.[29] Thus, it seems implausible that Weber would have thought that belief in enchantment had vanished completely in his own era.

Inarguably, Weber knew about the modern persistence of belief in magic. We do too. As I recount in *The Myth of Disenchantment*, there is a lot of sociological evidence that suggests that belief in ghosts, demons, magic, psychical powers, and the like are surprisingly widespread in contemporary America and Great

Britain. The consensus seems to be that "three in four Americans believe in the paranormal."[30] The data is less robust from Western Europe, but according to a German telephone survey of 1,500 people conducted by the Institut für Grenzgebiete der Psychologie und Psychohygiene in Freiburg in 2000, there was a widespread engagement with such beliefs in contemporary Germany. The study concluded that a surprising 73 percent of German interviewees were willing to tell an interviewer that they had personally experienced paranormal phenomena.[31] Belief in the paranormal and belief in magic are not identical, but even at this level of generality the sociological evidence puts pressure on most notions of a disenchanted modernity.

Even today, we can find a thriving occult scene just a few miles from the conference venue.[32] Theion Publishing, located in Munich, is a leading European esoteric publisher under the direction of a German practitioner named David Beth who writes about "Kosmic Gnosis" and "Gnostic Voudon." In addition to their interest in Afro-Caribbean traditions, his publishing house is keeping alive the work of Ludwig Klages and, indeed, published work on him shortly after my book came out. Beth contacted me and kindly offered to send me some of their latest publications about Klages.

Part II: The Disenchanting World

> The complete disenchantment of the world has only been carried out to its full conclusion [in Puritanism]. But that did not mean freedom from what we are today accustomed to call "superstition." Witch trials also flourished in New England … [The Puritans] came to believe all magic to be diabolical.
> —Max Weber, *Die Wirtschaftsethik der Weltreligionen*, 1916

For a variety of reasons, specialists and nonspecialists alike have had difficulty getting a handle on Weber's conception of disenchantment. Part of the issue is that later interpreters have been unduly preoccupied with "Science as a Vocation" (*Wissenschaft als Beruf*), often to the exclusion of Weber's other discussions of the subject. To be sure, "Science as a Vocation" was an important lecture and indeed crucial to Weber's subsequent canonization in the academy. But fixating on this lecture has been a mistake, in good part because it is not Weber's most systematic exposition of his notion of disenchantment and, moreover, as a speech for a popular audience it contains poetical flourishes that have misled later readers.

But the bigger source of confusion about disenchantment is that scholars have often presumed an opposition between rationality and magic that Weber did not share (see my discussion of Ghosh above). Moreover, they have often imputed to Weber the belief that magic had vanished (or would vanish) in modernity. To counter these misreadings of Weber, in this section, I'd like to focus on Weber's less read but more systematic discussion of the issue.

Weber's "disenchantment of the world" first appears in print in the article "Über einige Kategorien der verstehenden Soziologie" (Some Categories of Interpretive Sociology), which appeared in *Logos* in 1913.[33] This essay was Weber's first attempt to formulate a systematic account of his own vision for sociology. He does this by carefully distinguishing the objects of sociological knowledge from other disciplines, in particular psychology. It is in this context that Weber first refers to the relationship between magic and disenchantment. He is in the process of arguing that actions can be rational for a given actor, even if they are directed toward an aim that sociologists might not grant as rational. As he goes on to note:

> For instance, action that is oriented to magical notions is subjectively of an often much more instrumentally rational character than any non-magical "religious" conduct, since as the *disenchantment of the world* increases, religiosity is compelled increasingly to adopt subjectively, instrumentally irrational meanings [*Sinnbezogenheiten*] (for example, of a "conscientious" [*Gesinnungshaft*] or mystical kind).[34]

For Weber, magic is subjectively, instrumentally rational. Spells are intended for specific pragmatic purposes. We'll return to the second part of this quotation and his reference to disenchantment in a moment, but I want to further hit home Weber's notion of rational magic.

Weber frequently refers to magic and enchantment in the context of his later writings on religion, but the closest he comes to making an explicit definition of magic is in a footnote in the section *Die Wirtschaftsethik der Weltreligionen* (The Economic Ethics of the World Religions) dealing with the religions of China. In the relevant section of the text Weber remarks:

> A strict separation between what is "enchantment" [*Zauber*] and what is not is impossible in the world of pre-animistic [*präanimistische*] and animistic ideas. Even plowing and other everyday achievement-oriented activities were "enchantment" in the sense of employing specific "forces" and later "spirits."[35]

It appears that enchantment or magic (the German *Zauber* could mean either) was initially instrumentally rational. Indeed, Weber elsewhere associates magical powers with "world-mastery" (*Weltbeherrschung*).[36] At the very least, early magic was not different from practical technologies except insofar as it was connected to the notion of spirits and pre-animistic occult forces.[37] That Weber saw a connection between (at least early) enchantment and technology is worth underscoring because multitudes of contemporary theorists think they are one-upping Weber when they point to enchanting technology.[38] But Weber would not have been surprised by this, especially as this passage was not the only place where he theorized the coincidence of magic and technology.[39]

Significantly, Weber both provides his most systematic theorization of magic and even charts a whole trajectory of the history of enchantment in his incomplete final work, *Wirtschaft und Gesellschaft* (Economy and Society, 1922). In brief, here Weber reiterates that magic is originally this-worldly instrumentally rational, focused on producing particular ends like starting fires and calling rain.[40] Throughout his writings, Weber cautions his readers against anachronistically viewing the past from the standpoint of modern science and assuming that everything that looks irrational from that vantage is primitive magic. As he puts it, "[we cannot] objectively distinguish in such behaviors those which are 'correct' from those which are 'incorrect,' and then designate the [false] attributions of causality as irrational, and the corresponding actions as 'magic' [*Zauberei*]."[41] To underscore the main claim of this text, Weber was very explicitly arguing against the idea that magic is irrational or that primitive behaviors that don't make sense from the perspective of contemporary science were magical.

Weber argued that early magic was based on neither its irrationality nor a sense that magic violated the laws of nature. Instead, as he elaborated, belief in magic was rooted in the sense that some objects and people possess "extraordinary powers" (*außeralltäglichen Kräfte*) often referred to as "'mana,' 'orenda,' and the Iranian '*maga*' (which became '*magic*'), and which we will henceforth call 'charisma.'"[42] Crucially, in this passage magic and charisma are equivalent. Charisma, as Weber elaborates, can be an attribute of both people and objects, and is either claimed for one's self or bestowed, such as in an act of consecration.[43] Given that Weber is famous for importing the notion of charismatic authority into sociology, it is striking that in this early usage charisma is primarily a synonym for magic.

However, to be fair, Weber was not fully consistent in maintaining an equivalence between charisma and magic. While he often treats them as synonymous, Weber also argued that "charismatic authority" (*charismatische Herrschaft*) is "often thought of as resting on magical powers."[44] So in this passage at least, charisma and magic are being distinguished even if they are seen often to go together.[45] Moreover, in this passage Weber suggests that in its pure or primal form "charismatic authority is specifically irrational in the sense of being foreign to all rules."[46] There is lot more that could be said about how Weber's theories of magic and charisma fit together, but space prohibits a full explanation. Nonetheless, in the broadest of strokes we can say that while pure magic for Weber is instrumentally rational, pure charisma is antinomian and hence formally irrational (see the typology of rationality offered below). But that said, Weber was interested in how, despite charisma's inherent tension with institutional forms of rationality, it inevitably fell prey to them over time. Charismatic authority itself became divested from the person and attributed instead to the office or institution. In effect, antinomianism became the source of new norms and raw charisma was transposed into routine and even bureaucratic statecraft. Moreover, by way of foreshadowing, just as Weber wrote about the "routinization of charisma," he also referred to the rationalization of magic.[47]

To return to the "Kategorien" essay, it is only after having established the rationality of magic that Weber goes on to refer to the disenchantment of the world. I want to underscore that Weber's very first use of disenchantment is connected to his account of the rationality of magic. The two concepts are conjoined. Weber's main point is that, in contrast to the rationality of primitive magic, in an increasingly disenchanted world that has foreclosed meaning in nature, religiously motivated actors often perform actions that are instrumentally *irrational*: in other words, actions that are directed against their seemingly rational interests but are instead invested with subjective meaning rooted in their specific convictions or mystical experiences.

To get a better sense of what disenchantment meant in this context, we have to realize that Weber saw early human societies shifting their basic orientation toward the natural world, making it symbolic. The magical arts then come to occupy the position of interpretation (divination) and manipulation (spells) of this invisible, symbolic world. Later, magicians and priests will professionalize partially according to whether they compel gods or worship them, although Weber notes this differentiation is incomplete.[48] But the important thing is that humanity has come to read this world as symbolically significant by producing a contrasting other world.

Weber thought that human cultures eventually encounter a fork in the road. They can cling to their notion of magic, as he thinks happened in China and India (note the implicit Orientalism). This preserves the culture's image of the world as a meaningful "enchanted garden" (*Zaubergarten*), but it comes at a cost.[49] In part this is because Weber thinks that over time magic/charisma gets invested in particular institutions (like the Brahmans or the Chinese emperor), which then exert a conservative function on the culture that delays its growth.

According to Weber, however, the Occident took a different route, namely disenchantment. The history of the West's rejection of magic is a story that Weber sketched many times but never finished elaborating. One version occurs in a famous passage from the second edition of *The Protestant Ethic*:

> That great historic process in the development of religions, the disenchantment of the world, which had begun with the old Hebrew prophets and, in conjunction with Hellenistic scientific thought, had repudiated all magical means to salvation as superstition and sin, came here to its logical conclusion. The genuine Puritan even rejected all signs of religious ceremony at the grave and buried his nearest and dearest without song or ritual in order that no superstition, no trust in the effects of magical and sacramental forces on salvation, should creep in.[50]

Paraphrased, instead of producing an entrenched magical caste in the Occident, the Hebrew prophets' demonization of magic culminated in the Protestant, and especially Puritan, disenchantment of the world. The Puritans thus overcame not only the demonology of the Gentiles and the Catholic priesthood but also Jewish mysteries and rituals.

Weber's account of Protestant disenchantment has attracted the most attention in the secondary scholarship. But surprisingly, later interpreters have generally overlooked that Weber asserted that Puritans and Jews did not doubt "the reality of magic" and repeatedly reminded his readers that "witches were also burned in New England."[51] Moreover, Protestants continued to believe in angels and demons.[52] As Weber emphasized: "Nowhere, not even during the Reformation, was the existence of the spirit-world and demons permanently eliminated; rather, they were simply subordinated unconditionally to the one god, at least in theory."[53]

It is important to emphasize what the "disenchantment of the world" is not. It is not the end of belief in magic. It is not the end of belief in animating spirits. It is not a new pessimistic state of mind, nor is it the fragmentation of social cohesion. It is not the rise of instrumental reason because magic is itself instrumental. It is not yet secularization insofar as disenchantment happens earlier and is first and foremost internal to religion. It is not the evolution from magic to religion, and finally to science, because Weber repeatedly reminds his readers that magic and religion often coincide.[54]

Many scholars, even sophisticated Weberians, mistake disenchantment for the various things I have dismissed above.[55] A certain amount of the secondary literature promotes the idea that disenchantment means banishing the "mysterious" or losing a sense of wonder. But the parallel passage in the "Kategorien" essay where Weber spells out his theory makes no mention of mystery in reference to "savage" belief and instead refers to primitive attempts to influence the world. So it is hard to imagine that the "mysterious" is central to Weber's account.[56] Having rejected these, the question becomes: What then is disenchantment?

Many interpretations of Weber tend to assume that he was describing a world without magic. You can find this claim throughout the secondary literature even though some readers have complicated this account by discussing what they see as re-enchantment. At the very least, this reading of disenchantment is easy to dismiss in terms of both Weber's own understanding of the Puritan witch trials and knowledge of magical revivals. Indeed, I cannot emphasize this enough—the disenchantment of the world does not mean it has no magic. We understand Weber better if we read him as also theorizing the persistence of magic into modernity.

What Weber envisioned can be further clarified on basic philological grounds. *Entzauberung* in German signals something that is in process. As I argued in *The Myth of Disenchantment*, one of the most straightforward implications of revisiting Weber's famous frame is that it should be translated not as "the disenchantment of the world" but instead as "the disenchanting of the world." "Disenchantment" suggests an accomplished state of affairs. But what Weber has in mind is not just a process but also a program. All he's doing is identifying that this program is in place, not that it is completed. For there to be an active, ongoing disenchant*ing* of the world, magic has to be intact somewhere, among some groups. There must therefore be pockets, entire regions, groups, or classes where magic remains. If anything, disenchanting the world might seem destined to produce a "magic sphere" with a new host of professionals, subject to its own internal rationalization process.

Moreover, it is important to emphasize that for Weber to be right, the disenchanters do not have to deny the existence of magic. They merely have to demonize it. The disenchanting of the world is in place once there are some elites who want to cut out magic as a path to salvation. In the first instance, disenchanting does not strip the earth of supernatural beings so much as it depicts the world as demon-haunted. This allows us also to see that "the disenchanting of the world" is not identical to the (putatively) anonymous process of rationalization. Yet it is still alienating.

When Weber theorized rationalization, he argued that in the modern Occident, theoretical rationalization has, if anything, been further subsumed by the onset of formalized/institutionalized rationality, resulting in an "iron cage" (*stahlhartes Gehäuse*). Weber spent time discussing the many forms of domination and violence enshrined in the modern state. To these we could add the ideas of Marx and a host of different condemnations of the contemporary capitalist world order. I mention this here because the iron cage and disenchantment are often entangled. Framed this way, however, it seems unlikely that re-enchantment (either a naïve revival of magic or even a recovery of ethics) would solve any of these issues. Leaving aside his Orientalist binary between a magical Asia and a magic-less West, Weber himself seems to have believed that Asia had not yet been disenchanted, and yet he was ambivalent about this fact (as he was about enchantment/disenchantment in general).

To put this in more systematic terms, Weber's disenchanting world, as a characterization of popular mentality, had five levels:

1. *Metaphysical realism* (the belief that the world is what it is and does not represent anything else)
2. *Ontological homogeneity* (the belief that there are no truly extramundane objects or people)
3. *Ethical predeterminism* (that God has already decided each individual's soteriological fate) or *value nihilism* (the excision of value from the world of fact)
4. *Epistemic overconfidence* (the belief that everything in the material world is in principle knowable by means of intellectualization/theoretical rationality)
5. *The construction and rationalization of the magic sphere.*[57]

In previous writings, I have discussed the first four levels, but in what follows I want to focus on the construction and rationalization of the magic sphere.

Part III: The Magic Sphere, a Thought Experiment

Although Weber refers to the rationalization of magic, he never fully articulated what it would have looked like in a Western society. In this section, I want to explore what Weber might have meant by the rationalization of the magic sphere and then use Weber's theory in a kind of thought experiment or generative mode. This will put us in position to see where it looks different from a theory of secularization and will perhaps provide us with a more complete sense of what Weber might have thought of our current disenchanting world.

Two of Weber's most important contributions to sociology were his theory of rationalization and his notion of modernity as fragmented into distinct value spheres. Both can be critiqued; Weber's concept of rationalization tends to eliminate individual human agency from history, and his notion of the distinctiveness of the six value spheres or societal domains (*gesellschaftliche Ordnungen*) (often listed as religious, economic, political, aesthetic, erotic, intellectual), and his account of when they became differentiated historically, can also be criticized.[58] But I want to emphasize, on the one hand, that Weber had a complex account of rationalization, and, on the other, that he saw rationalization as occurring in different spheres which he described as coming increasingly to accord with their own logics and autonomous laws (*Eigengesetzlichkeit*).

Weber never explicitly discussed a magic sphere. He may not have conceived of one at all. But we can begin to reconstruct what he might have thought of a magic sphere in distinction from the other spheres by exploring his accounts of how other value spheres came to be differentiated and rationalized.

To explain, I first need to showcase the variety of types of rationalization in Weber's project. Later scholars have proposed radically divergent readings of Weber's system of rationalization, suggesting everything from sixteen versions of rationality to arguing that Weber essentially thought rationalization could mean anything. I parse Weber's notion of social orientations into instrumental, value, theoretical, and formalized rationality versus habitual and effectual irrationality.[59] I discuss these different types of rationality in greater detail and locate the specific references to them in Weber's corpus elsewhere.[60] But here I'd like to supply a brief overview: *instrumental rationality* (*Zweckrationalität*) is basically practical ends-means rationality. Weber's second type of rational orientation is what he referred to as *value rationality* (*Wertrationalität*), or rationality vis-à-vis a particular value or conviction (encompassing what philosophers have referred to as both teleological and deontological ethics). *Theoretical rationality* (generally referred to as "intellectual rationality" or "intellectualization") describes a type of rationality directed toward abstract conjecture and clarifying theoretical concepts. *Formalized rationality* is the institutionalization of various forms of rationality and their incarnation in courts, markets, and other bureaucratic organizations. Formalized rationality has two main sub-aspects: standardization and bureaucratization.

In addition, Weber's writings suggest his underlying notions about rationalization in general. He described the rationalization of the six different value spheres in terms of their coming increasingly into accord with their own particular ultimate values, means, and ends. As a general pattern, rationalization has led toward value spheres becoming increasingly autonomous and therefore fragmented. He also implied that different disciplines, professions, and so on could be rationalized according to their own internal logics. Further, Weber's use of rationalization intimated that it was in general a trend toward standardization, consistency, and decreased complexity (or decreased entropy). Moreover, Weber implied that all forms of rationality tended to absorb irrationality, in that respect liquidating habit, tradition, and emotion into rationalized (or we might say, repressed) norms of behavior.

What might the rationalization of the magic sphere have looked like according to Weber's theoretical apparatus? Our first clue can be found in Weber's writings themselves, in which can be found tentative gestures toward his account of the rationalization of magic. In the China portion of *Die Wirtschaftsethik der Weltreligionen,* Weber actually wrote a subsection titled "The Systematic Rationalization of Magic" (*Die rationale Systematisierung der Magie*). As he argued there:

> In general, it could be said that every sort of rationalization of archaic empirical knowledge and craft in China has moved toward a magical world picture [*magischen Weltbildes*]. Astronomy became astrology … Medicine, and connected with it pharmacology, once manifested estimable empirical accomplishments. They were completely rationalized in an animistic direction …. Chinese "universalist" philosophy and cosmogony transformed the world into a magic garden.[61]

In the first instance, what Weber seems to have had in mind was a set of calendrical reforms under the first Qin Emperor Shihuangdi (始皇帝, birth name Ying Zheng 嬴政, 259–210 BCE). Although today scholars would place the chronology differently, based on the sources he had available Weber believed that Shihuangdi's reign resulted in the systematization of omens, oracular divination, and astrological observations (alongside astronomical calculations) resulting in the production of calendrical almanacs that tracked fortunate and unfortunate days and the like.[62] Weber also argued that something similar happened in Chinese medicine, which became a kind of rationalized "animism" under the influence of notions of *qi* (気) energy and ideas of disease spirits.[63]

The main thrust of Weber's argument in the section on the rationalization of magic as a whole is that Chinese civilization rationalized toward, rather than away from, a meaningful cosmos. In his account, Chinese thinkers came to see the world as full of legible signs, but for Weber this was also a project of rationalization insofar as it produced what he saw as professional magical specialists, a fully bureaucratized enchanted government, and more importantly a standardization and intellectualization of magical forms of knowledge. To be sure, Weber saw this as a crucial difference between Occidental and Oriental civilizations. So in that respect the "magical garden" was the Orientalist alternative to the "disenchanting world." But nonetheless, Weber suggested that magic had been rationalized in the West as well, although he never described this process. In a disenchanting world, magic should be marginalized or at least contained in its own sphere and also rationalized. What might this have looked like according to Weber's model?

One clue can be found in Weber's *Die rationalen und soziologischen Grundlagen der Musik* (The Rational and Social Foundations of Music, 1911). Some of Weber's first explicit engagements with rationalization came in this early manuscript. In the work as a whole, Weber applies his sociological insights to the history of Western music. He began by describing an ideal "primitive" music, which he saw as being rooted in ritual performance, lacking particular note divisions, and being performed by nonspecialists. Then he wanted to explain how in his time, the octave scale, polyvocality, the role of the composer, and the specific instruments used all resulted from particular sociological factors that had altered these basic musical rites into modern forms. In his attempt to explore these, Weber began thinking about rationalization and in so doing he theorized about how different kinds of rationalization (or rational orientations) had produced Western music. For our purposes, the important thing to note is that each of the different kinds of rationalization explored above transformed the unspecialized music of antiquity into its modern form.

In the broadest of brushstrokes, *instrumental rationality* can be seen in the increasing professionalization of music. Instead of celebrating raw talent or local amateur musicians, modernization has meant the birth of whole systems of professionalization for musicians, vocalists, composers, producers, and the like. For Weber, the expression of *value rationality* in the history of Western music can be seen in the way it established its own values, such as aesthetic enjoyment (associated with euphony, harmony, and polyvocality), and then rationalized in order to maximize these values.[64] In this respect, Weber saw modernity as shifting from a less differentiated music, such as sacerdotal music whose function was rooted in praise of the divine, into a kind of music intended for listening pleasure. We can see *theoretical rationality* at work in the birth of music theory. We can see *formalized rationality* at work in both the standardization of music (e.g., musical notation) and the bureaucratization of music (Weber has in mind the orchestra as a kind of bureaucratic organization). In addition to these particular kinds of rationalizations, Weber also was interested in how mechanization or technological shifts contributed to producing modern forms of music.

What Weber said about the rationalization of music provides a blueprint for a discussion of what he might have thought of the rationalization of modern magic in a disenchanting world. Weber would have predicted that magic became increasingly separate from religion, as religion became increasingly contained in its own sphere, a.k.a. secularization. But alongside the secularization of religion, he would have expected to see the formation of a magic sphere with its own diverse types of professionals. The field would begin to cohere around a certain set of values. It would produce works that describe magic theory, so to speak. There would be both bureaucratic and standardization pressures. Finally, technology would result in changes in how the magic sphere operated.

To get a handle on what this magical sphere might look like, one has to begin with the *value rationality* of the magic sphere. Weber saw divination or a symbolic cosmos as a key part of his definition of enchantment. To be clear, I don't want to simplify his definition of magic excessively, but the above point suggests that fortune-telling might be one key site of analysis. One might imagine that as magic rationalized, its central value would be its ability to absorb the meaning-producing function shed by the de-ritualization of modern religion. Indeed, in parallel with Weber's example of Chinese divination above, I want to look at all the ways fortune-telling in the United States exhibits the various kinds of rationalization that Weber predicted.

First, I want to remind readers that despite grand secularization narratives, fortune-telling is widespread. Although surprisingly understudied by scholars, various forms of fortune-telling are big business in contemporary Europe and America. According to one survey from 2017, fortune-tellers and related fields make up an estimated 8 billion euros a year in Italy alone, and there is similar anecdotal evidence about the popularity of various forms of fortune-telling in the United States and Great Britain.[65] Indeed, one only has to travel to a sufficiently big urban area to find signs advertising "palm readers," "psychics," "clairvoyant readings," or "astrology." It is also easy to turn on the television to see celebrity psychics.

We only have a partial instrumental rationalization of this sphere since, despite attempts to the contrary, fortune-telling is still rather under-regulated in Europe and America.[66] That said, there are clearly different professional routes to the performance of fortune-telling due to the variety of different types of fortune-tellers—psychics, astrologers, palm readers, and so on. Looked at from the perspective of theoretical rationalization, there has been a profusion of New Age fortune-telling books that purport to explain astrology and psychical powers, or provide instructions on divination. We can also see standardization pressures at work in these various arenas, in which terminology, ritual, expectations, and (at a local level) pricing all have been standardized to some degree. Finally, it is clear that technological change is indeed motivating the transformations of fortune-telling. Astrology has branched out into iPhone apps and web subscriptions, and sellers on Etsy offer virtual "Spiritual Works" for a fee. To be sure, capitalist profit seems to be an underlying motivation, but one of the underemphasized aspects of Weber's analysis of the fragmentation of the value spheres is exactly that in modernity the economic sphere comes to dominate.

I do not want to claim that this reconstruction of Weber's theory necessarily describes contemporary American or European cultures, but it gives us a bare nub of what a Weberian account of such things might look like. At best magic is only partially rationalized in the contemporary context. We have fortune-tellers, energy workers, faith healers, New Age bookstores, and the like, but there are still many amateur magic practitioners. Moreover, the boundaries between magic and Weber's other value spheres (such as the religious or artistic) are at best incomplete. But it does suggest areas for future research.

Conclusion

The main thrust of this chapter has been an attempt to clarify various misunderstandings concerning Weber's notion of *Entzauberung*. In particular, I wanted to attack two common notions—that Weber thought magic would vanish in modernity and that Weber saw magic and rationalization as opposed. Instead, I have shown that the first is implausible both on biographical grounds and in reference to specific points in his writings. The second claim about the relationship between magic and rationality has required more explanation. But it should now be clear that a close reading of Weber's writings suggests that he specifically described the rationalization and systematization of magic.

Instead of a classic account of "the disenchantment of the world" that imagined either that belief in magic was gone or that it was displaced in favor of a subsequent revival, I have shown that Weber instead should be read as having posited a *disenchanting* world in which magic became demonized and located in its own sphere. In the above, I've sketched the barest of outlines of how he might have imagined this disenchanting world by looking at his account of the putative rationalization of magic in China and gesturing at fortune-telling in America and Western Europe.

3

Science as a Commodity

Disenchantment and Conspicuous Consumption

Egil Asprem

Introduction: The Continuing Relevance of "Science as a Vocation"

The most striking observation to make when reading Weber's lecture "Science as a Vocation" (*Wissenschaft als Beruf*) today is how little has changed in one hundred years. Aspiring scholars are still troubled by the precariousness of academic positions. Nepotistic hiring practices continue with impunity, even in the face of increasing bureaucratization and top-down management that, as Weber already lamented a century ago, work to the advancement of mediocrity rather than meritocracy. Both the American and the German models that Weber compared, with their unique drawbacks, are with us today: early-career scholars are exploited for their labor with unreasonable teaching demands for low salaries (as per the American model), but they are also pressured to achieve popularity and "success" in the quantitative sense, as per the German *Privatdozent* model. Arguably, the gamification of academic prestige through its increasing mediatization, especially in social media, contributes another, virtual dimension to this preexisting trend. The root problem remains economic, however: while the pressure to achieve quantifiable success existed for teaching in the past—at least for the *Privatdozent* who relied on lecture fees for their income—it is now also the case for publishing if one hopes to get tenure or some rough approximation of it. If there has been any development in the economic, social, and organizational aspects of academic life—its *external* conditions, to follow Weber's parlance—it is an intensification of these preexisting trends under the dual pressures of neoliberal governance in higher education and increased competition for scarce resources due to an overproduction of PhDs. The latter, of course, is a precondition for exploitative hiring practices to continue.

What, then, about the internal conditions of science, which were Weber's main concerns and which later scholars have continued to comment upon over the past century? Even here, the basic ideas remain familiar. Those of us who teach in history of religion departments, for example, still have to explain to students that we are not there to rank religions according to some criteria of "good" and "bad" or to deliver profound spiritual truths from the podium. Our business is not to tell students how to live their lives, which religion to join, or what party to vote for in the next election. Moreover, the feeling of embarrassment—and perhaps annoyance—when confronted with a colleague who plays on charisma, thrives in the spotlight of the media, and writes popularizing books that are rich in grand but poorly founded ideas remains familiar to many. Weber had little patience for this type of scholar, the one who asks, "How can I prove that I am something other than a mere 'specialist' and how can I manage to say something in form or in content that nobody else has ever said?"[1] This person is devoid of personality, Weber tells us, lacking in inner devotion to the task and refusing the lot that any scientist needs to accept: the fact that scholarship *is* specialized and limited, that advances are incremental at best, and that the ultimate fate is to have one's humble contributions superseded by future progress.

In short, even though Weber's notion of value-free science today seems untenable as a *descriptive* account of how the sciences actually work, many will still agree with him that neutrality is, at the very least, an *ideal* of science for which one ought to strive in one's teaching and publications.[2] In a world where science has again come under serious threat from governments as well as powerful corporations, many would agree with Weber that the key contribution of science today, that which gives it its particular value, is not primarily its ability to provide technologies for controlling and mastering life—although that is its most evident contribution—but more importantly, its development of methods for thinking and tools for training thought, and most of all, its contribution to achieving *clarity*. No matter what our subjective goals or ultimate values might be, clarity ought to be an unquestionable good in itself. Above all, the sort of *self-clarification* that Weber offered his audience at the end of the lecture is valuable because it lets one examine one's own presuppositions and one's conduct in life, exploring their consequences as well as their basic assumptions with as little bias as possible.

Unruly Academics and the Permeable Value Sphere of Science

While it is easy to be sympathetic with these points, they offer only one, quite particular view of the internal values of "proper science." Today, as in 1917,[3] the obvious problem is that academics do not all agree on the internal rules and values pertinent to scientific conduct. Put differently, the historical contingencies that have shaped the value sphere of science have not ceased operating. For example, Weber observed that the Renaissance view of science as a way to "true art" and to "true nature," and especially the idea still dominant in the early modern period that science could unveil the traces of the divine in nature, was largely relegated to the dustbin of history by the early twentieth century: "All these former illusions," he wrote, "the 'way to true being,' the 'way to true art,' the 'way to true nature,' the 'way to true God,' the 'way to true happiness,' have been dispelled."[4] And further: "Who—aside from certain big children ... still believes that the findings of astronomy, biology, physics, or chemistry could teach us anything about the *meaning* of the world?"[5] In his own day, Weber argued, the value sphere of science is predicated on the "disenchanted" view that positive knowledge of any phenomenon is possible, but leaves us devoid of metaphysics and with no ability to speak about meanings, values, or how to live our lives.

Nevertheless, it is not hard to come by scientists and even entire institutions and disciplines dedicated precisely to reinstating some of these older assumptions. Natural theology was, for example, experiencing a renaissance in Weber's own days.[6] This might be exemplified by the increasing prestige of the Gifford Lectures in Natural Theology, which encouraged a long list of esteemed academics across the disciplines to recover their inner "big child," violate the axiological and metaphysical skepticism of science's assumed internal disenchantment, and speculate freely on the implications of natural knowledge for values, metaphysics, and spirituality.[7] Prospective new disciplines, like psychical research or parapsychology, were founded on the very notion that the reach of empirical science extends into the realms of metaphysics, which should have been forbidden to those taking the dictums of a disenchanted world seriously. Indeed, while parapsychology eventually failed as a scientific discipline (in part *because* of its metaphysical appetite), it is notable that this collection of big children also inspired intellectual currents that have been much more successful, such as American pragmatism.[8] Even well-established and presumptively fully disenchanted disciplines like physics would (opportunistically, I argue) embrace an aura of enchantment in order to reinvent their public standing and relevance in the world under the pressure of anti-intellectualism.[9]

Weber was of course well aware that these "impure aberrations" existed. His point was precisely to stand up for a particular view of scientific values, according to which these mixes of scholarship and activism represented a *threat* to science in the long haul. When "the youth," which Weber addressed throughout his lecture, come to the lecture hall looking for charismatic personalities, authentic experience, and leadership, they are asking for something that scientists who remain true to their values simply cannot provide. The point, then, is moral: it concerns the *epistemic virtues* appropriate to science and education. Scholars *ought* to resist the temptation to oblige, and the youth *ought* to turn the attention of their seekership elsewhere—whether to "the old churches" or to individual mysticism.

My own agenda at present will be a different one. Leaving aside the question of what attitude scholars ought to have, I take as my point of departure the fact that scientists do occasionally break these epistemic virtues. Moreover, I argue that these breaches have been culturally significant, in that they have created a range of "scientific enchantments" that are popular with the educated middle classes. Finally, I propose to approach this social fact in a fairly Weberian way, asking simply *what socioeconomic conditions* have made this phenomenon possible.

By way of clarification, I do not take "disenchantment" to be a historical process by which the Occident progressively sheds its "magical" past—that narrative, as Jason Josephson-Storm has argued,[10] is a myth. It is, however, a myth that has shaped how moderns think about themselves, the world, and the nature of (scientific) knowledge.[11] When I talk about disenchantment, then, I refer to the mythical, or ideological, conception (1) that humans (through science) can in principle explain the natural world (I call this "epistemological optimism"); (2) that the sciences cannot produce metaphysical knowledge ("metaphysical skepticism"); and (3) that knowledge of nature cannot give knowledge of how we ought to live our lives ("axiological skepticism").[12] When I refer to re-/enchantment it is as shorthand for the negation of any of these three tenets, a negation typically grounded in the suspicion that nature does, after all, contain "mysterious incalculable powers," in Weber's sense.

In previous work, I have studied the relationship between science and spiritual practices, broadly conceived, from the perspective of intellectual history. In *The Problem of Disenchantment* (2014), I looked at how a number of science-internal disputes in the early twentieth century—such as the vitalism and organicism controversies in biology, the shattering of the Daltonian theory of matter following the discovery of radioactivity, and the discussion about causality and determinism in the context of quantum mechanics—encouraged a minority of scientists to counter a disenchanted view of the world, paving the way for a range of new natural theologies.

While some of this material will form a backdrop to my present argument, the approach taken here will be a different one. I propose to turn once more from the *internal* conditions of science to its *external* conditions in order to get at the social mechanisms and the motivations of actors that drive the production and dissemination of "scientific enchantments," focusing on the *commodification* and *consumption* of science in a consumer economy. I will do this by bringing another voice into our conversation: the iconoclastic Norwegian-American theorist of the "leisure class," Thorstein Veblen.

Thorstein Veblen and the Conspicuous Consumption of Higher Education

Veblen's contribution to social theory is best characterized as that of the provocateur, the "disturber of the intellectual peace," as his recent biographer put it.[13] As such we do not find a complete, workable theory in Veblen's work that can be applied without modification to our problem at hand. We do, however, find some useful concepts that help us explain why science in the twentieth century failed to be an unambiguously disenchanting force and was instead regularly coopted by various re-enchantment projects. In order to see this, we should first have a brief look at three aspects of Veblen's work: the notion of the "leisure class," the role of "conspicuous consumption," and the relevance of both concepts to trends in higher education and science.

Classic economic theory sees wealth as a sign of virtue: the capitalist has accumulated wealth through industrious work and smart investments. Veblen's analysis, based on anthropological and historical work, draws a different conclusion: the origin of wealth lies not in hard work but in the "predatory habit" of seizing the goods of others, whether by brute force or more subtle forms of exploitation.[14] When a society with a "predatory class" also manages to produce a surplus of subsistence that make it possible for some members of society to be economically unproductive, societies will tend to diversify along the lines of those who pursue economically productive work and those who enjoy leisure. The "leisure class" that emerges from the predators in this way tends to invent elaborate prestige systems, which are recognized throughout society but require a significant waste of time and resources to master. In other words: leisure becomes an economic precondition for partaking in prestige; hence, productive labor becomes low status, while the economically wasteful behavior of the unproductive upper classes is rewarded with high status. The leisure class perpetuates its influence and power in society by pursuing economically nonproductive occupations, of which Veblen lists government, warfare, religious observance, and sports as the main examples.

In foregrounding the accumulation of wealth through predatory exploitation that produces class hierarchies, Veblen's economic theory is closer to a Marxian tradition than to Weber's more nuanced focus on individual ethics and values as a variable that creates different economic outcomes.[15] Veblen's analysis of how the uneven distribution of leisure is related to prestige and distinction prefigures some of Pierre Bourdieu's key insights concerning cultural capital[16] and provides us with a better grounding for analyzing some of the unintended social and cultural consequences of higher education and learning. In the final chapter of *The Theory of the Leisure Class* (1899)—and again in his farcical analysis of *The Higher Education in America* (1918)—education, and particularly the humanities, is portrayed as an integrated part of how the leisure class produces and sustains rigid prestige hierarchies. As Veblen saw it, higher education in fact had so little to do with serious intellectual curiosity that he titled an earlier version of the manuscript *A Study in Total Depravity*.[17] To Veblen, humanities education had little function other than allocating class distinctions and perpetuating patterns of privilege.

Veblen's most enduring contribution to social theory was his account of the social functions of economically wasteful behavior, and it is summed up in the concept of "conspicuous consumption." We can view conspicuous consumption as the socioeconomic equivalent of what evolutionary biologists now call "costly signaling": the meaning of wasteful consumption—from fancy dress to fine dining to lighting up cigars with dollar bills—is completely lost if analyzed from a strictly economic perspective. Its meaning lies in the signaling of prestige. Around such signaling in- and out-groups are produced—those who can afford the waste and those who can't—and from group formations, arenas for socialization arise through which different values can be inculcated and strategies learned. Consumption is intricately linked with the production and transmission of class privileges.

Extending this analysis to academia, Veblen held that the leisure class's interest in higher education was driven not by a quest for erudition but by the pursuit of signs of merit, distinction, and honor. Moreover, since an occupation accrues more prestige the more wasteful it is, Veblen singled out the humanities, and particularly the classics, as the discipline of choice for idle, leisured gentlemen:

> There can be little doubt that it is their utility as evidence of wasted time and effort, and hence of the pecuniary strength necessary in order to afford this waste, that has secured to the classics their position of prerogative in the scheme of higher learning .... They serve the decorative ends of leisure-class learning better than any other body of knowledge, and hence they are an effective means of reputability.[18]

Looking at rituals and dress codes in institutions of higher education in late nineteenth-century North America, Veblen noted the tendency toward an increase in ritualism and impractical dress codes that varied directly with the wealth of the constituency of the school. Moreover, when a school transitioned from offering only technical education to also providing liberal arts education, an increase of wasteful ceremony and dress would follow. Humanities education, wasteful fashions, and irrational rituals are all part of the same signaling of prestige by upper-class people, in Veblen's view.

In contrast to this cynical view of the humanities, Veblen displays a remarkable naivety about the status of the natural sciences. The medieval feudal system—and particularly the church's place in it—had been peak leisure class, and the upheavals wreaked by industrialization, capitalism, and the intimate connection between science and technology were upsetting the old order. In this schema, the humanities were seen as a continuation of feudal leisure class arrangements in capitalist modernity, while the sciences were aligned with economically productive, industrious work. In later publications, Veblen would cast the engineers as the potential saviors of human civilization—those who would finally crush the remnants of aristocracy and replace it with a fairer, more rational, and more advanced socioeconomic order that values productivity over wasteful prestige.[19]

We may once again contrast Veblen's account of economic history with Weber's: whereas Weber sought the causes of material change in the mental and moral transformations of individuals and groups, Veblen flirts with technological determinism. His confidence in the rationalizing potential of technical education goes a long way toward suggesting that mere proximity to industrial work and thinking instills in people a rational and pragmatic attitude to *other* areas of life. This notion of operating machinery as a transferable cognitive skill is psychologically naïve; Weber's nuanced work on the paradoxical role of technology in the rationalization process is therefore, as I shall argue later, much preferable to Veblen's.

The place of natural science and technical education in society has taken a different course from the one Veblen envisioned. The nature of consumption has also changed in important ways. Veblen was writing before the full-scale emergence of the consumer economy, before the rise of the tertiary or service sector, and most importantly, before the *expansion* of leisure with the rise of the middle class. Leisure was more unevenly distributed in his time than it has since become. Veblen's account of conspicuous consumption is therefore also too simply connected to a binary separation of the "upper" and "lower classes," where social mobility through consumption is thought to take place on a single vertical axis.

Nevertheless, Veblen's tools can be shaped to deal with these shifts. Two simple modifications appear sufficient: first, the expansion of leisure and transition to an economy based largely on private consumption have *not* taken away the identity-constructing and identity-protective functions of conspicuous consumption. However, when the entire economy runs on waste, conspicuous consumption is diversified and no longer the prerogative of a monolithic "upper class." In addition to the signaling of "high class"—which undoubtedly still occurs, especially among the *nouveau riche* and *petit bourgeoisie* who transform economic capital into social capital in order to match the born advantage of the inheriting classes[20]—the identity-producing function of consumption has been broadened and expanded to include an ever-widening number of "alternative" identities, "lifestyles," and subcultural affiliations. The strategic consumption of goods still determines access to in-groups, whether we are thinking of metal music subcultures or fitting in at Burning Man, but the distinctions they create are now more horizontal than vertical.[21] This sort of analysis can be extended to religious identities, where patterns of consumption signal degrees of commitment and determine in-group status, whether in terms of what is *avoided* (e.g., vegetarianism over meat consumption, alternative therapies over school medicine) or the cultural capital accrued through, for example, the kinds of popular or high culture consumed (books, films, music, festivals, etc.).[22] In short, in a world of a rapidly expanding number of "identities" eager to distinguish themselves from each other, strategic consumption is a social skill.

The second modification is that natural science, too, must be viewed as a commodity-producing activity. This goes equally for science *education* as for the various marketable products branded as "science": from technological consumer products and works of *popular* science to big government spending on prestigious but wasteful projects, like the race to the moon or to identify the smallest particles of matter. One part of the picture here is, of course, that a drastic change has happened with the prestige system in higher education since Veblen's time of writing, which makes his discussion of "useless dead languages" as the pinnacle of prestige sound particularly quaint. Constantly under threat from diminishing departmental budgets, the classics professor today is unlikely to feel they are guarding the prestige of the ruling elites. One indicator of this shift is the sheer difference in monetary value and hence pecuniary prestige put on technical educations and humanities disciplines. On average, an engineering student in the United States can expect an almost 50 percent higher starting salary than a humanities graduate.[23] Given Veblen's role in inspiring the early technocracy movement, which wanted to overthrow capitalism by replacing the price system with an energy-based system of value and install engineers and scientists as the ruling class,[24] it is possible that he would have viewed the current defunding of the humanities with some ambiguity. While he would have welcomed the higher prestige of utilitarian and technical educations, he would no doubt have been alarmed to find that it is still the same predatory "captains of industry" who call the shots, from government to university boards. Productivity may have become more prestigious, but the engineer is still the serf of the capitalist.

Science as a Commodity: Re-Enchantment through Consumer Behavior

Let us now return to the problem at hand: How might this view of science as a commodity help us understand the role that science continues to have as an agent not of disenchantment but of re-enchantment? To deal with this question in a systematic way, we might attack it from two angles. First, how should we understand the motivations of those producers of science who promote discoveries in an enchanted mode, that is, Weber's "big children"? Second, what are the effects of the commodification of science on the consumers of science? Together, let us ask, what are the strategic drives that lead to a selective consumption of scientific products in the service of creating what we might think of as enchanted identities?

If we start with the motivations of the big children, we can return to an important aspect of Weber's lecture—namely, the conflict that it sets up between the internal demands of proper science and the demands of the scientist's *audience*. Veblen's cynical view of the consumers of higher education can help us analyze this situation. As noted already, Weber is repeatedly addressing "the youth" that flock to lecture rooms with what he considers to be inappropriate and unrealistic expectations of what the docents and professors ought to provide. The youth are looking for experience, authenticity, personality, and leadership. They are looking for charisma, and they are looking for purpose. Moreover, the youth are unimpressed with the mere *technical* and *practical* benefits that science has to offer; they want something less tangible and more deeply meaningful. In the end, Weber elegantly diverts their demand for meaning by offering them self-clarity and the ability to better judge for themselves what is meaningful and what is not. Meanwhile, he also has mocked those professors who would give in to the original demand of the youth, and, in no uncertain terms, dismissed them as crowd pleasers who, unfortunately, are encouraged to violate the internal conditions of the scientific profession due to its rough external conditions.

We might note that in this respect, Weber's attitude is every bit as cynical as Veblen's. But, with Veblen, we might add a dimension to the analysis of the situation: Who are the youth but the leisure class consumers of higher education? And who are the consumers but the market for lecturers who, at least in the German system, depend on lecture room consumption for personal financial security? The youth movements' dissatisfaction with the purely pragmatic utility of science belongs, of course, to the broader wave of antimodern sentiments of the era, but the wave of antimodernism itself rests precisely on the sort of cultural conservatism and contempt for industrial productivity that Veblen associated with the leisure class. On this view, it is little wonder that the consumer side of science demanded "higher," more "cultured," and more "prestigious" goods than mere facts and calculations.

Weber may have lamented the fact, but many scientists of the period would give in to the leisure class's cravings for more "meaning" in science. The best example of this is perhaps the effort to rebrand physics as philosophy and culture. As the historian of science Paul Forman famously argued, the inventors of quantum mechanics in the interwar years went through a process of cultural accommodation by which they created interpretations of microphysics that went much beyond the scientific data and served to harmonize the new physics with the antimechanistic, antimodern, and broadly romantic attitudes that permeated society at the time.[25]

Sometimes, this led physicists to draw on the storehouse of associations evoked by Western esotericism. References to "the question of the old alchemists" or even to the "cabbalists" are found in public addresses by physicists in the Weimar years.[26] Arnold Sommerfeld attempted to make the impenetrable mathematics of the new physics more palatable by casting it as a species of "Pythagorean number mysticism"[27]; Werner Heisenberg could frame the uncertainty principle as a flat-out rejection of "causality" from nature[28]; Niels Bohr could draw on Kierkegaard to explain "complementarity" and, moreover, extend it to thoroughly disconnected areas such as the "problems of consciousness" and the irreducibility of life[29]; while Pascual Jordan and eventually Wolfgang Pauli would insist on the relevance of quantum mechanics to parapsychology and paranormal phenomena.[30] The effect of all these attempts to marry physics with philosophical and esoteric concepts was the birth of "quantum mysticism," which would be rediscovered by the counterculture and the emerging New Age movement in the postwar period to form a significant impulse of science-oriented re-enchantment.[31] From the perspective of the consumer economy, we should understand this phenomenon as a successful branding strategy that hit a nerve in the growing middle-class reading market and catapulted the "mystical physicist" to international stardom.

This brings us to another important aspect of the commodification of science, namely popularization. In Germany there has historically been a wider chasm between the *producers* of science and its *popularizers* than in the Anglo-American context.[32] Weber's skepticism against crowd pleasers makes sense in this context, but less so in the context of the long British tradition of popular-scientific lectures, which frequently included questions of value and worldview—I am thinking, for example, of the famous "Lay Sermons" given by Victorian scientists such as John Tyndall or Thomas Henry Huxley, preaching the wonders of science along with antireligious sentiments and the ethical implications of Darwinism. The first decades of the twentieth century saw a new golden age of science popularization. Leading scientists were now writing inexpensive trade monographs explaining new discoveries in physics and cosmology in plain language. It is notable that, in order to pique the interest and increase the general value for the audience, these books would typically veer into philosophy, metaphysics, and spirituality. A particularly successful example of such consumer goods was James Jeans's *The Mysterious Universe* (1930), in which the leading astrophysicist argued that the emerging world picture implied what can best be characterized as a Pythagorean and Platonic universe where mathematics is eternal, time is unreal, and ultimate reality a "world of pure thought."[33] The book became a bestseller, surpassing all science titles to date; judging from its reviews, this was in large part *because* of its ability to present what is really on close inspection an austere form of physical determinism as something beautiful and spiritually significant.

What Jeans and other scientists deft at popularizing understood was that the reading public craves something more than cold facts and explanations; they want science to be mystery, culture, and beauty. So the scientists provided these. Over the rest of the century, this led to a veritable industry of science writing in an enchanted mode—sometimes with an explicit re-enchantment agenda, at other times more opportunistically seizing on tropes that sell. For an example of the latter: the Higgs boson was labeled *The God Particle* (1993) only on the recommendation of a publisher's marketing department. As the Nobel Prize–winning physicist Leon Lederman and his coauthor Dick Teresi wrote: "The publisher wouldn't let us call it the Goddamn Particle, though that might be a more appropriate title, given its villainous nature and the expense it is causing."[34]

This case leads me to a final observation regarding the effects of commodification in the form of popular science. In order to communicate successfully with a lay audience, scientists and science writers must reduce the complexity of scientific results and translate these into a language that is not only understood by but also appealing to the audience. Frequently, this means using metaphors and allegories that transform difficult-to-process material into graspable categories closer to everyday life. In previous work, I looked at these translation processes as a crucial step in a broader epidemiology of science-based representations, drawing on insights from the cognitive science of religion.[35]

According to this model, a function of popular science is to *select* a small segment of the total pool of research that is particularly attention-grabbing and to *transform* it into "cognitively optimal" representations (Figure 1). This, then, is the shape in which most consumers will tend to encounter scientific representations and which they will then elaborate upon in whatever local ideational context they find themselves. The problem, of course, is that the translations offered by popularizers will already tend to use metaphorical language that, in fact, invites the audience to engage the science in question with intuitions and background assumptions that lead to inferences quite at odds with the original scientific concept. If we think about the distinction between cognitively costly reflective thought, on the one hand, and "fast and frugal"

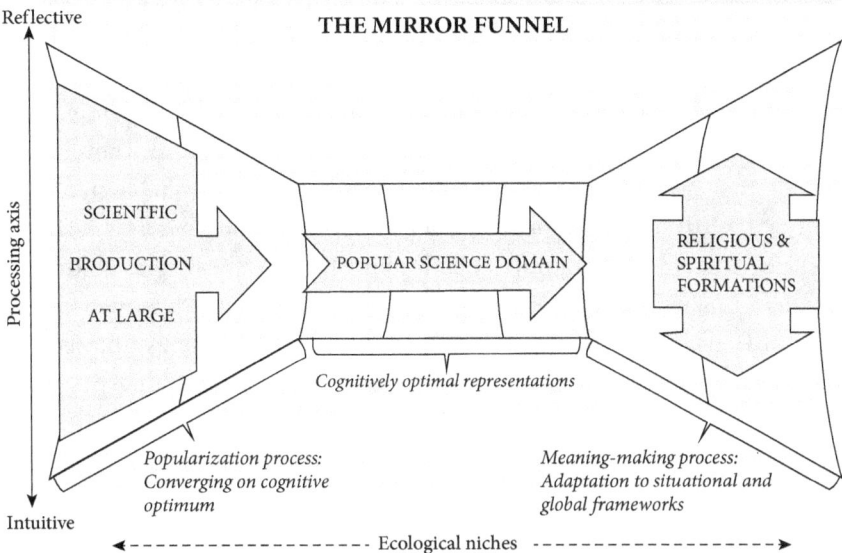

Figure 1 The Mirror Funnel Model: Attractor spaces for science-based representations along a processing axis (intuitive-reflective) and an ecological axis (scientific institutions—popular science—religious/spiritual formations).

Note: For a full explanation, see Asprem, "How Schrödinger's Cat Became a Zombie," 123–6.

intuitive inferences based on evolved systems for processing—for example, the intentions of agents or the behavior of physical objects—on the other, we see that popularizers typically draw on a combination of *agentive language* and *naïve physics* when presenting causally complex subject matters. In other words, authors appeal to our biases and heuristics, leading to a skewed processing of scientific content.

For example, Richard Dawkins popularized the gene-centered view of evolution in the 1970s, which is a complex but thoroughly *mechanistic* theory, by inventing the metaphor of the "selfish gene"—that is, a molecule with intentions and mental states.[36] This invites readers to talk about evolution in psychologistic and teleological terms that run exactly opposite to the core idea of evolutionary theory. In a different example, when Erwin Schrödinger invented the famous thought experiment of a cat locked inside a steel box together with a Geiger counter, some unstable radioactive material, and a hammer that will break a glass tube containing prussic acid whenever the radioactive material decays, his intention was to show the *absurdity* of the Copenhagen school's interpretation of indeterminacy. The both-dead-and-alive cat is a reductio ad absurdum: it is designed to show that the premises of the Copenhagen interpretation lead to a contradiction. Through its popularization, however, the complexity of this argument has been reduced and the thought experiment became simply a *description* of a cat that is both dead and alive—indeed a "minimally counterintuitive concept," akin to zombies, ghouls, and ghosts—and now mostly functions as an emblem of the mysterious weirdness of quantum physics.

The tragedy of even the most sincere science popularizer is that the metaphorical translations and simplifications that are their most useful tool also lead to a fetishization of scientific representations that hides their central content from view and invites more "enchanted" interpretations. Incidentally, the problem is exactly the same as what Pascal Boyer has termed "the tragedy of the theologian" in the context of religious doctrines.[37]

Technology and Commodity Fetishism

So far we have been talking about ideational commodities, in the form of education, lectures, and literature. But we should also consider *technological* commodities, not least because they occupied central roles in both Weber's and Veblen's theories of rationalization. As I let on earlier, Weber is much preferable to Veblen on this topic. Veblen appears to suggest that technology rationalizes by contagion. Weber, by contrast, noticed that the effect of the technologization of society on the *users* of technology is generally *not* a better, clearer understanding of the conditions of one's daily life but rather the opposite. As he wrote in 1913, we have

> the generally established belief that the conditions of civilized everyday life, be they streetcar or lift or money or court of law or military or medicine, are *in principle rational*, that is, are *human artifacts accessible to rational knowledge, creation, and control*.[38]

But even so, there is a basic socio-cognitive alienation to this rationalization process which, as Weber continued to note,

> means a wholesale widening separation of those practically affected by rational techniques and rules from the rational foundation of those rules, which, on the whole, is likely to be more mysterious to those affected than the meaning of the sorcerer's magical procedures is to the "primitive."[39]

The rationalization of society in general (including through bureaucratization) produces the conditions for a sort of re-enchantment of the everyday life of modern citizens. All it takes is to forget, reject, or ignore the very *artificiality* of the institutions and technological objects that populate the modern ecological niche and treat them as irreducible, essential things.

That, taking a cue from Marx, is precisely what *commodity fetishism* achieves: labor is transformed into "transcendent," "social things," that is, commodities.[40] With today's technological consumer products, fetishization occurs along three pathways, which reflect three types of alienation: the basic Marxian commodity fetishism (alienation of labor from its fruits), the socio-cognitive alienation that Weber described (users do not have access to the rational principles underlying the products), and finally the *deliberate* fetishization of technology through product design and marketing that plays strategically on psychological and affective biases. Today, there is probably no better example of the fetishization of consumer technology in all three aspects than Apple products. Through carefully designed user interfaces, few removable parts, and the cultivation of an image that "it just works," these devices aspire to present themselves as magical artifacts that have fallen from the skies—hiding, in the process, their vast supply and production chains that rely on environmental destruction through mineral extraction and severely exploitative labor practices in Chinese factories. An Apple product is "designed in California," not simply "made in China."

I mention this to make two related points. First, that there is (as Marx already noted) a continuity between the sort of "fetishism" that early anthropologists like E.B. Tylor were talking about, that is, the subset of animism (the belief in spirits) in which material objects are *ensouled*, and simple commodity fetishism by which a product presents itself to the consumer as sui generis. When commodities are designed and marketed, as they are today, with the help of psychologists' and cognitive scientists' knowledge about how best to arrest the consumer's attention, coopt their affective responses, and exploit biases in social cognition, the fetishizing effect can be made very convincing indeed, and the product presents itself to us as a social creature that inspires touch, talk, and care. It may even produce the illusion of consciousness, as was the case with the "conscious iPod" mytheme of the late 2000s (the iPods apparently "chose" songs in shuffle mode with uncanny appropriateness). In these latter cases, we have arrived at a full-blown "technofetishism," where commodity fetishes have developed into old-school Tylorian animated artifacts.

The *second* point I want to make is that this fetishization of technology makes possible a more explicit form of enchantment. From Kirlian photography to Scientology E-meters, quite ordinary technology is customarily embedded in enchanted worldviews that are enacted through ritualization. They become what historian of religion Olav Hammer calls "technological ritual objects."[41]

Thus in Scientology, electrical circuits measuring galvanic skin response become potent "E-meters," capable of measuring "mental mass" and providing technological backup for "auditing" one's way to salvation. To the engineer, however, it is simply a galvanometer with fancy design and sky-blue coating. Similarly, in Kirlian photography, the use of a charged photographic plate— the same technology used in office copy machines—reveals the texture of the soul. Moreover, devices for "technologized" and "scientized" healing practices abound in alternative and complementary medicine. The "quantum healing" SCIO machine, for example, is said to "harmonize" mysterious "bio-energetic" forces to create optimal wellness, blending "ancient healing" with "modern technology."[42] When our skeptical engineer wrenches the box open, however, she finds an ordinary biofeedback device, capable of measuring heartbeats and muscle contractions.[43] In all these cases, ritualization and displacement of goals from the material to the soteriological make the technological commodity present itself as invested with meanings and powers that are nowhere to be found in its internal circuitry.

Conclusion: Science and Enchantment in the Consumer Economy

The technological ritual objects of new religious movements achieve two things. They are deployed as fetishes, or "charismatic objects"[44] with special powers, but they also become tokens of scientificity, signaling a certain kind of prestige to other potential consumers. This brings me to my final considerations.

The idea of "science" now enjoys high prestige, and the conspicuous consumption of science—whether through products that are read as indexical of scientific literacy (books, university degrees) or through the display of apparently advanced technology—has effects similar to those of other adorning possessions that elevate their owners' status. In the field of alternative spiritualities, the conspicuous consumption of science is everywhere. Some of the most successful authors of New Age material are those who can display PhD titles from prestigious academic institutions on the dust jacket—people like Fritjof Capra, with his PhD from the University of Vienna and former research position at Berkeley, to Rupert Sheldrake, with his doctorate from Cambridge. When the "Near Death Experience" discourse resurfaced to popularity a few years back, it was due to the writings of neurosurgeon Eben Alexander, whose argument puts the external trappings of "science" front and center to argue that the brain does not produce "consciousness."⁴⁵ In all these cases, the educational commodity of the PhD was integral to the structuration of prestige hierarchies in the supposedly "flat" scene of alternative spirituality.

This contemporary situation already existed in embryo in Weber's and Veblen's days, and came of age in the second half of the twentieth century. We have seen this in the shape of physicists rebranding their science as philosophy and mysticism, in the parapsychological vogue of the 1920s to the 1930s, in the new natural theology embodied by institutions such as the Gifford Lectures, as well as in the polemics against such blends of science and worldview by intellectuals like Weber. What characterized the religionist scientists of the early twentieth century was precisely a rejection of the idea that science must entail a disenchantment of the world: instead, they professed science in an enchanted mode and often argued in defense of the scientific method while doing so. The scientific method, and even naturalism itself, was, on this view, an open-ended endeavor with the potential to unveil not only cold mechanisms at work in nature but irreducible mystery and magic as well. This happened in a period when most people, and even many scientists, were feeling increasingly alienated from the results and the procedures of natural science, as well as from the technologized social world that was increasingly associated with science. It was increasingly difficult to imagine what the new scientific world picture really entailed, beyond the advanced equations and mathematical matrixes designed to describe it. Meanwhile, there was an unmistakable sense that the tangible products of science, in the form of mechanized production, urbanization, and, not least, industrialized warfare of the type unleashed during the Great War, entailed a fundamental alienation of humanity from nature. To preserve one's fascination with science in this climate, it became necessary to imagine science as opening up new meaningful possibilities.

Since then, both the prestige and the alienation of the natural sciences have increased, setting the right conditions for renegade interpretations of science as a legitimizing factor for new spiritual frameworks. One significant change has been the emergence of so-called Big Science: "big" in the triple sense that it is conducted by big organizations, uses big machines, and is involved in big politics.⁴⁶ In the 1920s, the frontier was still dominated by individual scientists or small teams of researchers, but as the objects of scientific enquiry became at the same time impossibly small (microphysics) and impossibly vast (cosmology), research has come to depend entirely on huge and expensive instruments that require vast funding from nation states and the collaboration of sometimes thousands of researchers and technicians. The 2015 paper that confirmed the discovery of the Higgs boson had 5,154 coauthors.[47] From Hubble to CERN, no single individual has the full picture anymore.

The rise of Big Science was largely a result of the government-funded military-industrial projects of the Second World War, like the Manhattan Project, and it continued to grow as the ideological blocks of the Cold War were locked in a struggle for scientific prestige as well as technological supremacy. This politicization of science helps explain how enchanted science came to be a central ingredient of the alternative spiritualities produced by the so-called counterculture that took shape in the 1960s.[48] One obvious factor is that the very same "problem of disenchantment" that emerged at the beginning of the century was at the forefront of the counterculture's criticisms of mainstream, establishment society, now with added ingredients like environmental and anti-nuclear activism. In this milieu, the writings and lectures of an earlier generation of intellectuals dreaming of a re-enchanted science aligned with mysticism and the esoteric fell on fertile soil. But more importantly still, a new generation of young scientists grew impatient with the bureaucratic, super-specialized, and inherently authoritarian structures of Big Science, and created new forums outside of the usual institutions in order to discuss "big picture" ideas. As the historian of science David Kaiser showed in his book, *How the Hippies Saved Physics* (2011), colorful and talented groups like the Berkeley-based Fundamental Fysiks Group succeeded in connecting physics to topics as diverse as information theory, psychedelics, and parapsychological abilities, and in making inroads to the Esalen Institute and the wider "human potential movement," as well as to the CIA and the Pentagon.[49] The counterculture in short gave birth to a new era of renegade physics that has remained particularly influential in the alternative spiritual scene, but also in the public imagination.

Given the radical roots of the contemporary "science and spirituality" discourse, it may seem out of place to insist that commodification and consumerism are key factors in explaining this phenomenon. The truth is that, like so much else originating in the radical counterculture, "quantum talk" and other signs of renegade physics are now part and parcel of what Thomas Frank has called "hip consumerism," used as marketing ploys in science popularization, spiritual self-help literature, and alternative medicine.[50] I suggest that we can deepen the standard history of religion perspective on references to "science" as a legitimation strategy[51] by approaching it as a form of conspicuous consumption, the prestige value of which is intimately tied up with the history of countercultural renegade science sketched above. One advantage of this view is that we have an easier time explaining the accumulation of adorning possessions from a wider range of fields: paratechnological objects and books imitating the authority of science share the New Age treasure chamber with religious statues, wisdom literature, radiant crystals, and works of art and music, collected by people who follow specific "lifestyles" that include consumer preferences in diet, clothing, and vacation destinations. Commodities suggesting "the scientific" are in this way a part of the general material culture of alternative spiritualities; possessing them signals prestige and potential authority within spiritual milieus and aligns the consumer with particular traditions in the milieu.

Looking at how science ends up in these contexts through the lens of commodification also brings attention to why and in what way people who have at some point been active in the sciences participate in the commodification process and prop up the conspicuous consumption of science in spiritual milieus. I have suggested a range of related reasons, but they all boil down to the relationship between producers (scientists, technologists, and science writers) and the real or imagined demands of consumers. The need to identify consumer needs and interests, and to tailor the product of their intellectual labor to satisfy these, arises simply because it is often expected of successful scientists that they have "outreach," "impact," and a social media strategy. The pressure on a budding scientist to do so in order to increase their career prospects and income potential is probably a lot larger today than it was in the 1920s. When catering to the demands of the market, then, it is not unusual to encase the product with a veneer of the spiritual and the enchanted, whether this is done playfully or in earnest.

Finally, the commodification perspective also invites us to look at the role of the commercial actors that frame and market commodified science, most notably the publishers. As in the case of "the God(damn) Particle," the fetishization and enchantment of scientific content are often the work of a publisher's marketing department rather than of the scientist-authors themselves. Either way, the fact that science in a consumer economy is so intimately tied up and networked with commercial interests goes a long way toward explaining why we see such a wide array of meanings attached to "science" in the broader culture that conflict with the internal ethos of communities of scientists. Under the socioeconomic and cultural conditions of consumerism, the fetishization of science and its use as an adorning possession are exactly what we should expect.

4

Multiple Times of Disenchantment and Secularization

Lorenz Trein

Introduction

The rise and dissemination of specifically modern historical concepts such as "progress" and "history" have been often treated as closely intertwined with a transformation of religious ideas into historicized experiences of temporality.[1] At the same time, there are substantial arguments claiming that theological ideas contained in the categories of secularization and disenchantment call into question their adequacy as scholarly means to understanding the historical nature of modernity properly.[2] More recently, and in a similar vein, the idea of secularization has been used to refer to a uniform historiographical time in itself; that is to say, the formation of modern historical concepts rather appears to be a problem of how to integrate a multiplicity of orderings of the historical exceeding the conceptual boundaries of a monolithic, historiographical time,[3] sometimes also referred to as "secular time."[4]

Whatever the significance of such an argument may be for the historical study of religion, it suggests a conceptual shift of secularization and disenchantment in understanding modern religious history. More specifically, one can ask whether we are witnessing a shift from understanding secularization as an explanation of the rise of specifically modern historical concepts and processes to a specifically modern form of historical self-description.[5] At the same time, it is becoming ever clearer that the category of secularization reflects a historico-theological discourse charged with genealogical claims that are in need of historicization and critique.[6] The category of secularization reflects a strong orientation toward "questions of continuity in the history of ideas"[7]; another implication is periodization and the intricate question of origins.[8]

This chapter interrogates a multiple temporalities approach to "the function of the historical in imagining"[9] modern religious history. The main focus will be on differentiating a few layers of inquiry for analyzing historico-temporal implications of the concepts of secularization and disenchantment as reflected in historiographical, philosophical, and sociological accounts of the interrelatedness of religion, modernity, and a disenchanted world. I begin with the problem that the historical imagining of religion and modernity is by no means reducible to a monolithic concept of historical time as expressed by the renewed genealogical quest for either the continuities or the discontinuities between secular modernity and its religious past. It seems far more likely to assume that modernity consists of various historical times interfering with each other and existing simultaneously in complex layers of synchrony.

Unpacking Historical Temporalities

Let me begin by raising a few questions that might help to clarify what is meant here by historical temporality. What, for example, is the significance of the past, if one's present is conceived of as thoroughly disenchanted? Does the historical assumption concerning a rupture or break always imply a moment of temporal differentiation? How is our making sense of history changed when religion appears to become more and more disenchanted? What, specifically, are the temporal conditions that constitute the presence of a supposedly bygone religious era in a disenchanted world, in relation to which narratives of disenchantment and secularization deploy their understandings of modernity as historically meaningful in the first place? To frame the question somewhat differently: Which premises and historical presuppositions determine the balance in what is conceived of within such narratives as the historical relation between our contemporary moment and the past?

Historians of religion might question such premises by looking at the temporal archives of disenchantment and secularization, that is, by studying historical semantics conveying relations of past, present, and future times in their respective sources and theories. I understand "semantics" here in a broad sense mainly as referring to forms of communication that are sedimented and subject to discursive-anthropological reorderings; metaphorically speaking, they are "the water[s] we swim in."[10] At the same time, a meta-historical critique is at stake when we acknowledge the problem that concepts of time and historicity involved in scholarly debates about secular modernity are themselves subject to historical change. Put somewhat differently, the starting point here is that narratives of disenchantment and secularization differentiate and conflate both historical self-descriptions of and specifically theoretical (i.e., historiographical) assumptions about temporality; the latter here refers to explicit reflections on "a theory of possible history,"[11] as well as to enunciations of our historical moment vis-à-vis historically semanticized religious origin narratives of modernity.

This blend of historical ideas with the historical can be put in even more general terms: "That which makes a history into the historical cannot be derived from the sources alone: a theory of possible history is required so that the sources might be brought to speak at all."[12] Whereas scholars of religion and those from other disciplines might use Reinhart Koselleck's hermeneutical proposition as a starting point to discuss the structural implications of a sharp scientific separation of their data from historical theories, this chapter asks whether one can interrogate ideas of disenchantment and secularization vis-à-vis historical presuppositions of meaning in history. What it aims to contribute is an unfolding of the historical temporalities, which are productive in narratives of disenchantment and secularization, by looking at the possible histories of such narratives. The idea is therefore not to remove the distinction between the historical and its possible histories but to treat such presuppositions as a possible object for the study of narratives of religious history.

As a first step, I will address only briefly the historical ambiguity of the category of secularization as reflected in Koselleck's historiographical narrative of modernity. Although religion was certainly not a major topic for Koselleck, I shall argue that his quest to theorize historical time is highly instructive for approaching the presence of past times of religious history in notions of disenchantment and secularization. Using recent discussions over the significance of Koselleck's theory of historical times, I will take a closer look at Karl Löwith's discussion of Max Weber's take on the meaninglessness of modern progress as it relates to Löwith's contention that modernity is both secular and non-secular at the same time. Finally, I will address a historico-temporal moment constituting the presence of a bygone religious past in Weber's idea of disenchantment, which has attracted attention recently in genealogical accounts that assume a largely overlooked presence of theological ideas in narratives of disenchantment and secularization. As a result, I will extend my problematization of the temporal implications of the categories of disenchantment and secularization to more recent approaches interrogating religious inheritances of secular modernity.

Secularization and the Modern Concept of History

While studying in Heidelberg, young historian Reinhart Koselleck was engaged in translating portions of a book from English into German that became the subject of a heated debate in the years after its publication.[13] The author of the work in question, who did a report on Koselleck's doctoral thesis,[14] returned in the early 1950s to Germany after having lived for several years in exile in Italy, Japan, and the United States.[15] If we follow historian Niklas Olsen, philosopher Karl Löwith deeply influenced the younger Koselleck.[16] Löwith's critique of "the idea of modern historical philosophy as secularized eschatology" reflects "a profound skepticism" toward the possibility of "Meaning in History."[17] This skepticism was directed against the idea "of imposing on history a reasoned order" such as "the belief that God or some world-process intends [individuals as well as whole nations] ... to achieve this or that and to survive while others are going under"; for Löwith, "there is always something pathetic, if not ludicrous, in beliefs of this kind."[18]

Indeed, there is a link between Löwith's *Meaning in History* (1949) and Koselleck's doctoral thesis.[19] In his preface to the English edition, Koselleck pointed to "the early postwar" context of his approach to "the historical preconditions of German National Socialism."[20] Also influenced by Carl Schmitt,[21] Koselleck aimed to understand the historical relation between the political structures of absolutism and the emergence of utopian notions of historicity.[22] As the absolutist state faced its discontinuance in the wake of the French Revolution, utopian modernity emerged.[23] This process was accompanied by radical criticism directed at fields like art and literature, but also at Christianity, which furthered the temporalization of the historical through the emerging "bourgeois philosophy of history."[24] At this point Koselleck refers to "the charismatic-historical heritage [*das heilsgeschichtliche Erbe*] that was subsumed into the future-oriented world-view." "We know the process of secularisation," Koselleck noted, "which transposed eschatology into a history of progress."[25] At the same time, the plan of divine salvation was transformed into a philosophical mode of appropriating the future by means of historical imagination and thereby "applied to history itself."[26]

Although he depicted Christianity both as an object of philosophical critique and as stimulating the rise of progressive notions of history, one can ask whether Koselleck conceived of religion as vanishing in modern times.[27] His overall aim was to historicize and theorize "persistent structures of the modern age."[28] One of them refers to a temporal experience of acceleration ("the sense that we are being sucked into an open and unknown future, the pace of which has kept us in a constant state of breathlessness ever since the dissolution of the traditional *ständische* [estate-based] societies"); the other refers to "the pressure on our post-theological age to justify politics and morals without us being able to reconcile the two."[29] The differentiation between morality and politics was understood to be a direct outcome of and a crucial condition for the failing of the absolutist state, in consequence of which utopian meanings of history became more and more (de-)politicized. By the same token, the modern age was conceived of as developing in the direction of "de-theologization."[30] In a Schmittian register, the idea of secularization appears to convey an antiliberal critique of modernity; it is a narrative of decline demanding a future re-politicization and re-theologization of a particular polity to come, and therefore, a totalizing (i.e., a monolithic and linear) idea of the historical signaling simultaneously a rupture of the contemporary political order and a genealogical interest in continuities in the history of ideas. For Koselleck, "the notion of modern time" is an "attempt to deduce the criteria of time from the course of history itself"; historical imagination "gained a genuinely historical meaning, distinct from mythical, theological, or natural chronological origins,"[31] so to speak.

At the same time, there are references challenging the idea that Koselleck's narrative of modernity is centered on a rigid dualism of Christian understandings of history and modern philosophical notions of progress. The historical relation of religious and secular ideas of history appears in Koselleck's account not simply as radical rupture or total replacement but rather as mutual reference and coexistence in complex historical settings of synchrony. For example, the idea of "rational prognosis" was depicted at once as the counterpart to "prevailing prophecy" and as "refer[ring] back to the expectations of salvation."[32] By the same token, Koselleck construes the rise and dissemination of the modern philosophy of historical progress as shaped by "a typical eighteenth-century mixture of rational prediction and salvational expectation."[33]

Theorizing Multiple Times

Koselleck's historical understanding of modernity (*Neuzeit*) has been criticized for expressing a periodization that, as Kathleen Davis suggested, posits an all too "linear transition" from medieval to modern times and from "religious to secular" discourse.[34] By contrast, other scholars have emphasized that Koselleck's interest in historical time opposes simplifying models of periodization. According to John Zammito, "What Koselleck's theory of historical times in fact should mean is that there is no 'total otherness of the past,' nothing like total incommensurability, but instead stratum upon stratum of the past flows in and through the present at varying velocities."[35]

Striking about Helge Jordheim's argument "Against Periodization" is the degree to which it challenges recent interpretations of Koselleck's picture of modernity. What seems to be more significant, however, and this is not taken into account by Jordheim himself, is how it broadens our understanding of narratives of secularization and disenchantment as consisting of and referring to a complex overlapping of various historical temporalities. If there is no total otherness of the past to imagine, then a linear notion of secularization—according to which a specific religious past and its secular other are clearly distinguished in terms of what has been before and what will follow afterward—collapses. Of course, this argument is not against the pragmatics of periodization as such. It is rather a call to consider a synchrony of various times (think of ruptures, continuities, and recurrences[36]) when disenchantment and secularization are (and are not) talked about in historical debate. Furthermore, an interest in multiple temporalities signals that these times are themselves subject to historical change and reordering.

As much as I agree with Jordheim's take on Koselleck, and as much as his argument proves helpful for setting up a multiple temporalities approach to narratives of disenchantment and secularization, there are also reasons to assume that his approach implies exactly the opposite, which is a displacement of religion and secularization from our historiographical imagining of modernity.[37] Evidence for this "modernist" implication of his argument can be found in another essay where Jordheim argues for the rise and dissemination of specifically modern historical concepts during the eighteenth century as a problem of "synchronization."[38] Jordheim makes his case also with regard to Karl Löwith and Hans Blumenberg:

> In both cases ... the unity of time itself was never questioned or discussed. As soon as we presume that historical and social time are not one, but always many, another image of the eighteenth century emerges in which ideas of progress do not come into being due to secularization or intellectual curiosity, but due to a complex and ongoing adjustment and synchronization of different times.[39]

One implication of this argument is a displacement of secularization as a historiographical explanation of modernity. By the same token, one can ask whether Jordheim's critique gestures at displacing secularization, and thereby religion, as objects in favour of culture as a basis from which to study the rise and dissemination of specifically modern historical concepts of temporality.

The reference to Löwith and Blumenberg implies a conceptual differentiation between a uniform historical temporality of the secular, on the one hand, and a plurality of historical times beyond secularization, on the other hand. Understood as the epitome of a monolithic historical time, secularization appears in Jordheim's account first and foremost as a matter of "continuity between Christian eschatology and Hegelian historicism."[40] By contrast, he proposes to understand "the experience of *Ungleichzeitigkeit* [non-simultaneity] within and between cultures, and the work of synchronization" as "the most important new contribution in eighteenth-century thinking about time, temporality, and history."[41]

Even though one might be skeptical about transferring Jordheim's approach onto the historical study of disenchantment and secularization,[42] his theoretical focus on the interrelatedness of various historical temporalities matches the overall concern of this chapter to study the temporal conditions that constitute the historical presence of a bygone religious past within such narratives. I take it to be a main challenge for scholars of religion to achieve a view of the senses of historical time conveyed through narratives of disenchantment and secularization. By the same token, this approach may allow us to have a fresh look at issues of historical continuities and discontinuities. Whereas a binary logic of historical time forces scholars to opt for either the continuities or the discontinuities between secular modernity and its religious past, a multiple temporalities approach to disenchantment and secularization aims to expand our imagining of the temporal relations in which the continuities and discontinuities of religion and the secular are taking shape and being constantly contested and rearranged at the same time.

Sharpening historico-temporal implications of disenchantment and secularization may also help to see better the positions that scholars assign to religion within their historical imagining of secular modernity vis-à-vis historically semanticized ideas about the presence of a bygone religious past.

"The modern world is as Christian as it is un-Christian"

One can consider a whole series of implications informing Karl Löwith's interpretation of Max Weber's famous Munich lecture "Science as a Vocation" in order to unfold the various temporalities reflected in Löwith's critique of utopian notions of progress and history.[43] Genealogically speaking, the most general assumption concerns one of the conclusions drawn by Löwith from his inquiry into *Meaning in History*: "The modern world is as Christian as it is un-Christian because it is the outcome of an age-long process of secularization.... our modern world is worldly and irreligious and yet dependent on the Christian creed from which it is emancipated."[44]

The idea of a simultaneity indicating the historical presence of Christianity within, as well as its absence from, the modern age represents a constitutive feature of genealogical accounts of secular modernity. Löwith's aim was to excavate the historical and theological implications of a specifically modern concept of the future, understood as a goal to be achieved within a historical world-process. At the same time, Löwith's reflection on the theological condition of secular modernity conveys a highly critical stance toward historicizing mediations of Christianity,[45] which was also a reflection about exploring possible exits from the perceived "catastrophe of progress."

This last phrase might be helpful for translating the German expression "*Das Verhängnis des Fortschritts*,"[46] which is an essay complementing Löwith's earlier engagement with Weber,[47] along with an article Löwith originally did on the occasion of the centenary of Weber's birth.[48] Note how Löwith reproduces Weber's discussion of Leo Tolstoi in "Science as a Vocation" vis-à-vis "the problem of whether or not death is a meaningful phenomenon."[49] Weber's passage reads as follows:

> Abraham, or some peasant of the past, died "old and satiated with life" because he stood in the organic cycle of life; because his life, in terms of its meaning and on the eve of his days, had given to him what life had to offer; because for him there remained no puzzles he might wish to solve; and therefore he could have had "enough" of life. Whereas civilized man, placed in the midst of the continuous enrichment of culture by ideas, knowledge, and problems, may become "tired of life" but not "satiated with life." He catches only the most minute part of what the life of the spirit brings forth ever anew, and what he seizes is always something provisional and not definitive, and therefore death for him is a meaningless occurrence. And because death is meaningless, civilized life as such is meaningless; by its very "progressiveness" it gives death the imprint of meaninglessness.[50]

Löwith's take on the "immanent meaning" ascribed by Weber to the idea of "infinite 'progress'" as a historical experience of secular modernity[51] suggests a slightly different interpretation. Quite similarly, Löwith understands the meaninglessness of historical progress, which expresses a persistent orientation toward a future that has not yet been achieved. At the same time, his interpretation of Weber resonates with the concern that secularization is tantamount to an indissoluble historical ambiguity, namely that religion is simultaneously present and absent in the historical experience of secular modernity:

> Any peasant in days gone by died "old and satiated with life" because, at the end of his days his life had brought him all that it had to offer. For the representative of an insatiably progressive civilization, death is a premature breaking-off, an absurdity [*eine sinnwidrige Begebenheit*]. Human beings may become "tired of life," but not "satiated with life"; for their existence is always oriented towards an as yet unfulfilled future [*im Hinblick auf eine noch unerfüllte Zukunft*].[52]

Löwith's approach to Weber refers directly back to his concern about the disaster of historical progress. For genealogy, Löwith points to the specifically modern ambivalence toward secularized eschatology: "Although the Christian confidence towards a future fulfilment vanished for the modern historical consciousness, the view toward the future itself and towards an indeterminate fulfilment has remained dominant."[53] At the same time, his genealogical concern is accompanied by an attempt to indicate possible exit signs from the perceived fatality of modern progress. For Löwith, the idea of progress is conceivable only within a concept of time that is essentially oriented toward the future.[54] By contrast, historical ideas of "development and progress are nullified in a time of eternal presence."[55] As a result, Löwith contrasts "our obsession with the future" (*unsere Besessenheit von der Zukunft*) with an idea of "perpetual world-time" (*immerwährende Weltzeit*) toward imagining a more permanent ordering of the historical.[56] The connotation used by Löwith to hint at this exit comprises several notions such as cancelling, preserving, and lifting up.[57]

Given these broader implications of Löwith's engagement with the idea of historical meaninglessness, it becomes questionable to assume a monolithic temporality of the historical in his account. Rather it appears that Löwith's understanding of the meaninglessness of modern progress closely relates to his overall concern that modernity is secular and non-secular at the same time, due to its ambivalent relation to Christianity and the historical and theological process of its secularization. For Löwith, there is a presence of a supposedly bygone Christian past in a "disenchanting" world.[58] This past is present in the hegemony of progress, which has some of its historical origins in categories of salvational history but is at the same time distinct from these theological origins. Furthermore, secular modernity is imagined through a dialectical historical reasoning that oscillates between a temporality of progress, that "is a straight line into an endless future and past," and a time of eternal presence referring to "the eternal recurrence of all things, whose time is an ever present circle."[59]

The Presence of a Bygone Past

When finishing his lecture "Science as a Vocation," Max Weber pointed to a specific historico-temporal moment constituting the presence of a bygone religious past in a disenchanting world:

> The fate of our times is characterized by rationalization and intellectualization and, above all, by the "disenchantment of the world." Precisely the ultimate and most sublime values have retreated from public life either into the transcendental realm of mystic life or into the brotherliness of direct and personal human relations. It is not accidental that our greatest art is intimate and not monumental, nor is it accidental that today only within the smallest and intimate circles, in personal human situations, in *pianissimo*, that something is pulsating that corresponds to the prophetic *pneuma*, which in former times swept through the great communities like a firebrand, welding them together.[60]

What is conceived of here as disenchantment is by no means a radical rupture with a religious past, which is imagined as the opposite of a thoroughly disenchanted present of secular modernity. If we understand disenchantment primarily as a historical concept of temporality, which presupposes layers that interrelate the past with present and future times, then the meaning of Weber's reference to prophetic *pneuma* encompasses more than a certain ordering principle of community formation vanishing over the course of religious history. By contrast, the imagining of this relation between former times and present days should be taken firstly as referring to a specific set of historical presuppositions.

From a genealogical point of view, these premises have been discussed as a negotiation of religious belonging and exclusion by imagining historical and theological differentiations between the traditions of Christianity and Judaism.[61] By the same token, such a temporality establishes historical imaginings of the rise and fall of religious traditions à la supersessionist narratives. Genealogical approaches to secularization and disenchantment have taken up Protestant narratives of primitive Christianity in order to disclose the theological inheritances of secular modernity.[62] It seems therefore important to ask about the historico-temporal implications of such arguments by looking at interrelations of past, present, and future times as reflected in historical sources and possible histories invoked in recent genealogies of disenchantment and secularization.

There are several examples in Weber's sociology of religion that indicate a temporal imaginary, which construes the historical relation between a bygone era and later times as a state of closure or which assigns a particular prophetic orientation of religion primarily to its historical beginnings. This is the case, for example, when Weber discusses the relation between priest and prophet with a view to the formation of the canon and the systematizing of particular teachings and traditions as one means of religious boundary work:

> The closing of the canon was generally accounted for by the theory that only a certain epoch in the past history of the religion had been blessed with prophetic charisma. According to the theory of the rabbis this was the period from Moses to Alexander, while from the Roman Catholic point of view the period was the Apostolic Age. On the whole, these theories correctly express recognition of the contrast between prophetic and priestly systematization.[63]

This clearly corresponds with Weber's observation that it is "the first stage of a religious community's formation ... when the pneumatic manifestations of charisma are valued as hallmarks of specifically religious exaltation," whereas subsequent "routinization and regimentation of community relationships" mean "a reaction ... against" such appearances.[64]

As is known from the secondary literature, Weber's interest in charisma mirrors contemporary theological debates[65] about primitive Christianity and prophetic charisma with regard to the problem of whether the early church is to be understood as a legal or charismatic collectivization, or as both. For Rudolph Sohm, the ordering principle of the *ecclesia* was first of all "not legal, but charismatic organization,"[66] whereas Adolf Harnack highlighted both competing pneumatic and law-making aspects in the formation of early Christian communities.[67] Harnack and Sohm shared the assumption that primitive Christianity reflected charismatic dispositions;[68] the contested issue was instead whether charisma is an ordering principle of the *ecclesia* in itself and by what ordering principle—charismatic and/or legal?—authority was established in the primitive epoch of Christianity.[69]

The historico-theological semantic of this last phrase already signals an early loss of significance of miracles and other charismata, which Harnack expressed as follows:

> Towards the close of the first century, when people came to look back upon the age in which the church had been established, the course of events was summed

up in these words (Heb. ii. 3): "Salvation began by being spoken through the Lord, and was confirmed for us by those who heard it, while God accompanied their witness by signs and wonders and manifold miracles and distribution of the holy Spirit."[70]

Only a couple of decades later these signs had ceased[71]:

> Eusebius is not the first … to look back upon the age of the Spirit and of power as the bygone heroic age of the church, for Origen had already pronounced this verdict on the past out of an impoverished present. Yet this impoverishment and disenchantment [*Verarmung und Ernüchterung*] hardly inflicted any injury now upon the mission of Christianity.[72]

Harnack's account of the cessation of miracles was by no means a marginal position around the turn of the twentieth century. We find similar ideas in Carl Weizsäcker's work on the apostolic age[73] or in Adolf Jülicher's account of primitive Christianity.[74] Focusing on the second century CE, Jülicher stresses that "enthusiasm" and "prophecy" were soon ebbing away in Christian communities, thereby inaugurating an experience of "disenchantment" (*Ernüchterung*).[75] At the same time, he disagrees that this period reflects "the beginning of a disastrous process of secularization [*Verweltlichung*]"; rather it shows "a lack of spirit and power" (*eine Zeit des Mangels an Geist und Kraft*) after a time representing an "excess of" enthusiastic exaltation.[76]

Imagining the historical development of Christianity through the cessation of charismata was by no means a novel theological manoeuvre. Heinrich Heppe's 1857 account of sixteenth-century Protestant dogmatism references the idea of a "cessation of miracles" (*das Aufhören der Wunder*): "Once Christ and the gospel were sufficiently authenticated by miracles, there was no further miracle to expect."[77] Another textbook of dogmatic history notes that

> among the old church fathers one can also find passages about a cessation of miracles in the church, invoked later by the Protestants; but what these passages simply convey is that Christendom now shouldn't be founded any longer on and proved through miracles, but upon itself.[78]

Historically (or should I rather say genealogically?) speaking, one can ask whether it makes sense to link Weber's idea of disenchantment, which conveys a historical presence of a bygone religious past, to theological imaginaries of religious history.[79] This past is present insofar as the claim that miracles and other spontaneous pneumatic manifestations are "the hall-mark"[80] of an earlier period—"the age of miracles … lay for Origen in earlier days"[81]—reflects a temporal imaginary that is itself genealogical.[82]

By the same token, one can argue that theological narratives of religious history have served as the basis for imagining contemporary and future orderings of Christianity.[83] In 1907, Harnack received a letter from his colleague Julius Wellhausen expressing distrust toward the possibility that a new prophecy would arise in modern times: "I ... trust in the steadiness of uncomplaining scholarship more than in the sudden flare-up of a new religion, such as through a socialist prophet. While in earlier times tremendous things arose from it, the days of enthusiasm seem to be over."[84] Here the idea of disenchantment resonates with a narrative of religious history that claims that Judaism had alienated itself from the natural religion of ancient Israel and had thereby deteriorated into ritualistic legalism. For Weber, "the genuine 'spirit' of the old prophecy was in eclipse. ... It vanished because the priestly police power in the Jewish congregation gained control over ecstatic prophecy in the same manner as did the bishopric and presbyterian authorities over pneumatic prophecy in the early Christian congregation."[85] At the same time, Wellhausen and other fellow Liberal Protestant theologians assumed that "Christianity ... is the authentic historical heir of biblical monotheism or of the original early religion of Israel as revealed in the ethical teachings of the prophets and in the Psalms, reaching its fulfillment in the glad tidings of Jesus Christ, the Messiah."[86]

The Times of Genealogy

The narratives that lead us to assume a perpetual theological underpinning of modern historical imagination challenge scholars of religion and neighboring disciplines to constantly rethink and retheorize the temporal framings of their interest in religious inheritances of secular modernity. Löwith's interest in the historical meaninglessness of modern progress conveys a temporality of dialectical transitions ("dialectic of transitions") referring directly back to Georg Wilhelm Friedrich Hegel's philosophy of history:

> In actual existence, progress ... appears as an advance from the imperfect to the more perfect, although the former should not be understood in an abstract sense as merely imperfect, but as something which at the same time contains its own opposite ... as a germ or impulse .... Thus the imperfect, in so far as it contains its own opposite within itself, is a contradiction; and although it certainly exists, it must just as surely be overcome [*aufgehoben*] and resolved.[87]

The genealogical concern to disclose the modern idea of historical progress reaffirms the criticized temporality in question because genealogy implies the idea of a historical ordering of specific ideas developing over the course of time.[88] At that same time, Löwith was very aware that the idea of a "'standstill of time'"[89] affirms a historical concept of the "future," both as its opposite and as something that has not been achieved yet, and therefore, according to his own genealogy, presupposes a specific "modern,"[90] that is, at once Christian and un-Christian disposition toward possible meanings of the historical. Put somewhat differently, Löwith's approach to the meaninglessness of modern progress affirms a meaningful idea of history insofar as it implies opposite times existing simultaneously in relations of cancelling and preserving each other.

A similar historical temporality is prevalent in recent scholarly attempts to historicize narratives and ideas of disenchantment and secularization. For example, it has been argued that disenchantment signals a loss of significance of gods, rituals, and magic practices as well as an increased ordering of the magical in secular modernity.[91] As to the temporality implied in such an argument, one is tempted to ask whether opposing magic and rationality as mutually exclusive provides the meaningful framework (the Hegelian imperfect, so to say) that identifies and allows for a magical interpretation of Weber's idea of disenchantment in the first place: "For there to be an active, ongoing disenchanting of the world, magic has to be intact."[92]

Arguing that "Weber's idea of 'disenchantment' represented a direct continuation of earlier Christian tropes ... redeployed by Protestants during the Reformation" and "gradually secularized to the point where their theological origins were obscured"[93] conveys a similar ordering of the historical insofar as the secular, along with the secularizing of theological origins of disenchantment, is conceived of as both preserving and annulling. The latter here refers to an obscuring transformation of religion under the historical conditions of secular modernity, which is secularization. At the same time, rebuilding a revised genealogy of disenchantment provides a meaningful framework for theological ideas of continuity in the history of religions. Put somewhat differently, secular genealogy has invoked a narrative of Protestants drawing on earlier Christian origin narratives in order to disclose religious inheritances of an ostensibly disenchanting world.

Note also that recent attempts to separate a multiplicity of historical times from an ascribed uniformity of secular time hold on to the idea that a specific former period of the historical has come to an end in our contemporary historical moment. The end of the philosophy of history as presupposed by Löwith has been replaced by the end of historical time and of progressive historical worldviews.[94] Perhaps this is another version of the same history. The historiographical rejection of older models of genealogy and secularization reestablishes the historical logic of linear time that it aims to supersede vis-à-vis historically semanticized narratives of the rise and fall of specifically modern historical concepts. Whatever the historical meaning of secular modernity may be, it remains hard to imagine its religious history outside of any set of temporal narratives. This circular trajectory of historical reasoning certainly deserves scholarly attention.

Interrogating historical and theological assumptions about historical time comes full circle to the starting point of this chapter, which claimed that narratives of disenchantment and secularization presuppose and conflate both historical self-descriptions and theoretical assumptions about the historical. This overlap can help to illustrate the intricacy of imagining disenchantment and secularization by pointing to the difficulties of a clean break between historical data and theories of possible history. This is also evident from the fact that we can read Löwith and Weber, as well as Koselleck, on both levels, as historiographical theories and as historical sources of disenchantment and secularization.

But the opposite is also true: there is no such reading without a possible history that informs narratives of disenchantment and secularization. One might therefore think of a historical theory of the secular that is concerned with reflecting explicitly such possible histories. What I conceive of as one possible (to avoid the somewhat abused phrase *meaningful*) history is to explore the historico-temporal implications of disenchantment and secularization as referring to historical sediments on which "our" histories of the secular are constantly rebuilt. The challenge is therefore to get a hand on the presence of past times of religious history in imagining the historical. Thinking disenchantment and secularization through the idea of historical times might help scholars of religion to identify possible explanations for the rise and dissemination of a temporality that is simultaneously a historical self-description and a possible mode of theorizing modern religious history. So, what is modernity?

5

The Disenchanted Enchantments of the Modern Imagination and "Fictionalism"

Michael Saler

Max Weber's understanding of Western modernity as "disenchanted" has mesmerized scholars for much of the twentieth century. It attractively combined the "Enlightenment" narrative of the West as progressively rational (although Weber himself did not believe in teleology) with the "Romantic" critique of the corrosive effects this tendency had on everyday life (although Weber did not consider himself a Romantic).[1] Weber's disenchantment paradigm became the basis for post-1945 Modernization Theory, which was less ambivalent than he about the rational direction of the West.[2] At the same time, it informed less celebratory accounts of Western modernity, such as those by Max Horkheimer and Theodor Adorno (especially their 1944 *Dialectic of Enlightenment*) and Michel Foucault (notably his 1975 *Discipline and Punish*). These accounts echoed Weber's exposure of reason, in its instrumental-rational form, as a potential tool of domination rather than emancipation.

Weber thus formulated a definition of Western modernity as primarily rational or "disenchanted" that pervaded scientific and humanistic discourses through the late twentieth century. In its exaggerated emphasis on reason, it exemplified Weber's concept of an explanatory "ideal type": "An ideal type is formed by the one-sided accentuation of one or more points of view."[3] The paradigm remained the dominant understanding of modernity within the academy until the past two decades, when scholars from multiple disciplines began to question the nature and extent of modern disenchantment, and how it related to concepts of enchantment and re-enchantment.

For many of these revisionists, Weber's definition became untenable precisely because it was too one-sided in its emphasis on rational disenchantment. They highlighted the persistence of traditional enchantment, in terms of religious, spiritual, and magical beliefs, as well as new forms of "re-enchantment" compatible with modern reason, secularism, and capitalism.[4] In place of Weber's binary and hierarchical opposition between rational, modern disenchantment and irrational, atavistic enchantment, these scholars emphasized the more complementary interplay between disenchantment and enchantment. "Enchantment" has long had the dual meanings of "to delight" and "to delude"; while Weber stressed delusive enchantments, recent scholarship has focused on "disenchanted enchantments," which ideally delight without deluding.[5]

The findings of this revisionary school go far beyond a simple recovery of forgotten or marginalized expressions of enchantment within an allegedly disenchanted modernity. They posit a more robust and complex definition of Western modernity than that advanced by Weber and many of his epigones.[6] The new definition sees modernity as combining both the Enlightenment faith in reason and Romanticism's embrace of the creative imagination. It has become clear during the past century that modernity is not defined primarily by rationality in its positive and negative aspects, as Weber and others would have it, but rather by the reciprocity between reason and imagination. And the major tension within modernity is not Weber's focus on the irrational consequences of rationalization—although this is a critical issue—but rather the difficulties of harmonizing reason and the imagination into a productive synthesis.[7]

One advantage of this capacious approach to Western modernity is that it not only redresses the relative marginalization of the imagination in many earlier accounts but also restores its numinous, spiritual dimension alongside more secular understandings of its nature. Weber had famously proclaimed in his 1917 lecture "Science as Vocation" that within modernity, "there are no mysterious incalculable forces that come into play, but rather that one can, in principle, master all things by calculation. This means that the world is disenchanted."[8] Ironically, he made this assertion at a time when its core assertions began to face new challenges: Newtonian calculations now had to contend with quantum probabilities and the imagination was being elevated by psychologists, philosophers, politicians, and artists into the quintessential "mysterious, incalculable force" of modernity.

Weber was aware of the latter current, interpreting the widespread "aesthetic turn" of the *fin de siècle* as an emotional reaction against the sway of increasing rationalization. He viewed the enthusiasm for the imagination as well as concurrent forms of *Lebensphilosophie* as understandable yet subjective evasions of the hard truth of the modern "iron cage" nature of existence, which was emerging from instrumental reason, bureaucratic governance, and the splintering of shared meaning into mutually exclusive value spheres. The progressive disenchantment of the world was simply a fact of life that must be confronted as a matter of, in his words, "intellectual integrity."[9]

Yet Weber's positioning of reason as dominant and the imagination as residual in Western modernity was incorrect. The imagination had become an emergent force within modernity as a result of Romanticism, which overturned the imagination's long history of being subordinated to reason since classical antiquity.[10] The imagination also filled the spiritual vacuum created by the secularization of Western culture because it provided both spiritual and secular solace. As a mysterious, incalculable force, it usefully incorporated metaphysics at one extreme and metafictions at the other. It could be seen as the human faculty connecting the individual with the divine or as a cognitive process generating the symbols undergirding phenomenological reality. Both possibilities were expressed by two influential poets who explored the nature of the creative imagination. In 1817, Samuel Taylor Coleridge articulated a religiously inflected, essentialist notion of it as the "repetition in the finite mind of the eternal act of creation in the infinite act of I AM." In 1942, the poet Wallace Stevens expressed a more secular faith in the imagination's capacity to create foundational, yet provisional, fictions of human meaning: "The final belief is to believe in a fiction, which you know to be a fiction, there being nothing else. The exquisite truth is to know that it is a fiction and that you believe in it willingly."[11] In modernity, the mysterious, incalculable force of the imagination spoke to the religious and secular alike, retaining the elements of magic, mystery, and enchantment that Weber implied had been vanquished through rationalization.

In what follows, I will chart how Weber's one-sided definition of modern disenchantment downplayed the mysterious force of the imagination and then outline how the imagination's influence actually inflated since the Enlightenment to become the coequal of reason. If Weber rightly stressed the rationalization of modernity, there was a corresponding process of "imaginalization" that he, and some of his followers, unjustly marginalized and stigmatized. In *Dialectic of Enlightenment*, for example, Horkheimer and Adorno simply assert that most imaginative expressions are colonized insidiously by the rationalized "Culture Industry," leaving only an avant-garde remnant to resist commodification and instrumentalization.

The gradual intertwining of reason and imagination has resulted in a specifically modern form of enchantment, one that is critically self-reflexive about its status and therefore deserves to be called "disenchanted enchantment." After providing some secular examples of the turn to imaginative fictions as instances of this disenchanted enchantment, which I call "fictionalism," I will discuss its non-secular, spiritual orientation in the thought of Dorothy L. Sayers. Like Stevens, she believed in the centrality of fictions, but unlike Stevens, she did not believe there was "nothing else" than fictions. For her and many other spiritually inclined individuals, fictions can directly express or lead to apprehensions of the sacred. And for Sayers, no less than for Weber, "intellectual integrity" was the primary concern when it came to modern enchantment. The issue of how to maintain the intellectual integrity necessary to sustain disenchanted enchantment—a form that ideally delights without deluding—remains a difficult challenge in an allegedly "post-truth" world, where the imagination has not only caught up with reason but threatens to supplant it.

The Weberian Ethic and the Spirit of Disenchantment

Weber's "Science as a Vocation" vividly associated disenchantment with the spread of a rational worldview rather than a secular one. Religion and disenchantment could be compatible, as in the cases of the monotheistic, iconoclastic religions of Judaism and Protestantism.[12] However, his accounts of disenchantment were not only histories of the past but also—perhaps primarily—diagnoses of his own, rapidly secularizing era. Contemporary religion, he showed, remained one source of value among others. But it was no longer the primary one: religion, along with art, personal relations, and other "value spheres," was overshadowed by the dominance of theoretical and instrumental reason. Religious beliefs and spiritual states were no longer default outlooks but often desperate reactions to the arid materialism of rationalization. As he argued about his own time, "the fundamental presupposition of living in union with the divine" is "redemption from the rationalism and intellectualism of science."[13]

It's not only magic that has been lost: shared meanings and purposes have also been shattered through the development of distinct value spheres with their own rules and terminologies. The only commonality in this atomistic culture is the language of reason—although it too assumes different forms—and a bureaucratic lifeworld. Weber is ambivalent about this situation, not rejecting it entirely. Modernity has established procedural norms advancing equality and justice, and scientific norms yielding material and medical advances. Yet his ultimate tenor is dark, congruent with late nineteenth-century cultural pessimism. For all of his nuanced qualifications, the disenchanted world Weber depicts is one in which affective wonder is replaced by rote quantification, ultimate ends by efficient means, and freedom by bureaucracy. This picture is beholden to earlier Romantic elegies about modern disenchantment, and it spoke to the lived experience of his contemporaries. Indeed, it continues to resonate today in our own silicon cage of Big Data, algorithms, and STEM education.

While Weber's narrative was essentially replicated in academic discourses through the 1980s, the world it described was already disappearing by Weber's death in 1920. For example, his confident assertion that everything could, in principle, be known through calculation expressed a Newtonian perspective that would be challenged by the quantum physics of the interwar period.[14] Weber's traditional outlook aligned with that of physicists like Albert Michelson, who proclaimed in 1894 that "most of the grand underlying [scientific] principles have been firmly established and ... future truths of Physical Science are to be looked for in the sixth place of decimals."[15] Yet Heisenberg's uncertainty principle, and the mysteries of quantum entanglement, challenged earlier mechanistic accounts of nature and the presumption that science would ever arrive at a final "theory of everything." Thanks in part to the New Physics of the new century, the Western world remained wedded to a rational perspective, but it could no longer confidently assert that everything, in principle, was amenable to calculation.

Further, certain interpretations of quantum mechanics challenged the Aristotelian logic underlying Weber's concepts, notably the principle of non-contradiction—that it is impossible to hold that the same thing can be A and not-A simultaneously. Weber and his Victorian contemporaries tended to think in binary, either/or terms: enchantment versus disenchantment, reason versus the irrational, and so on. The New Physics of the early twentieth century challenged such binary oppositions by permitting both/and complementarities. The most famous example is of Schrödinger's ontologically challenged cat that is both alive and dead until it is observed. Non-Aristotelian logic was also explored by early twentieth-century analytic philosophers and popularized more broadly at mid-century by Alfred Korzybski's General Semantics and works of science fiction, such as A.E. van Vogt's *The World of Null-A* (1945). Walter Benjamin defended a logic of complementarity in his concepts of "constellations" and "force fields," in which apparent opposites coexist in fruitful tension within a broader configuration.[16] Sigmund Freud's unravelling of the logic of the unconscious in *The Interpretation of Dreams* (1899) likewise argued that dreams employ their own peculiar non-Aristotelian logic (to say nothing of revealing the centrality of the imagination, or *Phantasie*, in both conscious and unconscious life).

The twentieth-century recognition of complementarities made it easier to accept that enchantment and disenchantment could coexist, and that an apparent oxymoron like "disenchanted enchantment" needn't be dismissed out of hand. This term better describes how many of Weber's contemporaries thought of the enchantment and disenchantment of the world. As will be explored below, they were able to be affectively enchanted and rationally disenchanted simultaneously, just as film-viewers can be horrified by a monster on screen while knowing at the same time that it's merely a special effect.

Scholars have done signal service in recent years by exploring the potential dangers of modern enchantment as well as its benefits. Such complementary considerations arise from Talcott Parsons's English translation of Weber's original term, *Entzauberung* as "disenchantment." Weber's term is narrower—it literally means "de-magicifying"—but Parsons's choice was felicitous because it captured the broader, and darker, connotations of Weber's perspective of modernity as an "iron cage" shorn of illusions and bereft of common meanings and purposes. While recent revisions of Weber's paradigm rightly highlight more optimistic interpretations of modern enchantment, his warnings about the potential dangers of irrational enchantments (including the emergence of charismatic leaders, who are as likely to be a Genghis Khan as they are to be a Jesus) have not been ignored. Contemporary scholars note that enchantment is an inherently ambiguous condition, combining positive and negative valences. Positive enchantment signifies a state of affective delight, wonder, and possibility, whereas negative enchantment connotes a state of delusion—literally, to be cast under a spell. Both resonate powerfully within modernity, from the affective "sense of wonder" capable of being generated by science and art to the delusive incantations frequently found within politics and commerce.

Thus, by stressing the ambivalent nature of enchantment, scholars have redressed the unilateral nature of Weber's disenchantment paradigm, which shunted affective enchantment to the private sphere while characterizing the public domain as an arid prison with a dystopian future: "Not summer's bloom lies ahead of us, but rather a polar night of icy darkness."[17] Affective enchantment is clearly cold comfort here.

Today's revised understanding of enchantment presents an ideal type of its own, one that acknowledges enchantment's dual nature and commends forms that delight without deluding. This vision is beholden to Friedrich Nietzsche, who conceived a similar concept in his call for the creation of modern myths explicitly marked as fictions, which could nevertheless provide meaning and generate wonder within a secularizing world. Such a self-reflexive art, he maintained, was compatible with modern rationalization and science, delighting but not deluding: "In art the lie becomes consecrated, the will to deception has good conscience at its back."[18] Nietzsche's version of disenchanted enchantment became influential by the late nineteenth century, particularly through the new orientation toward "fictionalism," both of which will be discussed below.

Toward Disenchanted Enchantment

Nietzsche stressed the interplay of reason and imagination in his understanding of human meaning as a personal and cultural creation, a contingent "perspective" rather than an eternal Truth. For him, modern myths, art, and other ways to orient oneself in the world combine rational disenchantment with imaginative enchantment; they delight without deluding. He was able to balance Enlightenment and Romantic outlooks more capably than those who were otherwise indebted to him, such as Weber, Horkheimer and Adorno, and Foucault. These latter thinkers present the imagination as largely passive in the face of reason's incursions, an attitude beholden to traditional assumptions about the imagination in Western culture. From classical antiquity through the Enlightenment, the imagination has usually been defined as reason's irrational and subordinate servant. (There were exceptions to this view, of course, including Renaissance Neo-Platonism and modern esotericism.) Generally speaking, the imagination's function was to translate sensations into visual or conceptual schema for reason's judgment. But it could be deceptive, misleading by generating false images, as in dreams; it could also incite desires undermining reason's dictates and social norms. Many warned that the imagination must be disciplined rather than indulged.

Beginning in the eighteenth century, however, Enlightenment thinkers like David Hume, Adam Smith, and Immanuel Kant challenged this notion, advancing more positive evaluations of the imagination and its essential contributions to cognition. By the late nineteenth century, the imagination was increasingly defined as reason's equal and inextricable partner. Yet the earlier, and more prejudicial, conception of the imagination as reason's "Other" remained as well, as Weber's example suggests. He certainly appreciated the imagination, associating it with intuition and inspiration; he even granted it a seminal role in the arts and sciences. In "Science as a Vocation," he stated that mathematical and scientific insights emerge from "intuitive flashes of imagination." While the imagination of a scientist and an artist differs in "orientation" and "quality," "the psychological processes do not differ. Both are frenzy."[19] But "frenzy," of course, is the giveaway: this is the traditional Western view of the imagination as irrational. Indeed, it distinguishes imagination's "magic" from that of so-called "primitive" magic, which in Weber's view was not irrational. One wonders if Weber's binary, hierarchical opposition of reason and imagination had a personal dimension to explain its tenacity. He was certainly aware, as an imaginative scholar and ruminative depressive, of the imagination's seductive powers; while he often stated his own preference for "matter-of-factness" and "reality" as a point of personal integrity, he remained entranced by subjectivity and its imaginative expressions. As one of his intimates noted after his death, "One never knew which was stronger in him: the keen-eyed realist without illusions or the great dreamer."[20]

On the whole, then, Weber didn't perceive the contemporary turn to enchantments of the imagination, including that of Nietzsche, as a challenge to a rationally disenchanted modernity. Instead, the imagination provided residual compensations in a routinized world. It enabled individuals to cope by retreating into the subjective realms of art, religion, and friendship. And, for good and for ill, it generated the irrational force of charismatic authority, which had a particular appeal in a modern world starved for meaning and purpose.

From today's vantage, however, the imagination is not residual but dominant: virtual reality vies with material reality, fantasy pervades the media, and "creativity" is the gold standard in business and technology. Modernity has been called the Age of Reason, but it is equally the Age of the Imagination. This is a remarkable development, especially since we still aren't sure what the imagination is: the capacity to visualize what doesn't exist? The ability to posit alternatives to the given? Intuition and inspiration? The imagination remains a "mysterious, incalculable force": arguably the functional equivalent to the Gods and spirits of earlier ages, with powers and energies that we hope to invoke and control.[21]

Fortunately, we don't need to know what the imagination is in order to trace how its moralistic regulation has been largely replaced today by its uninhibited liberation. The gradual legitimation of the imagination as reason's equal was a complex process, but we can highlight a few of the ways that middle-class attitudes toward the imagination changed between the nineteenth century and the present in the West, paving the way for the disenchanted enchantments of modernity.

At the turn of the nineteenth century, German and English Romantics emphasized the nature of the imagination as a divine faculty, in which humans had been made in the image of the Supreme Creator to be sub-creators. At this time the imagination was redefined as active rather than passive and as reason's partner rather than servant. However, this revolutionary redefinition of a creative imagination initially didn't make much headway among the middle classes influenced by the Protestant work ethic. They feared its exercise was frivolous at best and at worst would unleash ungodly desires and escapist habits. Even the progenitors of Romanticism couldn't escape this view. Rousseau echoed a common understanding: "The real world has its limits; the imaginary world is infinite. Unable to enlarge the one, let us restrict the other."[22] We see a similar restriction in Coleridge's account of how we apprehend fantastic poesy through "the willing suspension of disbelief."[23] Disbelief is assumed to be the default mode of an enlightened individual, which is then consciously suspended for brief periods to entertain the unreal.

Another factor impeding the recognition of the imagination as being coterminous with reason was the professionalization of science during the nineteenth century. Newly defined "scientists" (the term was not coined until 1833) insisted that science was the sole conveyor of "positive," objective knowledge, in contrast to the more imaginative, subjective assertions of theologians and "men of letters," the cultural authorities scientists sought to displace. Whereas the arts had not been excluded from the sciences within the earlier practice of science as "natural philosophy," professionalizing scientists did exclude them from the new idea of rational and empirical "objectivity" that they advanced starting in the mid-nineteenth century.[24]

Nevertheless, during the course of the nineteenth century, more secular currents of thought, new theories of cognition, and the rise of mass culture challenged many of these strictures on the imagination. An important turning point came at mid-century, when psychologists and philosophers argued that individuals have a "double consciousness," permitting the exercise of rationality and the imagination simultaneously. In 1844, a British psychologist explained that an individual could be consciously aware that he experienced illusory perceptions, because humans in effect had "two distinct and perfect brains: One brain was, as we so often see, watching the other, and even interested and amused by its vagaries."[25] In *Human, All-Too-Human* (1878), Nietzsche discussed double consciousness in similarly corporeal terms. "Therefore, a higher culture must give man a double-brain," he wrote, "two brain chambers, so to speak, one to feel science, the other to feel non-science."[26]

These discussions about double consciousness were reassuring to the wider public: one could freely exercise one's imagination without losing one's reason.

It wasn't a new practice; the capacity for "meta-representation" is an innate human ability, which children develop around the age of four. But by labeling this ability as "double consciousness," Victorian scientists and philosophers gave individuals permission to exercise their imaginations more freely: the unbounded imagination that Rousseau feared was monitored by reason. Nietzsche and others could now insist that fictions were not entertained through the willing suspension of disbelief, as Coleridge had claimed, but rather through the willing activation of pretense. This practice also allowed Nietzsche, Georges Sorel, and others to praise consciously held illusions as vital for survival in a disenchanted age. As Nietzsche argued in his brief for recognizing "untruth as a condition of life" in *Beyond Good and Evil* (1886):

> We are fundamentally inclined to claim that the falsest judgements ... are the most indispensable for us; that without accepting the fictions of logic, without measuring reality against the purely invented world of the unconditional and self-identical, without a constant falsification of the world by means of numbers, man could not live—that renouncing false judgements would mean renouncing life and a denial of life.[27]

The imagination was not simply irrational intuition or inspiration, they showed; nor was it the subordinate of reason, organizing perceptions for rational judgment. In self-reflexive modernity, imagination and reason work in tandem.

This conception of the imagination was not confined to psychologists and philosophers: it permeated mass culture. By the late nineteenth century, it was exemplified in a new definition of magic, which had become an exemplary "disenchanted enchantment" for the modern age. A magician was no longer a sorcerer with a long beard and pointed hat, waving a wand to invoke spirits; it was now a man in elegantly formal attire, standing on stage and performing tricks, which delighted an audience that knew they were tricks. The first modern magician was the French conjurer Robert Houdin, who in the mid-nineteenth century wrote that "a magician is an actor playing the part of a magician."[28] Similarly, the great American hoaxer P.T. Barnum knew that the audience for his duplicitous attractions were aware that they were being tricked; they enjoyed trying to figure out rationally how the trick was done. Barnum encapsulated the double-minded nature of disenchanted enchantment in his wry observation that the public is "disposed to be amused even when they are conscious of being deceived."[29]

Another manifestation of the liberated imagination was the new children's literature of the mid-century, which shifted from earlier didactic tales to whimsical fantasies celebrating imaginative free play, such as Lewis Carroll's

Alice in Wonderland (1865). Rational, responsible adults adopted this spirit of make-believe in the late nineteenth century, continuing the make-believe they enjoyed as children reading *Alice* and similar works. For example, starting in the 1890s, adult fans of Sherlock Holmes began to "live" in Arthur Conan Doyle's imaginary world for prolonged periods of time, often in the company of others, while retaining firm footing in the real world. They wrote nonfiction histories claiming that Holmes was real and Arthur Conan Doyle was fictional, as well as formed new public spaces to bring the imaginary world to virtual life, such as clubs, fanzines, and the first journals dedicated entirely to a fictional being. They "believed" in Holmes in the realm of the imagination, while knowing he was fictional in the realm of the real. (This disenchanted enchantment, delighting but not deluding, ironically contrasts with Arthur Conan Doyle's interwar belief in the existence of fairies, a form of delusive enchantment.)

Holmes fandom became the model for subsequent transformations of imaginary worlds into virtual worlds, from Middle-earth through Hogwarts. The public spaces dedicated to these imaginary worlds did more than generate an escapist form of enchantment. Because they provided safe harbors, fans often used imaginary worlds to discuss real-world issues. Once a cliquish pursuit, this practice has become widespread: the *New York Times*, for example, has hosted weekly online discussions of fantasy series like *Game of Thrones* and *Twin Peaks*. In effect, modern imaginary worlds have become "public spheres of the imagination," where serious issues about the real world are discussed rationally and often respectfully, because the diverse participants all share something that binds them together: their passion for an imaginary world.

The practice had another salutary consequence at the turn of the twentieth century. Enthusiasts of imaginary worlds reflected on how these places were created and sometimes helped construct the world by filling in gaps or reconciling contradictions left by the author. In so doing, fans became more self-aware of how the "real" world was, at a phenomenological level, an imaginary world created by a combination of reason and fantasy. Such self-reflexive insights about the social construction of reality at the popular level were similar to the late nineteenth-century "revolt against positivism" among scholars, including Weber.[30] So-called "elite" and "mass" cultures shared common ground in seeking a balance between objectivity and subjectivity, reason and imagination.

Sherlock Holmes perfectly represented the wider recognition that reason and the imagination were inextricable allies. He boasted that he bested other detectives through "the scientific use of the imagination."[31] Holmes could have the frenzied, intuitive leaps of insight that Weber described, but he more frequently trained an imagination-imbued reason on everyday life to solve its mysteries. While on a case, he scrutinized every detail in terms of potential meanings; he was not simply intuiting or ratiocinating but imagining different configurations that would best fit the evidence. This process of rapt attention transformed the ordinary into the magical: a matchstick or an envelope became as mysterious and alluring as the footprint of a giant hound. Holmes's reasoning process transcended Weberian calculation: he turned instrumental reason into a vivifying, animistic reason.

This was a major reason why Holmes appealed so strongly to adult readers at the time. Many of his most fervent admirers, who would create clubs and journals dedicated to him, were among the newly established professional classes. They identified with Holmes: like them, the great detective was enmeshed in a disenchanted world of instrumental reason and bureaucratization that lacked magic, meaning, or purpose. Without a case to combat ennui, Holmes resorted to drugs as a way to escape the iron cage. It was only when he could exercise his animistic reason, combining logic and imagination, that the world became re-enchanted. For Holmes and his contemporary readers, rationality was both the problem and the solution. (Indeed, many of his fans exercised their animistic reason on him, rendering him virtually alive by writing playful essays that reconciled contradictions in the stories or speculated about his character based on hints left by Conan Doyle.)

The new twentieth-century genre of science fiction also celebrated the intertwined nature of reason and the imagination. It first became a recognized literary genre in the late 1920s, when publisher Hugo Gernsback gave the literature its name and published the first magazine devoted to it, *Amazing Stories*. Since many contemporary scientists continued to deny or minimize the role of the imagination in science, Gernsback proclaimed that science fiction would unite the two, as "Scientifiction." This genre would complement science, providing it with speculative ideas for new technologies and theories. An editorial in a 1928 issue of *Amazing Stories Quarterly* opined, "Scientifiction ... takes the basis of science, considers all the clues that science has to offer, and then adds a thing that is alien to science—imagination. It goes ahead and lights the way. And when science sees the things made real in the author's mind, it makes them real indeed."[32]

Scientists themselves began to challenge the separation of the Two Cultures, especially after 1945, when that phrase emerged. The mathematician and poet Jacob Bronowski became a vocal proponent of the unity of the imagination and reason, making his most public case for it in the popular 1973 BBC television series, *The Ascent of Man*. Carl Sagan's 1976 television series *Cosmos* was inspired by it, and Sagan made a point of exploring various scientific topics through his "ship of the imagination." Today, Richard Dawkins and other scientists openly acknowledge that science is beholden to the mysterious, incalculable force of the imagination: it does not exclusively disenchant or, in Dawkins's words, "unweave the rainbow."[33] Science disenchants and re-enchants the world simultaneously.

The broad turn to the imagination in the twentieth century gained momentum, thanks to the new media of film, radio, and television, and new theories of psychology that made fantasy intrinsic to everyday life. Some approaches to the imagination continued to regard it as entirely irrational, but many didn't, including the influential avant-garde movement of Surrealism. In 1924, its founder, André Breton, defined it in complementary terms as exploring the midpoint at which reason and the imagination, reality and dream, merge. (The surrealists even established a "Bureau of Surrealist Research," and Surrealism itself became a stimulus for important theories in social science.)[34] Breton further wondered if "the imagination is on the verge of recovering its rights."[35]

Breton's intimation was certainly true in twentieth-century France, challenging the profound cultural heritage of Cartesian rationality. In 1936, Jean-Paul Sartre wrote the first work of philosophy devoted exclusively to the imagination, *L'Imagination,* and in 1968, student protestors in Paris plastered walls with the slogan, "All Power to the Imagination." Outside of France, the imagination finally recovered its rights as well, notably within academia. It became a central explanatory device in such influential works as Lionel Trilling's *The Liberal Imagination* (1950), C. Wright Mills's *The Sociological Imagination* (1959), and Martin Jay's *The Dialectical Imagination* (1966); other important studies delved into "imagined communities" and "social imaginaries."

"Fictionalism" and the Spiritual Spectrum of Modern Enchantment

The legitimation of the imagination thus enabled many strategies for re-enchanting a secular, disenchanted world in ways that were compatible with reason, science, and spirituality. Let me turn now to one of the most capacious of all, "fictionalism." Fictionalism signifies how terms like "narrative" and "story" have become master metaphors for how we organize experience and define ourselves.[36] This strategy can be traced back at least to the Renaissance: one recalls Shakespeare's adage that all the world's a stage, Montaigne's conflation of his ever-changing sense of self with his constantly revised *Essays*, and Cervantes's satiric warning against eliding life with fiction. The role of fictions in ordinary life was also discussed intently by Enlightenment thinkers, including Adam Smith, David Hume, and Jeremy Bentham.[37]

The eighteenth-century rise of the novel was accompanied by a new recognition of "fictionality," in which literary fiction was understood to be believably "real" but not referentially actual. Catherine Gallagher has argued that prior to the development of this stance, fiction was understood in two ways: stories that were clearly unbelievable, such as fables, fairy tales, and romances, and stories that were barely disguised depictions of reality, in which real people could be identified, and the real author could be sued for real damages. Perhaps tired of the lawsuits, early novelists in Britain had a conceptual breakthrough: Why not write about believable but purely imaginary characters and plots? They publicly discussed their aesthetic innovation, which had been anticipated earlier by a few writers such as Cervantes, thereby training their readers to accept novels as "believable stories that [do] not solicit belief."[38]

"Fictionality" is restricted to literature, whereas "fictionalism" as I am defining it is more capacious. It applies the idea of fiction as "truthful artifice" to everyday life: the awareness that human reality is always mediated through consciousness and language, and is therefore ineluctably constructed, albeit in different degrees. The extent of artifice can vary from being constrained, as in the natural sciences, to expansive, as in the arts. The tipping point for the shift from fictionality limited to literary expression, to fictionalism extended to the apprehension of existence, was the late nineteenth century, and it was related to the new understanding of the central role of the imagination discussed above. Terms like "narrative" and "story" started to be applied to life as a whole, alongside new, hybrid terms that captured the merger. "Autobiografiction" first appeared in 1906 to describe the blurred line between autobiography and fiction; "bibliotherapy" first appeared in 1916 to discuss the healing properties of fiction.[39] Some individuals even began to consciously live their own lives as fiction, following Oscar Wilde's half-jesting admonition, "One should either be a work of art, or wear a work of art."[40] This peculiar company of aesthetes anticipated today's use of avatars and other guises on the internet, and included Frederic Rolfe, who wrote and lived as the fictional "Baron Corvo"; the poet Fernando Pessoa, who created over seventy personas or "heteronyms"; and the author Philip K. Dick, who ended his life wondering if he might actually be a character from one of his earlier novels.[41]

The term "fictionalism" itself was coined in 1911 by the philosopher Hans Vaihinger in *The Philosophy of "As If": A System of the Theoretical, Practical and Religious Fictions of Mankind*. It signified the deliberate employment of provisional fictions to represent wide swaths of experience that had yet to be demonstrated empirically, ranging from scientific hypotheses about the material world to abstract values like freedom and justice. Vaihinger's book was widely influential in the early decades of the twentieth century. It inspired Konstantin Stanislavski, who extolled "the magic if" in his pioneering technique of method acting, whereby actors use make-believe to "become" the characters they play, and the historian Carl Becker, whose Presidential Address to the American Historical Association in 1932 proclaimed history as a form of true myth.[42] (William H. McNeil consciously echoed Becker in his 1986 AHA Presidential Address, "Mythistory."[43]) Vaihinger's work was followed by many others with their own versions of fictionalism. These include Kenneth Burke's "Dramatism," Hans Blumenberg's "Metaphorology," Hayden White's "Metahistory," and Walter Fisher's "Narrative Paradigm," in which he tellingly redefined *Homo sapiens* as *Homo narrans*.[44]

These master metaphors of "story" and "narrative" become omnipresent once you are alerted to them. They're in the lyrics of the Broadway show "The Book of Mormon," which compares religion to fantasy fiction; they're at the core of the HBO series *Westworld*, starring Anthony Hopkins as a scientist in charge of a fantasy theme park, who likens existence to stories that he will revise with the aid of homicidal robots. In terms of real people advocating fictionalism, we can limit ourselves to a scientist endorsing the views of a poet, simply because such a confluence would have shocked Weber. As he scoffed in "Science as a Vocation," "Science as a way to art? Here no criticism is even needed."[45] Modern fictionalism, however, has reunited them. Thus the astrophysicist Sean Carroll cited with approval the poet Muriel Rukeyser's line, "the universe is made of stories, not of atoms." According to Carroll, "That is absolutely correct. There is more to the world than what happens; there are the ways we make sense of it by telling its story."[46] Carroll's fictionalist approach to science, which he called "Poetic Naturalism," is a far cry from Weber's positivist emphasis on all questions being solved, in principle, through calculation.

Like science, religion too has taken an overtly fictionalist turn. T.M. Luhrmann's study of an American evangelical community shows that fictionalism can be an effective tool for religious conversion, and that committed religious practitioners are conscious of how artifices, from creeds and rituals to explicit fictions, mediate their belief in transcendent reality. She explored how religious evangelicals utilized fictionalism to help individuals experience Jesus as a living presence in their lives. Seekers were encouraged to consider Jesus as an "imaginary friend" and have ongoing conversations—even date nights—with him. Over time, this fictionalist game of "make believe" shaded into the conviction that Jesus did speak directly to the questing individual.

Once this metaphysical berth is attained, presumably the ladder of fictionalism would be discarded for a self-reinforcing faith in an incalculable, supernatural force, "enchantment" in Weber's sense. Yet Luhrmann shows that such faith does not necessarily preclude doubts that it may be nothing more than wish-fulfillment, a hopeful fiction: "Many Christians struggle, at one point or another, with the despair that it all might be a sham."[47] Religious belief can emerge from the self-conscious practice of fictionalism, but its fictionalist trappings don't necessarily disappear. Double consciousness can characterize believers in transcendent realms as well as ironic believers in imaginary worlds.

And just as belief in the creeds of established religions does not preclude fictionalism, new religions founded on acknowledged fictions can provide the existential meaning and social solidarity that characterize traditional faith-based practices. These fictionalist religions include the "Church of All Worlds," based on Robert Heinlein's 1961 novel *Stranger in a Strange Land*; the "Otherkins," based on the *Lord of the Rings*; Chaos magic, inspired by the works of H.P. Lovecraft; "Jediism," based on *Star Wars*. They are solidly in the camp of disenchanted enchantment: practitioners know that their creeds are derived from overt fantasies, but this does not preclude such ironically held beliefs from generating transcendental experiences.[48] As Erik Davis observed about the American "New Age" milieu of the 1960s and 1970s from which several of these religions arose, "fictions were self-consciously instrumentalized for occult or spiritual purposes."[49]

Fiction-based religions may be new, but fictionalism itself started to have a pronounced effect on ideas about religion in the eighteenth and nineteenth centuries, alongside the growing legitimation of the imagination. At this time, enlightened humanists increasingly defined religion as literature rather than revealed truth, a case famously made by Matthew Arnold in *Literature and Dogma* (1873).[50] Arnold argued that despite the recession of the "sea of faith," the bedrock of morally instructive stories remained.[51] And in response to the idea that religion was literature, devout writers in the early twentieth century, including J.R.R. Tolkien, C.S. Lewis, and Dorothy L. Sayers, insisted that all literature was religious. Echoing Coleridge, they maintained that literary works expressed divine Truth: God the Creator was mirrored by humanity as subcreators, capturing facets of revealed Truth in their art.

While these British writers discussed fiction in religious terms, they did so in different ways, revealing the broad spectrum of a fictionalist orientation to religion. Such distinctions had less to do with doctrinal views than with personal interpretations of them. Prior to his conversion to Christianity, for example, C.S. Lewis turned to fiction for meaning and purpose in a disenchanted world. In his autobiography he recalled that he "[cared] for almost nothing but the gods and heroes, Launcelot and the Grail, and [believed] in nothing but atoms and evolution and military service."[52] Yet Lewis also craved metaphysical solace. Characteristically, he went from one belief to another based on his wide reading. He became engrossed in occultism after reading William Butler Yeats, but eventually rejected it and considered himself an atheist. He then read a work of fantasy by the Christian writer George MacDonald, which helped him see ordinary life as numinous rather than as a meaningless confluence of atoms. His disenchanted, materialist outlook was further challenged when he read G.K. Chesterton, Henri Bergson, and the British Neo-Hegelians. He became an agnostic, open to the possibility of divine or spiritual agency and was gradually drawn to Christianity through his studies of medieval literature and friendship with Christian writers like Tolkien. By 1929, Lewis accepted the existence of God, but defined himself as a theist, not a Christian. Christianity in particular appealed to his fictionalist side: he considered it to be mythic, as beautiful, mysterious, and inspiring as all the other epics and heroic legends that he loved.

That, however, was also the problem. Lewis thought of Christianity as a myth, not a religion that he could believe in with the conviction of a convert. He entertained Christianity as he entertained all fiction, with the double consciousness that made them real to his imagination and fictitious to his reason. Lewis's secular fictionalism, with its emphasis on the interpretation of experience through multiple stories, prevented him from adopting an absolute, final point of view.

In the end, Lewis was converted to Christianity by the theistic understanding of fictionalism upheld by Tolkien. The two discussed Lewis's belief that myths are lies, not eternal truths. Tolkien responded that Christianity was indeed a myth, as fantastic as all others—but it was the only myth that was also a historical fact and thus truer than all the others. For the fiction-loving Lewis, this was a fatally attractive notion: he could single-mindedly commit himself to a myth, rather than merely enjoy it in a double-minded fashion. Shortly after this conversation with Tolkien, Lewis accepted Jesus as his personal savior.[53] Some have argued that Lewis became less catholic in his literary tastes after becoming a fervent Protestant, interested only in fictions that accorded with his religious belief. Certainly, the novels that he subsequently wrote were didactic expositions of a Christian worldview. He had come to Christianity through fictionalism and then renounced fictionalism in favor of the One True Story.

Tolkien represents an interesting contrast, because his lifelong Catholicism didn't conflict with his continued fictionalist orientation. For him, existence was a story authored by God. True, it had a foregone conclusion, but its multiple story arcs were baffling, tragic, and thrilling, just like a good fantasy epic. Unlike the Protestant Lewis, who was supremely confident in his own unmediated interpretations of Christianity, the Catholic Tolkien had a humbler attitude before the supreme mysteries of creation. For him, fallen humanity could only address metaphysical questions by fallible, or at least provisional, stories. Tolkien's skeptical attitude accords with a fictionalist outlook and helps to explain why he was able to maintain it. Life for him was an enchanting, mysterious story, a view authorized by Tolkien's faith. When his son Christopher was serving in the RAF during the Second World War, Tolkien counseled him to interpret his frightening military duties in terms of a heroic narrative: "Keep up your hobbitry in heart, and think that all stories feel like that when you are in them. You are inside a very great story!"[54]

Dorothy L. Sayers's religious views were also fundamentally shaped by fictionalism. A mystery novelist and, like Lewis, a prominent Christian apologist in the interwar period, Sayers's fictionalism was so extreme that it could be said that she was more devoted to fiction than Christianity. Whereas fictionalism brought Lewis to Christianity, whereupon he discarded it, Sayers's dutiful Christianity as a youth only became a passionate conviction in the second half of her life, when she was able to reconcile it with her love of stories and make-believe. Christianity became truly meaningful to her at this time because she was able to interpret it as authorizing artistic creativity as the supreme good, as sanctioning her self-image as a writer, and as imbuing literature with a holy status and purpose. While Sayers appeared to have abandoned writing secular mystery novels in the 1930s for popularizing religious dogma, in actuality her focus was always on the importance of fiction: in the end as in the beginning, religion justified literature. This becomes most apparent in her essay *The Mind of the Maker* (1941), in which she takes the romantic idea of imagination being humanity's reflection of the Supreme Creator to an unusual extreme. She argued that works of fiction replicate and embody the Trinity, transubstantiating even detective novels into an exemplification of God the Father, the Son, and the Holy Spirit. This is an unusual interpretation of Trinitarian theology, to say the least, but when *The Mind of the Maker* is situated within the broader cultural turn of fictionalism, it appears as less of a sport and more characteristic of a diffuse yet increasingly pronounced cultural trend.

Sayers, "Intellectual Integrity," and the Enchantments of Fictionalism

While Sayers was raised as a Christian—her father was an Anglican minister—for much of her life her belief in its teachings was more dutiful than committed. Her parents didn't provide her much religious instruction, assuming she would assimilate it through osmosis, which she did. But her true love was not the patristics she found in her father's well-stocked library but the volumes of alluring fiction. An only child, she lived in her imagination, putting on theatricals and living in imaginary worlds. For example, after performing her adaptation of *The Three Musketeers* for her parents and relatives—some of whom she roped in as players—she maintained the artifice for over a year, signing her letters "Athos."[55] She never abandoned such make-believe, devouring fiction omnivorously and engaging in literary hoaxes and multiple self-dramatizations. All of this was done through double-consciousness, as she admitted: "I was always readily able to distinguish between fact and fiction … I dramatised myself, and have at all periods of my life continued to dramatise myself, into a great number of egotistical impersonations … but at all times with a perfect realization that I was the creator, not the subject, of these fantasies."[56]

Her commitment to Christianity was more perfunctory. She resented being confirmed at her parents' insistence, arguing that belief was being inflicted upon her when she had yet to determine her stance. And the uninspired, low-Church teachings she endured during her secondary school education nearly made her abandon religion entirely. She persevered only because she read G.K. Chesterton, who presented Christianity as "one whirling adventure … in which the heavenly chariot flies thundering through the ages, the dull heresies sprawling and prostrate, the wild truth reeling but erect."[57] Christianity as pulp fiction attracted her enormously.

Sayers continued to question the degree of her attachment to religion in college and after, although she remained in the fold. She never questioned her calling as a writer, however. After graduation, she worked for several years in an advertising firm, excelling at creating fictions inciting desires for unnecessary products. She loved the creative work but was troubled by the fuzzy line between truth and fictions. In her free time, she began to write mystery novels about Lord Peter Wimsey, who ferreted out the truth about crime through a form of animistic reason similar to Sayers's own hero, Sherlock Holmes.

As his name suggests, Wimsey used logical reason combined with imaginative forms of deliberation, and he was ultimately able to determine the truth by an analysis of facts. For Sayers and her detective hero, not everything is a fiction: empirical truth does exist, but it is always framed and interpreted through stories. Wimsey frequently ponders how to distinguish real stories from lies or fantasies, especially in the novel *Murder Must Advertise* (1933), where Sayers puts him through the paces she experienced as a copywriter. The novel suggests at times that advertising is a form of delusive enchantment, although it holds out the hope that consumers are less deceived than willing participants in a game of selling and buying. The more creative side of advertising, which Sayers herself excelled at, is given more play by an author who wanted to see the best side of fictionalism. At this point in her life, her fictional detective could seem as alive and responsive to her as Jesus was to the evangelicals studied by Luhrmann. As she wrote in 1937, "[Wimsey] has become a permanent resident in the house of my mind. His affairs are more real to me than my own; his domestic responsibilities haunt my waking hours, and I find myself bringing all my actions and opinions to the bar of his silent criticism."[58]

As she continued to write fiction, Sayers wrestled with more existential questions about her own beliefs and behavior. Her penchant for self-dramatization and fantasy resulted in several painful love affairs and an illegitimate child, whose existence she hid from nearly everyone for over thirty years. (Her son was brought up by a close relative who was sworn to secrecy.) She thrived on the creative life, but was troubled by the morality of advertising and the frivolity of the mystery genre. She came close to resolving these questions in her novel *Gaudy Night* (1935), in which the protagonist Harriet Vane—a character similar in many ways to Sayers—has related doubts about her calling as a mystery writer. Vane resolves them, Sayers explained, in terms of "intellectual integrity as the one great permanent value in an emotionally unstable world."[59] One must pursue one's creative talents, regardless of what they are, provided they are done for the good of the work and not for egoistic reasons. In other words, self-abasement before a higher cause—which is as much a religious attitude as a secular one. Sayers, like Vane, chose intellectual integrity as her lodestar in a world where fiction and reality were frequently intertwined, which also happened to be Max Weber's primary allegiance within similar existential circumstances.

Her religious belief, on the other hand, was never passionate but strictly intellectual. This was true when she was young, and it was also true at the end of her life, when she acknowledged, "Since I cannot come at God through intuition, or through my emotions, or through my 'inner light' ... there is only the intellect left."[60] When critics accused her of being interested in Christian theology for its "intellectual pattern," she admitted, "That is quite true. I remember once saying [to a friend], 'I do not know whether I believe in Christ or whether I am only in love with the pattern.'"[61] She then tried to justify this "intellectual passion" for Christian dogma as being equivalent to an emotional conversion: "I do not know whether we can be saved through the intellect, but I do know that I can be saved by nothing else."[62]

This profession of rational faith was made sincerely, but when we look at the process by which Sayers became intellectually passionate about Christianity, we see that it didn't gel until she could interpret its doctrines as justifying her love of fiction and her calling as a writer. This was a matter of happenstance. In the late 1930s, she wrote a play about Wimsey, which restored her childhood love of the theater. She didn't just love the make-believe but also praised the common unity and purpose of the theatrical enterprise, which she had yet to find in religious rites. Her play was a success, and in 1937 the Canterbury Cathedral commissioned her to write on a religious subject for one of their annual productions. Sayers chose the life of a Cathedral architect, because she was more interested in exploring the artistic calling than she was in expounding theology. The message of this play was similar to that of *Gaudy Night*, except cast in an explicitly Christian framework. Here she expressed for the first time the romantic idea of God as Creator, the individual as sub-creator.

This early foray into Christian apologetics might not have continued, except that the Press was intrigued by the notion of a mystery writer engaged in religious apologetics. An editor asked her to justify her new work, and she did so in an article entitled "The Greatest Drama Ever Staged." Sayers argued that Christian dogma, rather than being scholastic and dull, was as exciting as any potboiler: God, incarnate as man, was both hero and victim, murdered by his own creation. Jesus was not meek and mild but a "dangerous firebrand," and since "He was God, there can be nothing dull about God either."[63]

Her argument that Christianity was a great story—in fact, a hard-boiled mystery with a dramatic killing—caused a sensation. She was asked to write more articles about questions of Christian belief and more plays about the life of Christ for BBC radio. Her career as a defender of the faith had been unanticipated, but it afforded her a wider audience for a topic more respectable than detective fiction. And it allowed her to interpret Christianity as justifying not simply creativity but fictionalism, the holiness of story. Sayers had found a supernatural sanction for fictionalism in addition to the more fallibly human bulwark against deceit represented by "intellectual integrity." She was finally able to combine Christian orthodoxy with her long-held and most passionate faith in the enchantments and moral truths of fiction.

This was a neat trick, sometimes too neat, as in the case of *The Mind of the Maker*, which simplified the notoriously complex Trinitarian doctrine by equating the different aspects of God to the elements of a good novel. She argued that the novelist's initial idea for the work, viewed as a whole from beginning to end, was analogous to the Father, encompasser of eternity; the incarnation of that idea in a manuscript was analogous to the Son, the "word made flesh"; and the power of that story to move people was analogous to the Holy Spirit. Just as the three aspects of the novel cannot be prised apart, so too was the Trinity three-in-one. Sayers claimed that *The Mind of the Maker* was meant to make an abstract doctrine relatable to the common reader and to stress the foundational injunction to be creative that Sayers found and celebrated in Christianity.

The work may not be entirely convincing as theology, but it is representative of the modern turn to fictionalism by religious thinkers. In their individual ways, Lewis, Tolkien, and Sayers were drawn to traditional creeds as much for their attraction as stories as for their claims to eternal truth. Contemporary fiction-based religions also capitalize on the innate power of narratives to provide meanings, albeit provisional and contingent ones, while also fostering the fellowship and rites built on mutual appreciations of such narratives. For religious believers, the fictions gesture to essential truths, mediated through a glass darkly. And for those seeking more secular forms of inspiration, fictions can provide provisional hypotheses and contingent guidelines to be validated against the test of experience. In both cases, beliefs are held in a double-minded way, with an awareness of the interplay of truth and artifice, enchantment and disenchantment.

Conclusion

In terms of narratives of secularism and disenchantment, Weber provided profound questions, although his more limited answers reflected his own personal predilections and historical context, which was changing radically even as he addressed them. This is why he wasn't able to see the imagination as an emergent rather than residual phenomenon and one soon to be dominant. It has become a central mysterious and incalculable force in its own right, authorizing the self-reflexive turn to fictions in all their ambiguity.

Disenchantment and enchantment are thus ineluctably intertwined in modernity: the ideal is to balance reason with imagination, to be delighted without being deluded. However, with the spread of mass culture since the late nineteenth century, and the impact of information technologies since the late twentieth century, it has become more difficult to prevent the desires and illusions of the imagination from overwhelming rationality. Our contemporary dilemma appears to be the reverse of that which Weber posited during his *fin de siècle*: rather than being disenchanted by instrumental rationality, we are more likely to be enchanted by the imagination, even as we are aware of its artifices. We have replaced the iron cage with a fun-house mirror, with only the intellectual integrity endorsed by Weber and Sayers to counter the glare of its labyrinthine reflections.

6

Narratives of Disenchantment, Narratives of Secularization

Radical Enlightenment and the Rise of the Illiberal Secular

Jonathan Israel

Arguably, one of Max Weber's principal lessons for the modern historian (and political philosopher) is that we must avoid confusing the rapid receding of older forms of magical thinking, mystique, and organized religion—which he termed *Entzauberung*, or "disenchantment"—with any supposed weakening of quasi-theological and powerfully mythical patterns of thought in the modern context. Given that organized religion and theology have lost much of their grip over Western modernity, it is by no means also the case that superficially secularized but actually quasi-theological patterns of thought, in Weber's sense, or modern Western "credulity" as a populist phenomenon denounced by generations of Enlightenment thinkers, have similarly weakened or ceased to menace modern freedoms and democracy. We should worry, of course, especially with respect to new, secularized forms of older theological approaches that have, or are apt to have, highly illiberal consequences. Indeed, in this context there is a sense in which modern democracy may actually enhance the power of popular credulity to operate in illiberal directions even more powerfully than before. Whatever the strengths and weaknesses of Weber's identification of the social and cultural roots of modern capitalism with the Protestant ethic, there are incontestably excellent grounds for arguing that post-1800 forms of credulity have been just as powerful and sometimes more destructive of political stability and basic freedoms than even the most bigoted and uncompromising manifestations of medieval Crusader faith or the Spanish and Portuguese Inquisitions. Arguably, nothing is more insidious and dangerous than secularized theology when it becomes an unsubstantiated but dramatic summons for society's general salvation and redemption, although stripped of any genuinely theological appeal to the divine or supernatural.

An inherent part of such a "secularized theology" is the type of political and general leadership of the people that acquires unlimited authority arising from the fascinating, overwhelming, and exceptional appeal of the leader's person and projected image despite the absence of any legal, religious, or traditional basis for that appeal, that is, from "charisma," another concept introduced by Weber and one which he linked to the wider process of disenchantment. Viewing "charisma" as one of the three main types of authority in the social sphere—traditional, legal-rational, and charismatic—he linked this phenomenon to secularized modernity by postulating that the sway of "charisma" must gradually fade away over time owing to the inexorable advance of legal, administrative, and governmental "routinization" gradually depriving it of what he considered its positive potential as much as its destabilizing and dangerously authoritarian capability.[1] Reality, though, soon pointed in a very different direction from Weber's prediction. That the people should be swayed, amid great fervor, to believe their misfortunes and grievances were due to the pernicious machinations of a particular group, and that finally a Redeemer had arrived possessing the strength of will to save the people from this curse, and extirpate that allegedly pernicious social element ruthlessly, and thereby save the nation from its wretchedness and misfortunes, namely the lure of Nazism, undoubtedly figures among the greatest and most powerful myths of the twentieth century. But it is important to view this political mass phenomenon as part of a much wider tendency commencing not with twentieth-century Fascism but rather reaching back to Robespierre's theory of the special moral purity and destiny of the "ordinary person."

Of course, many examples of the potency of popular myths devoid of basis in fact exerting a pervasive impact on the political scene today can be cited. As Ernst van den Hemel argued at this conference,[2] the post-2000s claim in the Netherlands that Dutch society has enjoyed a religiously inspired tradition of equality reaching back thousands of years, despite having no basis whatsoever in fact or theology, remains nevertheless a powerful trope in contemporary Dutch politics; people believe it and that is what counts when making something politically exploitable. Contemporary American society, where many insist there is no scientific evidence for Darwinian evolution theory or global warming, seemingly provides ample justification for Spinoza's comment, on the first page of the *Tractatus Theologico-Politicus*, that where their hopes and fears, their deepest longings, are concerned, "most people are quite ready to believe anything."[3]

However, it would be wildly mistaken to suppose that gross irrationality and prejudice pervade only the realm of the unschooled popular mind. A modern scholarly theory that distinctly troubled Weber was that put forward in 1911 by Werner Sombart in his book *The Jews and Economic Life*. For Sombart, "the genesis of the capitalist spirit" required a particularly "calculating" and speculative form of "rationalism," "money calculation" perverting higher forms of human ideals and coupling these with forms of exploitation specialized in by alien social groups, especially the Jews. As an "alien" minority, the Jews supposedly manifested a marked indifference to society and the state, so that conflicts between nations became a major source of "Jewish acquisition." According to Sombart, the root of modern capitalism should therefore be located not in the Protestant ethic, where Weber located it—though he did at times acknowledge a degree of affinity between Jews and Puritans, and therefore also of affinity between Jewishness and North American capitalism—but rather in Jewish money-lending. Here was a modern scholarly "myth," constructed with Weber in mind, fueled by theological traditions, powerfully energized by prejudice, that exerted a wide impact.[4]

Quasi- or post-theological, irrational ways of thinking have manifested an immensely powerful grip not just on the less-educated mind-set but equally on large sections of the Western intelligentsia. When, in the preface to his *Tractatus Theologico-Politicus*, Spinoza states that we cannot defeat tyranny and despotism without conquering "superstition" first, he was certainly not referring just to the organized religions of the early modern era. He meant every myth and superstition useful to despots as a tool for capturing power and controlling the people, all irrational and prejudiced ways of thinking devised to project popular grievances, account for setbacks, and explain the masses' wretched condition. The historian, accordingly, must be doubly on his guard against mistaking the weakening of older, more explicitly theological forms of credulity for the weakening of credulity per se. "Because the common people everywhere live in the same wretched state," adds Spinoza on his third page, "they never adhere to the same superstition for very long. It is only a new form of credulity that really pleases them, one that has not yet let them down."[5] The essence of "superstition" for Spinoza is not belief in one or another theology as such but the power of hope driven by fear and distress to find dramatic redemption, no matter how misplaced or incoherent the belief embraced.

The so-called "secularization" process embedded in the Enlightenment therefore needs to be treated with the utmost caution. Certainly, processes of disenchantment—dispelling the magical, mysterious, and miraculous from our public reasoning and of "secularization"—removing religious authority and theological criteria from public life, publicly supported education, and politics—are rightly viewed as integral and fundamental to the Enlightenment. We need only think of Balthasar Bekker's assault in his epoch-making book *De Betoverde Weereld* (The World Bewitched) (1691–3), on belief in witchcraft, sorcery, and demonic powers in the 1690s and the Haarlem Mennonite, Anthonie van Dale's demolition in his *De oraculis veterum ethnicorum dissertationes* (1683) and subsequent works, during the first decade of the eighteenth century, of the age-old conviction that the ancient pagan Oracles had infused the entire Roman world until the fourth century, that belief in demonic power combined with faith that it was Christ's coming that had silenced these supernatural powers, to see how central to the Enlightenment's progress the *Entzauberung* process was, though one could also argue that Christianity already manifested signs of moving in such a direction much earlier. These books undoubtedly reflected a changing social and cultural reality. After around 1670, accusations of witchcraft, for instance, occurred increasingly less often in the Dutch Republic and were increasingly taken less seriously even by Calvinist and other preachers.[6] However, as subsequent developments were to show, this was not the same as extinguishing popular superstition and credulity.

It is undoubtedly true, too, that the realization that "disenchantment" was fast dissolving the individual's belief in *supernaturalia*, the power of the supernatural in humanity's outlook, and that this process was catastrophically sapping theology's hold on the mind, itself became a powerful new rationalizing ecclesiastical myth and dominated the vigorous response to Bekker's and Van Dale's interventions. Bekker was massively denounced in Dutch society and eventually dismissed from his ministry for challenging belief in the reality of diabolical powers insinuating themselves into humans. Approximately 300 publications appeared in reply to Bekker's book, the vast majority drenching his efforts at "disenchantment" with strict Calvinist, liberal Calvinist (Coccean), Remonstrant, and Lutheran rebuke and insistence on theological "truth," reaffirming the power of the supernatural in our everyday world. Yet by their very efforts to defend church doctrines against the likes of Bekker and Van Dale, and still more in subsequent decades against the deists, Calvinist conservatives indubitably contributed too, if less spectacularly, to the process of *Entzauberung*, which they did by forging a considerably narrowed, reduced, and more carefully and strictly defined sphere of the supernatural, confined to the miracles and revelations recorded in scripture, with reduced scope for the efficacy of prayer, a defensive stance reinforced by a torrent of early "moderate Enlightenment" theological texts.

Hence, if secularization was basic to the Enlightenment in every Western society, it was rarely comprehensive or endorsed across the board; and insofar as it produced new, more guarded, and better defended lines of theological defense, expounded in powerfully influential "moderate" enlightened terms, it supplied a formidable fresh set of obstacles and a range of myths encouraging faith and reliance on the clergy. If John Locke's theory of toleration proved a landmark in the history of religious freedom, it was also an obstruction to modern equality, since it granted the "right" to full freedom of individual conscience only to selected categories of believers (the main exceptions being Catholics, atheists, and to a lesser extent Jews) within a contractualist framework that otherwise endorsed monarchy and assigned to the state not just responsibility for restricting toleration but also the duty to support the clergy's efforts to enforce church discipline on their congregations and preside over morals and lifestyle. Hence, it was not only the so-called "religious Enlightenment" that devised fresh defenses against impulses toward secularization; the non-religious "moderate Enlightenment" did so likewise. Arguably still more conducive to modern myths than Locke were Hume's endorsement of what people are accustomed to as the basis of the moral order, followed by Kant's and Christoph Meiners's novel theories of racial hierarchy, and Hegel's metaphysical notions of the "spirit of the age" and the relationship of the state to society.

In the case of another influential formula for limited toleration rivalling Locke's, that of the Lutheran jurist Christian Thomasius (1655–1728), a dominant voice at Halle, the power of state and church to coerce individuals, including declared heretics, was redefined and limited not on the basis of individual rights but in accordance with the doctrine that the state's prime function is to minimize civil discord especially in the religious sphere, and defuse and mute theological strife. It was a doctrine that fitted well within the Prussian context in which Lutheranism and Calvinism confronted each other, both being accorded a recognized, institutionalized standing.[7] The Lockean and Thomasian doctrines of toleration acted as engines driving a limited secularization while also entrenching the power of established churches and the role of theology in society on a new basis. Meanwhile, such arrangements to protect state power alongside a core of ecclesiastical authority, using "reason" in this defensive fashion, inevitably had a further cumulative weakening effect on older structures of authority. One would not need to go as far as Leo Strauss (1899–1973), who concluded that Locke's affirmations of the divine authority of scripture to underpin key parts of his theological-political system were not sincerely meant and ultimately subversive in character, to conclude that comprehensive secularization was being avoided. Strauss was right, though, to point to the disintegrative, unravelling intellectual potential for an "age of reason" to leave nothing in the way of rational justification for arguments championing the miraculous and divine character of scriptural authority.[8]

If narratives of disenchantment and secularization were foundational to the construction of "modernity" in our post-Enlightenment world, at the same time these generated an enduring tension between a moderate Enlightenment—one anxious to compromise with theology, the existing social hierarchy and in some instances in the late eighteenth century, likewise to help legitimize existing social structures as well as racial hierarchy—and a radical Enlightenment that made no concession to theology or secular credulity. Here was a tension already clearly identified and delineated by Strauss in the 1920s,[9] which during the 1930s became central to the ongoing dispute over the character of modern political theory between Strauss and Carl Schmitt (1888–1985).[10] At the same time, however, both the radical and moderate tendency found themselves locked in conflict with the theology of a resurgent Counter-Enlightenment, seemingly a formidably powerful modern force following Napoleon's defeat, during the years of the Restoration and the "Holy Alliance," a political-theological construct that threatened to dominate European political life in the decades after 1815 and was one of the sources, later, of Schmitt's illiberalism. The Holy Alliance and its ideologues, such as Joseph de Maistre and Louis Bonald, helped slow both "secularization" and rationalization but at the same time helped ensure these remained entirely separate things as well as incomplete and highly variegated in their consequences for politics, education, and the moral sphere.

As several key twentieth-century political thinkers described and made their contemporaries aware—above all Weber, Sombart, Schmitt, and Strauss—the advance of both "secularization" and "rationalization" in the West remained highly ambiguous both as abstract principles and in their effects. One of the principal founders of sociology as a discipline, Weber was a distinctly pessimistic analyst of our post-Marxian and post-Nietzschean world. Struck by the fact that Protestants in the Germany of 1900 were far more likely than Catholics to become entrepreneurs, industrialists, and business leaders, after winning his long battle with depression and mental illness, he went on to develop his famous theory that modern capitalism is essentially the secularized legacy of the "Protestant ethic," a perspective classically expounded in his *Die protestantische Ethik und der Geist des Kapitalismus* (1904–05). Key to Weber's theory was his idea that only the Protestant ethic can explain the complex sociological phenomenon of "this-worldly asceticism" that in his view buttresses the rise of modern industrial society and work routines, the self-enclosed dreariness of "the modern human class of specialists and occupationalists" (*das moderne Fach- und Berufsmenschentum*), together with the lifelong pursuit of profit through the rational organization of labor shaped by an intensely frugal personal lifestyle in the entrepreneur himself. For such effort required the entrepreneur to deny himself or herself personal rewards such as a consequent lifestyle of pleasure, luxury, and idleness. Shaped partly by Nietzsche's influence, Weber's analysis stressed, with alarm and a certain dreary horror,[11] the alienation and dismal effects of "modernity" and by doing so powerfully contributed to the increasingly negative image of the Enlightenment nurtured in certain quarters during the Weimar era, not least in the minds of Schmitt and Strauss, a negative critique taken several steps further in the famous Counter-Enlightenment diatribe of Horkheimer and Adorno, the *Dialektik der Aufklärung* (1944), a deeply unhistorical and even perhaps, in most Enlightenment experts' estimation (including my own), a dreadful book, but one with an astonishing influence nevertheless.[12] For Adorno and Horkheimer, "the program of the Enlightenment was the disenchantment of the world, the dissolution of myths and the substitution of knowledge for fancy."[13] Yet its final result, allegedly, was demoralizing: a general disaster culminating in the soul-destroying dreariness of modern mass culture and the erasure of genuine individuality.[14]

The Protestant ethic, explained Weber, encouraged men to approach God through frugal endeavor in this world: the concept of "vocation" (*Beruf*) powerfully fused, as he explained the phenomenon, with the secularized doctrine of predestination to realize individual salvation in the successful and ever-growing enterprise. Criticizing Karl Marx's iron laws of historical materialism and class warfare, which make no allowance for cultural or psychological factors, Weber brought cultural influences, and especially elements deriving from theology, directly into his causal schema for explaining "modernity."[15] In particular, he very effectively employed the concept of "instrumental reason" (*Zweckrationalität*) to help explain how "reason" can become the harnessed principal tool of an irrational quasi-theological agenda.[16] But such a conception is itself enshrouded in myth and as impossible to verify as Marx's doctrine of "class warfare." Leo Strauss (1899–1973), for one, held that Weber here stepped too far, that capitalism and the modern world were not born of the Protestant Reformation, nor specifically of Calvinism, certainly not to the extent that the "Weber thesis" contended. Strauss believed that Weber's conceptualization of the process implied a much greater degree of continuity than really existed and that the advent of modernity involved a much more radical break, one brought about chiefly by philosophers and political thinkers in the tradition of Machiavelli, Hobbes, and Spinoza, than Weber tended to admit.[17]

Specifying theological roots for modernity in turn poses a range of questions not just about the supposedly ultimate Christian origins of the elimination of miracles and mystery but about the legitimacy, direction, and moral orientation of the consequent process of "secularization." As a purely theoretical proposition, comprehensive secularization might have the effect of detaching society from all meaningful moral moorings and boundaries, plunging society and culture into Nietzsche's endless chaos of strife and struggles for power, spreading a deeply divisive, immoral, and anarchic culture of selfishness destructive of all cohesion, stability, and order. Weber, Schmitt—who had long felt fascination for Weber's theories[18]—and Strauss all averred that what Western modernity was experiencing was a process of adjustment and absorption, a "preservation of thought, feelings or habits of Biblical origin," as Strauss expressed it, "after the loss or atrophy of Biblical faith."[19] Secularization, for Weber, Schmitt, and Strauss, in other words entails a transfer of structures of theological thought and religious authority from the level of religious belief to the level of assumption, convention, and habits of mind, which the scholar analyzing the phenomenon might evaluate in either a positive or negative light. But where Weber with his Kantian perspectives and methodology viewed the persistence of the irrational and the mythical in modernity as vestiges of an irrational past linked to escapism from the "overly rationalized present," Schmitt, not unlike the neo-Marxist theorist Georg Luckács, contended that "irrationality and neomythology are intrinsically linked to the abstract rationality that Weber describes and practices."[20]

Hence arose the tendency during the Weimar era, from the 1920s on, to go beyond Weber in stressing the persistence of mythical irrationality in modernity. Schmitt famously contended that "all significant concepts of the modern theory of the state are secularized theological concepts" and that this was the case both historically and ontologically, that is not only because of their long and complex development—in which they were transferred from theology to the theory of the state, "whereby, for example, the omnipotent God became the omnipotent lawgiver"—but also due to their systematic form and structure (*systematischen Struktur*).[21] Recognition of this he deemed essential for any meaningful historical, philosophical, political-theoretical, or sociological consideration of these concepts. For modern "secularization" to be adequately understood and placed in the sphere of modern political theory, held Schmitt in his *Political*

Theology (1922), it must be contemplated in this double aspect—as a process by which conceptions of the modern state descend from religious systems, their historical evolution leading to their being progressively less embedded in theological doctrines, on the one hand, and, on the other, their underlying structures and organization of authority being rendered stronger. Schmitt, like Strauss, represented modern "secularization" as highly ambiguous, not really secular, and inherently divisive.[22]

It is hard to deny that some modern political systems, and especially those that persecute, oppress, and are destructive of human freedom, can usefully be analyzed in Schmittian terms. How else should one characterize Fascist ideologies that invest all the redeeming power of the state in the authority of the "leader" and other types of totalitarian regime that systematically crush all criticism and ideological dissent, and demonize ideological foes, except as secularized systems of theology powered by the phenomenon Weber labeled "charisma"? But Schmitt, who was disdainful of and denigrated the Weimar constitution and state, insisted that liberal constitutionalism too was a "secularized theology."[23] A resolute Schmittian theorist persuaded that all theories of sovereignty and of the modern state are in fact secularized theological systems might try, as he did, to construe even democratic republicanism as a "secularization," and particularly insidious form of "political theology," rather than as a logical outcome of an undeviating radical Enlightenment rationalization program and Spinozistic metaphysical monism.

Where Schmitt's notion of modern "political theology" has an obviously persuasive logic when applied to the Third Reich, for most it will seem considerably less compelling when applied, as he applied it, to the tradition of liberal democracy.[24] Liberal democracy Schmitt deemed the secularized descendant of eighteenth-century Protestantism and deism, excluding the sphere of the miraculous and ruling out exceptional divine interventions, thereby reducing God to the divine watchmaker who simply launches the cosmos into an unchanging clockwork regularity of fixed rules. Much as deism dismantled divine intervention outside the natural order of things, so liberal constitutionalism, according to Schmitt, banishes the sovereign's overarching and indispensable power of direct intervention against the routine administrative and legal order whenever a threat to society and state arises thereby disarming, unbalancing, and destabilizing society.[25] As Schmitt expressed this notion,

> The idea of the modern constitutionalist state triumphed together with deism, a theology and metaphysics that banished the miracle from the world. This theology and metaphysics rejected not only the transgression of the laws of

nature through an exception brought about by direct intervention, as is found in the idea of a miracle, but also the sovereign's direct intervention in a valid legal order.[26]

The prime philosophical architect of this banishing of the Miracle from the modern political arena, Schmitt did not fail to identify as "the Jewish philosopher," Spinoza, whom he therefore viewed as the supreme foe of authentic state authority.[27]

Unlike the classical tradition of German philosophy that, as one of the noteworthy Hungarian Jewish intellectuals of the mid-nineteenth century passionately committed to the 1848–49 revolutions, Ignác Einhorn (1825–75), complained, emphatically placed Spinoza at the center of the metaphysical speculations without paying any attention whatever to his political thought, Schmitt placed the figure of Spinoza at the center of his account of modern "political theologies" even while periodically adjusting his perspective over time. Einhorn, sometimes called Ignaz Einhorn Horn, the grandson of a rabbi of Vagújhely, in western Hungary near the Slovakian border, studied history, politics, and philosophy at Leipzig in 1849–50 and wrote a thesis on Spinoza's political thought published at Dessau in 1851, which became central to his revolutionary outlook. In this text he points to the absurdity, as he saw it, of absorbing Spinoza's philosophy into the core of modern thought, as Mendelssohn, Lessing, Goethe, Herder, Fichte, Schelling, Hegel, Bruno Bauer, and Feuerbach had all done, while totally ignoring his political ideas or else dismissing these, as many in a confused and superficial manner did, as merely derived from Hobbes.[28] Society, churches, government, and the academy still conspired as it were in the mid-nineteenth century to conceal from the general view something that was deeply relevant to everyone.

Even those thinkers, like Schelling and Hegel, most indebted to Spinoza's insights, objected Einhorn, took the opportunity provided by the unrelenting force of ecclesiastical condemnation and by popular distaste to marginalize and bury his political philosophy. Reprehensibly, considering the huge scale of their debt, Fichte, Schelling, and Hegel had all persisted with this startling lack of generosity in their publicly stated judgments about Spinoza.[29] The paradox of German idealism was hence that it simultaneously placed Spinoza at the center while pretending to do nothing of the kind, concealing the full implications of *Spinozismus*, especially Spinoza's political thought, from university students and from the reading public in general. They did so, argued the ex-rabbinical candidate Einhorn, as a collective antidemocratic popular, pro-theology defensive strategy to protect myth, religion, and unreason against philosophical reason.[30]

No such accusation could be leveled at Carl Schmitt. Contrary to Strauss, Schmitt correctly saw that where for Hobbes, his favorite early modern political thinker, the rights of the sovereign always "trump the rights of the individual, for the sake of the individual's salvation, in Spinoza this is no longer the case."[31] Schmitt correctly identified Spinoza rather than Hobbes as the true commencement of the modern separation of church and state and of liberalism from Christian values. In his early writings, Schmitt depicted Spinoza as reacting at a basic level against the "mechanical rationalism" of Descartes and of Hobbes, the political thinker he regarded as especially profound. Schmitt identified Spinoza as crucial to the idea of an undermining, revolutionary democratic *pouvoir constituant*, such as the Abbé Sieyès urged the French National Assembly to assume in 1789, an overriding power that transcends the bounds of the existing constitutional and legal system and that derives its force and validity from the collective power of society as a whole, the first deployment of the "general will" concept in its democratic political guise that Schmitt interprets as Spinoza's own transfer to the political sphere or systematic secularization of his metaphysics of *natura naturans* working on *natura naturata* (the power of nature working on produced nature). The problem with this philosophically, as Schmitt himself conceded, was that Spinoza's metaphysics of *natura naturans/natura naturata*, though designated by him a "theology" was at the same time, as Strauss insisted, clearly a "political theology" intended to end all theology.[32]

In Schmitt's thought of the early Weimar period, Spinoza is the originator of the modern democratic tendency, a fact that rendered him an essentially illiberal force since, in Schmitt's system of political thought, "democracy" is a principle that stands in opposition to the Weberian liberal constitutional state based on the rule of law. However, the illiberal, authoritarian implications of the "general will," as Schmitt soon had to admit, are found much more strikingly in Rousseau's concept of *volonté générale*, a substitution that helped him edge toward his revised perspective of the 1930s. Schmitt joined the Nazi party on May 1, 1933, just days after his Jewish and leftist colleagues were dismissed from their positions in Germany's universities. By 1938, Spinoza stood in Schmitt's political theory less as the fount of "democracy" than as the fount of modern liberal constitutionalism and a quintessentially "Jewish thinker," the embodiment of the "Jewish spirit" poisoning the state from within, with his democratic republicanism and doctrines of freedom of thought, expression, and criticism, eroding the unconditional status of obedience to the sovereign, and, finally, allegedly serving the interests of the "Jewish people" against those of "the Christian people."[33]

Meanwhile, democracy as such, at least the abstract principle of democracy, seemed to Schmitt something very different from parliamentary, representative government, something dangerously and massively destabilizing in a different way, especially when assuming the form Rousseau gave it in his *Social Contract* where he forges a "general will" that can at any time justify overriding laws and the constitution and changing society's institutional format by ex-parliamentary means. On one level, Fascist dictatorships and democratic republics remained very different kinds of entity in Schmitt's schema, but within the context of Rousseau's political theory, of which Schmitt was a discerning critic, no less than he was of Hobbes and Spinoza, a startling convergence occurs that leaves no significant gap. In moments of severe crisis, emergencies, or what Schmitt calls "states of exception," both Rousseau and Schmitt postulate the need for the dictator by popular assent to redeem and defend the body politic. Schmitt queries how it is possible in Rousseau's theory, for the "general will" ever to suspend itself, seeing his own theory of the supremacy of state sovereignty and dictatorship as more consistent here; but Rousseau perceived no contradiction between the dictator taking emergency measures, in exceptional circumstances, to ensure the survival of the state as already constituted, as an expression of the "general will," provided this dictatorship is understood as provisional and its true goal is to revert to the normal rule of law as soon as circumstances permit.[34]

The most vital and innovative element in Schmitt's political theology is his notion that what is bad in man and inherently antisocial cannot be suppressed altogether by human means or reason, but only contained by a state that defines its friends and enemies in much the same way that theology differentiates between believers and unbelievers, not according to any moral qualities that can be evaluated in terms of worldly principle but by decree or decision of the sovereign in a manner apt to be morally arbitrary but satisfying to popular credulity. The stability, cohesion, and durability of the state depend on this ultimately arbitrary "decisionism," and when need be, in emergencies, full-scale dictatorial sovereign power. All politics he views as conflict, all politics is dangerous, the danger being inescapably lodged in the limited and in part perverse nature of man, or in the doctrine of Original Sin, which he says that Donoso Cortés radicalized for polemical purposes.[35] If Weber's political thought is ultimately Kantian, Schmitt's, as Strauss pointed out, is based on Hobbes's "state of nature."[36] For Schmitt, blind apparently to the true character of democratic constitutionalism and modern parliamentary democracy, which most theorists would consider difficult to classify as political theologies, the only possible response to Weber's narrative of "disenchantment," unavoidably but deeply problematically, was either Hobbesian authoritarianism or disintegrative and defenseless liberal anarchy, a kind of Augustinian or even Manichaean theological schema secularized.[37]

If the chief function of the Führer was to establish by authoritarian decree who are the "friends" and who the "enemies" of the state, there were eminently cogent reasons, at least of a quasi-theological nature, why, in Schmitt's post-1933 view, the Jews should be proclaimed the supreme enemy. All modern political ideologies were "secularized theologies" according to Schmitt, but Jewish rationalism he viewed as an applied secularized theology more apt than any other to strangle sovereignty and healthy political theologies of action, such as that of Hobbes. The Jews, and especially Jewish influences and ideas, including all their writings, averred Schmitt from 1933 onward, represented the principle of subversion, disorder, and disintegration in the body of law and the institutions of the state and must therefore be purged from its functioning, juristic practice, and legal discourse, much as in the Middle Ages the Jews, considered perverse unbelievers, mockers, and killers of Christ, needed to be purged from the Christian body politic. State-authorized antisemitism he therefore held to be something valid and even indispensable in the same way that any fundamental theological doctrine conceives itself to be. The Jews, according to the Church's doctrine, had killed Christ, but according to Schmitt who had not expressed a virulent antisemitism along these lines before 1933, they had also taken the lead in undermining Christianity and Christian values during the Enlightenment and in turning the Hobbesian state from a life-giving, healthy myth into an overly rationalized machine. If Strauss aligned Hobbes and Spinoza, seeing both as foundational to the "radical Enlightenment," Schmitt directly pitted Spinoza against Hobbes, the first being the great false guide and the "first liberal Jew" and the second the true path to "Christian" political modernity. However distorted and grotesque much of this may sound, Schmitt was undoubtedly closer to the mark than Strauss in viewing Hobbes and Spinoza as political opposites, the latter as the fount of the Enlightenment strand that turned radical, anti-Christian, and liberal constitutionalist.[38] Here, then, we encounter a crucial intellectual intersection of the theories of Schmitt and Strauss with wide-ranging implications even today, which Adorno and Horkheimer adroitly skipped by that favorite dodge of Enlightenment historiography: leaving Spinoza out of the discussion virtually altogether.[39]

In this key context, Schmitt identifies Spinoza as the overarching violator, the figure who more than any other thinker sought not just to destroy myth, undermine and weaken theology, sap the clergy's moral dominance, fortify freedom of conscience, and break the bonds between theology and philosophy, and theology and politics, but who more than any other also introduced individualism, the freedom to criticize and to promote democratic republican thinking, the hegemony of individual rights over law, the primacy of the individual in relation to the state, all this being viewed, to an extent accurately, as the direct consequence of Spinoza's undermining of the moral, social, and political functions of theology and of sovereignty as vested in the state rather than in society.[40] Spinoza, allegedly, had done more than anything or anyone to dissolve and disrupt the cohesion, stability, and purity of nation and sovereign, and of theology and state. By removing belief, opinion, and the right to criticize from the control and purview of the state, Spinoza had fatally weakened it in a fashion backed up later by another Jewish philosopher, Moses Mendelssohn, who was also repeatedly the target of Schmitt's condemnation. According to Schmitt, who aligns Mendelssohn and Lessing with Spinoza in key respects, the former's *Jerusalem, oder über religiöse Macht und Judentum* (Jerusalem, or on Religious Power and Judaism) (1783) validates Spinoza's separation between inner disposition, ethical substance, and right from the external action of the law and the state, not just guaranteeing freedom of conscience but insidiously "undermining and hollowing the power of the state."[41]

If Schmitt's "Spinoza" was in part merely a convenient symbol, a modern political myth, one might argue that the reverse side of the coin, the way Weimar German Jewry enthusiastically adopted the Jewish heretic Spinoza as a symbol in their longing "for salvation," as David Wertheim expressed it, and "turned to Spinoza," was no less a political-theological myth.[42] Representative democracy seemed to Schmitt inherently and perennially weak and indecisive, being rooted in discussion and compromise, features that he believed harm the integrity of society. The expanded and now vehement Schmittian polemic against Spinoza during the Nazi period represented the Jewish thinker as now Schmitt's *Erz-Feind* (Arch-Fiend), the great author of the "liberal" tendency, as Marta García-Alonso stresses by identifying Schmitt's "Spinoza" as the ultimate antithesis of the Radical Enlightenment's liberating "Spinoza," who sought to create a new universalism of emancipation and equality that broke down all traditional barriers. Schmitt and Strauss both inherited much from Weber, and both nurtured strong reservations about the character of liberal democracy that today retain a continuing relevance.

But other ways of discerning "political theology" in parliamentary democracy have surfaced, building on Weber's vision in a quite different direction. American historian James Kloppenberg contends:

There are multiple reasons for taking seriously the role of religion in modern democratic discourse. Historically it is undeniable that the source of the animating ideals of modern democratic movements in the Atlantic world has been the Christian principle of agape, selfless love for all humans because all are created in God's image, which lies beneath the democratic ethic of reciprocity. ... Christian ideas of humility, mercy, forgiveness, and equal respect for other persons, the very values so despised by Spinoza and Nietzsche, form the backdrop against which modern concepts of autonomy and equality emerged, and they remain a crucial part of the cultural inheritance of North Atlantic democratic cultures.[43]

One must accept that the Enlightenment was fundamentally divided between its moderate and radical tendencies, concedes Kloppenberg, but he insists on defining the "radical enlightenment" excessively narrowly, not unlike Strauss, to mean just atheism and materialism; what he infers from the reality of this dichotomy is that it was the religious inspiration of the "moderate enlightenment," not the Spinozist irreligion of the "radical enlightenment," that was the true source of our modern ideals of equity, equality, individual autonomy, and republican democracy.[44]

If Schmitt, Strauss, and Kloppenberg all pushed Weber's insights further than did Weber, ultimately, the fundamental ambiguity and contested validity of the concept "secularization" derive from the inner tension between the Enlightenment's two rival agendas themselves, namely the chiseling down of the supernatural to its purported proper place versus total elimination of the supernatural altogether. For the moderate Enlightenment in a Lockean mode, for example, there exist two separate and unmixable spheres of reality, the empirical and the *supra rationem,* and any "secularization" that erases the sphere of the supernatural segment of reality is ipso facto blasphemous and sacrilegious as well as destructive; if legitimate secularization for Thomasius curtails the sphere of "superstition" and the ecclesiastical usurpation of powers that properly belong to the state, that is, in Lockean terms, adjusts the supernatural to its proper place and proportions, such a political, theological, educational, and moral adjustment must be conducted with the agreement and support of the state's tolerated religious congregations. Where approval by governments and endorsement by universities, as well as the pronouncements of churchmen, rendered moderate Enlightenment dualism widely endorsed and adopted, radical thought—the ideas Strauss was the first to label the *radikale Aufklärung* and adopt as a central theme in the 1920s—despite being always suppressed and illicit before 1789, seemed to him, on evaluating the rival arguments philosophically, to carry the main burden of "the truth" or real force of the Enlightenment.[45] The arguments of Mendelssohn, like those of Locke and Voltaire, in favor of divine revelation, the immortality of the soul, and the reality of the eternal and supernatural, struck Strauss as little more than forced and unconvincing defensive fixes. The "secularization" of Locke and Thomasius separating philosophy, science, and political theory, which rested on "reason" alone from theology where supernatural forces continue to operate, was rightly dismissed by Strauss as a feeble and arbitrary fence and hence itself a source of myth and dogma. As Strauss saw it, modern Jewry had to turn away from the path ahead that Mendelssohn had marked out: Jews faced a stark choice between aligning with Spinoza, assimilation, universalism and the "radical Enlightenment" or sticking with separate identity, orthodoxy, and the religious Law.[46]

Strauss was undoubtedly correct in arguing that in the intellectual controversies of the Enlightenment era there can be no clear, convincing borderline between the purely empirical based on natural laws and occurrences, and the supernatural. What of God's role, for instance, in guiding the course of history? One can "secularize" by steadily reducing the role of direct divine intervention and that of lesser supernatural forces, including the works of the Devil; but how can one legitimately, within a Christian or even the less belief-oriented Jewish context, eliminate divine intervention and the miraculous altogether? The answer, surely, is that one cannot. This meant, as Strauss emphasized, that there was always an in-built tendency to slippage towards the hegemony of "reason" in the moderate Enlightenment stance and a built-in intellectual advantage on the side of *radikale Aufklärung*. To counter this force of argument powering the slippage towards the radical in what most contemporaries regarded as the sole legitimate approach, the full force of the state, churches, and universities had to be brought to bear, that is, myth and popular credulity remained indispensable.

Since moderate enlighteners like Locke and Thomasius were consciously adapting the state, law, and institutions to the theological in a retracted format while radical enlighteners were eliminating miracles, revelation, divine providence, and the theological altogether, it makes sense, as Martin Mulsow has pointed out, to connect Schmitt's challenging use of the concept "political theology" to the actual early modern usage of the category *theologia politica* as this evolved between the seventeenth and eighteenth centuries.[47] Moderate and radical Enlightenment presented two rival kinds of political theology for critical judgment, but the complexity of the situation, the force of suppression of radical thought and its retreat into the clandestine underground, gave rise to a third class of *theologia politica* even without counting the resurgence, in the background of the theological politics of the Counter-Enlightenment and the "Holy Alliance." This additional category of modern mythology, responding to the unrelenting force of state and church repression of atheism, naturalism, and unbelief, was what Mulsow has aptly termed the "political theology of subterfuge."[48]

Mulsow poses the question whether this kind of clandestine strategy might perhaps have also been a means employed by skeptical minds genuinely seeking to evade a Spinozistic philosophical logic that equated God with nature and eliminated the miraculous at every level and, as Strauss accepted, remained extremely difficult to refute on a non-skeptical basis.[49] But, arguably, a more significant role for this third category, "political theology" as subterfuge, was to divert or blunt suspicions of "Spinozism" while actually endeavouring to salvage and vindicate that very current of thought and protect the adherents of the underground "Spinozist" sect. Here *prisca theologia* (the ancient theology) itself, the concept which religious thinkers like Kircher, Huet, and Morhof used to unify and universalize history as a whole since Adam, bringing everything into a single narrative pivoting on Christian truth and revelation, found itself subverted and reconstituted by writers like Wachter, Bayle, and Toland as an esoteric tradition of pantheism within the universal history of the world, including biblical history, the connecting thread of universal truth identified as "Spinozism," the story, in other words, of *Spinozismus ante Spinozam*, yet another potent modern myth coined in the late seventeenth century, albeit one that did not survive the eighteenth century.[50]

Meanwhile, the extreme peril for society and the modern democratic republic that the theories of dictatorship of Rousseau and Schmitt represent is evident both from the content of these theories themselves and the actual *Robespierriste* dictatorship that emerged during the Terror of 1793–94 using Rousseau's political thought as its principal justification for ending freedom of the press and suppressing all criticism of the regime. A secularized theology was undoubtedly at work here too. In his speeches, Robespierre continually reiterated the cosmic dualism infusing his political outlook, exalting the purity, disinterestedness, generosity, and "moderation" of ordinary folk and their being deceived by those intriguers (his Brissotin opponents) aiming to raise themselves above them. These deceivers of the common people, in his part-Augustinian, part-Manichaean world-view, included the *philosophes* and writers, the intellectuals, whom he accused of seeking to turn themselves into a new species of "aristocrats." Only one thinker, Rousseau, insisted Robespierre, in his great speech of May 7, 1794 (18 Floréal) to the French National Convention, in Paris, in which he looked back on the course of the Revolution and expounded the theology of his cult of the Supreme Being, revealed true grandeur prior to the Revolution, and true purity of doctrine. Only one system invoked "virtue," the ordinary person, and the Divinity as these truly exist in accord with nature—and in opposition to the false doctrines of his foes, the *philosophes*—that of Rousseau.[51]

Sometimes seen as a necessary safeguard and regulator, and at other times as a dire Rousseauist threat, Schmitt's insightful theory of the "dictator" by popular assent proved paradoxical, ironic, and fitting. To a discomforting extent, it covered both Rousseau's "dictator" in the shape of the Montaigne whose populist style, authoritarianism, ruthless immoralism, and extreme intolerance of other views foreshadowed Fascism in important respects, and the actual Fascist regimes assuming dictatorial powers and crushing all internal dissent around them. Whether it also corresponded in any way, as Schmitt claimed, to the emergency executives of constitutional states, girding them for exceptional circumstances and war, seems much less plausible. In any case, for those arguing that "rationalization" is something very different from modern "secularization," it makes a good deal of sense to place Robespierre alongside Hitler especially with regard to the role of popular anti-intellectualism, bigotry, and credulity in the construction of modern despotism.

The debates of the Weimar era seem to be regaining some of their former relevance today. More than a few recent commentators have discerned that "Schmitt's thought exerts a subterranean, yet pervasive, influence on conservatism in the postwar United States beyond the cultural conservatism of Straussianism."[52] Yet perhaps real politics is always a clash of myths and the modern secularized myth is not only a force for evil. In reacting against the insistence of nineteenth-century Jewish historians and scholars on the alleged rationality and freedom from superstition of the Jewish religion, Martin Buber made as good a case as any twentieth-century philosopher for the need of myth and mysticism among mankind to enshrine and promote a renewed cult, or array of cults, devoted to goodness, justice, and charity.

7

"An Age of Miracles": Disenchantment as a Secularized Theological Narrative

Robert A. Yelle

"Though I reverence those men of ancient time that either have written truth perspicuously, or set us in a better way to find it out ourselves, yet to the antiquity itself I think nothing due. For if we will reverence the age, the present is the oldest."

—Thomas Hobbes, *Leviathan*[1]

Introduction: Thesis and Delimitation of the Topic

The idea that ours is an age in decline—broken down, disaffected, but perhaps the better for having been disabused of some of its false notions—is scarcely new. It is a very ancient, even pre-Christian idea. Plutarch's account of the oracles falling silent is an example.[2] It may always seem to the older generation, as it did to Hobbes when he wrote the words above past the age of 60, that the world is less cheerful than it used to be, even if not less wise. However, this idea is a projection, one that we must be careful not to confuse with reality.

The same is true for Weber's own ideas of "disenchantment" (*Entzauberung*) and the "routinization of charisma" (*Veralltäglichung bzw. Rationalisierung der charismatischen Herrschaft*).[3] In a series of publications including *The Language of Disenchantment* (2013) and *Sovereignty and the Sacred* (2019), I have laid out a genealogy of the idea of disenchantment: its origins, meanings, transformations, and disseminations.[4] The broader context for these ideas lies in an older tradition of Christian claims, redeployed during the Reformation, that the Gospel had disenchanted the world by silencing the pagan oracles, ending miracles, revelations, and prophecies, and replacing the Mosaic ritual law, thus ushering in a New Age of enlightenment. It is only when we locate Weber in this longue durée history that he assumes the importance he rightfully deserves.

Reframing the matter in this way means, at the same time, going beyond an approach that would narrow our focus to "what Weber meant" by disenchantment. Although Weber may still serve as the point of departure for our discussion of these matters, and although (as we shall see) several of his historical contentions have held up very well, we must nevertheless go beyond the exegesis of the Weberian canon and its immediate context. Whether such a mode of exegesis is the result of the "great man" theory of history, of an innate tendency to conservatism within some disciplines, or of Weber's heroic status in the German tradition, the tendency to focus on Weber to the exclusion of a broader history of disenchantment is actually to make the man less important than he was. If Weber was merely expressing his own opinion, then we may safely regard this as irrelevant.

Although we shall have further indications that Weber echoed older Christian and specifically Protestant discourses, it should be noted at the outset that what concerns me is not to demonstrate with certainty that the real referent of Weber's idea of disenchantment was such older sources. Instead, my goal is to follow Weber further down the path that he opened by tracing the impact of Christian theological ideas on what we call "modernity" or the "secular." In *The Protestant Ethic and the Spirit of Capitalism*,[5] Weber skillfully deployed a genealogical method that he may have learned from such earlier thinkers as Friedrich Nietzsche and Georg Jellinek, and that he passed on to successors including Carl Schmitt and Bernhard Laum.[6] The largely successful attempt in some branches of sociology to present Weber as the founder of a positive science has come at the expense of this genealogical project.[7] To claim that modernity, including Weber's own restatement of what this represented, was influenced by Christian theological ideas is precisely to challenge, once again, the idea of the independence of secularism, science, and Enlightenment—an independence that Hans Blumenberg defended as "the legitimacy of the modern age" (*die Legitimität der Neuzeit*).[8] More recent and critical appraisals, also from the side of sociology, demonstrate an awareness of this challenge. Thus Philip S. Gorski and Ateş Altinordu state that "the notion that history consists of secular and religious phases simply stands Christian eschatology on its head by postulating that religious darkness will give way to secular enlightenment."[9]

If disenchantment is a theological trope, then surely it cannot be a neutral, scientific description of some event in historical time. Don't such genealogical arguments dodge the question of what really happened? And thereby replace careful empirical analysis with a purely deconstructive gesture of postmodern relativism? I think that such legitimate concerns motivate many objections against the idea that disenchantment or secularization is a narrative, a reaction expressed quite forcefully in this volume by Monika Wohlrab-Sahr.[10] I will try to answer such objections to the best of my ability in what follows. To preview my answer, it is that there is no such thing as a "mere" narrative; that especially such master narratives as that of disenchantment, and the soteriological idea of supersession on which it is ultimately based, have had profound consequences for our culture and society. In addition to inspiring significant changes in belief and practice, such ideas have affected our experience of modernity, of how we inhabit the world.[11] To give the impact of such ideas their full due is, once again, to follow in Weber's footsteps.

Part of the reason why these matters have not been reduced to clarity yet, a century after Weber's death, is that various levels of analysis that should be kept strictly separate have not been. To frame the analysis that follows, and to defuse the charge that my own position in these matters is unclear, I will organize this chapter around a series of questions:

What did Weber mean by "disenchantment"?
Did disenchantment happen?
What are the sources and meanings of the narrative of disenchantment?
Did Weber reflect these older sources; and from where or whom might he have taken them?
What remains of Weber's thesis for science?

In the course of addressing these and related questions, I will also introduce new evidence as well as summarize arguments that may be accessed in my works and those of other scholars.

What Did Weber Mean by "Disenchantment"?

Partly because this question has received so much attention already,[12] and partly because (for reasons given above) this question is less important than the longue durée history, I will spend little time on it. Weber did not use the word before 1913, well after the first version of *The Protestant Ethic* (1904–05).[13] In his 1917 lecture, "Science as a Vocation," he identified disenchantment with a general process of rationalization that has been going on for "thousands of years" in

Western culture and that is closely connected with the idea that everything can be calculated and controlled by technological means.[14] This coordinated with his contentions that special inspiration and gifts of grace are no longer needed in scientific work. Weber thereby connected disenchantment with the idea of a "routinization of charisma" that received elaboration in his posthumously published *Economy and Society*. The second edition of *The Protestant Ethic* (1920) contained several passages that connected disenchantment with the Reformers' attacks on the Catholic sacramental order, a development that Weber called "decisive" (*entscheidend*).[15] Weber found precedent for the attack on magic in ancient Israelite monotheism.[16] Puritan insistence on the remoteness of God recapitulated the ancient Hebrew attack on idolatry that had led to bans against most forms of magical manipulation of the world. Weber may have been thinking about laws that prescribed capital punishment for witchcraft (Exodus 22:18) or that banned most forms of divination apart from the war oracles, Urim and Thummim.

Weber's coinage of the word "disenchantment" (*Entzauberung*), which includes the German root *Zauber* ('magic'), has spawned an entire genre of studies addressing whether magic has really declined with the rise of modernity.[17] While productive at least in these terms, the question has also led to a certain impasse, as it can be answered in different ways. Arguably, this question has also distorted discussions of what modernization entailed. For example, the Protestant claim that miracles ceased articulated with a rejection of divine-right kingship, meaning the idea that the sovereign has absolute power and can not only break laws but also, like God, perform miracles.[18] One manifestation of this was the Royal Touch by which the kings of England and France formerly healed scrofula, a practice that declined after the Reformation, as described further below. However, as such, this development had at least as much to do with sovereignty as with magic; as much with politics as with the occult.[19] It reflected equally the process that Weber described as the routinization of charisma into legal or bureaucratic authority. A single-minded focus on the question of whether "magic" or "esotericism" has survived into modernity may cause us to neglect these other important dimensions of secularization.

Where did Weber get the word "disenchantment" from? Hans Kippenberg maintained that "until today nobody has been able to find a source from which Weber derived this concept."[20] However, a number of scholars have noted that the term *Entzauberung* (adj. *entzaubert*) was used in German previously, mainly to indicate what the word "disenchanted" still sometimes means in English: a mood of disinterest, disaffection, or disengagement.[21] The poet Friedrich Schiller (1759–1805) had used the term "the dis-godding (or de-divinization) of nature" (*die Entgötterung der Natur*) to describe a world devoid of sacred presence.[22] In a similar sense, but with the opposite intention, the Calvinist theologian Balthasar Bekker had earlier described and attacked the belief that the world is populated by spirits and demons, in his influential Dutch work *De betoverde Weereld* (1691) (The Enchanted World). The work was published in German as *Die bezauberte Welt* (1693). Bekker's polemic resembled Thomas Hobbes's earlier attack on "the demonology of the Gentiles"[23] and, like this, participated in skeptical critiques of contemporary superstitions. Because Bekker's work was well known in its day, Hartmut Lehmann's suggestion that Bekker may have been the source for Weber's coinage of *Entzauberung*, by inversion of the prefix and meaning of the word, appears plausible.[24] I am not aware that anyone has pointed out previously that Rudolf Otto seems to refer to Bekker in his *Gottheit und Gottheiten der Arier* (1932): "So began the second half of the Middle Ages with a demonization of the world that spread like an epidemic, which thereafter faded away again in the 'disenchanted world' [*enttoferde wereld*] of the Enlightenment."[25] Otto performs an inversion of Bekker's term, from "enchanted" to "disenchanted," similar to that posited for Weber. Otto also modifies the spelling; perhaps his Dutch was poor, and/or he was quoting from memory. It is quite possible that Otto had Weber's earlier usage in mind and was deliberately linking this with Bekker's, seventy years before contemporary scholars rediscovered this linkage. At the very least, this shows that Bekker was still remembered in Weimar Germany, rendering more plausible the thesis that he may have served as one of Weber's sources for the idea of *Entzauberung*.

Did Disenchantment Happen?

Weber's framing of the historical debate in terms of the question of whether there was a decline or even disappearance of magic has been tremendously influential. Until now, historians have not been able to agree on an answer. Keith Thomas's *Religion and the Decline of Magic* (1971) set the stage, in many ways, by documenting the loss of belief in magic following a sustained series of polemics against superstitious practices that began before the Enlightenment and led back, in some instances, to theological critiques.[26] In response to this work, the anthropologist Hildred Geertz argued that "magic" was an etic and polemical term that cannot validly be used as a descriptor of folk beliefs and practices that have been dismissed by elites and by later intellectual historians in reliance upon these elites.[27] There remains to this day a current of opinion in anthropology and religious studies that avoids the category of "magic" for similar reasons.[28] Such arguments offer an alternative refutation of Weber's disenchantment thesis: if the world was never full of magic, then it could never be divested of this quality. It should be noted that this critique of the idea of disenchantment is potentially at odds with the one made by such scholars as Egil Asprem and Jason Josephson-Storm, namely that we continue to be enchanted, believe in spirits, entertain cosmological beliefs incompatible with mechanism, and so on.[29]

Meanwhile, with respect to the early modern period, there persists a division of opinion among historians. Robert Scribner argued that popular folk magic outlived the Reformation.[30] Alexandra Walsham argued the same for the belief in miracles.[31] In an excellent review article from 2008, Walsham tried to take a middle path.[32] Despite "Protestant propagand[a]" that "miracles had ceased," "the world ... remained what Scribner called a 'moralized universe' and one, moreover, that continued to be populated by angels and demons."[33] On the other hand, she acknowledged that something potentially irrevocable happened: "Yet it cannot be denied that subtle shifts and developments took place over the course of the early modern period which, cumulatively, were decisive. ... [I]t is possible to detect signs of a process by which certain sacred rituals and practices were displaced out of the realm of religion and piety into the domains of leisure and recreation."[34] She also noted the semiotic dimensions of this transformation, which decoupled fact from fiction and sign from referent.[35] A key point here was debates over the Eucharist. Many Protestants, especially Puritans, viewed transubstantiation as a form of magical thinking, the epitome of the Catholic error that rituals were automatically effective (*ex opere operato*) for achieving salvation.[36] Huldrych Zwingli argued that the Eucharist was merely a sign, rather than the Real Presence. Walsham acknowledged evidence for the claim that, as a result of the sustained attack on ritual, religion retreated further into the private sphere.[37] She connected the decline of belief in miracles with the rise of deism[38] and further acknowledged that many of these developments were theologically driven, to the extent that "Christianity is gradually reclaiming its place at the heart of this project [of disenchantment] in a way that severs the assumed link between the forces of modernity and secularization."[39]

Coming from the other side of this debate, Euan Cameron emphasized that the ideas propounded by the theologians of the Reformation mattered.[40] These were not merely elite discourses but also influenced popular practices in ways that were far-reaching. While acknowledging that the belief in demons and witches continued[41]—indeed, the witchcraft craze lasted longer in certain Protestant areas, such as colonial New England—Cameron argued that the theology of the Reformation worked a profound disenchantment of Catholic rituals and ceremonies.[42] He responded directly to Scribner's argument that the belief in miracles persisted:

> Protestant polemic insisted that the true exorcism, the supernatural power to cast out demons with a command, had been a miraculous gift in the early centuries of the Church, and that this gift had long since ceased. Possibly no claim about Protestant teaching has been more thoroughly challenged in recent years than the claim that Protestants argued that the age of miracles was past. Certainly an abundance of evidence can be brought forward to show that ordinary people continued to look for extraordinary signs of divine intervention in the visible world. ... [Yet] Only by stubbornly refusing to read what Protestant theologians wrote on the subject can one overlook this basic principle: developed mainstream Protestant theology insisted that true miracles were no longer to be expected in the Church. ... How that theological proposition would diffuse itself through society was of course another question.[43]

Where Walsham referred to the Protestant idea that miracles had ceased as "propaganda," Cameron cited the widespread nature of this idea as evidence for disenchantment. The truth presumably lies somewhere in between. Both historians noted the need to distinguish between elite theological opinion and popular practice, and differed mainly with respect to the question how far the former permeated and influenced the latter. Significantly, both Walsham and Cameron agreed that the idea that miracles had ceased originated in Protestant theology. This shows already that it is not merely postmodernists who have recognized that disenchantment is, to some extent, a (theological) narrative: mainstream historians of different persuasions have also noted this, and in some cases, as a result called into question the scientific status of Weber's thesis that the Reformation brought about disenchantment. Walsham summed this up nicely: "the settled assumptions about medieval 'credulity' upon which the Weberian paradigm of disenchantment is predicated are becoming increasingly untenable. ... The idea of an enchanted middle ages ... perpetuate[s] the polemical contrast between 'darkness' and 'light' that has been the invidious legacy of this" paradigm.[44]

As evidence for the position that disenchantment was less than complete, Walsham cited "the fact that English monarchs continued to be seen as conduits of thaumaturgic power capable of healing diseases like scrofula, notwithstanding puritan doubts."⁴⁵ However, looking at the decline of the Royal Touch actually demonstrates the manner in which disenchantment, in this case meaning specifically the decline of miracles and sovereign charisma, coordinated with the Reformation as well as with the transition to more democratic modes of governance.⁴⁶ A convinced Protestant who presided over a new translation of the Bible, James I of England only reluctantly agreed to perform the Royal Touch.⁴⁷ After the Restoration, Charles II reintroduced this practice in a major way, healing thousands each year.⁴⁸ This may have been one of the factors prompting the Cambridge theologian John Spencer in 1663 to publish treatises against prodigies and other miraculous events.⁴⁹ He published in English, perhaps to persuade the general public among whom such superstitions were found, rather than in the scholarly language of Latin, as in the case of his later magnum opus, *De legibus hebraeorum* (1685). Lorraine Daston and Katherine Park argue that Spencer "was a *devoté* of the pleasures of wonder and curiosity," but was also aware of prodigies' "potential for political and religious subversion,"⁵⁰ particularly in the immediate aftermath of the Civil War. On the one hand, Spencer's theological and supersessionist argument that prodigies, like oracles and miracles, had ceased in Apostolic times represented a critique of religious enthusiasm, the revolutionary potential of which had earlier motivated Hobbes to embrace the idea that miracles and prophecy had ceased.⁵¹ On the other hand, it was possible that Spencer meant to caution the king himself. The end of his Preface warns of the dangers of "an overhasty pulling off (even) the wens and excrescencies from the body of Religion," which demystification could lead to the consequence that "persons once Sacred, found guilty of capital crimes, are solemnly degraded, before they are executed." Should these be read as references, respectively, to the Royal Touch and to the execution of Charles I? Miracles and enthusiasm could reinforce the majesty of the sovereign or lead to his downfall.

After the Glorious Revolution, William III refused to perform the Royal Touch, supposedly for religious reasons.⁵² Queen Anne was the last English monarch to perform the Touch, in 1714.⁵³ The kings of France did so more or less up until the 1789 Revolution, and there were even efforts to reinstate the practice later.⁵⁴ However, the Touch fell into abeyance there also. Marc Bloch argued that the practice declined for political as well as religious reasons: "The decline of the royal miracle was closely linked to the effort by persons, at least among the elite, to eliminate the supernatural and the arbitrary from the world order, and at the same to conceive political institutions under a uniquely rational aspect."⁵⁵ There could scarcely be a better definition of disenchantment, which described a politico-theological turn against divine right kingship, as Carl Schmitt noted.⁵⁶

What Are the Sources and Meanings of the Narrative of Disenchantment?

As just shown, historians have pointed to the Protestant idea that miracles had ceased as one of the drivers of disenchantment in early modernity. My own contribution to these debates has focused on the origin, meaning, and transformation of such narratives.[57] The narrative of disenchantment appears to have emerged from a complex of Christian ideas that were present already in the first centuries of the Common Era, but were then taken up early in the Reformation by Protestants and redeployed as arguments in theological debates. The idea that the oracles were silenced was present already in the first-century pagan Greek philosopher Plutarch but was reinterpreted by Eusebius in the early fourth century as the direct result of the Christ event. The idea that miracles ceased was originally a Patristic narrative. The claim that gifts of grace or of the Holy Spirit, such as speaking in tongues, would cease is present already in the canon of the New Testament (1 Corinthians 13). Such signs and wonders were the hallmarks of prophecy or revelation. The Passion itself was, according to the Gospels, attended by certain miraculous signs, such as an earthquake, a darkening of the sky, and the rending of the veil of the Temple at Jerusalem. But with the closure of the canon of scripture, the end of the Apostolic Age, and the establishment of the Church, some argued that these gifts of grace were no longer necessary. Already certain Church Fathers, such as Origen, argued that miracles had ceased. Originally an argument against the introduction of new revelations, this became, in the hands of Protestants, a key weapon against the claims of the Catholic Church to be able to certify and perform miracles. Both Luther and Calvin expressed this idea, which was normative in English Protestant theology by 1600.[58] D.P. Walker stated that both Luther and Calvin "assumed … that God does miracles only to establish a new religion, and that, as it becomes established, the miracles gradually cease."[59] Like the idea in ancient Judaism that prophecy had ceased,[60] the Christian version expressed the need to close the canon of scripture. Miracles certified the truth of the Gospel revelation and the authority of the Apostles, and supposedly were no longer necessary after Christianity was firmly established, especially in the form of the institutionalized Church. As we shall see, it is this idea in particular that anticipated Weber's notion of the routinization of charismatic authority into institutional forms. Weber himself acknowledged that this notion was taken partly from the Protestant theologian Rudolph Sohm's account of the decline from charismatic leadership to the legal election of bishops in the early Christian community, an account that represented a latter-day echo of these ancient theological debates.[61]

Additionally, Christians beginning with Paul argued that the Gospel had suspended and replaced part of the Mosaic law, particularly its ritual practices. The ceremonial laws, including those prescribing circumcision, the kosher dietary prohibitions, and sacrifices, were supposedly no longer binding on Christians. During the Reformation, Protestants used such ideas to attack the settled liturgy and to argue that even more rituals should be ended. According to the traditional typological interpretation, Mosaic ritual had been necessary only as a temporary measure that pointed, in symbolic and veiled fashion, to the more spiritual dispensation of the New Testament, which had now ended all such mysteries.

All three of these tropes (the cessation of miracles, oracles, and Mosaic ritual) were sometimes combined by Protestant theologians such as Spencer. These ideas were part of what we refer to as "supersessionism": the notion that the New Testament replaced the Old, ushering in an era of salvation and enlightenment. The idea itself was therefore inseparable from that of revelation. Despite their theological provenance, such ideas of temporal rupture and succession were secularized in the early modern period and became one basis for the notion of a general Enlightenment. As J.G.A. Pocock stated,

> It could quite plausibly have been maintained—although I don't know if it ever was—that Jesus Christ was the first modern: he had come to transform, to fulfil and in that sense to terminate the old Law, the old covenant and the old dispensation; and if attention shifted from the Hebrew to the Greek, he had come to wind up the old (Gentile) religion.[62]

In fact, a version of this claim was made by Bishop Thomas Sprat, who asserted a direct connection between Christianity and science in his apologetic *History of the Royal Society* (1667):

> It is now the fittest season for Experiments to arise, to teach us a Wisdome, which springs from the depths of Knowledge, to shake off the shadows, and to scatter the mists, which fill the minds of men with a vain consternation. This is a work well-becoming the most Christian Profession. For the most apparent effect, which attended the passion of Christ, was the putting of an eternal silence, on all the false oracles, and dissembled inspirations of Antient Times.[63]

This shows already that the boundary between Reformation and Enlightenment could be rather porous, particularly in the English context where, in the first half of the eighteenth century, deism developed further some of the basic tropes, such as the idea that miracles had ceased, in such a way as to undermine the status of Christianity itself as a revealed religion. Jonathan Israel has documented masterfully the emergence of a "radical" or nonreligious Enlightenment beginning in the seventeenth century, particularly in connection with the renegade Dutch Jewish philosopher, Baruch/Benedict Spinoza. However, we should not forget that the polemics against miracles and against oracles did not start where Israel begins his account of such ideas, namely with Spinoza and Bernard Fontenelle, respectively, but rather with explicitly theological polemics earlier in the Reformation.[64] This fact challenges the conclusion that the broader Enlightenment represented a break with, rather than a continuation of, Christian theology. In 2003, Jonathan Sheehan argued that historians had called into question the idea that religion had nothing to do with the Enlightenment, which appeared to be "incapable of surviving the introduction of religion [into its genealogy or biography] without some reduction in power."[65] This raises again the problem of the alleged "illegitimacy" of modernity addressed earlier by Hans Blumenberg.

The idea that the oracles had fallen silent was, as previously noted, found already in classical paganism. Plutarch proposed a number of explanations for this event, including that the vapors from underground that intoxicated the priestesses of the oracle had stopped flowing or that the gods themselves could eventually die, as signaled by the cry "Great Pan is dead!," a cry echoed much later by various Romantics.[66] Plutarch's explanations were more rationalist than Eusebius's insistence that the real reason for the demise of the demonic oracles was Christ; this was a variant of the supersessionist trope according to which the Gospel replaced paganism in a moment of revelation. Eusebius's account, however, was the one revived by Protestants early in the Reformation. The Christian theological trope depicted the death of the demons and the silencing of their oracles as an event simultaneous with its cause, namely either the birth or death of Christ. Fontenelle's critique of this trope attributed the decline of the oracles instead to the gradual progress of reason, which eroded the credibility of such superstitious practices.[67] Blumenberg rightly noted that Fontenelle's aim was to attack and replace the theological accounts: "That the heathen oracles should have fallen mute at the exact moment of Jesus' birth is just as much a myth of simultaneity [*Gleichzeitigkeit*] as that of the death of the shepherd god Pan at the exact moment of Jesus' Crucifixion."[68] The idea of simultaneity or synchronicity was in itself a form of magical thinking, which invoked miraculous, divine intervention in lieu of a properly scientific history and was therefore incompatible with secular reason, hence Fontenelle's critique of this idea.

There were similar problems with the secularization of the idea that miracles had ceased. This is because the idea of a sudden and complete cessation is just as miraculous, irruptive, and unnatural as the idea of the miracle itself. We can illustrate the difficulty of accommodating such inherently mythological ideas to a properly secular reason through Edward Gibbon's notorious account of the rise of Christianity in chapter 15 of *The Decline and Fall of the Roman Empire*.[69] Acknowledging the "dark cloud" that hangs over the history of the early Church, Gibbon nevertheless provided several reasons for the success of this institution. One of these was "the miraculous powers ascribed to the primitive church":

> Besides the occasional prodigies, which might sometimes be effected by the immediate interposition of the Deity when he suspended the laws of Nature for the service of religion, the Christian church, from the time of the apostles and their first disciples, has claimed an uninterrupted succession of miraculous powers, the gift of tongues, of vision, and of prophecy, the power of expelling daemons, of healing the sick, and of raising the dead.[70]

The problem, then, was how to identify the moment when such miracles had ended definitively. Noting the controversy over Conyers Middleton's book on this topic,[71] Gibbon acknowledged "our perplexity in defining the miraculous period," since

> the duty of an historian does not call upon him to interpose his private judgment in this nice and important controversy; but he ought not to dissemble the difficulty of adopting such a theory as may reconcile the interest of religion with that of reason, of making a proper application of that theory, and of defining with precision the limits of that happy period, exempt from error and from deceit, to which we might be disposed to extend the gift of supernatural powers. ... [S]ince every friend to revelation is persuaded of the reality, and every reasonable man is convinced of the cessation, of miraculous powers, it is evident that there must have been some period in which they were either suddenly or gradually withdrawn from the Christian church. Whatever era is chosen for that purpose, the death of the apostles, the conversion of the Roman empire, or the extinction of the Arian heresy, the insensibility of the Christians who lived at that time will equally afford a just matter of surprise. They still supported their pretensions [to miracles] after they had lost their power.

While playing coy so as not to exacerbate the already sufficiently great offense to orthodox Protestant sensibilities, Gibbon was pointing to the impossibility of reconciling any idea of the miracle with a scientific historical account.[72] The gap between reason and revelation could not be bridged. Gibbon's skepticism anticipated Jonathan Sheehan's rhetorical question, posed in response to Charles Taylor's *A Secular Age* (2007), "when was disenchantment?"[73] Sheehan indicated the impossibility of answering this question while at the same time arguing that Taylor's nostalgia for an enchanted past was part of a Catholic apologetic narrative. As we have seen, there were also Protestant versions of this narrative.

To point this out does not end the possibility of all historical inquiry, since we can trace the origin, meaning, dissemination, transformation, and effect of such mythological and apologetic narratives, just as we can in the case of any other ideas or discourses. So, for example, enough evidence has been adduced already to prove that "disenchantment" as such is not a product of the (radical) Enlightenment, nor of Romanticism (as Talal Asad claimed[74]); that it did not emerge only in the seventeenth century (*pace* Michael Saler[75]); and that, of course, neither was it the invention of Max Weber personally.

Did Weber Reflect These Older Sources; and From Where or Whom Might He Have Taken Them?

Weber echoed the Protestant idea that miracles are no more. In "Science as a Vocation" (1917), he invoked such ideas in a manner that linked disenchantment to the rationalization of charisma:

> Science ... does not know of the "miracle" and the "revelation." ... Science today is ... not the gift of grace of seers and prophets dispensing sacred values and revelations ... The fate of our times is characterized by rationalization and intellectualization and, above all, by the "disenchantment of the world."[76]

The reference to "gifts of grace" (*Gnadengaben*) links disenchantment precisely to the decline of charisma in an increasingly bureaucratic world. In other works, Weber referred to the idea that prophecy and miracles had ended in order to illustrate his concept of the routinization of charisma.[77] He connected this process with the institutional establishment of the Christian Church: "Finally, and above all, after the end of the charismatic epoch of the early church, the character of ecclesiastical lawmaking was influenced by the fact that the church's functionaries were holders of rationally defined bureaucratic offices."[78] Note already how, in this formulation, the "end of the charismatic epoch" has been transformed from a theological trope to a definite event in historical time.[79]

As noted above, the historical account of a progression from charismatic to legal authority in the early church was anticipated by older theological sources.

For Weber, a much more proximate and explicit source was the Protestant theologian and legal historian Rudolph Sohm.[80] Sohm embraced a "decline and fall" thesis of the rise of the Roman Catholic Church as an institution that betrayed the dependence of early Christianity on more personal or inspired modes of authority by exchanging such inspiration for legalism and bureaucratic hierarchy. Sohm's work on *Kirchenrecht* (The Law of the Church) was published in two volumes, the first of which appeared in 1892 and the second posthumously in 1923.[81] In this work, Sohm argued that leadership in the earliest Christian communities was invested in those teachers, such as apostles and prophets, whose authority sprang directly from God, as demonstrated by their possession of "gifts of grace" (*Gnadengaben; Charismen*).[82] This mode of organization was entirely opposed to the notion of a succession of authority according to an external legal principle[83]: "There can be no legal constitution and no legal legislative power in the church. The truly apostolic teaching, created by the divine word, regarding the constitution of the church is that the organization of Christianity is not a legal but a charismatic organization."[84] Sohm further described the devolution of this originally charismatic mode of organization into a legal one:

> The church (*ecclesia*) of primitive Christianity is nothing legal, political, or worldly. ... All the life of Christianity is religious, spiritual [*pneumatisches*], and comes from the spirit of God ... From this comes the purely spiritual (religious), unity of the church, the purely spiritual (charismatic and religiously founded) organization, the purely spiritually (not legally) effective theocracy of the spiritually gifted [*Geistbegabten*]. As soon as the number of inwardly non-self-reliant [*unselbständigen*] Christians grows, they demand forms and prescriptions for the life of the church, i.e. church law, which mechanically certify [*mechanisch sicher stellen*] the spiritual value of the Christian assembly through external signs. Church law will come. ... A legal order for visible Christianity (i.e. church law) ... will mean a transformation [*Umwandlung*] of Christian religion from a religion of belief to a religion of laws.[85]

The end point of this degeneration was, according to Sohm, the Catholic Church,[86] although the process began even earlier, with the confusion of "economic" and "administrative" officials with true "charismatics" (*Charismatiker*) such as "apostles, prophets, and teachers/preachers."[87] Sohm told a familiar Protestant story of the Fall, of the decline and corruption of the Gospel into Catholic legalism and ritualism. Ironically, Sohm expressed the yearning for a vanished charisma, one that his earlier Protestant forebears had explicitly foreclosed with the idea that miracles had ceased. Despite this difference, the frame of reference was still the same for Sohm and Weber as it had been for those writing in the seventeenth and eighteenth centuries. The idea of the cessation of miracles and other gifts of grace was connected closely to the question of how to represent the relationship between an original revelation and its institutional expression in the Church.[88] Sohm's insistence on a stark opposition between charisma and law, as well as on the devolution of the former into the latter, anticipated and informed Weber's later usage of these categories. Even in Weber's ostensibly more scientific formulation, charisma remains a mysterious and largely unexplained force, analogous to a miraculous event. Although there are differences between Weber's and Sohm's uses of these categories[89]—such as the fact that Weber detached the concept of charisma from morality to the extent of applying it to warriors and madmen—the structural parallels are clear.[90]

The term "charisma" was itself derived originally from Paul's contrast between "grace" (*charis*) and "law" (*nomos*), meaning Torah, Mosaic law, or *halakhah*.[91] This was, in its origins, the opposite of a scientific concept. It was a polemical concept deployed in the context of a power struggle in the early Christian movement. The radical dichotomy between grace and law posited by Paul has inspired a long series of Christian anti-Jewish polemics. It also manifestly shaped Sohm's history of church law and Weber's sociology. Weber carried such ideas of a diametrical opposition between charisma and law over into his book on *Ancient Judaism*, which was influenced, inter alia, also by the Protestant theologian Julius Wellhausen's reconstruction of the historical development of ancient Israelite religion, according to which prophecy had preceded and declined into law.[92] Wellhausen regarded the tradition of priestly law in the Hebrew Bible as a corruption and degeneration of an earlier, more natural form of Israelite religion. Like Sohm's account of the early Christian church, Wellhausen's account of the rise of Judaism betrayed a general Protestant bias against ritual, against law, and against the authority of the priesthood. Despite the brilliance of Wellhausen's historical reconstruction, it was marked by a profound anti-Jewish as well as anti-Catholic bias, as I have argued elsewhere.[93]

Weber appears to have adapted Wellhausen's account of the degeneration of natural, spontaneous religion into rigid legal prescriptions imposed by priests, which led to calculation and ossification. In its earlier stages, according to Weber, ancient Israelite religion was charismatic. The leaders called "Judges" (*shofetim*) were charismatic war chieftains[94] who controlled certain oracles, particularly for rendering military decisions.[95] Examples of battle-ecstasy, such as Samson or the biblical *ḥerem*, were also present at this stage.[96] Weber described the *ruach*—the "breath" or "wind" of God—as "the special divine force, which corresponding to *mana* and *orenda*, finds expression as charisma of extraordinary accomplishments in heroes, prophets, artists and, reversely, as demonic possession in grave affects and unusual psychic states."[97] Although much of this is Weber's own, we may detect a parallel in Wellhausen's contention:

> The history of the ancient Israelites shows us nothing so distinctly as the uncommon freshness and naturalness of their impulses. The persons who appear always act from the constraining impulse of their nature, the men of God not less than the murderers and adulterers: they are such figures as could only grow up in the open air. Judaism, which realized the Mosaic constitution and carried it out logically, left no free scope for the individual; but in ancient Israel the divine right did not attach to the institution but was in the Creator Spirit, in individuals.[98]

The next historical phase, according to Weber, was represented above all by the prophet (*nabi*), whose authority depended on neither office nor the performance of rituals, but was "a free gift of godly grace" that was often announced in ecstasy[99] or magical powers.[100] The prophet's status was "truly personal"[101] and opposed to every form of "office charisma" such as belonged to priests.[102] In emphasizing the opposition between prophets and priests, Weber was influenced not only by Wellhausen but also by other Protestant theologians such as Hermann Gunkel and Abraham Kuenen.[103]

However, prophecy in ancient Israelite religion too had waned, to be replaced by its very opposite: the ascendancy of the priestly class and of their successors, the rabbis.[104] Weber's account of this historical development paralleled Wellhausen's, while echoing Sohm's account of a similar decline in the early Christian church[105]:

> The genuine "spirit" of the old prophecy … did not disappear because of an "immanent" psychic law of [a] mysterious sort. It vanished because the priestly police power in the Jewish congregation gained control over ecstatic prophecy in the same manner as did the bishopric and Presbyterian authorities over pneumatic prophecy in the early Christian congregation. … Popular opinion upheld the divine nature of the gift of prophecy and all prophets were popular figures [*sic*]. The priests always opposed them. … In the post-exilic congregation the priests succeeded completely in destroying the prestige of the ancient Nabi ecstasy. … The increasing bourgeois rationalism of the people … had given the priests the opportunity to suffocate prophecy.[106]

To reinforce the idea of a conflict and diametrical opposition between priests and prophets, Weber also attributed to the prophets a strong rejection of the ritual institutions, including sacrifice, that were identified with the Levitical priesthood.[107] The early Christian movement supposedly inherited, or rather renewed, the charismatic tendencies of the older prophetic tradition,[108] which were anathema to the rabbis, who embraced the idea that prophecy had ceased.[109] Thus the old conflict between prophets and priests was repeated in the struggles of the early Christians against their opponents who remained within the Jewish fold; of the early Christian charismatics against the evolving hierarchy of the Church; and indeed of Protestants against Catholics. Christians—or Protestants, at least—could thus be viewed as the legitimate successors of the older prophetic tradition, displacing both Jews and Catholics. This was a version of a standard rhetorical strategy of disinheritance already deployed by Paul to favor Gentiles over Jews.[110] Weber in this way extended Sohm's account of the degeneration of the early Christian charismatic community into Catholic legalism, by combining this with Wellhausen's account of a similar and older degeneration in ancient Israelite religion. None of these scholars escaped the gravity of Paul's original opposition between charisma and law, which constituted precisely a condemnation of the Mosaic law, particularly in its ritual dimensions. As John Milbank notes, "The dualisms of Weber's religious categorizations (mystical/ascetic; priestly/prophetic) really derive from a crudified version of the liberal protestant 'higher-critical' reading of the Old Testament, which is now seen to be a serious distortion."[111]

Indeed, Weber echoed another strand of the Christian trope of supersession, namely the idea that the Gospel had abrogated the Mosaic law, at least in its ritual dimensions. He shared the negative view of Jewish ritual endemic to Christianity but especially virulent in certain strands of Protestantism. Judaism, like Roman Catholicism, could be read as a fall from prophetic charisma into a legalism that was incompatible with modernization due to its ritualistic dimensions. Weber contended that Hinduism, Judaism, and other Oriental religions confounded "legal prescriptions" with "ceremonial and ritual norms" and made all law sacred, which sharply limited the potential for the rationalization of both law and the economy.[112] Weber's (in)famous designation of the Jews as a "pariah people"[113] was paralleled in his labeling of certain Indian merchant castes as the "Jews of India"[114]: both were confined and ghettoized by ritual. Conversely, Paul's removal of such ritual barriers in his Apostolic mission to the Gentiles represented the conception, if not yet the fulfillment, of the Western notions of freedom and of universal citizenship.[115]

In *The Protestant Ethic*, Weber directly connected the rationalization of modern life with the abrogation of the Mosaic ceremonial law[116]:

The Puritans opposed the theory that the law of Moses had lost its legitimacy with the founding of Christianity. They argued instead that only those passages relating to Jewish ceremonial or historically conditioned statutes were invalid. Otherwise this law, they maintained, as an expression of *lex naturae* [natural law], possessed its validity from eternity and therefore must be retained. This interpretation allowed on the one hand the elimination of statutes not easily adaptable to modern life, and on the other a powerful strengthening of the spirit of self-righteousness and dispassionate legality suitable to Puritanism's this-worldly asceticism.[117]

Puritanism had developed the ethical dimensions of Jewish monotheism in such a way as to rationalize the world. This occurred through the abrogation of those ritual aspects of Jewish law that were hindrances to the universalization of its ethical message. As Weber argued elsewhere: "In consequence of the New Testament's eschatological withdrawal from the world, the basic writ of Christianity contains only such a minimum of formally binding norms of a ritual or legal character that the way was left entirely free for purely rational enactment."[118] This closely tracked one of the reasons Gibbon gave already in the eighteenth century for the triumph of Christianity, which "offered itself to the world, armed with the strength of the Mosaic law, and delivered from the weight of its fetters."[119] In both cases this was little more than an echo of Christian supersessionism. As David Ellenson has pointed out, Weber's analysis of ancient Judaism was typical of the modern "secularization of Christian universalism."[120]

What Remains of Weber's Thesis for Science?

Weber's ideas of disenchantment and of the routinization of charisma appear deeply indebted on multiple fronts to older theological polemics, according to which the Gospel revelation replaced the Mosaic law and also ended paganism. Weber expressed one, particularly influential version of a broader historical narrative according to which an enlightened present has transcended a superstitious past. Such narratives repeat, in secularized form, an originally theological idea of revelation and supersession. The paradox is that the very idea of a rupture or clean break with an outmoded past is precisely what has been carried over from theology. The supposed caesura actually describes a continuity. The claim of transcendence is meant to insulate the present from the taint of an impure past. When we find such tropes recoded as a central idea of social theory, we should recognize, in this act of distancing, forgetting, and repression, the gesture that genealogy seeks to counter. As a mode of uncovering the absence of absolute difference between posited metaphysical opposites—in this case, between science and theology or between secular and religious modes of thought—genealogy reveals both that "we were never really secular" and, at the same time, that these older modes of thought remain relevant for us, as expressions of either our own, still living past or perennial human tendencies.

A key question, after such genealogies have been taken into account, is what remains of Weber's theory that might still be regarded as useful for science? More than fifty years ago, Peter Berger already noted the influence of Protestant theology on Weber's stark opposition between prophets and priests: "The contra-position of prophet and priest, which Weber knew from the scholars of the Wellhausen school, vibrates through the entire theory of charisma."[121] Berger pointed out that contemporary biblical scholarship no longer supported such an opposition: the scholarly image of the prophet was now associated more closely with the cult and could, in its origins, be said to constitute a special kind of ritual office. Berger concluded that these new data "do not invalidate the ideal-typical construction of charismatic authority as against traditional and legal-rational authority. More importantly, these modifications in no way weaken Weber's sociologically crucial elaboration of the process of the routinization of charisma."[122] This attempt to salvage part of Weber's thesis now seems less convincing. Not only the dichotomy between prophet and priest but the broader opposition between charisma and law appears problematic, as does especially the very idea of "routinization," which as we have seen was deeply implicated in Protestant and more broadly Christian theological discourses.

Nor was Weber correct in arguing that the roots of disenchantment should be located in ancient Israelite religion. As we have seen, the main tropes that appear to have converged in the modern concept were derived instead from Christian supersessionism and were actually directed against both Judaism and paganism. This does not mean that Weber's claim had no basis. One of the theological grounds for the Protestant attacks on ritual was indeed a heightened emphasis on divine omnipotence, and a concomitant devaluation of the power of magic, which we may see already in the Hebrew Bible. Furthermore, the idea that prophecy had ceased developed in Judaism earlier than in Christianity. Yet the fact remains that disenchantment, at least in its early modern and modern forms, has been overwhelmingly conditioned by Protestant interpretations of older Christian ideas.

However, another part of Weber's account has held up very well. He diagnosed quite accurately what some more recent scholars have called the "repudiation of ritual" as a key step taken by the early Reformers en route to the modern world.[123] The apex of this repudiation was indeed in Puritanism, which represented only one strand of Protestantism but an important one. Although Protestant polemics against ritual relied heavily on the supersessionist narratives that Weber himself echoed,[124] these ideas nevertheless had a widespread and lasting impact on attitudes and practices. Cultural narratives are never merely stories; they also exert a powerful influence on the manner in which we inhabit the world. It is exactly as Clifford Geertz said of ritual: "The world as lived and the world as imagined, fused under the agency of a single set of symbolic forms, turn out to be the same world."[125]

Perhaps most importantly, the opposition that Weber posited between charisma and law cannot be dismissed as merely a myth or theological trope. As I suggested in *Sovereignty and the Sacred*, there appears to be a perennial tension between sovereignty and legality, one that is expressed or negotiated differently in different cultures. Weber's own opposition between charismatic and legal authority constitutes one particular formulation of this tension. The fact that Weber borrowed older words and concepts for his formulation does not, in and of itself, render it false. Any heuristic concept that is applied cross-culturally must have emerged first at one point in time in a particular culture. The question is whether such a concept has been liberated sufficiently from the historical conditions of its production to serve as a non-distorting lens on other cultures. My own conclusion is that Weber's concept does not meet this standard. However, it remains useful, inasmuch as it provides valuable evidence concerning the nature of the problem itself, namely, the problem of how to locate sovereignty (or charisma) in relation to a normative order.[126]

If Weber's sociology now appears partly theological, and less than fully scientific, then we must allow that the earlier, Christian concepts on which he drew also remain relevant for us, as part of a past that remains somehow present, if only by virtue of being sedimented in our language and conceptual categories. The absolute divide between theology and science cannot be maintained. This in itself undercuts the narrative of secularization, if such is taken to mean a rupture with a religious past. Part of the value of genealogy is that it shows us that we are merely mortal, and that we cannot escape the gravity of our history completely. Neither should we fear to face this history as, properly understood, it is a reflection of ourselves. This may be the true path to overcoming disenchantment.

8

Counter-Narratives to Secularization: Merits and Limits of Genealogy Critique

Monika Wohlrab-Sahr

Disenchantment and Secularization: Narratives and Counter-Narratives

Max Weber's famous and influential diagnosis of "disenchantment,"[1] which dates back to 1913 in his writings,[2] left a lasting imprint on the analysis and perception of modern society. Weber perceived "disenchantment" not simply as a metaphor for a substantial disruption but as a long-term trend in the real world with real causes and effects. He saw it rooted in a process of religious rationalization, of the de-magicalization of religion, starting with early Judaism and becoming fully fledged in ascetic Protestantism. Weber extended the use of the term beyond the process in the history of religion to a general diagnosis of the path into and of the modern world, intimately tied to rationalization. He regarded the marginalization and transformation of religion as the consequence of this process of rationalization and of the concomitant differentiation of value spheres. This might be labeled as secularization, though Weber himself used this term only rarely, mostly in relation to the historical expropriation of church property, and certainly not as a strong concept.[3] While he considered religion, and especially Protestantism, to be the decisive force behind the emergence of modernity due to its intrinsic rationalizing quality and its impact on methodical life conduct, he saw religion being transformed during this process into the "irrational or antirational transpersonal power per se."[4]

I would like to thank Todd Weir, Christoph Kleine, Hubert Seiwert, Daniel Kinitz, Marian Burchardt, Nader Sohrabi, Florian Zemmin, Neguin Yavari, Wolfgang Höpken, and the editors of this volume for their valuable comments on this chapter.

Several authors in this volume elaborate on the background to this narrative: its history, origins, and borrowings;[5] its plausibility;[6] and its implications. This chapter comes from a different angle. It will deal with a specific type of *critique* of diagnoses like secularization and, more recently, of the whole concept of the religious-secular divide. I will thereby concentrate mainly on the dominant postcolonial critique in the context of Islamic studies and Anthropology of Islam, as well as on a specific type of genealogical critique in the footsteps of Talal Asad.[7] This selection is, however, not incidental. In their genealogical approach, Asad and most of his followers put their attention especially on the way in which scholars in Religious Studies and the Social Sciences with their theoretical and methodological instruments (developed in Western contexts) deal with Islam; and how their conceptual gaze influences what they get to see. Majority and minority relations, issues of domination and subordination, play a central role in this strand of literature, and Muslims are in the center of this discussion. Thereby, the critique of scientific concepts and the critique of present political regimes and international politics are closely intertwined.

The critique of concepts and diagnoses and the discussion of their transferability to other contexts as a challenge for cross- and intra-cultural approaches to religion are part of the scientific endeavor. This especially holds true for the critique of the *narratives* behind such diagnoses that are—much too often—taken for granted and excluded from critical inquiry. So far, there have been valuable contributions and criticisms aimed at historicizing and contextualizing concepts like modernity/modernization, religion/secularity, secularism, and secularization,[8] and at highlighting complexities and ambiguities as well as the role of agency, power, and interests, from both Religious Studies and the Social Sciences.[9] Genealogical approaches have been important in these efforts at historicization, and post-colonial approaches have been decisive for questioning the alleged universalism of theories and categories developed within the West and first of all suitable for Western contexts. However, some of these critiques and their wide reception are much more than just attempts at scientific reflexivity: inasmuch as they argue against an "episteme" by referring to a totalizing, agent-like concept of *secularism*, they themselves tend to become *counter-narratives* to differentiation, secularization, and disenchantment. I argue that as a result—and often against their stated intentions—these critiques not only neglect the multiplicity of processes and regimes related to secularization and secular-religious distinctions and differentiations but also implicitly paint a picture of integration and identity in contrast to the religious-secular divide. As I will show in the following in more detail, this is the flip side of a perception of Islam (or of non-Western contexts like India or Japan) as the "opposite" of a secular-religious divide that emerged out of a Christian context—an Islam mainly considered as an integrated "way of life" and as such in contrast to a "compartmentalized" notion of Protestant-like religion or in depictions of a Muslim "habitus" that is hurt in toto when, for example, the prophet is ridiculed. Islam and Muslims—or interchangeably other types of non-Western religions and populations—are placed in the center of this "opposite side" and thereby implicitly become the representative figures of such integrity. Similar framings can be found with regard to other non-Western contexts, like the interreligious tolerance that is considered characteristic of the Indian precolonial past, whereas "Western" concepts of the secular or secularism allegedly remain alien to this context. Aamir Mufti, for good reasons, has criticized the "auratisation" of the precolonial past in some of the postcolonial writings.[10]

It is not my intention that the following should contribute to a ping-pong between contradicting normativities, nor is this an attempt at simply demystifying the demystifier. Since these counter-narratives, however, have become very influential, and have had serious effects on the field of research on religion, it seems important to deal with them in some detail.

There is no doubt that "classical" theories of modernization and secularization have, for a long time, too easily generalized from the developments in the West to those expected in the "rest" of the world. Often, secularization analyses were embedded in narratives of modernization with strong teleological underpinnings. This has led to the criticism that now seems to have become a new mainstream, pointedly labeled as "the post-secular turn."[11] The competition between narratives and counter-narratives in the field of research on religion, however, raises the question of whether a sociological or historical account is still possible that, without ignoring the accompanying narratives, nevertheless addresses questions that once were at the center of secularization analyses. Essential for them, I argue, are not only the—often cited—"decline of religion" analyses but also, and I think more important, the analyses of *social differentiation processes* related to religion. More precisely: of the *conceptual distinction and institutional differentiation* between "religion" (or related phenomena) and other spheres of activity. One of the main figures of historical sociology in the research on secularization, David Martin has stressed that in this research the "key concept is differentiation, not a once-for-all transition from religion to politics, or from religion to science—or even to personal utopia—backed up by other postulated transitions based on the nouns of process, like 'rationalisation,' 'modernisation' and, of course, 'secularisation' itself."[12] I argue that the critique of a discourse—like "secularization"—and its genealogy alone does not answer the question if distinctions and differentiations related to religion exist under the surface of these discourses or have existed in a vernacular version even before the encounter with the West and without using the term "secular." Jonathan Sheehan, for the early modern history of Christianity, speaks of the "resources of the nonreligious" in premodern periods, thereby questioning Taylor's narrative of a premodern religious past as opposed to the present "secular age."[13] However, whether intentionally or not, some types of critique tend to block research that explores such questions. My interest is to overcome this deadlock and reopen the possibility of comparative research on religion and the secular without, however, ignoring the role of strong narratives in that field.

Narrative as Sensemaking

What is suggested, explicitly or implicitly, when we speak of "narratives" or—with a more derogatory undertone—of "myths" of social developments? Certainly, there is a suggestion that these depictions refer to developments *that call for explanation*, legitimization, and critique. In short, there is a need for sensemaking, which is then produced by means of what are often grand narratives. These narratives stretch over a long time span, explain how present conditions came to be, and point out the forces that allowed them to emerge. They explain how we became who we are and, as such, they are myths in a very general sense: tales of origin.

Narratives like these have existed from early on, and, as Robert Yelle[14] has shown for Weber's disenchantment narrative, they connect with earlier narratives and reproduce older topics and older forms of sensemaking. It seems that the scope of possible narratives of sensemaking of the world is limited, and that topics like enchantment and disenchantment, wholeness and divide, embeddedness and disembedding,[15] origin and loss, have been recurring themes over the centuries, despite being provoked by very different developments and ruptures that made explanation necessary.

The terms for "secularization," in German divided into *Säkularisation* and *Säkularisierung*, have obviously been keywords and categories of interpretation within such narratives, referring to the historical expropriation of church property and the related legal term as well as to later theological, philosophical, and historical interpretations of the perceived changes,[16] partly equating the term "secularization" with "profanation" (*Verweltlichung*).[17]

When dealing with counter-narratives to secularization, it is reasonable to start with Germany as the country where the term *Säkularisation* was coined in advance of the Peace of Westphalia, long before the invention of the term "secularism."[18] Counter-narratives related to secularization became prominent in Germany from the early nineteenth century, when the counter-revolutionary movement began to perceive the "de-Christianization of Europe" as a problem.[19] The movement was responding to narratives of Enlightenment, but also to the longer-lasting differentiation between matters related to the church and *seculares causae*, especially with regard to the limitation of the legal and governmental power of the clergy and to the expropriation of church property in countries that were previously Catholic. This intellectual opposition was expressed in the writings of Joseph von Eichendorff, who in 1818 lamented the loss of the "wonderful fusion of spiritual and mundane matters,"[20] which destroyed "the legal influence of the clergy ... on war and peace, jurisdiction and administration, in general on the Christian institution of public and private life in Germany."[21] He considered the secularization of the states and of church property "a misfortune [*Unglück*] for Germany."[22] This indicates that in the early nineteenth century, an anti-secularization "narrative" already existed, which interpreted the expropriation of church property and the diminishing power of the Church in political and legal matters as the dissolution of a previous unity that was to be lamented.[23] This unity, symbolized by the Catholic Church, was perceived as the reflection of a superior, transcendent order in the world. To put it sociologically: it was secularization (*Säkularisation*), not only as an act of expropriation but also of *differentiation* between the church and the state, the dissolution of something retrospectively perceived as a unity, the loss of which was interpreted as a misfortune. Secularization and functional differentiation were commented upon with a grand narrative of decline: "The abolition of the sovereignty of bishops and abbots is a cultural-historical document of the decline of an epoch in the history of the Occident."[24]

This example indicates that narratives are not simply ideologies disconnected from historical events. They relate, in different ways and with different interpretations, to *epochal experiences,* as Wolfgang Eßbach put it.[25] Eichendorff's lament obviously makes reference to the historical experience of the French Revolution and the German Enlightenment ("religion of reason"[26]), as well as to the partial political disempowerment and expropriation of the churches and the related differentiation of functions between the bishops and the princes. However, this lament is much more than a sociohistorical depiction. By commenting on the changes, it draws a picture of what has been lost and alleges the unity of a world under Catholic regiment, Catholicism being the "soul" of the state.

While grand narratives do refer to historical events, events and narratives are not the same.[27] This is a primary and, in certain academic fields, unproblematic perspective on "narratives." Analysts usually hint at continuities between different types of narratives, relativize novelties, point out counter-tendencies, and thereby de-objectify interpretations that make sense of the world in its present state. Narratives are not replications of what occurred; they are strong and generalizing interpretations, some of which are able to create their own realities. Analysts of narratives as second-order interpreters may see things that the narrators themselves have not seen. They place them in context, show from where they have borrowed their lines of thought and thereby remind us that the narrators were children of their time, with interests and passions, and that their narratives are a reflection of these interests and influenced by these passions. Sometimes, however, the analysts themselves turn into narrators.

Narrative as *Concealment*: Process and Interpretation

A key question is *how* the narration relates to a sequence of historical events. In sociological debate in the 1980s, discussion of the "myth of secularization" explicitly addressed the tension between process and interpretation. Thomas Luckmann[28] came up with this phrase to point out that secularization is a narrative told by modern society to make sense of its own history: a modern myth of origin.

However, while he conceded that there was a connection between the narrative and an underlying historical experience, Luckmann did not pay much attention to the historical experience. For him, the term "myth" itself implied that it *concealed* what was really going on, namely the continued presence of religion. Luckmann therefore concluded that theories of secularization were ultimately misleading, at least as far as the religiosity of people was concerned. He conceded that there was something like secularization on the level of social institutions (societal differentiation). However, he linked religiosity on a very general level with the transcendence of the biological nature of human beings. Furthermore, he regarded "religion" as being connected to the existence of "society" in a Durkheimian sense, another form of self-transcendence.[29] For Luckmann, this implied that secularization at the level of the individual and of society as a whole was literally impossible, although he thought that transcendence was shifting from higher to lower levels.[30] In this sense, describing secularization as a *myth of modernity* implied that it was insinuating a false objectivity of social developments. What has been interpreted as religious decline was simply a misinterpretation of the changing institutional reality of religion.

Academically, this contribution was quite productive. The Luckmann school made many attempts to prove that religiosity was not declining but simply changing its shape, and collected evidence for new or little-acknowledged forms of spirituality, folk religiosity, magic, New Age, and so on.[31] However, Luckmann's argumentation was always based on the axiomatic assumption that religiosity ultimately *cannot* decline, that humans would not be humans if they were void of religiosity in a very general sense.

Critics of this approach were also productive in showing that there had *indeed* been religious decline (in membership, belief, and practice)—at least in Western Europe—and that what could be statistically measured as "spirituality" could not make up for this decline. The authors in question could show for several European countries that even if some parts of the population might have moved from church-bound religiosity to spirituality outside the churches, a much bigger proportion of the population were including spiritual interests within their church-bound religiosity, and the number of people who were non-religious and not interested in spiritual matters was also growing significantly. In short, they argued that secularization was not a mere narrative or myth but a real development.[32]

This is not the place to discuss the evidence for either position. Of relevance, however, is that secularization was described as a "myth of modernity" with the intention to question a development that others claimed to be empirically proven. Luckmann certainly did not present a fully developed anti-secularization narrative and certainly did not present an antimodern one. He presented a criticism of secularization that was embedded in an axiomatic assumption about the anthropological and sociological necessity of religion. Consequently, the secularization narrative *conceals* what is really going on with regard to religion.

There is no doubt that in the research on secularization, scholars tend to interpret their findings in the light of certain narrations, which may bear ideological imprints. Daniel Weidner has argued that the "rhetoricity" of secularization is an irreducible part of the form in which the proposition of "secularization" is presented. Without questioning the existence of the related historical processes, he argues that these processes are not simply described but transformed into texts, "which fluctuate between historical comprehension and self-description, evaluation, claim, and analysis, and which produce special meaning effects exactly due to this fluctuation."[33] To analyze these fluctuations, and to question the sometimes ideological imprints of narratives, however, does not per se call into question the validity of findings. In a certain strand of the debate, however, it is insinuated that the rejection of narratives also disproves the processes to which they relate.

Historian Ian Hunter, who has labeled secularization as a "combat concept," has made this argument.[34] Based on the historical analysis of various philosophical-historical conceptions of secularization in Germany since the 1830s, of Kantian, Hegelian and Marxian descent, he argues that these philosophies did not become influential due to actual secularization processes but due to processes of a very different kind:

> In one regard these circumstances were formed by the capacity of the rationalist philosophies and histories to imbue the leadership of political sects with the charismatic authority to propose installing their particular "theory" of secularization as the constitutional foundation of religion, law, and state. At the same time, it was only the military and political suspension of the existing constitutional order that permitted the rationalist philosophies to migrate from their tolerated academic enclaves and enter the political sects that were proposing to refound the pluralistic and relativistic religious constitution on the basis of a "true" theory of religion and politics. For just this reason, the rationalist philosophies could be swept out of political reality if, for example, political circumstances led to the reinstatement of the pluralist religious constitution as the modus vivendi between the rival cultural and political factions.[35]

The latter, according to Hunter, was the case in West Germany in 1949, when a secular and relativistic religious constitution was reinstated, different from the socialist East:

> In Soviet East Germany, however, the constitutional interregnum would be terminated through a program to impose the Marxist conception of secularization through the instrumentarium of a party state, thereby demonstrating the only form in which philosophical history could deal with both the nonexistence of the process of secularization and the historical persistence of confessional religions.[36]

At first glance, this sounds convincing. Despite being "secular," the West German constitution and its way of regulating religion certainly did not follow a "secularist" ideological program, quite the opposite. However, one must consider whether this indicates the "nonexistence" of a process of secularization.

Secularization—as José Casanova[37] has convincingly shown—refers to various processes that are not necessarily interlinked. Casanova lists *religious decline, functional differentiation,* and the *privatization of religion.* One might add— with reference to Hunter—the emergence of *secularist worldviews.* Hunter, without making use of Casanova's approach, only refers to the relationship between functional differentiation (here: church-state relations) and secularist worldviews. Other historians, however, have presented evidence for secularization as religious decline, especially in the northern and central regions of Germany. Lucian Hölscher has shown that in the area that later became the German Democratic Republic, the population was already somewhat detached from the church around 1910.[38] The regions with low participation in church activities were industrialized areas of Germany at that time, and secular movements were popular, not only among the intellectual elite or "sectarian" secularist groups but also in the Social Democratic Party that was preaching "a synthesis of Marxism and Darwinism."[39] Obviously, this region was a historical setting where different kinds of secularizing effects coincided—secularist movements being one of them. These influences created the soil on which the SED (Socialist Union Party of Germany) could later plant their secularist ideas. Secularist ideologies and a process of secularization in the population in that case *were* indeed related, and they were not only confined to a "sectarian" movement. Hugh McLeod[40] and José Casanova have highlighted the secularizing influence of social movements that propagated Enlightenment ideas in Europe, which they considered to be one important factor for the European secularization process.[41] The socialist period was not simply a "sectarian" episode without lasting effects. To this day, East Germany is one of the most highly secularized regions in the world. Survey data shows that the rationalist agenda of the socialist regime, expressed in the framework of a *wissenschaftliche Weltanschauung* (scientific world view), has left lasting imprints on the East German population.[42]

This example indicates that the relationship between secularization as a *combat concept* (or a narrative)—which it certainly *also* was—and secularization as an institutional and social reality is more complicated than Hunter suggests. Secularist ideologies may resonate in parts of the population against the background of certain historical experiences or class structures. They may be supported and spread by movements like the Social Democrats or more explicitly secularist movements. Against such backgrounds, authoritarian regimes, like the SED regime, may then foster a long-lasting change, and secularist philosophies may play a role in that. The contrast between science/rationality and religion may even survive the death of the regime. Combat concepts can be combined with "real" secularization even if the institutional background of church-state relations is supportive of the public presence of the Christian confessions, as was the case after the German reunification. This, at least, is what the example of East Germany tells us.

Hunter himself refers to a specific process of secularization, namely *functional differentiation*, when he points out that it is a *secular state* in Germany that maintains an amicable distance from both Christian confessions while not employing a secularist ideology. Such differentiation, accompanied to a greater or lesser extent by secular ideologies, occurred in different social spheres in the late nineteenth and twentieth centuries.[43] What we can draw from Hunter is the necessity to differentiate analytically between *secularism as an ideology*, the *institutionalization of certain church-state regulations*, and the *secular outlook or behavior of the population*. Ideological secularism, that is, a certain rationalist narrative, may create a lasting influence under certain conditions, whereas it may remain in a sectarian niche under different ones.

The fact that secularization exists as a *combat concept*, however, draws our attention to the field in which such combat takes place. We have already seen two historical positions in the late eighteenth and early nineteenth centuries: the romantic anti-secularist narrative, mourning for the lost unity of the Catholic German Reich, and the secularist, rational philosophical narrative based on certain Enlightenment philosophies, to which Hunter refers.[44] Also writing about Germany, Todd Weir[45] has pointed to clashes "over political practices and epistemological assumptions" between worldview secularism and the liberal project of secularization.[46]

That secularization or anti-secularization were combat concepts between conflicting ideological groups shows us that the processes were *serious enough* to cause conflicting actors to come up with extended narratives, political practices, and epistemological assumptions. It would be too easy, however, to treat them only as ideologies that *conceal* what was really going on. In our case, they were narratives related to a process of differentiation between church and state powers that was interpreted and valued in very different ways.

Narrative as Discourse, Secularism as Apparatus

Many critics of secularization theories who came up with the "narrative," "myth," or "combat concept" argument left one element of secularization analyses untouched. This was the element of *societal or functional differentiation*, the differentiation between religion and other social spheres and institutions, and the diminishing power of religious institutions and actors over other spheres of social life.[47] Rodney Stark, one of the most prolific proponents of the market model of religion and one of the harshest critics of secularization theories, writes:

> Secularization prophecies ... are *not* directed primarily toward institutional differentiation—they do not merely predict the separation of church and state or a decline in the direct, secular authority of church leaders. Their primary concern is with *individual piety*, especially *belief.* ... One definition, often referred to as the macro version ..., identifies secularization as *de-institutionalization* .... This refers to a decline in the social power of once-dominant religious institutions whereby other social institutions, especially political and educational institutions, have escaped from prior religious domination. If this were all that secularization means, there would be nothing to argue about.[48]

This is in line with José Casanova's disentanglement of the different components of secularization theory: *religious decline, functional differentiation,* and the *privatization of religion*. The first conclusion that Casanova draws is that these three elements are not necessarily connected in the process of modernity. Indeed, connections between them may be the exception rather than the rule. However, Casanova also concluded, at least earlier on,[49] that *functional differentiation* is a central element of any modern development and in this sense a generalizable feature of secularization theory and the theory of modernity.[50]

For some time, this seemed to be a basic point of agreement, but this idea too would ultimately come under attack. The attack took the *narrative-as-concealment* argument even further: not only was secularization perceived as a narrative or myth that conflicted with real developments, the idea that the underlying conceptual frame—the secular-religious divide—was a generalizable pattern was also called into question. It was Talal Asad[51] and the group of scholars who followed him, who were the agents of this attack. It was not that they considered this divide simply as a myth that could be contrasted with a vital religious or confessional reality, as Thomas Luckmann or Ian Hunter argued. The secular-religious divide was interpreted as a narration and a conceptual tool that was based on a very specific Christian history and made sense only against the background of this history.[52] This divide, the scholars argued, had then been imposed on non-Christian contexts, mostly within imperial or colonial settings, meaning that from the very beginning it was essentially linked to the power and violence of the (colonial) nation state. It was regarded as the only legitimate means of ordering the world and then applied in foreign contexts, resulting in non-Western contexts being perceived as deficient.

From this perspective, as Todd Weir has argued, secularization was identified

> not as a neutral social theory, but rather as a scientific auxiliary of a technique of statecraft developed and deployed in the nineteenth century to unify nations and divide colonial populations. By removing the "ization" and adding "ism," the new critical histories have signaled their effort to demystify or, better yet, to secularize the theory of secularization by revealing that what was once held for science was, in fact, ideology. Secularism, accordingly, encompasses the discourses, policies, and constitutional arrangements, whereby modern states and elites have sought to regulate religion and, in the process, contributed to the "immanent frame" in which religion is now located.[53]

As such, religion—meaning both the concept and the specific form that is perceived as legitimate from the secular viewpoint—is generated and aligned according to the principles of secularism.

The genealogical historicization and contextualization of the conceptual divide was unquestionably an important step in the study of religion and the secular. It forced scholars in this field to question what had widely been taken for granted. However, due to the strong theoretical link to nation-state power and violence, what started as an attempt at historicization immediately became an enterprise in the critique of ideology. Despite Asad's proclaimed scholarly curiosity,[54] there was little room for varieties and nuances. "Secularism" became a collective singular within a seemingly "linear process of continual adjustment without serious reversal."[55] For good reason, José Casanova has considered it "the most problematic aspect of Asad's genealogy of the secular," that he "has presented a stark picture of the secular, liberal democracy, and the human rights regime, all blurred into an undifferentiated totality of Western modernity."[56] If we consider the response to Asad's work, we find that "secularism" as a "discourse" became an all-encompassing term, necessarily carrying with it the vagueness of the concept of discourse itself. What began as an attempt to historicize and contextualize that which seemed universal and as such stimulated genealogical endeavors[57] turned into the totalizing metaphor of the "secular apparatus"[58] that eradicated contextual differences. Hadi Enayat,[59] in his critique, therefore sees the Asad-school characterized by a subversive genealogy, an essentialization of secularism, and a phobia against the state, and places it in the line of antiliberal theories in the tradition of Nietzsche, Heidegger, and Foucault.

In this latter sense, secularism became very influential in the present debate on religion. Whereas there are important comparative studies dealing with "secularisms" as institutionalized religion-state arrangements and related politics,[60] or with secularization as the possibly tri-fold process so aptly disentangled by Casanova, in its conceptualization as a "discourse," secularism tends to be present everywhere but has become difficult to observe and to prove or disprove empirically. This is not meant to deny the influence of discourses. However, if discourse analysis is done with methodological scrutiny, it should take conflicting strands of discourse into account and allow for surprises in the empirical data. This is hardly the case in present research that refers to secularism as a "discourse" or "apparatus." A paramount theoretical narrative, in which—as John R. Bowen has put it—"the secular" becomes a grammatical and historical subject,[61] tends to identify one unifying logic behind all actions and conceptions related to religion. From the perspective of the "powers of the secular modern,"[62] secularism dominates everything that does not seem in line with it, especially religion. Because it is placed, historically, at the origins of "the secular," the quest for something distant from or alternative to "religion" that predates explicit secular-religious distinctions as well as ideological secularism seems irrelevant.[63]

What becomes impossible from such a totalizing perspective is to differentiate between several processes or dimensions: secularization as a decline of religious participation and belief, certain forms of functional differentiation between religion and other social spheres, and, finally, secularist ideologies or "discourses" referring to the relation between religion and its others. What also falls out of sight are the variations and even oppositions between different types of reference to the secular.[64] A strong concept of "discourse" tends to lump all of these together.

This totalizing tendency is visible even where a plurality of "secularisms" is supposed to be taken into account. Jakobsen and Pellegrini in their attempt at pluralizing the "secularism" concept nevertheless end up with a unifying view:

> Particular secularisms are not just autonomous units grounded in their national contexts, or in relation to particular religious formations; precisely by being called "secularisms," they are also articulated in relation to the dominating discourse of universal secularism, which is tied to the Protestant secularism of the market.[65]

Without ignoring the global diffusion of certain concepts and institutional programs beyond the limits of nation states, one must question whether the secularism discourse is indeed so dominating and universal, if we compare China, Japan, India, France, the United States, and Germany, for instance. Aren't the historical settings and their development into the present very different even within Europe?[66] Don't we find contradictory practices and understandings even in a specific national context like France, as Bowen convincingly shows?[67] And, if there are unifying tendencies, should there not be an attempt to *explain* how they became dominant over other tendencies, as opposed to simply presupposing such a "dominating discourse?" Even the term "secularism" might be more widespread in scholarly literature than in societal and political practice. At least, the dominance of a discourse cannot be derived from the alleged omnipresence of certain terminology.

Finally, that Max Weber is supposed to be the foundational figure for the "Protestant secularism of the market," which is the allegedly dominant discourse, is even more irritating. Weber's essay, *The Protestant Ethic and the Spirit of Capitalism*, certainly deals with the marginalization of religion in the process of rationalization. However, to consider it the prototype of the secularism discourse, of the "co-origination of secularism and market-reformed Protestantism," is grossly mistaken.[68] While according to Weber's analysis, modern capitalism developed against the background of a certain, religiously grounded ascetic life conduct (*methodische Lebensführung*) and—when fully developed—became independent of this religious motivation, his essay is certainly not about "freedom from religion" that "was also freedom for the market."[69] "Freedom from religion" as a motif that we certainly find in secularist ideologies does not play any role in Weber's writing. For fully developed capitalism, religion is simply no longer necessary. As far as the market is concerned, it is *not secularism* that is required in this market, it is *methodical life conduct*, whatever its motivation may be. Its originally *religious* motivation in the long run simply becomes irrelevant. It is substituted neither by "secularism" nor by striving for "freedom from religion," but simply by an inner-worldly orientation toward work as a vocation.

Others have combined Asad's theorem with Edward Said's analysis of the "Orientalism" narrative. Said considered the narrative of Orientalism—a cultural tradition that divides the world into two uneven halves and that he regarded as having roots in antiquity—an explanation for the way Europe and the United States treated the Orient. Whereas Said was *not* writing about secularism, Gil Anidjar, for example, made a direct connection between Orientalism, Christianity, and secularism and tried to prove that this was actually in line with Said's intention:

> It is my contention ... that Said was participating in the general movement of opposition to religion carried by the terms *secular* and *secularism*. ... In waging

that battle Said simply appears to have forgotten the lesson taught by his most important of books, namely *Orientalism*. For if *Orientalism* teaches us anything, it is that Orientalism *is* secularism.[70]

Following this line of argument, Elizabeth Shakman Hurd[71] explains the international relations of the United States and Europe, for example, with Iran or Turkey, with the discursive confrontation between secularism and Islam. Such polarizations certainly exist. However, are they really that univocal? Can they actually *explain* U.S. foreign policy, taking into account the different relations with countries in the Islamicate world like Iran, Turkey, or Saudi Arabia? Again, it seems that in this line of argument, the secularist discourse becomes an agent in itself, which is supposed to *explain* political outcomes. Such an analysis hardly relies on actual sources or documents of foreign policy, like talks, interviews, statements, treaties, negotiations, or their depictions in the media, which could prove the influence of such discourse. It largely relies on academic literature that confirms the polarizing discourse. The metaphor of the "apparatus," taken from Asad's approach, used here as an interpretational frame, de facto substitutes for the analysis of actual international relations, as "the 'ideological conditions that give point and force to the theoretical apparatuses employed to describe and objectify' the secular and the religious. These theoretical apparatuses are identified (…) as laicism and Judeo-Christian secularism."[72]

Asad's depiction of secularism has become one of the most influential counter-secularization narratives in academia that deals with religion today. It has shaken the last, and for a long time seemingly safe bastion of secularization theory, the theory of functional differentiation. Genealogical interests in religion and the secular can certainly follow different paths than the Asadian. Presently, however, many follow in his footsteps. The genealogical critique of the "secularism discourse" has developed into a counter-narrative of its own.

Asad's genealogical approach stands in the tradition of a Foucauldian or Nietzschean genealogy. These approaches, as Martin Saar has pointed out,[73] aim not only at the analysis of *historical developments* but also at the analysis of a *certain kind of present subjectivity*. They call into question a subjectivity that seems indispensable and unquestionable to the recipient, and put it in the light of a contingent, even violent, historical development aligned with the power and the violence of the nation state and with colonialism.

Saar has argued that genealogical approaches like Foucault's or Nietzsche's are hyperbolic in character; that their interest is polemical and their style exaggeration. He underlines that this has to be taken into account. They want to show the contingency of a development to those who take it as a given. They aim at the possibility of critique of one's own form of subjectivity, at the possibility of self-reflection. With regard to our subject, this means: the critical reflection of one's own secular self-perception.

The works of Talal Asad and his followers tend to neglect this hyperbolism and give the critique a specific turn. The critique is about what has been done to "others." There is a risk, however, that this other side remains a passive victim of "Western" impositions. Consequently, in this line of critique, empirical research that could possibly produce counter-evidence is often absent, and its stance on the other tends to be apologetic.

The Blind Spot: The "Other Side" of the Imposed Divide

Focusing on the "powers of the secular modern," on hegemonic discourses and "apparatuses" of secularism and the secular-religious divide and their impacts on non-Western societies, provokes curiosity for the other side. What was there before the imposition of the "Western" type of divide? Or, if we take Weir's perspective: Wasn't there a "secular" before "secularism?"[74]

Important work has been done with regard to imperial and colonial encounters.[75] Unquestionably, Western notions of religion and the secular have exerted influence on what was found in the non-West, and power relations had a great impact on this encounter. Western concepts of religion as confession had implications for the evaluation of rituals and practices found elsewhere,[76] as was the case with Western concepts of the secular. Peter van der Veer, however, has stressed the need for an *"interactional perspective"*[77] instead of assuming one-sided impositions. He problematizes the "orientalist" notion of a confrontation between a holistic system of group religion in India and a system that has "separate values for separate spheres of life" and the "ideology of the individual" in England.[78] What he describes as an "interactional perspective" is mainly the impact that the imperial encounter left *on both sides*. This approach, however, is still too narrow. It should be extended to the interaction between different systems of knowledge even in the "colonized" regions. The "secular-religious divide" was not simply imposed upon but also corresponded with existing epistemes. It was supported, rejected, integrated, transformed, accommodated, and so on.[79] This makes it necessary, however, to look not only for differences but also for possible similarities between the indigenous and the new.

Furthermore, what van der Veer discusses regarding Western historiographies of India can also be related to present depictions of Islam and secularism. The generalizing picture of Western "secularism" in recent literature implicitly insinuates that the quest for distinctions and differentiations between "religion" and its other is per se inadequate for the analysis of non-Western contexts. It is not such a great step from there to conclude that what existed in this place before the encounter or what is violated in present encounters was some kind of undivided wholeness, a peaceful and tolerant coexistence of different religions,[80] a fluid ambiguity without clear distinctions, a harmonious integration of heavenly and mundane realms under one canopy. Another insinuation is that all this has been destroyed by the dividing impact of Western secularism—politically as well as conceptually—and that Western secularism still violates the Islamicate world and Muslims in the present. This is what I call the counter-narrative.

Pointing out this counter-narrative does not involve denying the impact of power and violence in the course of imperial or colonial encounters. Instead, it problematizes the broad neglect of an interactional perspective and—as a by-product of the rejection of differentiation perspectives—the implicit suggestion of non-differentiation on the "other side." This precludes the possible existence of the "secular" or of the "nonreligious" before "secularism." With regard to Islam, at least, such a possibility is not discussed in the context of secularism debates, which then insinuates that differentiation as such only exists due to the "apparatus" of secularism.

Instructive for the debate on Islam is the volume *Islam and Secularism in the Middle East*,[81] where several contributions relate an alleged unity in the past to the rejection of political secularism in the present. It is telling of this approach that scholarly and political positions are closely intertwined in a coalition of Muslim scholars critical of the West[82] and of political regimes in the Middle East, and American scholars of Islam who criticize their own political environment.[83] The critical discussion of specific, often authoritarian political regimes, labelled "secular fundamentalist," then becomes a blueprint for the critique of "secularism" as such: secularism of the West and of Western science. This hardly leaves room for differentiation, neither to analytically distinguish between "authoritarianism" and "secularism," nor to take processes of differentiation within the Islamic tradition into account.

John Esposito in this introduction explicitly brings these strands together, when he argues that this

> militant secular fundamentalism [and] the secular presuppositions which inform our academic disciplines and outlook on life, our Western secular worldview,

have been a major obstacle to our understanding and analysis of Islamic politics and have contributed to a tendency to reduce Islam to fundamentalism and fundamentalism to religious extremism … The post-Enlightenment tendency to define religion as a system of belief, rather than as a way of life, has seriously hampered our ability to understand the nature of Islam and many of the world's religions. It has artificially compartmentalised religion, doing violence to its nature, and reinforced a static, reified conception of religious traditions rather than revealing their inner dynamic nature.[84]

His coeditor Tamimi links this perspective to present politics:

If secularism was justifiable in the West due to the nature of religion there, it is entirely unnecessary in the Muslim world. Muslims can progress and develop without having to create a wall between their religious values and livelihood. Secularisation of Muslim societies, though short-lived, has been possible only through force as wielded by despotic governments.[85]

What we find here is a mixture of a critique of specific authoritarian regimes in the Middle East that are labeled "secularist," a totalizing caricature of Western "secularism" ("wall between their religious values and livelihood"), and the presupposition of a "nature of religion," in which Christianity and Islam are placed on two different sides: one side "needs" secularism, the other does not. It is difficult not to read this as also being a statement on the political struggles for a more secular society in different parts of the "Muslim world." It is obvious that such depictions are far from being solely scholarly. They are closely linked with political assessments of the past and present Islamicate world.

In other contributions to the volume, this is extended to the critique of a "metaphysics of immanence," on which Western modernity is allegedly founded, and which, as "comprehensive secularism," will lead to a complete annihilation of men and their cultural achievements, as the Egyptian scholar and political activist Abdelwahab Elmessiri argues.[86] This worldview strongly resonates with Protestant and Catholic European narratives in the early twentieth century about Bolshevism and "Cultural Bolshevism" (*Kulturbolschewismus*) as worldviews of radical immanence and godlessness originating in the rejection of Christianity and "above all in fallen liberalism."[87] Liberalism, radical secularism, and a dramatic cultural crisis were seen as different sides of the same coin.[88] It sounds very similar when some of the authors in *Islam and Secularism in the Middle East* see "secularism" not only as a threat to Islam but as a totalitarian immanent project.[89] The critique of concrete political, and sometimes authoritarian, conditions[90] turns into a general and totalizing critique of secularism and finally into an apologetic of religion.[91]

This holistic notion of Islam is also used with regard to the Muslim *person*. Saba Mahmood,[92] for example, in her critique of a secular type of blasphemy, comes up with the notion of a Muslim habitus, a Muslim "being" that is hurt in toto by this critique, not only in certain regions of the self, meaning Muslims are unable to distance themselves from the damaging impact of blasphemy:[93]

> The notion of moral injury I am describing no doubt entails a sense of violation, but this violation emanates not from the judgement that the law has been transgressed but that one's being, grounded as it is in a relation of dependency with the Prophet, has been shaken. For many Muslims, the offence the cartoons committed was not against a moral interdiction … but against a structure of affect, a habitus, that feels wounded. This wound requires moral action, but the language of this wound is neither juridical nor that of street protest because it does not belong to an economy of blame, accountability, and reparations.[94]

I do not want to question whether the moral injury that Mahmood mentions was felt by Muslims when confronted with the caricatures of Prophet Mohammad. In addition, the concept of "habitus" is not per se problematic if it is open to empirical inquiry and not meant to stop this. Max Weber, by the way, also used this concept with regard to the "Protestant ethic."

As Andrew March has rightly pointed out, it is problematic however that Mahmood proclaims this reaction to be experienced almost generally by Muslims, as if there were no other reaction—discursive, strategic, distanced intellectual, or ideological—at their disposal. This perspective becomes especially problematic when the assumption of a specific Muslim vulnerability results in demands for political and legal change in European public spheres in order to prevent such injuries from happening.[95] The academic analyst is then at risk of becoming an ally of identitarian politics.[96]

Mahmood herself does not argue for a solution via blasphemy laws. She leaves the consequences of her problematization open. In the international debate on human rights, however, such consequences have been demanded. As Barbara Rox[97] shows in her constitutional legal study, *violations of religious feelings* mainly entered the juridical debate via the jurisdiction of the European Court of Human Rights, and similar notions of the defamation of religions entered the debate via resolutions of the United Nations Human Rights Council. The defamation of religion originally referred to the defamation of Islam, introduced as a proposal for a UN resolution by Pakistan in 1999 for the Organization of the Islamic Conference (now Organization of Islamic Cooperation).[98] It was then extended to cover the defamation of religions in general. The respective resolutions urge states to combat the "defamation of religion, especially the defamation of Islam 'as such'."⁹⁹ Rox argues that in this debate we can observe an extension from physical to psychological attacks and, finally, to the "intoxication of the climate." This intoxication also encompasses "the intentional creation of negative stereotypes about religions, their adherents and their *saints* [!] in the media, politics, and society, and the related intentional provocations."¹⁰⁰ Parallel to this, one observes the equation of racial discrimination with the defamation of religions and of racial hate with hatred of religions. This equation of race and religion is reminiscent of Saba Mahmood's argument that it morally hurts Muslims in the center of their being if the prophet is ridiculed.

It seems that the genealogical perspective on the Christian-secular divide, which started with an attempt at reflection and self-critique, inadvertently became the incantation of Muslim totality. Of course, the incantation of totality as a counter-narrative has been part and parcel of secularization and secularism from the beginning. Just remember Eichendorff's romantic lament over the loss of the unity of the Holy Roman Empire. Such laments are part of the social process, and, sociologically, we have to take them seriously. In the discussion on secularism and secularization, however, we can observe that these counter-narratives enter academic debate in a way that makes it difficult to differentiate academic from political statements.

While such research considers itself to be "critical," it ends in the same aporia as the criticized. Research that perceives questions of secularization, secularity, and secularism, *exclusively* as ideological constructs of the West, tends to overlook distinctions and differentiations on the "other side," since these are immediately interpreted as expressions of estrangement, power, and violence.

In the counter-narratives that relate to Islam, we find many identitarian references: totalizing concepts of Muslim habitus, of Homo Islamicus, or of a collective political Islamic identity. Sociologically, these references cannot be ignored. They are part of the history of anticolonial intellectual debates in the Islamicate world and especially of the Islamization of these debates in the 1960s and 1970s in response to the Left. Here we might mention Ali Shariati's reception of Frantz Fanon; the notion of "Westoxification" in the writings of Al-e Ahmad and Behrangi; Foucault's fascination with the emerging Iranian Revolution in 1978, which he interpreted as an expression of "political spirituality"—something that seemed to have been forgotten since the Renaissance and the "great crisis of Christianity."¹⁰¹ It seems that unifying concepts like political spirituality also resonated in the political reception of Islamic thought. As part of an intellectual history, these references to Islam are social facts that need to be interpreted. However, narratives of resistance are *objects* of sociological observation, irrespective of the distance the observer may be from them. Sometimes, however, it seems that they enter analysis through the back door, such that the analysis itself becomes entangled with a counter-narrative to secularization.

The Universality of Distinctions and Differentiations

In concluding this chapter, I cannot question the influence of Western powers and Western academia on the non-Western world, nor should I simply equate the history of "Christian" nations with the histories of countries in the Islamicate world and other parts of the world. Equally, I cannot deny the role of power in the majority-minority relations of Western societies. However, excluding the search for "indigenous" religion-related distinctions and differentiations from the analysis of non-Western societies is no solution, nor is ignoring interaction processes between Western thought and indigenous knowledge systems that are not simply violent impositions.

Questions that tend to be forgotten in the dynamics of anti-secularization narratives are the following:[102]

1. Were there any forms of distinction and differentiation related to the sphere of "religion" in non-Western, non-Christian contexts before or during the encounter with Western regimes and ideas, maybe without using the term "religion" but referring to something related? These may include practices, everyday divisions of labor, forms of distancing or of critique, concepts that divided spheres of activity and related institutions. Christoph Kleine has argued for premodern Japan that, due to the distinctions that had already been established in early Buddhism, it was relatively easy to later integrate Western concepts like religious and secular into the pre-existing categories. Distinctions were made between the law of the emperor and the law of the Buddha—*obo* and *buppo*—and the related responsibilities for the mundane and the supra-mundane, *laukika* und *lokottara*.[103]
2. With regard to early Islam, Andrew March has pointed out two different legal realms in pre-modern Islam—*siyasa* as governance and *fiqh* as religious law—and has thus argued against the notion of a paradigmatic

harmonious Muslim past.[104] Neguin Yavari[105] has shown that politics and religion in early Islam overlapped, but were certainly not undifferentiated, and were not in line with the idea of a religio-political fusion.[106] Armando Salvatore has hinted at the distinction between *adab* and *sharia* as different types of normative order, which he interprets as the "mother of distinctions" in Islam.[107] Even if such differentiations are not "the same" as the religious-secular distinction in the West, they nevertheless show that even in early modernity, religion was not "everywhere."[108]

3. What were the influential historical events that introduced new forms of distinction and differentiation, often through colonial or missionary encounters or through regimes that take Western models as their blueprint? This question is partly in line with Talal Asad's original perspective. Where did the introduction of distinctions and differentiations related to Western secular concepts occur? What did this imply for existing practices and debates? Which kinds of interaction took place?

4. Since distinctions and differentiations are not disconnected from societal problems and historical circumstances, one might ask: Which societal reference problem is the introduction of distinctions and differentiation (or their rejection) related to?[109]

5. What were the guiding ideas (if any) with which this introduction was legitimized or called into question? Did these guiding ideas serve as umbrella ideas under which coalitions could be established or were they only the "battle concepts" of small political sects?

6. Who were the relevant actors in particular conflicts? How did they position themselves? How were critics and supporters related to each other?

7. What kind of resistance and support confronted the introduction of differentiations? What were the patterns of legitimation used by critics and supporters? To which sources did they refer? Did they refer to previous ("indigenous") forms of distinction and differentiation, or did they refer to ideals or negative examples "out there?"

8. And finally: Can we identify certain trajectories or paths in the institutionalization of boundaries and in the ways of dealing with distinctions and differentiations? In what way does the course of events structure the collective memory? Are there later references to previous forms of differentiation, and in what way are they interconnected?

Ultimately, the aim is to re-complicate the analysis of historical events and trajectories, and not to consider them as already being understood by hinting at "the power and violence of the secular nation state" or the "apparatus of the secular modern." An interdisciplinary informed historical sociology should replace narratives that are primarily struggling to fight other narratives. However, it owes to genealogical accounts as they have been suggested by Robert Yelle, Michael Bergunder, and others, the awareness that the history of concepts and their consequences has to be taken into account, and that concepts cannot simply be taken as innocent and unchangeable tools for historical sociological analysis.

Notes

Introduction

1. Max Weber, "Science as a Vocation," in *From Max Weber: Essays in Sociology*, ed. Hans H. Gerth and C. Wright Mills (New York: Oxford University Press, 1946), 138–9; on rationalization, see Max Weber, *Gesammelte Aufsätze zur Religionssoziologie*, vol. 1 (Tübingen: J. C. B. Mohr, 1972 [1920]), 1, hereafter cited as *GARS* I. As a number of our contributors note, Weber first used the term "disenchantment" in 1913.
2. Wouter J. Hanegraaff, *New Age Religion and Western Culture: Esotericism in the Mirror of Secular Thought* (Leiden: Brill, 1996); Wouter J. Hanegraaff, "How Magic Survived the Disenchantment of the World," *Religion* 33, no. 4 (2003); Egil Asprem, *The Problem of Disenchantment: Scientific Naturalism and Esoteric Discourse, 1900–1939* (Leiden: Brill, 2014); Jason Ä. Josephson-Storm, *The Myth of Disenchantment: Magic, Modernity, and the Birth of the Human Sciences* (Chicago: University of Chicago Press, 2017).
3. Talal Asad, *Formations of the Secular: Christianity, Islam, Modernity* (Stanford: Stanford University Press, 2003), 13–14; Michael Saler, "Modernity and Enchantment: A Historiographic Review," *The American Historical Review* 111, no. 3 (2006): 695.
4. Jonathan I. Israel, *Radical Enlightenment: Philosophy and the Making of Modernity 1650–1750* (New York: Oxford University Press, 2001).
5. Max Weber, *The Protestant Ethic and the Spirit of Capitalism* (New York: Charles Scribner's Sons, 1958).
6. Friedrich Nietzsche, *The Genealogy of Morals* (New York: Boni and Liveright, 1918 [1887]); Georg Jellinek, *Die Erklärung der Menschen- und Bürgerrechte: Ein Beitrag zur modernen Verfassungsgeschichte* (Leipzig: Duncker & Humblot, 1895). Regarding Weber's connection to Jellinek, see the references in Robert Yelle's chapter in this volume.
7. See, for example, Friedrich Wilhelm Graf, "Max Weber und die protestantische Theologie seiner Zeit," *Zeitschrift für Religions- und Geistesgeschichte* 39, no. 2 (1987); Thomas Kroll, "Max Webers Idealtypus der charismatischen Herrschaft und die zeitgenössische Charisma-Debatte," in *Max Webers Herrschaftssoziologie: Studien zu Entstehung und Wirkung*, ed. Edith Hanke and Wolfgang J. Mommsen (Tübingen: Mohr Siebeck, 2001).

8   Hans Kippenberg, "Dialektik der Entzauberung: Säkularisierung aus der Perspektive von Webers Religionssystematik," in *Alte Begriffe—Neue Probleme: Max Webers Soziologie im Lichte aktueller Problemstellungen*, ed. Thomas Schwinn and Gert Albert (Tübingen: Mohr Siebeck, 2016), 90n7. In an earlier work, Kippenberg had excluded the possibility that Weber borrowed some of these ideas from theology. Hans G. Kippenberg, *Die Entdeckung der Religionsgeschichte: Religionswissenschaft und Moderne* (Munich: Beck, 1997), 218: "Daß die moderne Kultur ein Produkt der Religionsgeschichte gewesen sein soll: diese überraschende These Max Webers verdankte sich keiner besonderen Nähe, persönlich oder wissenschaftlich, zur Theologie."
9   See Robert Yelle's chapter in this volume.
10 Hans Blumenberg, *The Legitimacy of the Modern Age* (Cambridge, MA: MIT Press, 1985 [1976]).
11 See, for example, Sjoerd Griffioen, "Modernity and the Problem of Its Christian Past: The *Geistesgeschichten* of Blumenberg, Berger, and Gauchet," *History and Theory* 55, no. 2 (2016).
12 Weber, "Science as a Vocation"; *GARS* I, 93–5; Weber, *The Protestant Ethic*, 13, 104–5.
13 See especially Monika Wohlrab-Sahr's chapter in this volume.
14 See, for example, Asad, *Formations of the Secular*; Gil Anidjar, "Secularism," *Critical Inquiry* 33, no. 1 (2006); Karl Löwith, *Meaning in History: The Theological Implications of the Philosophy of History*, 2nd ed. (Chicago: University of Chicago Press, 1950); Reinhart Koselleck, "Zeitverkürzung und Beschleunigung: Eine Studie zur Säkularisation," in Reinhart Koselleck, *Zeitschichten: Studien zur Historik* (Frankfurt am Main: Suhrkamp, 2013).
15 Charles Taylor, *A Secular Age* (Cambridge, MA: Belknap Press of Harvard University Press, 2007), 22.
16 Jonathan Sheehan, "When Was Disenchantment? History and the Secular Age," in *Varieties of Secularism in a Secular Age*, ed. Michael Warner, Jonathan VanAntwerpen, and Craig Calhoun (Cambridge, MA: Harvard University Press, 2010), 238.
17 Peter Harrison, "Introduction: Narratives of Secularization," *Intellectual History Review* 27, no. 1 (2017): 2.
18 An example of such an account is Andrew Dickson White, *A History of the Warfare of Science with Theology in Christendom*, 2 vols. (London: Macmillan and Co., 1896).
19 José Casanova, *Public Religions in the Modern World* (Chicago: University of Chicago Press, 1994).
20 Josephson-Storm, *The Myth of Disenchantment*.
21 Asprem, *The Problem of Disenchantment*.

22 See, for example, Joshua Landy and Michael Saler, eds., *The Re-Enchantment of the World: Secular Magic in a Rational Age* (Stanford: Stanford University Press, 2009).
23 Israel, *Radical Enlightenment*.

Chapter 1

1 Richard Swedberg, *Max Weber Dictionary: Key Words and Central Concepts* (Stanford: Stanford University Press, 2005), 62–3.
2 The notion of "secularization" appears ten times in Weber's writings, "secularizing" seven times, both as legal terms indicating a change of legal status independent of when it happened in history or the modern age. "Disenchantment" appears eleven times. CD-Rom *Max Weber im Kontext: Gesammelte Schriften, Aufsätze & Vorträge* (Berlin: Karsten Worm, 1999).
3 Marcel Gauchet, *The Disenchantment of the World: A Political History of Religion* (Princeton, NJ: Princeton University Press, 1999); Zoltan Hidas, *Entzauberte Geschichte: Max Weber und die Krise des Historismus* (Frankfurt am Main: Lang, 2004); Hartmut Lehmann, *Die Entzauberung der Welt: Studien zu Themen von Max Weber* (Göttingen: Vandenhoeck & Ruprecht, 2009); Wolfgang Schluchter, *Die Entzauberung der Welt: Sechs Studien zu Max Weber* (Tübingen: Mohr Siebeck, 2009); Volkhard Krech, "Secularization, Re-Enchantment, or Something in between? Methodological Considerations and Empirical Observations Concerning a Controversial Historical Idea," in *Religion and Secularity: Transformations and Transfers of Religious Discourses in Europe and Asia*, ed. Marion Eggert and Lucian Hölscher (Leiden: Brill, 2013); Egil Asprem, *The Problem of Disenchantment: Scientific Naturalism and Esoteric Discourse, 1900–1939* (Leiden: Brill, 2014).
4 Max Weber, "Science as a Vocation," in *From Max Weber: Essays in Sociology*, ed. Hans H. Gerth and C. Wright Mills (Oxford: Oxford University Press, 1958), 139; Max Weber, *Wissenschaft als Beruf* (1917/1919)/*Politik als Beruf, Max Weber Gesamtausgabe* I/17, ed. Wolfgang J. Mommsen and Wolfgang Schluchter (Tübingen: Mohr Siebeck, 1992), 86–7. The *Max Weber Gesamtausgabe* is cited hereafter as "*MWG*."
5 Hans Joas, *Die Macht des Heiligen: Eine Alternative zur Geschichte der Entzauberung* (Berlin: Suhrkamp, 2017).
6 Ibid., 207, 257, 282, 406.
7 A smart dismantling of Joas's line of argument appears in Hartmann Tyrell, "Das Narrativ von der Entzauberung der Welt," *Soziopolis* (February 15, 2018).
8 Peter Ghosh, in his acclaimed book *Max Weber and "The Protestant Ethic": Twin Histories* (Oxford: Oxford University Press, 2014), avoids the translation of "Entzauberung" by "disenchantment" and replaces it by "demagification" (249).

9   José Casanova, *Public Religions in the Modern World* (Chicago: University of Chicago Press, 1994); Jürgen Habermas and Joseph Ratzinger, *Dialectics of Secularization: On Reason and Religion*, trans. Brian McNeil (San Francisco: Ignatius Press, 2006).
10 Schluchter, *Die Entzauberung der Welt*, 7–13, makes a distinction between disenchantment in the history of science and in the history of religions.
11 See Friedrich H. Tenbruck, "Abschied von Wirtschaft und Gesellschaft," *Zeitschrift für die gesamte Staatswissenschaft* 133, no. 4 (1977); Wolfgang Schluchter, "Max Webers Religionssoziologie: Eine werkgeschichtliche Rekonstruktion," in *Max Webers Sicht des antiken Christentums: Interpretation und Kritik*, ed. W. Schluchter (Frankfurt: Suhrkamp, 1985); Wolfgang Schluchter, "'Wirtschaft und Gesellschaft': Das Ende eines Mythos," in Wolfgang Schluchter, *Religion und Lebensführung*, vol. 2 (Frankfurt: Suhrkamp, 1988).
12 Marianne Weber's preface to the posthumous manuscripts in the first edition of *Wirtschaft und Gesellschaft* between pp. 180 and 181. Marianne Weber states in a footnote that an occasional remark made by Weber in reference to a Dr. Frank was "written about 1912–1913." Max Weber, *Wirtschaft und Gesellschaft*, vol. 2, *Religiöse Gemeinschaften, MWG I/22-2*, ed. Hans G. Kippenberg, Petra Schilm, and Jutta Niemeier (Tübingen: J.C.B. Mohr Siebeck, 2001), 315. On the beginnings of the study, see further Guenther Roth's Introduction in Max Weber, *Economy and Society: An Outline of Interpretive Sociology*, ed. Guenther Roth and Claus Wittich (Berkeley: University of California Press, 1978 [1921–1922]), lxvii–c.
13 See the survey of authors and literature that Weber quotes directly or indirectly in *Religiöse Gemeinschaften*, 505–7 and 75–83.
14 Johannes Winckelmann, *Max Webers Hauptwerk* (Tübingen: Mohr Siebeck, 1986), 151; see the explanation by the editors of the *MWG* in Max Weber, *Wirtschaft und Gesellschaft*, vol. 2, *Religiöse Gemeinschaften; MWG I/22-2*, VIII.
15 Karl Bücher, Joseph Schumpeter, and Fr. Freiherr von Wiese, *Wirtschaft und Wirtschaftswissenschaft: Grundriß der Sozialökonomik*, part 1 (Tübingen: J.C.B. Mohr Paul Siebeck, 1914), x–xiii, reprinted in Winckelmann, *Max Webers Hauptwerk*, in appendix 3, 168–71.
16 Max Weber, "Religiöse Gemeinschaften: Klassenbedingtheit der Religionen; Kulturreligionen und Wirtschaftsgesinnung," in Weber, *Economy and Society*, G. Roth's Introduction, lxv–lxvi. Max Weber's *Economy and Society*, ed. Keith Tribe (Cambridge, MA: Harvard University Press, 2019), is a new translation of the first, later and younger part.
17 Max Weber, *The Protestant Ethic and the "Spirit" of Capitalism (1905) and Other Writings*, ed. Peter Baehr and Gordon Wells (Harmondsworth: Penguin, 2002); Max Weber, "Antikritisches zum 'Geist' des Kapitalismus," *Archiv für Sozialwissenschaft und Sozialpolitik* 30 (1910); Max Weber's "Anticritical Last Word on *The Spirit of*

Capitalism," *American Journal of Sociology* 83, no. 5 (1978), translates only the second part.

18 Max Weber, *The Protestant Ethic and the Spirit of Capitalism*, trans. Talcott Parsons, with a new Introduction by Anthony Giddens (London and New York: Routledge, 1992), 284n119.

19 Marianne Weber, *Max Weber: Ein Lebensbild* (Tübingen: Mohr Siebeck, 1926), 346; Marianne Weber, *Max Weber: A Biography*, ed. Harry Zohn (New Brunswick and Oxford: Transaction Books, 1988), 331.

20 See the surveys of authors and literature that Weber quotes directly and indirectly in *Religiöse Gemeinschaften*, 505–7 and 75–83.

21 Max Weber, Letter to the publisher Paul Siebeck, June 22, 1915; Weber, *Religiöse Gemeinschaften*, 91. For Weber's systematic of religion, see Hans G. Kippenberg and Martin Riesebrodt, eds., *Max Webers "Religionssystematik"* (Tübingen: Mohr Siebeck, 2001).

22 Max Weber, *Die Wirtschaftsethik der Weltreligionen: Konfuzianismus und Taoismus* (1915–1920), ed. Helwig Schmidt-Glintzer, *MWG* I/19 (Tübingen: Mohr Siebeck, 1989), 83–4.

23 *MWG* I/19, 83–4.

24 Max Weber, *Gesammelte Aufsätze zur Religionssoziologie*, vol. 1 (Tübingen: J.C.B. Mohr, 1972 [1920]), 15: "Einiges zu ihrer Ausfüllung hoffe ich bei einer systematischen Bearbeitung der Religionssoziologie tun zu können." See Weber, *The Protestant Ethic*, trans. Parsons, 30.

25 Edward W. Said, *Orientalism* (New York: Vintage, 1979).

26 Georg Stauth, *Islam und westlicher Rationalismus: Der Beitrag des Orientalismus zur Entstehung der Soziologie* (Frankfurt: Campus, 1993), 11.

27 Hermann Oldenberg, "Die indische Religion," in *Die orientalischen Religionen*, part 1.3.1 of *Die Kultur der Gegenwart: Ihre Entwicklung und ihre Ziele*, ed. Paul Hinneberg (Berlin and Leipzig: B. G. Teubner, 1906).

28 Hermann Siebeck, *Lehrbuch der Religionsphilosophie* (Freiburg and Leipzig: Mohr Siebeck, 1893), 49.

29 Edvard Lehmann, "Erscheinungswelt der Religion: Phänomenologie der Religion," in *RGG*, vol. 2 (1910), cols. 497–8 (translation HGK).

30 Hans G. Kippenberg, "The Study of Religions in the Twentieth Century," in *The Future of the Study of Religion: Proceedings of Congress 2000*, ed. Slavica Jakelić and Lori Pearson (Leiden: Brill, 2004), 58–63.

31 Max Weber, "Über einige Kategorien der verstehenden Soziologie (1913)," in *Gesammelte Aufsätze zur Wissenschaftslehre*, ed. Johannes Winckelmann (Tübingen: Mohr Siebeck, 1988); trans. Edith E. Graber, "Categories of Interpretive Sociology (1913)," *The Sociological Quarterly* 22, no. 2 (1981).

32 Weber, "Categories of Interpretive Sociology," 155.

33 Weber, *Economy and Society*, 403; Weber, *Religiöse Gemeinschaften*, 127.

34 Weber, *Economy and Society*, 401; Weber, *Religiöse Gemeinschaften*, 124. Weber here relied on Erwin Rohde, *Psyche: Seelencult und Unsterblichkeitsglaube der Griechen* (Freiburg im Breisgau: Mohr, 1894), behind whom we discern the shadow of Friedrich Nietzsche.
35 Weber, *Economy and Society*, 411; Weber, *Religiöse Gemeinschaften*, 140.
36 Weber, *Economy and Society*, 430; Weber, *Religiöse Gemeinschaften*, 165.
37 Weber, *Economy and Society*, 431; Weber, *Religiöse Gemeinschaften*, 167.
38 Weber, *Economy and Society*, 447–50; Weber, *Religiöse Gemeinschaften*, 189–90.
39 Weber, "Categories of Interpretive Sociology," 155.
40 Weber, *Economy and Society*, 447–9; Weber, *Religiöse Gemeinschaften*, 189–90.
41 Weber, *Economy and Society*, 499; Weber, *Religiöse Gemeinschaften*, 265.
42 The notion of religiosity (*Religiösität*) appears 435 times in Weber's writings, much more frequently than the notion of religion, which occurs 293 times. CD-Rom *Max Weber im Kontext*.
43 Gerth and Mills, *From Max Weber*, 290, 282; MWG I/19, 103.
44 Gerth and Mills, *From Max Weber*, 281; MWG I/19, 102–3.
45 MWG I/19, 450.
46 Hans Joas regards such statements as "dangerous notions": Hans Joas, "Gefährliche Prozessbegriffe: Eine Warnung vor der Rede von Differenzierung, Rationalisierung und Modernisierung," in *Umstrittene Säkularisierung: Soziologische und Historische Analysen zur Differenzierung von Religion und Politik*, ed. Karl Gabriel, Christel Gärtner, and Detlef Pollack (Berlin: Berlin University Press, 2012), 610; and repeatedly in Joas, *Die Macht des Heiligen*, e.g., 364. Dirk Käsler has pointed out that Weber who strictly denied any laws in human history systematized earlier findings of his inquiries by such formulations. Dirk Käsler, "Max Weber," in *Klassiker der Soziologie*, ed. Dirk Käsler, vol. 1 (Munich: C.H. Beck, 2006), 199–200.
47 Volkhard Krech, "Magischer Orient und rationaler Okzident? Eine metaphorologische Notiz zum 'Zaubergarten,' 'stahlharten Gehäuse' und zur 'Welt als Text,'" *Bochumer Jahrbuch zur Ostasienforschung* 38 (2015).
48 MWG I/19, 450–1. The theological prehistory of his ideas (cessation of magic, miracles, charismata) is the subject of "The Disenchantment of Charisma: The Theological Origins of Secular Polity," chap. 2 in Robert A. Yelle, *Sovereignty and the Sacred: Secularism and the Political Economy of Religion* (Chicago and London: University of Chicago Press, 2019).
49 Stefan Breuer, "Magie, Zauber, Entzauberung," in *Max Webers "Religionssystematik,"* ed. Hans G. Kippenberg and Martin Riesebrodt (Tübingen: Mohr Siebeck, 2001).
50 Weber, *Economy and Society*, 576; MWG I/22-2, 367: "Die Erlösungsreligiosität bedeutet, je systematischer und 'gesinnungsethisch' verinnerlichter sie geartet ist, eine desto tiefere Spannung gegenüber den Realitäten der Welt."

51 Swedberg, *Max Weber Dictionary*, 90: "According to Guenther Roth, 'ethic of responsibility' is a literal rendering of *Verantwortungsethik*, but there is no equally easy translation for *Gesinnungsethik* ... Alternatives to the usual translation *Gesinnungsethik* as 'ethic of ultimate ends' include 'ethic of conviction'... 'ethic of single-minded conviction' and 'ethic of principled conviction.'"

52 It is a misunderstanding that an ethic of responsibility is an ethic without conviction. Wolfgang Schluchter has vigorously shown that Weber does not regard the ethics of responsibility and the ethics of conviction as related to different values. There can be *no* ethical action *without* a conviction. Consequently, an ethics of responsibility can exist only where belief in the validity of *particular* absolute ethical values on which conviction about an action is based is already present. Wolfgang Schluchter, "Gesinnungsethik und Verantwortungsethik: Probleme einer Unterscheidung," in *Religion und Lebensführung*, vol. 1, *Studien zu Max Webers Kultur- und Werttheorie* (Frankfurt am Main: Suhrkamp, 1988), 198.

53 Gerth and Mills, *From Max Weber*, 323–59.

54 Marianne Weber, *A Biography*, 333 (translation with emendations by HGK); Weber, *Ein Lebensbild*, 348.

55 Gerth and Mills, *From Max Weber*, 345, 347; Weber, *Die Wirtschaftsethik der Weltreligionen*, MWG I/19, 504, 507.

56 Gerth and Mills, *From Max Weber*, 341, Weber, *Die Wirtschaftsethik der Weltreligionen*, MWG I/19, 500: "Trägerin magischer Wirkungen."

57 For example, Morris Berman, *The Reenchantment of the World* (Ithaca, NY: Cornell University Press, 1981).

58 Introduction to "The Economic Ethic of the World Religions," in Gerth and Mills, *From Max Weber*, 278; MWG I/19, 83–127.

59 Weber, *Economy and Society*, 544–5; Weber, *Religiöse Gemeinschaften*, 324.

60 Gerth and Mills, *From Max Weber*, 357; Weber, "Zwischenbetrachtung," in MWG I/19, 519–20.

61 Weber, *Economy and Society*, 399–400; "Religiöse Gemeinschaften," MWG I-22-2, 121.

62 Weber, *The Protestant Ethic*, trans. Parsons, 8–9; Weber, *Die protestantische Ethik und der Geist des Kapitalismus*, vollständige Ausgabe, ed. Dirk Käsler (Munich: C.H. Beck, 2013), 74.

63 Marianne Weber, *A Biography*, 333 (translation with emendations by HGK); Weber, *Ein Lebensbild*, 348–9.

64 Schluchter, *Die Entzauberung der Welt*, 2–3.

65 Ibid., 13 (translation HGK).

66 Jason Ā. Josephson-Storm, in a conclusion titled "Disenchantment Disenchanted" to a strong and well-argued chapter "Max Weber and 'The World of Enchantment'" in his book *The Myth of Disenchantment: Magic, Modernity, and the Birth of the Human Sciences* (Chicago: University of Chicago Press, 2017), 300.

67   Robert A. Yelle, *The Language of Disenchantment: Protestant Literalism and Colonial Discourse in British India* (New York: Oxford University Press, 2013).
68   This loss of meaning by natural sciences is studied by Lorraine Daston, *Wunder, Beweise, Tatsachen* (Frankfurt: Fischer, 2001). However, the belief in signs and wonders remains unbroken also in modern society, as Thomas Kern makes explicit in *Zeichen und Wunder: Enthusiastische Glaubensformen in der modernen Gesellschaft* (Frankfurt: Lang, 1997).
69   Schluchter, *Die Entzauberung der Welt*, 11.
70   Gerth and Mills, *From Max Weber*, 281; *MWG* I/19, 102.
71   Weber, *Economy and Society*, 403; Weber, *Religiöse Gemeinschaften*, 127.
72   These are the first lines of the introduction to the volume edited by Craig Calhoun, Mark Juergensmeyer, and Jonathan VanAntwerpen, *Rethinking Secularism* (Oxford: Oxford University Press, 2011).
73   Charles Taylor, *A Secular Age* (Cambridge, MA: Harvard University Press, 2007), part 4.
74   Ibid., 593.
75   Ibid., 553.
76   Weber, *Economy and Society*, 506; Weber, *Religiöse Gemeinschaften*, 273.
77   Max Weber, *Critique of Stammler*, trans. Guy Oakes (New York: Free Press, 1977), 110–11; Max Weber, "R. Stammlers 'Überwindung' der materialistischen Geschichtsauffassung" (1907), in *Gesammelte Aufsätze zur Wissenschaftslehre*, ed. Johannes Winckelmann (Tübingen: Mohr Siebeck, 1988), 332–3. The English translation is debatable; it ignores the active role of the investigator. The original German reads: "'Natur' wird ein Vorgang, wenn wir bei ihm nach einem 'Sinn' nicht fragen." Also, the phrase "cannot raise the question" is not quite exactly what Weber says: "der 'Sinn,' der einem Vorgang oder Objekt zugesprochen, 'in ihm gefunden werden kann.'"
78   Kocku von Stuckrad, *The Scientification of Religion: An Historical Study of Discursive Change, 1800–2000* (Berlin: De Gruyter, 2014).
79   Asprem, *The Problem of Disenchantment* (Leiden: Brill, 2014).
80   Ibid., 6.
81   Von Stuckrad, *The Scientification of Religion*.
82   Asprem, *The Problem of Disenchantment*, 58–60.
83   Ibid., 424–5.
84   Ibid., 279–86 and 421–5; see also Wouter J. Hanegraaff, *Esotericism and the Academy: Rejected Knowledge in Western Culture* (Cambridge: Cambridge University Press, 2012).
85   Asprem's book has triggered a debate in the *Journal of Religion in Europe* 8, no. 3–4 (2015). My own contribution to this debate, "Tracing Modern Roots of Esotericism: Discussing the Limits of Disenchantment," focused on Weber's dialectic and its consequences (281–7); Asprem's answer, "The Disenchantment

of Problems: Musings on a Cognitive Turn in Intellectual History," 304–19, added new key issues regarding the disenchantment of nature.

86   Kocku von Stuckrad, *Western Esotericism: A Brief History of Secret Knowledge* (London and Oakville: Equinox, 2005), 3–4.
87   Ibid.
88   Weber, *Critique of Stammler,* 110–11; Weber, "R. Stammlers 'Überwindung,'" 332–3.
89   For Weber's theory of history and his rejection of historicism, with its assumption of an objective social progress, see Thomas Burger, "Deutsche Geschichtstheorie und Webersche Soziologie," in *Max Webers Wissenschaftslehre: Interpretation und Kritik*, ed. Gerhard Wagner and Heinz Zipprian (Frankfurt: Suhrkamp, 1994); Hidas, *Entzauberte Geschichte,* 78–97.
90   Lucian Hölscher, *Weltgericht oder Revolution: Protestantische und sozialistische Zukunftsvorstellungen im deutschen Kaiserreich* (Stuttgart: Klett, 1989), 32–4; Lucian Hölscher, *Die Entdeckung der Zukunft* (Frankfurt am Main: Fischer, 1999).
91   Karl Löwith, *Weltgeschichte und Heilsgeschehen: Die theologischen Voraussetzungen der Geschichtsphilosophie* (Stuttgart and Heidelberg: Metzler, 1953).
92   Hans Blumenberg, *Die Legitimität der Neuzeit* (Frankfurt: Suhrkamp, 1966), 225.
93   Malcolm Bull revisited the debate in 1995 and concluded that both concepts developed together by challenging each other. Malcom Bull, ed., *Apocalypse Theory and the Ends of the World* (Oxford: Oxford University Press, 1995), 1–17.
94   Martin E. Marty and R. Scott Appleby, eds., *The Fundamentalism Project*, 5 vols. (Chicago: University of Chicago Press, 1991–1995).
95   Martin E. Marty, "Fundamentalism as a Social Phenomenon," *Bulletin of the American Academy of Arts and Sciences* 42, no. 2 (1988); Bruce Lawrence, *Defenders of God: The Fundamentalist Revolt against the Modern Age* (San Francisco: Harper & Row, 1989); Martin Riesebrodt, *Fundamentalismus als patriarchalische Protestbewegung* (Tübingen: Mohr Siebeck, 1990); Eng. trans., *Pious Passion: The Emergence of Modern Fundamentalism in the United States and Iran*, trans. Don Reneau (Berkeley: University of California Press, 1993).
96   Lawrence, *Defenders of God*, 27.
97   Ernest R. Sandeen, *The Roots of Fundamentalism: British and American Millenarianism 1800–1930* (Chicago: University of Chicago Press, 2008).
98   See, for example, David S. Katz and Richard H. Popkin, *Messianic Revolution: Radical Religious Politics to the End of the Second Millennium* (New York: Hill and Wang, 1998).
99   Weber, *Economy and Society,* 580; *MWG* I/22-2: 372.
100 Rainer M. Lepsius, "Eigenart und Potenzial des Weber-Paradigmas," in *Das Weber-Paradigma: Studien zur Weiterentwicklung von Max Webers Forschungsprogramm*, ed. Gert Albert, Agathe Bienfait, Steffen Sigmund, and Claus Wendt (Tübingen: Mohr Siebeck, 2002).

101 *MWG* I/22-1, 122: "Nachbarschaft bedeutet praktisch… Aufeinander angewiesen sein in der Not. Der Nachbar ist der typische Nothelfer, und 'Nachbarschaft' daher Trägerin der 'Brüderlichkeit' in einem … unpathetischen vorwiegend wirtschaftsethischen Sinn des Wortes."
102 *MWG* I/22-1, 121.
103 Weber, *Economy and Society*, 452; for the difficulty in translating Weber's notion of "Gemeinschaft" with the English "community" or "congregation," see Swedberg, *Max Weber Dictionary*, 44–5.
104 Gerth and Mills, *From Max Weber*, 330; *MWG* I/19, 488: "Der Kosmos der modernen rationalen kapitalistischen Wirtschaft wurde daher, je mehr er seinen immanenten Eigengesetzlichkeiten folgte, desto unzugänglicher jeglicher denkbaren Beziehung zu einer religiösen Brüderlichkeitsethik."
105 *MWG* I/22-2, 373-6, makes it clear that the concept of "Liebeskommunismus" has its origin with Ernst Troeltsch.
106 Weber, *Economy and Society*, 576: "The more a religion of salvation has been systematized and internalized in the direction of an 'ethic of ultimate ends' [*Gesinnungsethik*], the greater becomes its tension in relation to the world"; *MWG* I/22-2, 367: "Die Erlösungsreligiosität bedeutet, je systematischer und, 'gesinnungsethisch' verinnerlichter sie geartet ist, eine desto tiefere Spannung gegenüber den Realitäten der Welt."
107 Gerth and Mills, *From Max Weber*, 329–30; Weber, *Die Wirtschaftsethik der Weltreligionen*, 486–7.
108 *MWG* I/19, 48.
109 *MWG* I/19, 487.
110 Donald E. Miller and Tetsunao Yamamori, *Global Pentecostalism: The New Face of Christian Social Engagement* (Berkeley: University of California Press, 2007).
111 Habermas and Ratzinger, *Dialectics of Secularization: On Reason and Religion*, 51.
112 Ibid., 41.
113 Ibid., 19.
114 Casanova, *Public Religions*, 6, 57–8.
115 See Hans G. Kippenberg, "Religionswissenschaft," in *Handbuch Moderneforschung*, ed. Friedrich Jäger, Wolfgang Knöbl, and Ute Schneider (Stuttgart: Metzler, 2015).

Chapter 2

1 Peter Ghosh, *Max Weber and "The Protestant Ethic": Twin Histories* (Oxford: Oxford University Press, 2014), 259, 264.
2 This quote also appears in Jason Ä. Josephson-Storm, *The Myth of Disenchantment: Magic, Modernity and the Birth of the Human Sciences* (Chicago: University of Chicago Press, 2017), 271.

3   Translated by JJ-S.
4   See Josephson-Storm, *The Myth of Disenchantment*, 211–12.
5   Raymond Furness, *Zarathustra's Children: A Study of a Lost Generation of German Writers* (Rochester, NY: Camden House, 2000), 77.
6   Reventlow discusses Delius (a.k.a. Schuler) and his conception of psychometry (*Psychometer*) basically meaning that soul-substances (*Seelensubstanzen*) cling to objects across time waiting to be unlocked. Franziska Reventlow, *Herrn Dames Aufzeichnungen, oder, Begebenheiten aus einem merkwürdigen Stadtteil* (Munich: Langen, 1913), 68–9.
7   Alfred Schuler, *Alfred Schuler: Fragmente und Vorträge aus dem Nachlass*, ed. Ludwig Klages (Leipzig: Barth, 1940), 159.
8   At least, based on a number of letters that reveal a correspondence between the two men. See Gustav Willibald Freytag, "Rainer Maria Rilkes Briefe an Alfred Schuler," *Jahrbuch der deutschen Schillergesellschaft* 4 (1960).
9   Josephson-Storm, *The Myth of Disenchantment*, 210.
10 Reventlow, *Herrn Dames Aufzeichnungen*, 142–3. See Josephson-Storm, *The Myth of Disenchantment*, 212.
11 Here the Kosmikers were likely evoking Johann Jakob Bachofen's *Das Mutterrecht* (1861), which we know they read and shared among each other.
12 Josephson-Storm, *The Myth of Disenchantment*, 275.
13 *Max Weber Gesamtausgabe* (Tübingen: Mohr Siebeck, 1984–2012; hereafter cited as *MWG*). For Wolfskehl, see *MWG*, II/8, 115; Friedrich Voit, *Karl Wolfskehl: Leben und Werk im Exil* (Göttingen: Wallstein-Verlag, 2005), 48–9.
14 Josephson-Storm, *The Myth of Disenchantment*, 287–96.
15 *MWG*, II/6, 560. See also Thomas Karlauf, *Stefan George: Die Entdeckung des Charisma* (Munich: Blessing, 2007), 412; Thomas Kroll, "Max Webers Idealtypus der charismatischen Herrschaft und die zeitgenössische Charisma-Debatte," in *Max Webers Herrschaftssoziologie: Studien zu Entstehung und Wirkung*, ed. Edith Hanke and Wolfgang Mommsen (Tübingen: Mohr Siebeck, 2001).
16 Ludwig Klages, *Rhythmen und Runen* (Leipzig: Barth, 1944), 312. The footnote on that page explains that what is at stake in the rejection of identity is the intelligibility of reality, not reality as such, because there is a disconnect between thinking and the flow of reality. Hence my interpolation of "flux" above.
17 First quote: Ludwig Klages, *The Biocentric Worldview: Selected Essays and Poems of Ludwig Klages*, trans. Joseph Pryce (London: Arktos Media, 2013), 32; Ludwig Klages, *Sämtliche Werke*, ed. Ernst Frauchiger (Bonn: H. Bouvier, 1964–1992) 3, 618 (hereafter *KSW*). Second quote: Klages, *The Biocentric Worldview*, 42; *KSW*, 3, 628.
18 Klages, *The Biocentric Worldview*, 42; *KSW*, 3, 628.
19 Klages, *The Biocentric Worldview*, 32; *KSW*, 3, 619.

20 *KSW*, 3, 479: "Der Wille zur verstandesmäßigen Wahrheit ist der Wille zur Entwirklichung der Welt."
21 *KSW*, 1, 2. See also *KSW*, 4, 699.
22 *KSW*, 6, 652.
23 Martin Green, *The Von Richthofen Sisters* (New York: Basic Books, 1974), 235.
24 Common acquaintances of Max Weber and Ludwig Klages included Else Jaffe, Reventlow, and the ex-fellow Kosmikers Stefan George and Karl Wolfskehl. *MWG*, II/8, 660.
25 Green, *The Von Richthofen Sisters*, 352.
26 *KSW*, 3, 482.
27 For example, Max Weber, *The Protestant Ethic and the Spirit of Capitalism* (New York: Routledge, 1992), 130n10.
28 *MWG*, I, 530.
29 For newspaper evidence, see Josephson-Storm, *The Myth of Disenchantment*, 298.
30 David Moore, cited in ibid., 25.
31 Ina Schmied-Knittel, "Außergewöhnliche Erfahrungen: Repräsentative Studien und aktuelle Befunde," *Zeitschrift für Anomalistik* 8, no. 1–3 (2008): 107. In their analysis of this data, the German sociologists Schmied-Knittel and Schetsche also reject the idea of contemporary Germany as disenchanted, emphasizing their larger conclusion that "postmodern people" often have magical experiences. Ina Schmied-Knittel and Michael T. Schetsche, "Everyday Miracles: Results of a Representative Survey in Germany," *European Journal of Parapsychology* 20, no. 1 (2005): 3–4. See also Schmied-Knittel and Schetsche, "Psi-Report Deutschland: Eine repräsentative Bevölkerungsumfrage zu außergewöhnlichen Erfahrungen," in *Alltägliche Wunder: Erfahrungen mit dem Übersinnlichen: Wissenschaftliche Befunde*, ed. Eberhard Bauer and Michael Schetsche (Würzburg: Ergon, 2003).
32 The conference at which this paper was presented was held at LMU Munich.
33 Johannes Winckelmann, "Die Herkunft von Max Webers Entzauberungs-Konzeption," *Kölner Zeitschrift für Soziologie und Sozialpsychologie* 32, no. 1 (1980).
34 Max Weber, *Gesammelte Aufsätze zur Religionssoziologie* (Tübingen: Mohr, 1922), 409.
35 *MWG*, I/19, 175.
36 *MWG*, I/19, 483–4.
37 I agree with Stefan Breuer that *Magie* and *Zauberei* are functionally synonymous in Weber's writings. Stefan Breuer, "Magie, Zauber, Entzauberung," in *Max Webers "Religionssystematik,"* ed. Hans G. Kippenberg and Martin Riesebrodt (Tübingen: Mohr Siebeck, 2001).
38 To be fair, in a late lecture, Weber remarked: "Prophecies have released the world from magic and in so doing created the basis for [occidental] modern science and

technology, and capitalism." Max Weber, *General Economic History* (New York: Collier Books, 1961), 205.

39 See *MWG*, I/19, 403–7. Although, to be fair, Weber especially associated the coincidence of magic and science/technology with China and sometimes suggested that it held Asia back from the same kind of rationalization that unfolded in the West.

40 *MWG*, I/22-2, 121–2.

41 *MWG*, I/22-2, 122.

42 Ibid.

43 *MWG*, I/22-2, 122–3.

44 Max Weber, *The Theory of Social and Economic Organizations* (New York: Oxford University Press, 1947), 360.

45 Weber's notion of charisma seems to have been intended to evoke the notion of charismata or divine gifts. See John Potts, *A History of Charisma* (New York: Palgrave, 2009), esp. 35–6.

46 Ibid., 361.

47 For an alternate account of how to repurpose Weber's notion of charismatic authority, see Robert A. Yelle, *Sovereignty and the Sacred: Secularism and the Political Economy of Religion* (Chicago: University of Chicago Press, 2019), 37–73.

48 *MWG*, I/22-2, 157–8.

49 *MWG*, I/19, 407.

50 Weber, *Protestant Ethic*, 61. I have restored "the disenchantment of the world" but otherwise reproduced Parsons's translation.

51 For example, *MWG*, I/19, 349, 450.

52 Weber, *Protestant Ethic*, 57.

53 Max Weber, *Wirtschaft und Gesellschaft* (Tübingen: Mohr, 1922), 237. Trans. JJ-S.

54 For example, Weber argues that Jesus was "above all a magician." *MWG*, I/22-2, 441.

55 For a solid appraisal of the orthodox Weberian concept of disenchantment and its obvious flaws, see Richard Jenkins, "Disenchantment, Enchantment and Re-enchantment: Max Weber at the Millennium," *Max Weber Studies* 1, no. 1 (2000).

56 Weber, *Wirtschaft und Gesellschaft*, 449. The passage literally states "functionally irrational." However, I read it with the same meaning as the "Science as a Vocation" lecture, namely, focused on unpredictability.

57 I list the first four of these in Josephson-Storm, *The Myth of Disenchantment*, 286. There is also a similar list in Egil Asprem, *The Problem of Disenchantment: Scientific Naturalism and Esoteric Discourse, 1900–1939* (Boston: Brill, 2014), 32.

58 Weber differentiates them in "The Religious Rejections of the World and Their Directions" (the *Zwischenbetrachtung* or "Intermediate Reflection"). See *MWG*, I/19.

59 Here I am largely following Stephen Kalberg, "Max Weber's Types of Rationality: Cornerstones for the Analysis of Rationalization Processes in History," *American Journal of Sociology* 85, no. 5 (1980).
60 Josephson-Storm, *The Myth of Disenchantment*, 272–4.
61 *MWG*, I/19, 171.
62 Weber's main source for this seems to have been the work of the Dutch sinologist Jan Jakob Maria de Groot, especially de Groot, *Universismus: Die Grundlagen der Religion und Ethik, des Staatswesens und der Wissenschaft Chinas*. For more recent scholarship on the history of Chinese astrology, see Christopher Cullen, *Heavenly Numbers: Astronomy and Authority in Early Imperial China* (New York: Oxford University Press, 2017).
63 Again, Weber's main source seems to have been de Groot.
64 Western music was one aspect but not the totality of the aesthetic sphere for Weber.
65 For journalistic accounts, see "U.S. Faces Growing Problems in Regulating Fortune Tellers," *BBC News* (September 28, 2010); Nick Squires, "Boom Time for Fortune-Tellers and Tarot Card Readers in Italy as Economic Crisis Bites," *Telegraph* (October 2, 2017); Julie Beck, "The New Age of Astrology," *The Atlantic* (January 16, 2018). See also William Little, "Britain's Psychic Turn," *The Guardian* (May 19, 2009), which asserts that more than half of the population of the UK believes in psychic powers.
66 See Charles McCrary, "Fortune Telling and American Religious Freedom," *Religion and American Culture* 28, no. 2 (2018). For Germany and the Netherlands, see Willem De Blécourt and Cornelie Usborne, "Women's Medicine, Women's Culture: Abortion and Fortune-Telling in Early Twentieth-Century Germany and the Netherlands," *Medical History* 43, no. 3 (1999). See also Faith Wigzell, *Reading Russian Fortunes: Print Culture, Gender and Divination in Russia from 1765* (Cambridge: Cambridge University Press, 2015).

Chapter 3

1 Max Weber, "Science as a Vocation," in *From Max Weber: Essays in Sociology*, ed. Hans H. Gerth and C. Wright Mills (London: Routledge and Kegan Paul, 1948), 137.
2 There is now, of course, an enormous literature on the value-ladenness of science—including normative critiques and reformulations—following the waves of historical, sociological, anthropological, philosophical, and psychological studies of the place of science and technology in contemporary societies that have appeared for more than half a century. For a fairly recent overview of positions on science and value from philosophically informed perspectives, see, for example, the

contributions to Harold Kincaid, John Dupré, and Alison Wylie, eds., *Value-Free Science? Ideals and Illusions* (Oxford: Oxford University Press, 2007). On the fact/value dichotomy specifically—so central to much of Weber's argument regarding science's role in a process of disenchantment—see Hilary Putnam, *The Collapse of the Fact/Value Dichotomy and Other Essays* (Cambridge, MA: Harvard University Press, 2002). See also Egil Asprem, *The Problem of Disenchantment. Scientific Naturalism and Esoteric Discourse 1900–1939* (Leiden and Boston: Brill, 2014), 32–40.

3. The conference at which this paper was presented was held at LMU Munich in October 2017, around the centenary of Weber's lecture, which also happened in Munich.
4. Weber, "Science as a Vocation," 142.
5. Ibid.
6. Asprem, *The Problem of Disenchantment*, 91–286; see also Peter J. Bowler, *Reconciling Science and Religion: The Debate in Early Twentieth-Century Britain* (Chicago: University of Chicago Press, 2001).
7. For an overview of its first hundred years (1887–1987), see Stanley L. Jaki, *Lord Gifford and His Lectures: A Centenary Retrospect* (Edinburgh: Scottish Academic Press, 1987).
8. See the recent doctoral dissertation by Sarah Gail Sussman, *Pragmatic Enchantment: William James, Psychical Research, and the Humanities in the American Research University, 1890–1910* (PhD diss., Faculty of the Graduate School, University of Texas at Austin, 2017). For a fully developed version of this argument as it pertains to the humanities rather than the natural sciences, see Jason Ā. Josephson-Storm, *The Myth of Disenchantment: Magic, Modernity, and the Birth of the Human Sciences* (Chicago and London: University of Chicago Press, 2017).
9. Asprem, *The Problem of Disenchantment*, 128–41.
10. Josephson-Storm, *The Myth of Disenchantment*.
11. Egil Asprem, "Dialectics of Darkness," *Inference: Review of Science* 4, no. 2 (2018).
12. Asprem, *The Problem of Disenchantment*, 32–9; see also Egil Asprem, "The Disenchantment of Problems: Musings on a Cognitive Turn in Intellectual History," *Journal of Religion in Europe* 8, no. 3–4 (2015).
13. John Patrick Diggins, *Thorstein Veblen: Theorist of the Leisure Class* (Princeton, NJ: Princeton University Press, 1999), 16.
14. Thorstein Veblen, *The Theory of the Leisure Class* (New York: Macmillan, 1899).
15. Max Weber, *The Protestant Ethic and the Spirit of Capitalism* (New York: Charles Scribner's Sons, 1958).
16. Pierre Bourdieu, *Distinction: A Social Critique of the Judgment of Taste* (Cambridge, MA: Harvard University Press, 1984).
17. Diggins, *Thorstein Veblen*, 170. The first draft of the manuscript was written as early as 1900, immediately following *The Theory of the Leisure Class*.

18 Veblen, *The Theory of the Leisure Class*, 256.
19 Most notably in his later works, such as *The Engineers and the Price System* (New York: B.W. Huebsch, 1921) and *Absentee Ownership and Business Enterprise in Recent Times: The Case of America* (New York: B.W. Huebsch, 1923).
20 See Pierre Bourdieu, "The Forms of Capital," in *Handbook of Theory and Research for the Sociology of Education*, ed. John G. Richardson (New York: Greenwood Press, 1986).
21 See, for example, Thomas Frank, *The Conquest of Cool: Business Culture, Counterculture, and the Rise of Hip Consumerism* (Chicago: University of Chicago Press, 1997).
22 For one example of socialization into an "alternative" religious identity (Satanism) through consumption, see Asbjørn Dyrendal, "Devillish Consumption: Popular Culture in Satanic Socialization," *Numen* 55, no. 1 (2008).
23 According to Statista, BAs of engineering science could expect a starting salary of $66,097 in 2017, while a freshly minted humanities BA could expect $48,733. These fields also represent the top and the bottom of the scale.
24 William E. Akin, *Technocracy and the American Dream: The Technocrat Movement, 1900–1941* (Berkeley: University of California Press, 1977).
25 Paul Forman, "Weimar Culture, Causality, and Quantum Theory: Adaptation by German Physicists and Mathematicians to a Hostile Environment," *Historical Studies in the Physical Sciences* 3 (1971).
26 Citations of Richard von Mises's introductory lecture at the Technische Hochschule in Dreseden in 1920, quoted by Forman, "Weimar Culture, Causality, and Quantum Theory," 49.
27 Arnold Sommerfeld, 1925 address to the Bavarian Academy of Sciences; see Forman, "Weimar Culture, Causality, and Quantum Theory," 50.
28 Werner Heisenberg, "The Physical Content of Quantum Kinematics and Mechanics," in *Quantum Theory and Measurement*, ed. and trans. John Archibald Wheeler and Wojchiech Hubert Zurek (Princeton, NJ: Princeton University Press, 1983).
29 See, for example, Niels Bohr, *Atomic Physics and Human Knowledge* (New York: John Wiley & Sons, 1958).
30 For example, Pascual Jordan, *Die Physik und das Geheimnis des organischen Lebens* (Braunschweig: Friedr. Vieweg, 1941); Wolfgang Pauli, "Der Einfluss archetypischer Vorstellungen auf die Bildung naturwissenschaftlicher Theorien bei Kepler," in *Naturerklärung und Psyche*, ed. Carl Gustav Jung and Wolfgang Pauli (Zürich: Rascher Verlag, 1952).
31 For an extensive discussion, see Asprem, *The Problem of Disenchantment*, 141–9, 259–78. See also Wouter J. Hanegraaff, *New Age Religion and Western Culture: Esotericism in the Mirror of Secular Thought* (Albany, NY: SUNY Press, 1998), 62–76.

32 See especially Peter J. Bowler, *Science for All: The Popularization of Science in Early Twentieth-Century Britain* (Chicago: University of Chicago Press, 2009); see also for the German context Andreas W. Daum, *Wissenschaftspopularisierung im 19. Jahrhundert: Bürgerliche Kultur, naturwissenschaftliche Bildung und die deutsche Öffentlichkeit 1848–1914*, 2nd ed. (Munich: Oldenburg Wissenschaftsverlag, 2002).

33 James Hopwood Jeans, *The Mysterious Universe* (Cambridge: Cambridge University Press, 1930), 140.

34 Leon M. Lederman, with Dick Teresi, *The God Particle: If the Universe Is the Answer, What Is the Question?* (Boston and New York: Houghton Mifflin Harcourt, 1993), 22.

35 Egil Asprem, "How Schrödinger's Cat Became a Zombie: On the Epidemiology of Science-Based Representations in Popular and Religious Contexts," *Method & Theory in the Study of Religion* 28, no. 2 (2016).

36 Richard Dawkins, *The Selfish Gene*, 30th Anniversary edition (Oxford: Oxford University Press, 2006).

37 Pascal Boyer, *Religion Explained: The Evolutionary Origins of Religious Thought* (New York: Basic Books, 2001), 285.

38 Max Weber, "Some Categories of Interpretive Sociology," *The Sociological Quarterly*, 22, no. 2 (1981), 179.

39 Ibid.

40 Karl Marx, *Capital*, vol. 1 (London: J. M. Dent & Sons, 1930), 43–58, 45.

41 Olav Hammer, *Claiming Knowledge: Strategies of Epistemology from Theosophy to the New Age* (Leiden and Boston: Brill, 2001), 241–2.

42 See anon., *SCIO: Ancient Healing Meets Modern Technology*: https://www.scio.co.za/how-does-it-work (accessed February 7, 2018).

43 See Stephen Barrett, "Some Notes on the Quantum Xrroid (QXCI) and William C. Nelson," *Quackwatch* (July 12, 2009).

44 Ann Taves, "Non-Ordinary Powers: Charisma, Special Affordances and the Study of Religion," in *Mental Culture: Classical Social Theory and the Cognitive Science of Religion*, ed. Dimitris Xygalatas and William W. McCorkle, Jr. (Chesham: Acumen, 2013).

45 Eben Alexander, *Proof of Heaven: A Neurosurgeon's Journey into the Afterlife* (London: Piaktus, 2012). Incidentally, the "Near Death Experience" discourse is itself heavily indebted to the technologization of medicine and the social ramifications of the displacement of death and dying from the home to the hospital that it caused. See Jens Schlieter, *What Is It Like to Be Dead? Near-Death Experiences, Christianity, and the Occult* (Oxford: Oxford University Press, 2018).

46 See, for example, Olof Hallonsten, *Big Science Transformed: Science, Politics, and Organization in Europe and the United States* (London: Palgrave Macmillan, 2016).

47 George Aad et al., "Combined Measurement of the Higgs Boson Mass in *pp* Collisions at $s\sqrt{}=7$ and 8 TeV with the ATLAS and CMS Experiments," *Physics Review Letters* 114 (2015).
48 On the birth of "New Age science" from the 1960s counterculture, see Hanegraaff, *New Age Religion*.
49 David Kaiser, *How the Hippies Saved Physics: Science, Counterculture, and the Quantum Revival* (New York and London: W. W. Norton & Co., 2011).
50 Frank, *The Conquest of Cool*.
51 For example, Hammer, *Claiming Knowledge*, 206.

Chapter 4

1 Karl Löwith, *Meaning in History: The Theological Implications of the Philosophy of History*, 2nd ed. (Chicago: University of Chicago Press, 1950), 202–3 at 203; Lucian Hölscher, *Die Entdeckung der Zukunft* (Frankfurt am Main: Fischer, 1999), 40–1; Reinhart Koselleck, "Zeitverkürzung und Beschleunigung: Eine Studie zur Säkularisation," in Reinhart Koselleck, *Zeitschichten: Studien zur Historik*, 3rd ed. (Frankfurt am Main: Suhrkamp, 2013), 189–90; Sebastian Conrad, "A Cultural History of Global Transformation," in *An Emerging Modern World 1750–1870*, ed. Sebastian Conrad and Jürgen Osterhammel (Cambridge, MA: The Belknap Press of Harvard University Press, 2018), 572, 574–6.
2 Hans Blumenberg, *The Legitimacy of the Modern Age* (Cambridge, MA: MIT Press, 1985 [1976]); Jonathan Sheehan, "When Was Disenchantment? History and the Secular Age," in *Varieties of Secularism in a Secular Age*, ed. Michael Warner, Jonathan VanAntwerpen, and Craig Calhoun (Cambridge, MA: Harvard University Press, 2010), 225: "For the story of the 'secular age' is not a history."
3 Helge Jordheim, "Introduction: Multiple Times and the Work of Synchronization," *History and Theory* 53, no. 4 (2014): 514. See also Conrad, "A Cultural History," 535–7, 574–9. Note, however, that Conrad does not exclude religion from the picture.
4 Michael Warner, Jonathan VanAntwerpen, and Craig Calhoun, "Editors' Introduction," in *Varieties of Secularism in a Secular Age*, 18.
5 Conrad, "A Cultural History," dedicates an entire chapter to religion (582–659), including a section "World Religions as a Product of Secularization" (621–6; see also 626–33). For Conrad, however, it is "not the usual narrative of secularization" but "the increasing involvement of religious life in transnational exchanges and the contact and competition with other religions" that explain the dynamics of religious history between the late eighteenth and the late nineteenth centuries: "Certainly, secularization played an important role too, albeit less as a natural process that

went hand-in-hand with modernization than as a strategy of social elites who had a vested interest in implementing a segregation of different social spheres" (658).

6   Lorenz Trein, "'Weil das Christentum nie eine Geschichte hat haben wollen': Theologische Voraussetzungen und eschatologische Ambiguität der Säkularisierung in religionswissenschaftlicher Sicht." *Theologische Zeitschrift* 76, no. 1 (2020).

7   These are rather downplayed by Conrad, "A Cultural History," 646.

8   For beginnings, Conrad, "A Cultural History," 633, follows Manuel Borutta, "Genealogie der Säkularisierungstheorie: Zur Historisierung einer großen Erzählung der Moderne," *Geschichte und Gesellschaft* 36, no. 3 (2010).

9   Sheehan, "When Was Disenchantment?," 219.

10 I borrow this phrase from anthropologist Charles Hirschkind, "Is There a Secular Body?," *Cultural Anthropology* 26, no. 4 (2011): 634. See also Wolfgang Eßbach, *Religionssoziologie 1: Glaubenskrieg und Revolution als Wiege neuer Religionen* (Paderborn: Wilhelm Fink, 2014), 18–19, 22. For references to conceptual history approaches, see also Reinhart Koselleck, ed., *Historische Semantik und Begriffsgeschichte* (Stuttgart: Klett-Cotta, 1978).

11 Reinhart Koselleck, "Perspective and Temporality: A Contribution to the Historiographical Exposure of the Historical World" [1977], in Reinhart Koselleck, *Futures Past: On the Semantics of Historical Time* (Cambridge, MA: MIT Press, 1985), 154.

12 Koselleck, "Perspective and Temporality," 155.

13 Niklas Olsen, *History in the Plural: An Introduction to the Work of Reinhart Koselleck* (New York: Berghahn Books, 2012), 22–3. See also Willibald Steinmetz, "Nachruf auf Reinhart Koselleck (1923–2006)" [2006], in *Begriffene Geschichte: Beiträge zum Werk Reinhart Kosellecks*, ed. Hans Joas and Peter Vogt (Berlin: Suhrkamp, 2011), 62.

14 Olsen, *History in the Plural*, 22, 101–2.

15 Ibid., 22.

16 Ibid., 21–3. See also Reinhart Koselleck, "Formen der Bürgerlichkeit: Reinhart Koselleck im Gespräch mit Manfred Hettling und Bernd Ulrich," *Mittelweg 36: Zeitschrift des Hamburger Instituts für Sozialforschung* 12, no. 2 (2003): 77; Koselleck, "Zeitverkürzung und Beschleunigung," 193; Hans Joas, "Die Kontingenz der Säkularisierung: Überlegungen zum Problem der Säkularisierung im Werk Reinhart Kosellecks," in *Begriffene Geschichte: Beiträge zum Werk Reinhart Kosellecks*, ed. Hans Joas and Peter Vogt (Berlin: Suhrkamp, 2011), 327–8.

17 Olsen, *History in the Plural*, 23.

18 Löwith, *Meaning in History*, vii.

19 Joas, "Die Kontingenz der Säkularisierung," 327; Olsen, *History in the Plural*, 53.

20 Reinhart Koselleck, *Critique and Crisis: Enlightenment and the Pathogenesis of Modern Society* (Cambridge, MA: MIT Press, 1988 [1959]), 1.

21 Koselleck, "Formen der Bürgerlichkeit," 75–6; Olsen, *History in the Plural*, 23–6, 53. See also Jan Werner Müller, *A Dangerous Mind: Carl Schmitt in Post-War European Thought* (New Haven, CT: Yale University Press, 2003), 104–7, 111–13.
22 Reinhart Koselleck, *Kritik und Krise: Eine Studie zur Pathogenese der bürgerlichen Welt* (Frankfurt am Main: Suhrkamp, 2013 [1959]), 9; Koselleck, *Critique and Crisis*, 12.
23 Koselleck, *Critique and Crisis*, 7; Koselleck, *Kritik und Krise*, 3.
24 Koselleck, *Critique and Crisis*, 10; Koselleck, *Kritik und Krise*, 6–7.
25 Koselleck, *Critique and Crisis*, 10; Koselleck, *Kritik und Krise*, 7.
26 Koselleck, *Critique and Crisis*, 10; Koselleck, *Kritik und Krise*, 7.
27 Joas, "Die Kontingenz der Säkularisierung," 334.
28 Koselleck, *Critique and Crisis*, 3.
29 Ibid. (emphasis in the original). See also Joas, "Die Kontingenz der Säkularisierung," 334.
30 Gavin Rae, "The Theology of Carl Schmitt's Political Theology," *Political Theology* 17, no. 6 (2016): 559.
31 Reinhart Koselleck, "Concepts of Historical Time and Social History" [1982], in Reinhart Koselleck, *The Practice of Conceptual History: Timing History, Spacing Concepts* (Stanford: Stanford University Press, 2002), 119.
32 Reinhart Koselleck, "Modernity and the Planes of Historicity" [1968], in *Futures Past: On the Semantics of Historical Time*, 12–13.
33 Ibid., 17.
34 Kathleen Davis, *Periodization and Sovereignty: How Ideas of Feudalism and Secularization Govern the Politics of Time* (Philadelphia: University of Pennsylvania Press, 2008), 93–4.
35 John Zammito, "Koselleck's Philosophy of Historical Time(s) and the Practice of History," *History and Theory* 43, no. 1 (2004): 133; quoted in Helge Jordheim, "Against Periodization: Koselleck's Theory of Multiple Temporalities," *History and Theory* 51, no. 2 (2012): 157.
36 See, for example, Aleida Assmann, *Zeit und Tradition: Kulturelle Strategien der Dauer* (Köln: Böhlau, 1999), 12–13.
37 The loss of significance of historical concepts in the study of religion vis-à-vis the dissemination of a secularizing idea of religious history has been addressed by Hans Kippenberg, "Religious History, Displaced by Modernity," *Numen* 47, no. 3 (2000).
38 Jordheim, "Introduction," 514: "In the course of the eighteenth century, the plurality of historical times characteristic of the emerging modernity was synchronized into the linear, homogeneous, teleological time of progress. This synchronization was achieved by means of a set of different genres, for example, universal histories, encyclopedias, novels, world maps."
39 Ibid.

40 Ibid.
41 Ibid. (emphasis in the original).
42 I am fully aware that my discussion of Jordheim largely leaves aside the cross-cultural implications of his approach.
43 Due to limited space, I can mention here only briefly a few trajectories of Löwith's interest in Weber.
44 Löwith, *Meaning in History*, 201.
45 Trein, "'Weil das Christentum.'"
46 Karl Löwith, "Das Verhängnis des Fortschritts" [1963], in Karl Löwith, *Vorträge und Abhandlungen: Zur Kritik der christlichen Überlieferung* (Stuttgart: W. Kohlhammer, 1966).
47 See, for example, Löwith, *Meaning in History*, 202–3. See also Joachim Vahland, *Max Webers entzauberte Welt* (Würzburg: Königshausen & Neumann, 2001), 21–26.
48 Karl Löwith, "Die Entzauberung der Welt durch Wissenschaft: Zu Max Webers 100. Geburtstag," *Merkur: Deutsche Zeitschrift für europäisches Denken* 18, no. 6 (=issue 196) (1964); partially translated as Karl Löwith, "Max Weber's Position on Science" [1965], in *Max Weber's "Science as a Vocation*," ed. Peter Lassman, Irving Velody, and Herminio Martins (London: Unwin Hyman, 1989). This translation is taken from a later version entitled Karl Löwith, "Max Webers Stellung zur Wissenschaft" [1965], in Karl Löwith, *Vorträge und Abhandlungen: Zur Kritik der christlichen Überlieferung* (Stuttgart: W. Kohlhammer, 1966). For bibliographical references, see also Löwith, *Vorträge und Abhandlungen*, 290.
49 Max Weber, "Science as a Vocation," in *From Max Weber: Essays in Sociology*, ed. H.H. Geerth and C. Wright Mills (New York: Oxford University Press, 1946), 139.
50 Ibid., 140.
51 Ibid., 139–40.
52 Löwith, "Max Weber's Position on Science," 140–1. One can ask whether Löwith's reference to the absurdity of a specifically modern historical existence prefigures the impact of existentialism on Koselleck's historical thinking as discussed by Jan Eike Dunkhase, *Absurde Geschichte: Reinhart Kosellecks historischer Existentialismus* (Marbach am Neckar: Deutsche Schillergesellschaft, 2015).
53 Löwith, "Das Verhängnis des Fortschritts," 143: "Die christliche Zuversicht auf eine künftige Erfüllung ist zwar dem modernen Geschichtsbewusstsein abhanden gekommen, aber die Sicht auf die Zukunft als solche und auf eine unbestimmte Erfüllung ist herrschend geblieben" (translation by the author).
54 Ibid., 139, 155.
55 Ibid., 155: "In einer ewigen Gegenwart sind Entwicklung und Fortschritt aufgehoben" (translation by the author).
56 Ibid. (translation by the author).

57 With reference to Marx and Hegel, see K. Westphal, "Aufhebung," in *A Dictionary of Continental Philosophy*, ed. John Protevi (New Haven, CT: Yale University Press, 2006), 42: "to cancel or nullify, to preserve, and to lift or raise up"; Karl Löwith, "Hegels Aufhebung der christlichen Religion" [1962], in Löwith, *Vorträge und Abhandlungen*, 55–6.
58 For insightful remarks on translating Max Weber's notorious phrase, see Jason Ā. Josephson-Storm, *The Myth of Disenchantment: Magic, Modernity, and the Birth of the Human Sciences* (Chicago: University of Chicago Press, 2017), 300. See also Löwith, "Max Weber's Position on Science," 140.
59 Löwith, *Meaning in History*, 217 (from the appendix on Friedrich Nietzsche).
60 Weber, "Science as a Vocation," 155 (emphasis in the original).
61 Ari Joskowicz and Ethan B. Katz, "Introduction: Rethinking Jews and Secularism," in *Secularism in Question: Jews and Judaism in Modern Times*, ed. Ari Joskowicz and Ethan B. Katz (Philadelphia: University of Pennsylvania Press, 2015), 3.
62 Robert Yelle, "Secularism Reconsidered: Three Approaches," *Politics, Religion & Ideology* 17, no. 4 (2016): 431–2.
63 Max Weber, *Economy and Society: An Outline of Interpretive Sociology*, vol. 1 (Berkeley: University of California Press, 1978 [1956]), 459–60. See also Max Weber, *Ancient Judaism*, ed. Hans H. Gerth and Don Martindale (New York: Free Press, 1967 [1921]), 380–2.
64 Weber, *Economy and Society*, 489.
65 Thomas Kroll, "Max Webers Idealtypus der charismatischen Herrschaft und die zeitgenössische Charisma-Debatte," in *Max Webers Herrschaftssoziologie: Studien zu Entstehung und Wirkung*, ed. Edith Hanke and Wolfgang J. Mommsen (Tübingen: Mohr Siebeck, 2001).
66 Rudolph Sohm, *Kirchenrecht*, vol. 1, *Die geschichtlichen Grundlagen*, reprint ed. (Munich: Duncker & Humblot, 1923 [1892]), 26: "Die aus dem göttlichen Wort geschöpfte, in Wahrheit apostolische Lehre von der Verfassung der Ekklesia ist die, daß die Organisation der Christenheit nicht rechtliche, sondern charismatische Organisation ist" (translation by the author).
67 Adolf Harnack, "Art. Verfassung, kirchliche, und kirchliches Recht im 1. und 2. Jahrhundert," in *Realencyclopädie für protestantische Theologie und Kirche*, vol. 20, ed. Albert Hauck, 3rd ed. (Leipzig: J.C. Hinrichs Buchhandlung, 1908), 513–14. See also Peter Haley, "Rudolph Sohm on Charisma," *The Journal of Religion* 60, no. 2 (1980): 191–2.
68 Kroll, "Max Webers Idealtypus der charismatischen Herrschaft," 56–7.
69 Ibid., 55–9.
70 Adolf Harnack, *The Mission and Expansion of Christianity in the First Three Centuries*, 2nd ed., vol. 1 (London: Williams and Norgate, 1908), 199–200.
71 Ibid., 204.

72　Ibid., 205; Adolf Harnack, *Die Mission und Ausbreitung des Christentums in den ersten drei Jahrhunderten*, vol. 1, *Die Mission in Wort und Tat*, 2nd. ed. (Leipzig: J.C. Hinrichs Buchhandlung, 1906), 177.

73　Carl Weizsäcker, *Das Apostolische Zeitalter der christlichen Kirche*, 3rd ed. (Tübingen: J.C.B. Mohr, 1902), 583. I am grateful to Christoph Auffarth for bringing this work to my attention.

74　Adolf Jülicher, "Die Religion Jesu und die Anfänge des Christentums bis zum Nicaenum," in J. Wellhausen et al., *Die christliche Religion mit Einschluss der Israelitisch-Jüdischen Religion* (=*Die Kultur der Gegenwart, ihre Entwicklung und Ziele I/IV*, ed. Paul Hinneberg) (Berlin: B.G. Teubner, 1906).

75　Ibid., 97–8 at 98 (translation by the author).

76　Ibid., 98 (translation by the author).

77　Heinrich Heppe, *Dogmatik des deutschen Protestantismus im sechzehnten Jahrhundert*, vol. 3 (Gotha: Friedrich Andreas Perthes, 1857), 22–3 (translation by the author).

78　Gotthold Neudecker, *Dr. Wilhelm Münschers Lehrbuch der christlichen Dogmengeschichte*, vol. 2/2 (Kassel: Joh. Chr. Krieger, 1838), 181n (translation by the author).

79　Yelle, "Secularism Reconsidered," 431–2.

80　Harnack, *The Mission and Expansion*, 204.

81　Ibid., 205n2.

82　For references to Martin Luther, see Neudecker, *Dr. Wilhelm Münschers Lehrbuch*, 171–2 and 173n1; Heppe, *Dogmatik des deutschen Protestantismus*, 23–4. See also F.W. Lomler et al., eds., *Geist aus Luthers Schriften oder Concordanz der Ansichten und Urtheile des großen Reformators über die wichtigsten Gegenstände des Glaubens, der Wissenschaft und des Lebens*, vol. 4 (Darmstadt: Karl Wilhelm Leske, 1831), 804; Martin Luther, *Werke: Kritische Gesamtausgabe*, vol. 41 (Weimar: Hermann Böhlaus Nachfolger, 1910), 20–1.

83　This also applies to Löwith's critique of the historicization of Christianity: Trein, "'Weil das Christentum.'"

84　Julius Wellhausen, *Briefe*, ed. Rudolf Smend, Peter Porzig, and Reinhard Müller (Tübingen: Mohr Siebeck, 2013), 519 (translation by the author).

85　Weber, *Ancient Judaism*, 380.

86　Uriel Tal, *Christians and Jews in Germany: Religion, Politics, and Ideology in the Second Reich, 1870–1914* (Ithaca, NY: Cornell University Press, 1975 [1969]), 191–5 at 192. I am grateful to Susannah Heschel for bringing this work to my attention.

87　Georg Wilhelm Friedrich Hegel, *Lectures on the Philosophy of World History: Introduction: Reason in History* (Cambridge: Cambridge University Press, 1984), 131 (whole passage italicized in the original).

88　See, for example, Löwith, "Das Verhängnis des Fortschritts."

89 Löwith, *Meaning in History*, 217.
90 Ibid., 221.
91 Josephson-Storm, *The Myth of Disenchantment*.
92 Ibid., 300.
93 Yelle, "Secularism Reconsidered," 431–2.
94 See, for example, Jordheim, "Multiple Times," 499–502.

Chapter 5

1 Joachim Radkau, *Max Weber: A Biography* (Cambridge: Polity Press, 2009), 71, maintains that in his cultural pessimism, "Weber found alien the modern belief in progress." However, Richard Jenkins, "Disenchantment, Enchantment and Re-Enchantment: Max Weber at the Millennium," *Max Weber Studies* 1, no. 1 (2000), 11–12, notes that Weber did see progressive facets within modernity and believed "that history has some direction in the sense of being cumulative and largely non-reversible."
2 Jeremiah Dibua, *Modernization and the Crisis of Development in Africa: The Nigerian Experience* (London: Ashgate, 2006), 20–1.
3 Max Weber, "'Objectivity' in Social Science and Social Policy," in *The Methodology of the Social Sciences*, ed. E.A. Shils and H.A. Finch (New York: Free Press, 1949), 90.
4 Joshua Landy and Michael Saler, eds., *The Re-Enchantment of the World: Secular Magic in a Rational Age* (Stanford: Stanford University Press, 2009).
5 The literature on "modern enchantment" and "re-enchantment" is large: for a survey through 2006, see Michael Saler, "Modernity and Enchantment: A Historiographic Review," *The American Historical Review* 111, no. 3 (2006); for a more recent overview, see Michael Saler, "Enchantment," *Oxford Research Encyclopedia of Literature* (New York: Oxford University Press, forthcoming).
6 In addition to Horkheimer, Adorno, and Foucault, see Peter Berger, Brigitte Berger, and Hansfried Kellner, *The Homeless Mind: Modernization and Consciousness* (New York: Vintage Books, 1974); Stephen Toulmin, *Cosmopolis: The Hidden Agenda of Modernity* (Chicago: University of Chicago Press, 1990); Jürgen Habermas, *The Structural Transformation of the Public Sphere: An Inquiry into a Category of Bourgeois Society* (Cambridge, MA: MIT Press, 1991).
7 The classic account of this attempt during the *fin de siècle* is H. Stuart Hughes, *Consciousness and Society* (New York: Alfred A. Knopf, 1958).
8 Weber, "Science as a Vocation": https://trialectics.net/projects/political-theory/max-weber/science-as-vocation/(accessed July 14 2019).
9 Lawrence A. Scaff, *Fleeing the Iron Cage: Culture, Politics, and Modernity in the Thought of Max Weber* (Berkeley: University of California Press, 1989), 113.
10 For discussions of the spiritual and secular approaches to the imagination in Western culture, see Eva Brann, *The World of the Imagination: Sum and Substance*

(Lanham, MD: Rowman and Littlefield, 1992) and Richard Kearney, *The Wake of Imagination* (New York: Routledge, 2003).

11 Samuel Taylor Coleridge, *Biographia Literaria*, vol. 1, ed. James Engell and W. Jackson Bate (Princeton, NJ: Princeton University Press, 1983), 304; Wallace Stevens, *Opus Posthumous*, ed. M.J. Bates (New York: Alfred A. Knopf, 1989), 189. For Stevens's capacity to entertain metaphysical as well as metafictional orientations, see Patricia Rae, *The Practical Muse: Pragmatist Poetics in Hulme, Pound, and Stevens* (Lewisburg, PA: Bucknell University Press, 1997).

12 Weber, *The Protestant Ethic and the Spirit of Capitalism* (New York: Penguin, 2002), 111–12.

13 Weber, "Science as a Vocation."

14 Egil Asprem surveys "the plurality of epistemological positions available within post-Enlightenment intellectual culture," including the rise of quantum mechanics. Asprem, *The Problem of Disenchantment: Scientific Naturalism and Esoteric Discourse, 1900–1939* (Leiden: Brill, 2014), 4, 260–78.

15 https://en.wikiquote.org/wiki/Albert_A._Michelson (accessed July 14, 2019).

16 For "Constellation," see Walter Benjamin, *The Origin of the German Trauerspiel* (Cambridge, MA: Harvard University Press, 2019), 10; for "force field," see Walter Benjamin, *The Arcades Project* (Cambridge, MA: Harvard University Press, 1999), 470.

17 Max Weber, *From Max Weber: Essays in Sociology*, ed. Hans H. Gerth and C. Wright Mills (London: Routledge, 1991), 128.

18 Friedrich Nietzsche, *The Birth of Tragedy & The Genealogy of Morals*, ed. Francis Golffing (New York: Anchor Books, 1956), 290.

19 Weber, "Science as a Vocation."

20 Radkau, *Max Weber*, 116.

21 Evolutionary psychologists and cognitive scientists are attempting to define the imagination empirically and functionally. For a recent overview, see Felipe Fernández-Armesto, *Out of Our Minds: What We Think and How We Came to Think It* (Berkeley: University of California Press, 2019).

22 Jean-Jacques Rousseau, *Emile, or on Education* (Hanover, NH: Dartmouth College Press, 2010), 211.

23 Samuel Taylor Coleridge, *Biographia Literaria*, vol. 2, ed. James Engell and W. Jackson Bate (Princeton, NJ: Princeton University Press, 1984), 6.

24 See Lorraine Daston, "Fear and Loathing of the Imagination in Science," *Daedalus* 127, no. 1 (Winter 1998); Lorraine Daston and Peter Galison, *Objectivity* (Cambridge, MA: Zone Books, 2007), 37, 120–54.

25 Michael Saler, *As If: Modern Enchantment and the Literary Prehistory of Virtual Reality* (New York: Oxford University Press, 2012), 40.

26 Nietzsche, *Human, All-Too Human* (New York: Dover, 2006), 136.

27 Friedrich Nietzsche, *Beyond Good and Evil* (New York: Vintage Books, 1989), 12.
28 Jean-Eugène Robert-Houdin, *Secrets of Conjuring and Magic*, ed. Louis Hoffman (Cambridge: Cambridge University Press, 2011), 43.
29 Phineas Taylor Barnum, *The Life of P.T. Barnum, Written by Himself* (New York: Redfield, 1855), 171.
30 In terms of this "fictionalist" turn in sociology, see Hughes, *Consciousness and Society* and Wolf Lepenies, *Between Literature and Science: The Rise of Sociology* (Cambridge: Cambridge University Press, 1988).
31 Arthur Conan Doyle, *The Hound of the Baskervilles*, ed. W.W. Robson (Oxford: Oxford University Press, 1998), 33.
32 Jack Williamson, "Scientifiction, Searchlight of Science," *Amazing Stories Quarterly* 1, no. 4 (1928): 435.
33 Richard Dawkins, *Unweaving the Rainbow: Science, Delusion and the Appetite for Wonder* (New York: Houghton Mifflin, 1998).
34 For surrealist science, see Derek Sayer, *Surrealism and the Human Sciences* (Chicago: Prickly Paradigm Press, 2015).
35 https://www.tcf.ua.edu/Classes/Jbutler/T340/SurManifesto/ManifestoOfSurrealism.htm (accessed July 16, 2019).
36 I have appropriated the term "fictionalism" from Hans Vaihinger, discussed below. Beginning in the early twentieth century, fictionalism was also used by analytic philosophers in a very different sense, to analyze the logic of propositions.
37 Robert Yelle demonstrates that Bentham and others drew on a longer tradition of Protestant literalism, which influenced Baconian empiricism. Yelle, "Bentham's Fictions: Canon and Idolatry in the Genealogy of Law," *Yale Journal of Law & the Humanities* 17, no. 2 (2005).
38 Catherine Gallagher, "The Rise of Fictionality," in *The Novel*, vol. 1, *History, Geography and Culture*, ed. Franco Moretti (Princeton, NJ: Princeton University Press, 2006), 340.
39 For the origin of "autobiografiction," see Max Saunders, *Self-Impression: Life-Writing, Autobiografiction, and the Forms of Modern Literature* (New York: Oxford University Press, 2010), 167–70; for "bibliotherapy," see Grainne McKenna, David Hevey, and Elaine Martin, *Patients' and Providers' Perspectives on Bibliotherapy in Primary Care*: https://www.hse.ie/eng/services/list/4/mental-health-services/powerofwords/patientsbibliotherapy.pdf (accessed July 16, 2019).
40 Oscar Wilde, "Phrases and Philosophies for the Uses of the Young," *The Chameleon* 1, no. 1 (1894), 3.
41 Erik Davis, *High Weirdness: Drugs, Esoterica, and Visionary Experience in the Seventies* (Cambridge, MA: MIT Press, 2019), 348–9.
42 For Stanislavski, see Edward Dickinson, *Dancing in the Blood: Modern Dance and European Culture on the Eve of the First World War* (Cambridge: Cambridge

University Press, 2017), 140–3; for Becker, see Carl Becker, "Everyman His Own Historian," *The American Historical Review* 37, no. 2 (1932).

43 William H. McNeill, "Mythistory, or Truth, Myth, History, and Historians," *The American Historical Review* 91, no. 1 (1986).

44 Walter R. Fisher, *Human Communication as Narration: Toward a Philosophy of Reason, Value and Action* (Columbia, SC: University of South Carolina Press, 1989).

45 Weber, "Science as a Vocation."

46 https://www.preposterousuniverse.com/poetic-naturalism/ (accessed July 18, 2019).

47 Tanya M. Luhrmann, *When God Talks Back: Understanding the American Evangelical Relationship with God* (New York: Alfred A. Knopf, 2012), Kindle edition, location 84.

48 For discussions of so-called "hyper-real religions," see Carole M. Cusack, *Invented Religions: Imagination, Fiction and Faith* (New York: Routledge, 2016) and the special thematic issue, dedicated to the theme of religion and fiction, of *Religion* 46, no. 4 (2016).

49 Davis, *High Weirdness*, 63.

50 Jonathan Sheehan, *The Enlightenment Bible: Translation, Scholarship, Culture* (Princeton, NJ: Princeton University Press, 2005).

51 Matthew Arnold, "Dover Beach."

52 C.S. Lewis, *Surprised by Joy: The Shape of My Early Life* (New York: Harcourt Brace & Company, 1955), 201.

53 Kirsten Johnson, "Tolkien's Mythopoesis," in *Tree of Tales: Tolkien, Literature and Theology*, ed. Trevor A. Hart and Ivan Khovacs (Waco, TX: Baylor University Press, 2007).

54 J.R.R. Tolkien, *The Letters of J.R.R. Tolkien*, ed. Humphrey Carpenter (Boston: Houghton Mifflin Company, 2000), 78.

55 Barbara Reynolds, *Dorothy L. Sayers: Her Life and Soul* (New York: St. Martin's Press, 1997), 21.

56 David Coomes, *Dorothy L. Sayers: A Careless Rage for Life* (New York: Lion Books, 1992), 31.

57 G.K. Chesterton, *Orthodoxy*: https://www.pagebypagebooks.com/Gilbert_K_Chesterton/Orthodoxy/The_Paradoxes_of_Christianity_p13.html (accessed July 23 2019).

58 Dorothy L. Sayers, "Gaudy Night," in *The Art of the Mystery Story*, ed. Howard Haycraft (New York: Carroll & Graf, 1974), 220.

59 Ibid., 213.

60 Marc Baer, *Mere Believers: How Eight Faithful Lives Changed the Course of History* (Eugene, OR: Cascade Books, 2013), 146.

61 James Brabazon, *Dorothy L. Sayers, A Biography* (New York: Scribner, 1981), 263.

62 Ibid., 263.

63 Dorothy L. Sayers, *Christian Letters to a Post-Christian World: A Selection of Essays* (Grand Rapids, MI: Eerdmans, 1969), 15.

Chapter 6

1. J.W. Burrow, *The Crisis of Reason: European Thought, 1848-1914* (New Haven, CT: Yale University Press, 2000), 145-6; Robert Yelle, "The Trouble with Transcendence: Carl Schmitt's 'Exception' as a Challenge for Religious Studies," *Method & Theory in the Study of Religion* 22, no. 2-3 (2010): 200.
2. Ernst van den Hemel's paper was presented at the conference at LMU Munich in October 2017 but is not included in these proceedings.
3. Benedict de Spinoza, *Theological-Political Treatise*, ed. Jonathan Israel (Cambridge: Cambridge University Press, 2007), 3.
4. Fritz Ringer, *Max Weber: An intellectual Biography* (Chicago: University of Chicago Press, 2004), 128-9; Chad Alan Goldberg, *Modernity and the Jews in Western Social Thought* (Chicago: University of Chicago Press, 2017), 64-5.
5. Spinoza, *Theological-Political Treatise*, 5.
6. Jacob van Sluis, *Bekkeriana: Balthasar Bekker biografisch en bibliografisch* (Leeuwarden: Fryske Akademy, 1994), 13-14.
7. Ian Hunter, *The Secularisation of the Confessional State: The Political Thought of Christian Thomasius* (Cambridge: Cambridge University Press, 2007), 159, 162-7.
8. Corine Pelluchon, *Leo Strauss and the Crisis of Rationalism* (Albany, NY: SUNY Press, 2014), 79, 197, 277n52; Victor Nuovo, *Christianity, Antiquity and Enlightenment: Interpretations of Locke* (Dordrecht: Springer, 2011), 58-65.
9. Leo Strauss, *Spinoza's Critique of Religion*, trans. E.M. Sinclair, 2nd ed. (Chicago: University of Chicago Press, 1997), 35; Steven B. Smith, *Spinoza's Book of Life* (New Haven, CT: Yale University Press, 2003), 191; Pelluchon, *Leo Strauss*, 77-84. I myself was unaware, Nicolas Dubos rightly notes, in my earlier Enlightenment volumes that the basic radical-moderate dichotomy effectively commences with Strauss in the 1920s; see Dubos, "Hobbes et les Lumières radicales," *Lumières* (Publication du Centre interdisciplinaire bordelais d'étude des Lumières) 13 (2009): 38-41.
10. Miguel Vatter, "Strauss and Schmitt as Readers of Hobbes and Spinoza: On the Relation between Political Theology and Liberalism," *The New Centennial Review* 4, no 3. (2004): 163, 202-3.
11. Burrow, *Crisis of Reason*, 144; Goldberg, *Modernity and the Jews*, 67-8.
12. Helmuth Kiesel, "Aufklärung und neuer Irrationalismus in der Weimarer Republik," in *Aufklärung und Gegenaufklärung in der europäischen Literatur, Philosophie und Politik von der Antike bis zur Gegenwart*, ed. Jochen Schmidt (Darmstadt: Wgb Academic, 1989), 513-15.
13. Max Horkheimer and Theodor Adorno, *Dialectic of Enlightenment* (New York: Continuum, 2000), 3.
14. Ibid., 154-6; Vatter, "Strauss and Schmitt," 168-9.

15 Peter Watson, *The German Genius: Europe's Third Renaissance, the Second Scientific Revolution, and the Twentieth Century* (New York: HarperCollins, 2010), 455–7.
16 Irene Gaddo and Edoardo Tortarolo, *Secolarizzione e modernità* (Rome: Carocci, 2017), 30.
17 Pelluchon, *Leo Strauss*, 11; Daniel Tanguay, *Leo Strauss: An Intellectual Biography*, trans. Christopher Nadon (New Haven, CT: Yale University Press, 2007), 113–14.
18 John P. McCormick, "Legal Theory and the Weimar Crisis of Law and Social Change," in *Weimar Thought: A Contested Legacy*, ed. P.E. Gordon and J.P. McCormick (Princeton, NJ: Princeton University Press, 2013), 55, 61.
19 Tanguay, *Leo Strauss*, 114.
20 John P. McCormick, *Carl Schmitt's Critique of Liberalism: Against Politics as Technology* (Cambridge: Cambridge University Press, 1997), 34.
21 Carl Schmitt, *Political Theology: Four Chapters on the Concept of Sovereignty* (Chicago: University of Chicago Press, 2007), 36.
22 Marta García-Alonso, "Jonathan Israel et Carl Schmitt : Révolution philosophique versus contre-révolution théologique," in *Les Lumières radicales et le politique: Études critiques sur les travaux de Jonathan Israel*, ed. M. García-Alonso (Paris: Honoré Champion, 2017), 357.
23 McCormick, "Legal Theory and the Weimar Crisis," 62, 67; Richard Wolin, *The Seduction of Unreason: The Intellectual Romance with Fascism from Nietzsche to Postmodernism* (Princeton, NJ: Princeton University Press, 2004), 239, 286–7.
24 Vatter, "Strauss and Schmitt," 203.
25 Yelle, "The Trouble with Transcendence," 191–92; García-Alonso, "Jonathan Israel et Carl Schmitt," 358.
26 Schmitt, *Political Theology*, 37.
27 Vatter, "Strauss and Schmitt," 189–92; García-Alonso, "Jonathan Israel et Carl Schmitt," 356, 366–9.
28 Ignaz Einhorn, *Spinoza's Staatslehre: Zum ersten Male dargestellt* (Dessau: Gebrüder Katz, 1851), 7.
29 Ibid., 10.
30 Ibid., 9–10.
31 Vatter, "Strauss and Schmitt," 189.
32 Manfred Walther, "Carl Schmitt contra Baruch Spinoza oder Vom Ende der politischen Theologie," in *Spinoza in der europäischen Geistesgeschichte*, ed. Hanna Delf, Julius H. Schoeps, and Manfred Walther (Berlin: Edition Hentrich, 1994), 426–7; Pelluchon, *Leo Strauss*, 26, 37–40, 160–4.
33 Vatter, "Strauss and Schmitt," 192–3, 202; Walther, "Carl Schmitt contra Baruch Spinoza," 433–4.
34 David Bates, "Rousseau and Schmitt: Sovereigns and Dictators," in *Thinking with Rousseau: From Machiavelli to Schmitt*, ed. Helena Rosenblatt and P. Schweigert

(Cambridge: Cambridge University Press, 2017), 292–4; Wolin, *Seduction of Unreason*, 286–7, 312.
35 Schmitt, *Political Theology*, 57.
36 Pelluchon, *Leo Strauss*, 162–71; McCormick, *Carl Schmitt's Critique*, 258–65.
37 Yelle, "The Trouble with Transcendence," 192–93; García-Alonso, "Jonathan Israel et Carl Schmitt," 362.
38 Vatter, "Strauss and Schmitt," 170–1, 183, 189; McCormick, "Political Theory," 841–42.
39 Pierre-François Moreau, "Adorno und Horkheimer als Spinoza-Leser," in *Aufklärungs-Kritik und Aufklärungs-Mythen: Horkheimer und Adorno in philosophiehistorischer Perspektive*, ed. Sonja Lavaert and Winfried Schröder (Berlin: De Gruyter, 2018), 113, 120.
40 McCormick, *Carl Schmitt's Critique*, 269–70, 273.
41 Vatter, "Strauss and Schmitt," 193.
42 David Wertheim, *Salvation through Spinoza: A Study of Jewish Culture in Weimar Germany* (Leiden: Brill, 2011), preface.
43 James T. Kloppenberg, *Toward Democracy: The Struggle for Self-Rule in European and American Thought* (New York: Oxford University Press, 2016), 16.
44 On my differences with Kloppenberg, see Jonathan Israel, *The Expanding Blaze. How the American Revolution Ignited the World, 1775–1848* (Princeton, NJ: Princeton University Press, 2017), 15–17.
45 Or what Tanguay dubs the Enlightenment's "radical tradition," see Tanguay, *Leo Strauss*, 101; on Strauss's role in coining the concept "Radical Enlightenment," see in particular Jonathan Israel, "'Radical Enlightenment': A Game-Changing Concept," in *Reassessing the Radical Enlightenment*, ed. Steffen Ducheyne (London: Routledge, 2017), 18; Frederik Stjernfelt, "'Radical Enlightenment': Aspects of the History of a Term," in idem, 95–8; and Jonathan Israel, "Leo Strauss and the Radical Enlightenment," in *Reading Between the Lines: Leo Strauss and the History of Early Modern Philosophy*, ed. Winfried Schröder (Berlin: De Gruyter, 2015).
46 Pelluchon, *Leo Strauss*, 34–40; Steven B. Smith, *Reading Leo Strauss: Politics, Philosophy, Judaism* (Chicago: University of Chicago Press, 2006), 71, 189.
47 Martin Mulsow, *Enlightenment Underground: Radical Germany, 1680–1720* (Charlottesville, VA: University of Virginia Press, 2015), 111–13.
48 Ibid., 165–70.
49 Ibid., 165–6.
50 Ibid., 171; further on "Spinozismus ante Spinozam" see the section "China and *Spinozismus ante Spinozam*," in Jonathan Israel, *Enlightenment Contested: Philosophy, Modernity, and the Emancipation of Man 1670–1752* (Oxford: Oxford University Press, 2006), 640–52.
51 Jonathan Israel, "Rousseau and d'Holbach: the Revolutionary Implications of *la philosophie anti-Thérésienne*," in *Thinking with Rousseau: From Machiavelli*

to Schmitt, ed. Helena Rosenblatt and Paul Schweigert (Cambridge: Cambridge University Press, 2017), 166–7, 173.
52 McCormick, "Political Theory," 847.

Chapter 7

1 Thomas Hobbes, *Leviathan*, "A Review and Conclusion," §15. All references are to the edition by Edwin Curley (Indianapolis: Hackett Publishing Co., 1994).
2 Philippe Bourgeaud, "The Death of the Great Pan: The Problem of Interpretation," *History of Religions* 22, no. 3 (1983).
3 The connection between these two Weberian ideas, namely disenchantment and the routinization of charisma, has been made previously and in any case is present in "Science as a Vocation," as indicated below. See, for example, William H. Swatos, Jr., "The Disenchantment of Charisma: A Weberian Assessment of Revolution in a Rationalized World," *Sociological Analysis* 42 (1981); Peter Ghosh, *Max Weber and "The Protestant Ethic": Twin Histories* (Oxford: Oxford University Press, 2014), identifying disenchantment with rationalization (257–74) and charisma as the magical quality par excellence (263; see also 307).
4 Robert A. Yelle, "The Trouble with Transcendence: Carl Schmitt's 'Exception' as a Challenge for Religious Studies," *Method & Theory in the Study of Religion* 22 (2010); Robert A. Yelle, "Moses' Veil: Secularization as Christian Myth," in *After Secular Law*, ed. Winnifred F. Sullivan, Robert A. Yelle, and Mateo Taussig-Rubbo (Stanford: Stanford University Press, 2011); Robert A. Yelle, *The Language of Disenchantment: Protestant Literalism and Colonial Discourse in British India* (New York: Oxford University Press, 2013), 18–32; Robert A. Yelle, *Sovereignty and the Sacred: Secularism and the Political Economy of Religion* (Chicago: University of Chicago Press, 2019), 44–7, 52–73.
5 The original version of this work appeared in two parts in 1904–05. The second edition was published in 1920. I have used Max Weber, *The Protestant Ethic and the Spirit of Capitalism, with Other Writings on the Rise of the West*, 4th ed., trans. Stephen Kalberg (New York: Oxford University Press, 2009), which translates the second German edition.
6 On the connection with Jellinek, see Johannes Winckelmann, "Die Herkunft von Max Webers 'Entzauberungs'-Konzeption," *Kölner Zeitschrift für Soziologie und Sozialpsychologie* 32 (1980): 13; Friedrich Wilhelm Graf, "The German Theological Sources and Protestant Church Politics," in *Weber's Protestant Ethic: Origins, Evidence, Contexts*, ed. Hartmut Lehmann and Guenther Roth (Cambridge: Cambridge University Press, 1993), 32; Martin Riesebrodt, "Dimensions of the Protestant Ethic," in *The Protestant Ethic Turns 100: Essays on the Centenary of the Weber Thesis*, ed. William H. Swatos, Jr., and Lutz Kaelber (Boulder, CO: Paradigm

Publishers, 2005), 38–9. On Weber's connection with Schmitt, see references in Yelle, *Sovereignty and the Sacred*, 46–7. On Weber's connection with Laum, see Bernhard Laum, *Heiliges Geld: Eine historische Untersuchung über den sakralen Ursprung des Geldes* (Tübingen: Mohr, 1924), 160–1.

7   Briefly, I agree with Friedrich W. Graf's statement that Weber's "heavy dependence on the theological discussion indicates that more value judgments, and specifically denominational ideology, are present in *The Protestant Ethic* than Weber himself realized or present interpreters are aware." Graf, "The German Theological Sources," 31.

8   Hans Blumenberg, *The Legitimacy of the Modern Age* (Cambridge, MA: MIT Press, 1983).

9   Philip S. Gorski and Ateş Altinordu, "After Secularization?," *Annual Review of Sociology* 34 (2008): 60.

10 See Monika Wohlrab-Sahr's chapter in this volume. Prof. Wohlrab-Sahr and I agree on many points. Due to limitations of space, and my focus on disenchantment, I do not address here her main argument regarding the reality of secularization as a differentiation of religion from politics and other domains. This is an important and complex issue that I hope to take up in future work.

11 Yelle, *Language of Disenchantment*, 14–16; Yelle, *Sovereignty and the Sacred*, 70–3.

12 See, for example, Hartmut Lehmann, *Die Entzauberung der Welt: Studien zu Themen von Max Weber* (Göttingen: Wallstein, 2009), 9–16; Hans Joas, *Die Macht des Heiligen: Eine Alternative zur Geschichte von der Entzauberung* (Berlin: Suhrkamp, 2017), 201–77.

13 Max Weber, "Über einige Kategorien der verstehenden Soziologie" [1913], in *Gesammelte Aufsätze zur Wissenschaftslehre*, ed. Johannes Winckelmann (Tübingen: Mohr Siebeck, 1988).

14 Max Weber, "Science as a Vocation," in *From Max Weber: Essays in Sociology*, ed. Hans H. Gerth and C. Wright Mills (London: Routledge, 1991), 139.

15 Weber, *Protestant Ethic*, 107.

16 Ibid.

17 Jason Josephson-Storm argues, in his chapter for this volume, that Weber did not mean to imply that magic would disappear.

18 Yelle, *Sovereignty and the Sacred*, 53–5, 68–9; and Carl Schmitt, *Political Theology: Four Chapters on the Concept of Sovereignty* (Chicago: University of Chicago Press, 2005), 36–7.

19 As recognized by Carl Schmitt, *The Leviathan in the State Theory of Thomas Hobbes* (Chicago: University of Chicago Press, 2008), 54–5; and by J.C.D. Clark, "The Re-Enchantment of the World?: Religion and Monarchy in Eighteenth-Century Europe," in *Monarchy and Religion: The Transformation of Royal Culture in Eighteenth-Century Europe*, ed. Michael Schaich (Oxford: Oxford University Press, 2007).

20 Hans Kippenberg, "Dialektik der Entzauberung: Säkularisierung aus der Perspektive von Webers Religionssystematik," in *Alte Begriffe—Neue Probleme: Max Webers Soziologie im Lichte aktueller Problemstellungen*, ed. Thomas Schwinn and Gert Albert (Tübingen: Mohr Siebeck, 2016), 90. See also Hans Kippenberg, *Die Entdeckung der Religionsgeschichte: Religionswissenschaft und Moderne* (Munich: C.H. Beck, 1997), 233–7, disclaiming any theological influence on Weber. Thanks to Lorenz Trein for these references.

21 Andreas Anter, "Entzauberung der Welt und okzidentale Rationalisierung (Weber)," in *Religion und Säkularisierung: Ein interdisziplinäres Handbuch*, ed. Thomas M. Schmidt and Annette Pitschmann (Stuttgart: J.B. Metzler, 2014), 14.

22 See Winckelmann 15, citing this usage in Marianne Weber, *Max Weber: Ein Lebensbild* (Tübingen: J.C.B. Mohr [Paul Siebeck], 1926), 348. Lehmann, *Die Entzauberung der Welt*, 13, rejects Morris Berman's argument for a connection but does not discuss the passage cited by Winckelmann. Alexandra Walsham, "The Reformation and 'The Disenchantment of the World' Reassessed," *Historical Journal* 51, no. 2 (2008): 526, mistakenly attributes the coinage of *Entzauberung* to Schiller himself. More generally, the idea of a vanishing of the gods, as this appeared in Classical and Romantic poetry, often echoed the ideas of the silence of the oracles and the death of Pan that, as described below, had earlier been common theological tropes.

23 Hobbes, *Leviathan*, chap. 45.

24 Lehmann, *Die Entzauberung der Welt*, 13. Wiep van Bunge, "Balthasar Bekker," in *Encyclopedia of the Enlightenment*, ed. Alan Kors, 4 vols. (Oxford: Oxford University Press, 2003), 1: 132–3, makes the same connection to Weber. See Euan Cameron, *Enchanted Europe: Superstition, Reason, and Religion, 1250–1750* (Oxford: Oxford University Press, 2010), 264–9, for a discussion of Bekker. Ibid., x, cites Bekker as the inspiration for the title of his own book. For further discussion of Bekker, see Jonathan Israel's chapter in this volume.

25 Rudolf Otto, *Gottheit und Gottheiten der Arier* (Gießen: Alfred Töpelmann, 1932), 38n1: "So begann mit der zweiten Hälfte des Mittelalters eine wie eine Epidemie sich ausdehnende Dämonisierung der Welt, die dann in der 'enttoferde wereld' der Aufklärung wieder abklang."

26 Keith Thomas, *Religion and the Decline of Magic* (New York: Charles Scribner's Sons, 1971). Thomas cites Weber's disenchantment thesis at 88 and 657.

27 Hildred Geertz, "An Anthropology of Religion and Magic, I," *Journal of Interdisciplinary History* 6 (1975).

28 See, for example, Randall Styers, *Making Magic: Religion, Magic, and Science in the Modern World* (New York: Oxford University Press, 2004).

29 Jason Ā. Josephson-Storm, *The Myth of Disenchantment: Magic, Modernity, and the Birth of the Human Sciences* (Chicago: University of Chicago Press, 2017);

Egil Asprem, *The Problem of Disenchantment: Scientific Naturalism and Esoteric Discourse 1900–1939* (Leiden: Brill, 2014). All of which may well be true to a certain extent. In going through my late mother-in-law's papers, we discovered some handwritten prayers for the health of infants, etc., that evidenced the persistence of folk magic among Italian-Americans in Brooklyn, New York, in the 1940s.

30 Robert Scribner, "The Reformation, Popular Magic, and the 'Disenchantment of the World,'" *Journal of Interdisciplinary History* 23, no. 3 (1993).
31 Alexandra Walsham, "Miracles in Post-Reformation England," in *Signs, Wonders, Miracles: Representations of Divine Power in the Life of the Church*, ed. Kate Cooper and Jeremy Gregory (Woodbridge: Boydell Press, 2005).
32 Walsham, "The Reformation."
33 Ibid., 509.
34 Ibid., 517–18. For the role of deism in disenchantment, see Yelle, *Sovereignty and the Sacred*, 38–9, 42–3, 56–61, 64–7.
35 Ibid., 518. See further Brian Vickers, "Analogy versus Identity: The Rejection of Occult Symbolism, 1580–1680," in Brian Vickers, *Occult and Scientific Mentalities in the Renaissance* (Cambridge: Cambridge University Press, 1984); and Michael Saler's chapter in this volume.
36 Robert A. Yelle, *Semiotics of Religion: Signs of the Sacred in History* (London: Bloomsbury, 2013), 93.
37 Walsham, "The Reformation," 521.
38 Ibid., 524.
39 Ibid., 525.
40 Cameron, *Enchanted Europe*. Ibid., 10, explicitly invokes Weber's disenchantment thesis.
41 Ibid., 12. Jason Josephson-Storm makes the same point in his chapter in this volume.
42 Ibid., 157, 196–210.
43 Cameron, *Enchanted Europe*, 206–7. See also ibid., 257–8 (discussing Hobbes's critique of miracles).
44 Walsham, "The Reformation," 503–4.
45 Ibid., 511. The classic work on this topic is, of course, Marc Bloch, *Les rois thaumaturges* (Paris: Armand Colin, 1961).
46 Bloch, *Les rois thaumaturges*, 381–405. See also Keith Thomas, *Religion and the Decline of Magic*, 192–8.
47 Bloch, *Les rois thaumaturges*, 336–9. See also Walker, "Cessation," 121; Paul Kléber Monod, *The Power of Kings: Monarchy and Religion in Europe, 1589–1715* (New Haven, CT: Yale University Press, 1999), 68. Yelle, *Sovereignty and the Sacred*, 53–5, discusses James I's own repetition of the idea that miracles and oracles ceased

with the establishment of the church, as an analogy for the manner in which kings temper their absolute power in submitting to a frame of laws.

48 Bloch, *Les rois thaumaturges*, 375–9. See also Schmitt, *Leviathan*, 54, noting the rite's political dimensions; Monod, *Power of Kings*, 226; Walsham, "The Reformation," 512.

49 John Spencer, *A Discourse concerning Prodigies* (Cambridge, 1663). For a discussion of Spencer, see Yelle, *Sovereignty and the Sacred*, 59–61. Another factor may have been the activity of such popular wonder-workers as Valentine Greatrakes; see already Bloch, *Les rois thaumaturges*, 384.

50 Lorraine Daston and Katharine Park, *Wonders and the Order of Nature 1150–1750* (New York: Zone Books, 1998), 321; see also ibid., 335.

51 Hobbes, *Leviathan*, chap. 32, §9. Cf. ibid., chap. 37, "Of Miracles, and Their Use," which is more equivocal, yet submits the certification of miracles to the sovereign, thus defusing precisely their revolutionary potential. As noted below, Hobbes also echoed the idea that oracles ceased. Similarly, Francis Atterbury argued that "since the Age of Miracles ceas'd, as it did, when the Testimony of the Gospel was fully Seal'd," the main evidence of divine providence now is political revolutions. Atterbury, "The Wisdom of Providence manifested in the Revolutions of Government. A Sermon Preach'd before the Honourable House of Commons … May the 29th, 1701," in *Sermons and Discourses on Several Subjects and Occasions* (London, 1723), 1: 251ff., quoted in Gerald Strake, "The Final Phase of Divine Right Theory in England, 1688–1702," *English Historical Review* 77 (1962): 645–6.

52 Bloch, *Les rois thaumaturges*, 390. See also Michael Schaich, ed., *Monarchy and Religion: The Transformation of Royal Culture in Eighteenth-Century Europe* (Oxford: Oxford University Press, 2007), Introduction, 27, stating that the Royal Touch in England "was finally discontinued after 1714, having first fallen into disuse under William III and only very briefly been revived under Anne. This was mainly for religious reasons, as [J.C.D.] Clark convincingly suggests. Neither the Calvinist William III nor the Lutheran George I (1714–27) wished to carry out a rite that was tainted by connotations of superstition and, from the reign of James II (1685–8), even Catholicism."

53 Bloch, *Les rois thaumaturges*, 391.

54 Ibid., 402, notes that Charles X attempted to revive the practice in 1825.

55 Ibid., 385.

56 Schmitt, *Leviathan*, 54–6; Schmitt, *Political Theology: Four Chapters on the Concept of Sovereignty*, translated by George Schwab (Chicago: University of Chicago Press, 2005), 36–7.

57 See the references above at note 4.

58 See also Jane Shaw, *Miracles in Enlightenment England* (New Haven, CT: Yale University Press, 2006), 22–5; Jean Calvin, *"Epistre"* to the *Institutions de la religion*

chrestienne (Geneva, 1541), cited in Daston and Park, *Wonders*, 247 and 424n118. D.P. Walker noted that Luther "sometimes preached the cessation of miracles," but that neither he nor Calvin absolutely excluded further miracles. Walker, "The Cessation of Miracles," in *Hermeticism and the Renaissance: Intellectual History and the Occult in Early Modern Europe*, ed. Ingrid Merkel and Allen G. Debus (Washington, DC: Folger Books, 1988), 111–12. For further references and discussion, see Yelle, *Sovereignty and the Sacred*, 52–61.

59 Walker, "Cessation of Miracles," 114.
60 See, for example, Amos Funkenstein, *Theology and the Scientific Imagination From the Middle Ages to the Seventeenth Century* (Princeton, NJ: Princeton University Press, 1986), 247: "Because the apocalyptic visionaries shared with the normative Jewish establishment the conviction that prophecy had ceased with the end of the ancient monarchy—a conviction that had guided the process of canonization of biblical books—they were inhibited from prophesying."
61 See the discussion and references in the next section of this chapter.
62 J.G.A. Pocock, "Perceptions of Modernity in Early Modern Historical Thinking," *Intellectual History Review* 17 (2007): 55.
63 Thomas Sprat, *History of the Royal Society* (London, 1667), 362–3.
64 Jonathan Israel, *Radical Enlightenment: Philosophy and the Making of Modernity, 1650-1750* (Oxford: Oxford University Press, 2001), 599–609 (Spinoza), 359–74 (Fontenelle). I should note that Prof. Israel, in his chapter in this volume, acknowledges the existence of such earlier theological polemics.
65 Jonathan Sheehan, "Enlightenment, Religion, and the Enigma of Secularization: A Review Essay," *The American Historical Review* 108 (2003): 1067.
66 See references in Yelle, *The Language of Disenchantment*, 22.
67 On Fontenelle, see J. Samuel Preus, *Explaining Religion: Criticism and Theory from Bodin to Freud* (Atlanta: Scholars Press, 1996), 40–55. See also Hobbes, *Leviathan*, chap. 12, §31: "And whereas in the planting of the Christian religion, the oracles ceased in all parts of the Roman empire, and the number of Christians increased wonderfully every day and in every place, by the preaching of the Apostles and Evangelists, a great part of that success may reasonably be attributed to the contempt into which the priests of the Gentiles of that time had brought themselves, by their uncleanness, avarice, and juggling between princes." See also ibid., chap. 37, §12.
68 Hans Blumenberg, *Arbeit am Mythos*, 2nd ed. (Frankfurt am Main: Suhrkamp, 1981), 121 (my translation): "Daß die heidnischen Orakel im Augenblick der Geburt Jesu verstummt seien, ist ebenso ein Mythos der Gleichzeitigkeit wie der vom Tode des Hirtengottes Pan im Augenblick der Kreuzigung Jesu." See also ibid., 292.
69 Edward Gibbon, *The Decline and Fall of the Roman Empire* (London, 1776). See also Conyers Middleton, *A Free Inquiry into the Miraculous Powers, Which Are Supposed to Have Subsisted in the Christian Church* (London, 1749).

70 Gibbon, *The Decline and Fall*, chap. 15, §3.
71 Ibid.
72 J.G.A. Pocock, *Barbarism and Religion*, vol. 1, *The Enlightenments of Edward Gibbon, 1737–1764* (Cambridge: Cambridge University Press, 1999), 44, states that Gibbon was involved in the debates over miracles already in his adolescence. Gibbon, *The Decline and Fall*, chap. 15, cites both Middleton and Johann Lorenz von Mosheim. See note 88 below for a discussion of Mosheim.
73 Jonathan Sheehan, "When Was Disenchantment? History and the Secular Age," in *Varieties of Secularism in a Secular Age*, ed. Michael Warner, Jonathan VanAntwerpen, and Craig Calhoun (Cambridge, MA: Harvard University Press, 2010).
74 Talal Asad, *Formations of the Secular: Christianity, Islam, Modernity* (Stanford: Stanford University Press, 2003), 13–14.
75 Michael Saler, "Modernity and Enchantment: A Historiographic Review," *The American Historical Review* 111, no. 3 (2006): 714.
76 Weber, "Science as a Vocation," 147, 152, 155.
77 Max Weber, *Ancient Judaism*, trans. Hans H. Gerth and Don Martindale (New York: Free Press, 1967), 379, 395, 412; and Max Weber, *Economy and Society*, ed. Guenther Roth and Claus Wittich, 2 vols. (Berkeley: University of California Press, 1978), 819, 828. However, as we know, Weber did not adopt the position that charisma had ended entirely. It remained possible as one ideal type of authority. Even in "Science as a Vocation," 155, Weber allowed the possibility of further charismatic movements, if only in small groups and *"in pianissimo."*
78 Weber, *Economy and Society*, 828. See also Lorenz Trein's discussion of this passage in his chapter.
79 As I pointed out in *Sovereignty and the Sacred*, 70, John Potts followed Weber in making the same mistake. See Potts, *A History of Charisma* (New York: Palgrave Macmillan, 2009), 80–1.
80 Weber, *Economy and Society*, 216, 1112. See Peter Haley, "Rudolph Sohm on Charisma," *Journal of Religion* 60 (1980); Friedrich Wilhelm Graf, "Max Weber und die protestantische Theologie seiner Zeit," *Zeitschrift für Religions- und Geistesgeschichte*, 39, no. 2 (1987): 132–3; David Norman Smith, "Faith, Reason, and Charisma: Rudolph Sohm, Max Weber, and the Theology of Grace," *Sociological Inquiry* 68 (1998); Thomas Kroll, "Max Webers Idealtypus der charismatischen Herrschaft und die zeitgenössische Charisma-Debatte," in *Max Webers Herrschaftssoziologie: Studien zu Entstehung und Wirkung*, ed. Edith Hanke and Wolfgang J. Mommsen (Tübigen: Mohr Siebeck, 2001), 50–1; Joshua Derman, "Max Weber and Charisma: A Transatlantic Affair," *New German Critique* 113 (2011): 56–7.
81 Rudolph Sohm, *Kirchenrecht*, vol. 1, *Die geschichtlichen Grundlagen* (Leipzig: Duncker & Humblot, 1892); Rudolph Sohm, *Kirchenrecht*, vol. 2, *Katholisches Kirchenrecht*

(Munich and Leipzig: Duncker & Humblot, 1923). Walter Lowrie, *The Church and Its Organization in Primitive and Catholic Times: An Interpretation of Rudolph Sohm's Kirchenrecht* (London and Bombay: Longmans, Green, and Co., 1904), is partly a translation and partly a paraphrase and extension of Sohm's work. Carl Schmitt responded to the second volume of Sohm's treatise the same year in which it appeared (1923), in *Roman Catholicism and Political Form*, trans. G.L. Ulmen (Westport, CT: Greenwood Press, 1996), which attacked the idea of a dichotomy between charisma and legal authority in the Roman Catholic Church, criticizing Sohm in particular (29, 32) while mentioning Weber in more positive terms (14).

82 Sohm, *Kirchenrecht*, 1: 26.
83 Ernst Troeltsch contested this point. See Troeltsch, *The Social Teaching of the Christian Churches*, trans. Olive Wyon, vol. 1 (Chicago: University of Chicago Press, 1981), 98n44: "Until now, he [Sohm] has not yet proved that it is possible to have a Church and an organized religious fellowship without some kind of Church order." For related reasons, the Protestant church historian Adolf Harnack conducted a debate with Sohm regarding the nature of the early Christian church, discussion of which would take us too far from our topic. On this debate, see Kroll, "Max Webers Idealtypus"; Haley, "Rudolph Sohm," 188. However, Harnack's position could also, on occasion, resemble Sohm's. See Harnack, *What Is Christianity?* (New York: Harper Torchbooks, 1957), 264: "as an outward and visible Church and a State founded on law and on force, Roman Catholicism has nothing to do with the Gospel, nay, is in fundamental contradiction with it." For further discussion of Harnack and his debate with Sohm, see Lorenz Trein's chapter in this volume.
84 Sohm, *Kirchenrecht*, 1: 22–3 (my translation).
85 Ibid., 2: 168–9, 180–2 (my translation).
86 Ibid., 2: 182.
87 Ibid., 2: 170–1 (my translation).
88 Gibbon, *The Decline and Fall*, chap. 15, §5, had already described a remarkably similar trajectory. At first early Christians had no set form of government: "the apostles declined the office of legislation …" Leadership was supplied by prophets, whose "extraordinary gifts were frequently abused or misapplied … As the institution of prophets became useless, and even pernicious, their powers were withdrawn, and their offices abolished. The public functions of religion were solely intrusted to the established ministers of the church, the bishops and the presbyters." In this respect, Gibbon partly followed Johann Lorenz von Mosheim's account of the history of the early church as a decline from the apostles and their disciples and followers, who possessed miraculous powers, to bishops who ruled over expanding domains. Johann Lorenz von Mosheim, *Institutes of Ecclesiastical History* (London: William Tegg, 1867 [1755]), part 1, chap. 1–2.
89 Derman, "Max Weber and Charisma," 65–6; Martin Riesebrodt, "Charisma in Max Weber's Sociology of Religion," *Religion* 29, 1 (1999): 7–8. Haley, "Rudolph

Sohm," 196, argues mainly for this reason that Weber "generaliz[ed Sohm's] concept 'charisma' ... [and] emptied the idea, gift of grace, first of its Christian meaning, finally of all religious content." Smith, "Faith, Reason, and Charisma," 50, exaggerates the difference when he states that "nowhere is Weber's deviation from Sohm clearer than in his appreciation of the Catholic idea of office charisma. Sohm fulminated against the very idea that an office can have charisma." Actually, Weber made the same sharp distinction as Sohm between *Amtscharisma* and true charisma.

90 I follow Kroll, "Max Webers Idealtypus," esp. 70–1, in this regard.

91 See, for example, Potts, *History of Charisma*, 81, 107, 115; Anthony Carroll, *Protestant Modernity: Weber, Secularisation, and Protestantism* (Scranton, PA: University of Scranton Press, 2007), 184–90.

92 Max Weber, *Ancient Judaism*. See Julius Wellhausen, *Prolegomena to the History of Ancient Israel* (Cleveland: Meridian Books, 1957 [1878]). For Wellhausen's influence on Weber, see Ernst Michael Dörrfuß, *Mose in den Chronikbüchern: Garant theokratischer Zukunftserwartung* (Berlin: De Gruyter, 1994), 87; Hubert Treiber, "Anmerkungen zu Max Webers Charismakonzept," *Zeitschrift für Altorientalische und Biblische Rechtsgeschichte* 11 (2005); Peter Ghosh, *A Historian Reads Max Weber: Essays on the Protestant Ethic* (Wiesbaden: Harrassowitz, 2008), 158–9; Friedemann Voigt, "Das protestantische Erbe in Max Webers Vorträgen über 'Wissenschaft als Beruf' und 'Politik als Beruf,'" *Zeitschrift für Neuere Theologiegeschichte* 9, no. 2 (2002): 253, 256: "Webers und Wellhausens Prophetenbild ist freilich selbst ein protestantisch-theologisches Konstrukt. ... Indem Weber mit Wellhausen den ursprünglichen, rein religiösen Charakter der prophetischen Offenbarungen und die institutionellen, priesterlichen Folgen unterschied, bleib er jener Differenz von Religion und Theologie verpflichtet, die der 'positiven' Theologie als Grundthema halt." For qualifications of this dependence, see Eckart Otto, *Max Webers Studien des Antiken Judentums: Historische Grundlegung einer Theorie der Moderne* (Tübingen: Mohr Siebeck, 2002), esp. 98–9, 270–1. Ibid., 99, states: "M. Weber folgt nicht der J. Wellhausen noch leitenden Differenzierung zwischen vorexilischem 'Hebraismus' und nachexilischem 'Judaismus,' die mit negativem Werturteilen in bezug auf das Judentum versehen ist." Despite the erudition that Otto displays in his command of Weber's writings and sources on ancient Judaism, this conclusion appears to me highly questionable. Weber's negative opinions regarding Judaism are described further below. For further discussion of Weber's ideas on ancient Judaism, see Wolfgang Schluchter, ed., *Max Webers Studie über das antike Judentum* (Frankfurt am Main: Suhrkamp, 1981).

93 Robert A. Yelle, "From Sovereignty to Solidarity: Some Transformations in the Politics of Sacrifice from the Reformation to Robertson Smith," *History of Religions* 58 (2019).

94 Weber, *Ancient Judaism*, 83–4.

95 Ibid., 84–6.
96 Ibid., 93–4, 411.
97 Ibid., 140.
98 Wellhausen, *Prolegomena*, 412.
99 Weber, *Ancient Judaism*, 294; see also ibid., 286, 381.
100 Ibid., 297. Christopher Adair-Toteff, "Max Weber's Charismatic Prophets," *History of the Human Sciences* 27 (2014), emphasizes Weber's dependence on the Old Testament prophets, rather than on Sohm, for his concept of charisma.
101 Weber, *Ancient Judaism*, 293.
102 Ibid., 284.
103 Graf, "Max Weber und die Protestantische Theologie," 129–31.
104 On the uncharismatic nature of the rabbis, see Weber, *Ancient Judaism*, 395, 411–12, 414.
105 Voigt, "Das protestantische Erbe," 255, notes the parallel already in Wellhausen: "Schon Wellhausen hatte in diesem Prozeß mehr als einen einmaligen historischen Vorgang gesehen. Vielmehr sei dies ein entwicklungsgeschichtlicher Realisierungsvorgang religiöser Ideen, der in der Transformation des Individualismus der Predigt Jesu in die hierokratischen Strukturen des Frühkatholizismus eine Analogie findet."
106 Weber, *Ancient Judaism*, 381–2. See also Lorenz Trein's discussion of this passage in his chapter.
107 Ibid., 284.
108 Ibid., 379, 412.
109 Ibid., 411–12; see also ibid., 395.
110 Romans 9.
111 John Milbank, *Theology and Social Theory: Beyond Secular Reason* (Oxford: Blackwell, 1990), 94.
112 Max Weber, *The Sociology of Religion* (Boston: Beacon Press, 1964), 207–8.
113 Max Weber, *The Religion of India: The Sociology of Hinduism and Buddhism*, trans. Hans H. Gerth and Don Martindale (New York: Free Press, 1958), 37–8. For a discussion, see Ghosh, *Max Weber and "The Protestant Ethic"*, 166–7.
114 Weber, *The Religion of India*, 112.
115 Ibid., 37–8.
116 For discussions of the contribution of the Christian critique of Mosaic ceremonial law to the development of secularization, see Yelle, "Moses' Veil"; Robert A. Yelle, "The Hindu Moses: Christian Polemics against Jewish Ritual and the Secularization of Hindu Law under Colonialism," *History of Religions* 49 (2009); Robert A. Yelle, "Imagining the Hebrew Republic: Christian Genealogies of Religious Freedom," in *Politics of Religious Freedom*, ed. Winnifred Fallers Sullivan, Elizabeth Shakman Hurd, Saba Mahmood, and Peter Danchin (Chicago: University of Chicago Press, 2015).

117 Weber, *Protestant Ethic*, 147.
118 Weber, *Economy and Society*, 820.
119 Gibbon, *The Decline and Fall*, chap. 15, §1.
120 David Ellenson, "Max Weber on Judaism and the Jews," in David Ellenson, *After Emancipation: Jewish Religious Responses to Modernity* (Cincinnati: Hebrew Union College Press, 2004), 94. For different perspectives, see Gary A. Abraham, *Max Weber and the Jewish Question: A Study of the Social Outlook of His Sociology* (Urbana and Chicago: University of Illinois Press, 1992); Hans Liebeschütz, "Max Weber's Historical Interpretation of Judaism," *The Leo Baeck Institute Year Book* 9, no. 1 (1964).
121 Peter L. Berger, "Charisma and Religious Innovation: The Social Location of Israelite Prophecy," *American Sociological Review* 28 (1963): 949.
122 Ibid., 949.
123 See discussion and references in Yelle, *The Language of Disenchantment*, 15, 110, 139–40, 160.
124 Further examples that directly connect the Puritan ideology of supersession with the end of sacrifice and the end of liturgical music as practiced under the Mosaic law can be found respectively in Yelle, "From Sovereignty to Solidarity," 331–8; and Robert Yelle, "Protestant (An)aesthetics," in *Bloomsbury Handbook for the Cultural and Cognitive Aesthetics of Religion*, ed. Anne Koch and Katharina Wilkens (London: Bloomsbury, 2019), 247–50.
125 Clifford Geertz, "Religion as a Cultural System," *Anthropological Approaches to the Study of Religion*, ed. Michael Banton (New York: Tavistock, 1985), 28.
126 Yelle, *Sovereignty and the Sacred*, suggests an alternative way of formulating the tension between sovereignty and legality while also providing further specific criticisms of Weber's sociology of religion.

Chapter 8

1 Max Weber, *Wissenschaft als Beruf*, Nachwort von Friedrich Tenbruck (Stuttgart: Reclam, 2002), 19; Max Weber, *Wirtschaft und Gesellschaft* (Tübingen: Mohr Siebeck, 1985); Max Weber, "Die protestantische Ethik und der Geist des Kapitalismus," in *Gesammelte Aufsätze zur Religionssoziologie* I (Tübingen: Mohr Siebeck, 1988), 94ff.
2 Max Weber, "Über einige Kategorien der Verstehenden Soziologie," in *Gesammelte Aufsätze zur Wissenschaftslehre* (Tübingen: Mohr Siebeck, 1922), 409.
3 Daniel Weidner, "Zur Rhetorik der Säkularisierung," *Deutsche Vierteljahresschrift für Literaturwissenschaft und Geistesgeschichte* 78, no. 1 (2004): 103.
4 Max Weber, "Zwischenbetrachtung," in *Gesammelte Aufsätze zur Religionssoziologie* I (Tübingen: Mohr Siebeck, 1988), 564 (translation MWS).

5   Robert Yelle, in this volume.
6   Jason Josephson-Storm, in this volume.
7   For Talal Asad and his school of thought, see, for example, Talal Asad, *Genealogies of Religion: Discipline and Reasons of Power in Christianity and Islam* (Baltimore: Johns Hopkins University Press, 1993); Talal Asad, *Formations of the Secular: Christianity, Islam, Modernity* (Stanford: Stanford University Press, 2003); Talal Asad, Judith Butler, and Saba Mahmood, *Is Critique Secular?: Blasphemy, Injury, and Free Speech* (Berkeley: Townsend Center, 2009); Saba Mahmood, "Religious Reason and Secular Affect: An Incommensurable Divide?" *Critical Inquiry* 35, no. 4. (2009); Saba Mahmood, *Religious Difference in the Secular Age: A Minority Report* (Princeton, NJ: Princeton University Press, 2015); Elizabeth Shakman Hurd, *The Politics of Secularism in International Relations* (Princeton, NJ: Princeton University Press, 2008).

    For the postcolonial strand of critique, related to secularism and Islam, see John L. Esposito and Azzam Tamimi, eds., *Islam and Secularism in the Middle East* (London: Hurst & Company 2000); for India, see Ashis Nandy, "An Anti-Secularist Manifesto," *India International Centre Quarterly* 22, no. 1 (1995). For critical accounts of the Asadian school and of other postcolonial accounts of secularism and secularization, see Hadi Enayat, *Islam and Secularism in Post-Colonial Thought: A Cartography of Asadian Genealogies* (Cham: Springer International Publishing, 2017); Sindre Bangstad, "Contesting Secularism/s: Secularism and Islam in the Work of Talal Asad," *Anthropological Theory* 9, no. 2 (2009).
8   Philip Gorski, "Historicizing the Secularization Debate: Church, State, and Society in Late Medieval and Early Modern Europe, ca. 1300 to 1700," *American Sociological Review* 65, no. 1 (2000); Michael Bergunder, "Comparison in the Maelstrom of Historicity: A Postcolonial Perspective on Comparative Religion," in *Interreligious Comparisons in Religious Studies and Theology: Comparison Revisited*, ed. P. Schmidt-Leukel and A. Nehring (London: Bloomsbury, 2016); Wolfgang Knöbl, *Die Kontingenz der Moderne: Wege in Europa, Asien und Amerika* (Frankfurt and New York: Campus, 2007).
9   Christian Smith, "Introduction: Rethinking the Secularization of American Public Life," in *The Secular Revolution: Power, Interests, and Conflict in the Secularization of American Public Life*, ed. Christian Smith (Berkeley: University of California Press, 2003).
10 Aamir Mufti, "The Aura of Authenticity," *Social Text* 18, no. 3 (2000).
11 Gregor McLennan, "The Postsecular Turn," *Theory, Culture, and Society* 27, no. 4 (2010).
12 David Martin, "What I Really Said about Secularization," *Dialog* 46, no. 2 (2007).
13 Jonathan Sheehan, "When Was Disenchantment? History and the Secular Age," in *Varieties of Secularism in a Secular Age*, ed. Michael Warner, Jonathan VanAntwerpen, and Craig Calhoun (Cambridge, MA: Harvard University Press, 2013).

14 Robert Yelle, in this volume.
15 See Ian Hunter, "Charles Taylor's *A Secular Age* and Secularization in Early Modern Germany," *Modern Intellectual History* 8, no. 3 (2011). Hunter has convincingly argued that Charles Taylor's philosophical history of secularization is "a single linear before-and-after narrative in which the 'before' has both normative and chronological priority in relation to the 'after'" (627). See also Sheehan, "When Was Disenchantment?"
16 For the analysis of such narratives, see Peter Harrison, "Introduction: Narratives of Secularization," *Intellectual History Review* 27, no. 1 (2017).
17 For the history of these categories of interpretation, see Hermann Zabel, *Verweltlichung/Säkularisierung: Zur Geschichte einer Interpretationskategorie*, PhD diss. (Westphalian Wilhelms University, Münster, 1968).
18 The term in its legal meaning goes back to 1646. It was the French envoy Longueville, who used "séculariser" for the first time to refer to the expropriation of Church property. The practice that it referred to, however, is much older. See Zabel, *Verweltlichung*, 11.
19 Werner Conze, Hans-Wolfgang Strätz, and Hermann Zabel, "Säkularisation, Säkularisierung," in *Geschichtliche Grundbegriffe: Historisches Lexikon zur politisch-sozialen Sprache in Deutschland*, ed. Otto Brunner, Werner Conze, and Reinhart Koselleck, vol. 5 (Stuttgart, 1984), 791.
20 Joseph von Eichendorff, "Über die Folgen von der Aufhebung der Landeshoheit der Bischöfe und der Klöster in Deutschland" (1818), in Joseph von Eichendorff, *Historische und politische Schriften*, historisch-kritische Ausgabe, vol. 10.1, ed. Antonie Magen (Tübingen: Max Niemeyer Verlag, 2007), 5 (translation MWS).
21 Ibid., 28–9 (translation MWS).
22 Ibid., 35 (translation MWS).
23 Ibid., 6 (translation MWS).
24 Conze, Strätz, and Zabel, "Säkularisation, Säkularisierung," 812 (translation MWS). This is not to say, however, that previous forms of distinction and differentiation did not exist. Early forms of distinction were between spiritual and temporal power, the two swords, etc., and existed in the Middle Ages and early modernity in regions influenced by Christianity, Islam, or Buddhism. What is new is that they are addressed (from the religious side) as a process of secularization that is perceived as problematic.
25 Wolfgang Eßbach, *Religionssoziologie 1: Glaubenskrieg und Revolution als Wiege neuer Religionen* (Munich: Wilhelm Fink, 2014), 25.
26 Ibid., 16 (translation MWS).
27 In this regard, see Robert A. Yelle, *The Language of Disenchantment: Protestant Literalism and Colonial Discourse in British India* (Oxford: Oxford University Press, 2013). Yelle argues (14) that disenchantment "has created its own reality, has induced its own break or rupture with history."

28 Thomas Luckmann, "Säkularisierung—ein moderner Mythos," in Thomas Luckmann, *Lebenswelt und Gesellschaft: Grundstrukturen und gesellschaftliche Wandlungen* (Paderborn: utb, 1980).
29 This is derived from Émile Durkheim, *The Elementary Forms of Religious Life*, trans. Karen E. Fields (New York: Free Press, 1995), especially book 2, chapters 6 and 7, pp. 190–241. For forms of individual and collective self-transcendence, see also Hans Joas, *Die Macht des Heiligen: Eine Alternative zur Geschichte von der Entzauberung* (Frankfurt am Main: Suhrkamp, 2017), chapter 7, p.419f.
30 Thomas Luckmann, "Schrumpfende Transzendenzen, expandierende Religion?," in Thomas Luckmann, *Wissen und Gesellschaft: Ausgewählte Aufsätze 1981–2002* (Konstanz: UVK, 2002).
31 Hubert Knoblauch, *Populäre Religion: Auf dem Weg in eine spirituelle Gesellschaft* (Frankfurt am Main: Campus, 2009). Jason Ä. Josephson-Storm, *The Myth of Disenchantment: Magic, Modernity, and the Birth of the Human Sciences* (Chicago: University of Chicago Press, 2017), uses a similar argument against Weber's thesis of de-magicalization, when he hints at the magic produced in Weber's own time.
32 See Detlef Pollack, *Säkularisierung—ein moderner Mythos?: Studien zum religiösen Wandel in Deutschland* (Tübingen: Mohr Siebeck, 2003).
33 Weidner, "Zur Rhetorik," 107 (translation MWS).
34 Ian Hunter, "Secularization: The Birth of a Modern Combat Concept," *Modern Intellectual History* 12, no. 1 (2015).
35 Ibid., 32.
36 Ibid.
37 José Casanova, *Public Religions in the Modern World* (Chicago: University of Chicago Press, 1994). See also José Casanova, "Secularization Revisited: A Reply to Talal Asad," in *Powers of the Secular Modern: Talal Asad and His Interlocutors*, ed. David Scott and Charles Hirschkind (Stanford: Stanford University Press, 2006), 19; José Casanova, "Rethinking Secularization: A Global Comparative Perspective," *The Hedgehog Review* 8, no. 1–2 (2006).
38 Lucian Hölscher, ed., *Datenatlas zur religiösen Geographie im protestantischen Deutschland: Von der Mitte des 19. Jahrhunderts bis zum Zweiten Weltkrieg*, 4 vols. (Berlin and New York: De Gruyter, 2003), 7. See also Kurt Nowak, "Staat ohne Kirche?: Überlegungen zur Entkirchlichung der evangelischen Bevölkerung im Staatsgebiet der DDR," in *Christen, Staat und Gesellschaft in der DDR*, ed. Gert Kaiser and Ewald Frie (Frankfurt am Main: Wallstein, 1996).
39 Hugh McLeod, "Secular Cities?: Berlin, London and New York in the Later Nineteenth and Early Twentieth Centuries," in *Religion and Modernization: Sociologists and Historians Debate the Secularization Thesis*, ed. Steve Bruce (Oxford: Oxford University Press, 1992), 66. See also Jochen-Christoph Kaiser, "Organisierter Atheismus im 19. Jahrhundert," in *Atheismus und religiöse*

Indifferenz, ed. Christel Gärtner, Detlef Pollack and Monika Wohlrab-Sahr (Opladen: Leske+Budrich, 2003), 120.

40 McLeod, "Secular Cities."
41 José Casanova, "Global Trends at the Turn of the Millennium" (lecture at Max-Weber-Kolleg, University of Erfurt, Germany, July 7, 2003); McLeod, "Secular Cities."
42 Monika Wohlrab-Sahr and Thomas Schmidt-Lux, "Science versus Religion: The Process of Secularization in the GDR as a Specific Response to the Challenges of Modernity," in *Religion and Politics in Europe and the United States: Transnational Historical Approaches*, ed. Volker Depkat and Jürgen Martschukat (Washington, DC and Baltimore: Johns Hopkins University Press, 2013).
43 See Hermann Lübbe, *Säkularisierung, Geschichte eines ideenpolitischen Begriffs* (Freiburg and Munich: Alber, 1975). Regarding history, see, as an example from the early twentieth century, Richard Fester, "Die Säkularisation der Historie," *Historische Vierteljahrschrift* 11 (1908).
44 Hunter, "Charles Taylor," 621, writes that the modern history of secularization is bound up in a "specific (neo-Thomist) view of secularization as a theological and ecclesiological 'disembedding' of rational subjectivity from its prior embodiment in a sacral body, community (church), and cosmos." Hunter sees this view represented in Charles Taylor, *A Secular Age* (Cambridge, MA: Harvard University Press, 2007).
45 Todd Weir, "Germany and the New Global History of Secularism: Questioning the Postcolonial Genealogy," *The Germanic Review: Literature, Culture, Theory* 90, no. 1 (2015). One might point out that the Enlightenment philosophies that Hunter deals with were also not necessarily anti-Christian.
46 Ibid., 8.
47 I cannot delve into the general debate on the concept of religion that has been going on in religious studies for decades. See, for example, Timothy Fitzgerald, "A Critique of 'Religion' as a Cross-cultural Category," *Method & Theory in the Study of Religion* 9, no. 2 (1997).
48 Rodney Stark, "Secularization, R.I.P.," *Sociology of Religion* 60, no. 3 (1999).
49 In later publications, Casanova himself shifted between questioning the generalizability of functional differentiation and considering "structural differentiation" as a general feature of modernity. See José Casanova, "Public Religions Revisited," in *Religion: Beyond a Concept*, ed. Hent de Vries (New York: Fordham University Press, 2008), 103; and Casanova, "Secularization Revisited," 19.
50 Casanova, *Public Religions*.
51 See esp. Talal Asad, "Religion, Nation-State, Secularism," in *Nation and Religion: Perspectives on Europe and Asia*, ed. Peter van der Veer and Hartmut Lehmann (Princeton, NJ: Princeton University Press, 1999); Asad, *Formations of the Secular*; and recently, Talal Asad, "Reflections on Violence, Law, and Humanitarianism," *Critical Inquiry* 41, no. 2 (2015).

52 As a criticism of this perspective, see also Enayat, *Islam and Secularism*; Reinhard Schulze, "Die Dritte Unterscheidung: Islam, Religion und Säkularität," in *Religionen—Wahrheitsansprüche—Konflikte: Theologische Perspektiven*, ed. Walter Dietrich and Wolfgang Lienemann (Zürich: TVZ, 2000).
53 Weir, "Germany," 7.
54 Asad, *Formations of the Secular*, 17.
55 Weir, "Germany," 10.
56 Casanova, "Secularization Revisited," 28.
57 See Robert A. Yelle, "The Hindu Moses: Christian Polemics against Jewish Ritual and the Secularization of Hindu Law under Colonialism," *History of Religions* 49, no. 2 (2009).
58 On this use of the term "apparatus," see Ruth Mas, "Why Critique?" *Method & Theory in the Study of Religion* 24 (2012): 405. The term "apparatus" has been used in many ways in relation to the secular.
59 Enayat, *Islam and Secularism*, 3.
60 See, for instance, Matthias Koenig, "How Nation-States Respond to Religious Diversity," in *International Migration and the Governance of Religious Diversity*, ed. Paul Bramadat and Matthias Koenig (Montreal: McGill-Queen's University Press, 2009); Ahmet T. Kuru, *Secularism and State Policies toward Religion: The United States, France, and Turkey* (Cambridge: Cambridge University Press, 2009).
61 John R. Bowen, "Secularism: Conceptual Genealogy or Political Dilemma?" *Comparative Studies in Society and History* 52, no. 3 (2010): 682.
62 David Scott and Charles Hirschkind, eds., *Powers of the Secular Modern: Talal Asad and His Interlocutors* (Stanford: Stanford University Press, 2006).
63 I very much agree with Jonathan Sheehan's comment on Charles Taylor and his plea to explore the resources of the nonreligious. Sheehan, "When Was Disenchantment?" 242.
64 See Weir, "Germany," 13ff.
65 Janet R. Jakobsen and Ann Pellegrini, "Introduction: Times Like These," in *Secularisms*, ed. Janet R. Jakobsen and Ann Pellegrini (Durham and London 2008: Duke University Press), 13.
66 See Weir, "Germany."
67 See Bowen, "Secularism."
68 Jakobsen and Pellegrini, "Introduction," 3.
69 Ibid., 2.
70 Gil Anidjar, "Secularism," *Critical Inquiry* 33, no. 1 (2006): 56.
71 Hurd, *The Politics of Secularism*.
72 Ibid., 2. The passage quoted within the quote is from Scott and Hirschkind, "Introduction," 2.
73 Martin Saar, "Genealogy and Subjectivity," *European Journal of Philosophy* 10, no. 2 (2002).

74 See, for example, Christoph Kleine, "Religion and the Secular in Premodern Japan from the Viewpoint of Systems Theory," *Journal of Religion in Japan* 2, no. 1 (2013). Different conceptualizations of the secular and the religious or their predecessors, similar to different notions of transcendence, could also be related to the debate on the Axial Age.

75 See, among others, Peter van der Veer, *Imperial Encounters. Religion and Modernity in India and Britain* (Princeton, NJ: Princeton University Press, 2001); Yelle, "The Hindu Moses," etc.

76 Yelle, "The Hindu Moses."

77 Van der Veer, *Imperial Encounters*, 8.

78 Ibid., 4. Van der Veer discusses this with regard to Louis Dumont's major work on the Hindu caste system, *Homo Hierarchicus* (1966).

79 See also Bergunder, "Comparison."

80 This argument has been made by Ashis Nandy, "The Politics of Secularism and the Recovery of Religious Tolerance," in *Secularism and Its Critics*, ed. Rajeev Bhargava (New Delhi: Oxford University Press, 1998).

81 Esposito and Tamimi, *Islam and Secularism*.

82 A significant example is Azzam Tamimi's provocative interview with La Vanguardia after 9/11: "Admiro a los talibán: son unos valientes," *La Vanguardia*, November 8 (2001), 88.

83 John Esposito is the director of The Prince Alwaleed bin Talal Center for Muslim-Christian Understanding at Georgetown University, Washington, DC.

84 John Esposito, "Introduction: Islam and Secularism in the 21st Century," in *Islam and Secularism*, 10–11.

85 Azzam Tamimi, "The Origins of Arab Secularism," in *Islam and Secularism*, 28.

86 Abdelwahab Elmessiri, "Secularism, Immanence, and Deconstruction," in *Islam and Secularism*, 58, 69.

87 Weir, "Germany," 17. Weir quotes here from Kurt Hutten, *Kulturbolschewismus: Eine deutsche Schicksalsfrage* (Stuttgart: Kohlhammer, 1932), 4.

88 See Hutten, *Kulturbolschewismus*, 4–5.

89 See Parvez Manzoor, "Desacralising Secularism," in *Islam and Secularism*.

90 Authoritarianism, however, is confined not only to "secularist regimes" in the Middle East but also to those which call themselves "Islamic" states or republics.

91 The general assumption is that religion is much better able than the secular state to guarantee tolerance toward other religions. See Mahmood, *Religious Difference*. You can find a very similar argument in the Indian debate, usually referring back to Ashoka. See Nandy, "The Politics of Secularism."

92 Mahmood, "Religious Reason," 848–9. For a critique of this argument, see Andrew F. March, "Speaking about Muhammad, Speaking for Muslims," *Critical Inquiry* 37, no. 4 (2011).

93 Mahmood, "Religious Reason."
94 Ibid., 848f.
95 Andrew F. March, "Is Critique Secular? Poppies and Prophets," *The Immanent Frame*, March 2011: http://blogs.ssrc.org/tif/2011/03/17/poppies-and-prophets/?disp=print (last access: December 8, 2019).
96 Ibid.
97 Barbara Rox, *Schutz religiöser Gefühle im freiheitlichen Verfassungsstaat?* (Tübingen: Mohr Siebeck, 2012).
98 Ibid., 313.
99 Ibid., 319.
100 Ibid., 318 (translation MWS).
101 Michel Foucault, "What Are the Iranians Dreaming About?," in *Foucault and the Iranian Revolution: Gender and the Seductions of Islamism*, ed. Janet Afary and Kevin B. Anderson (Chicago: University of Chicago Press, 2005).
102 These questions are reflected in the research being conducted by the Humanities Centre of Advanced Study "Multiple Secularities—Beyond the West, Beyond Modernities" at the University of Leipzig, funded by the DFG since 2016. The center is directed by Christoph Kleine and myself.
103 Christoph Kleine, "Zur Universalität der Unterscheidung religiös/säkular: Eine systemtheoretische Betrachtung," in *Religionswissenschaft: Ein Studienbuch*, ed. Michael Stausberg (Berlin: De Gruyter, 2012).
104 Andrew F. March, "What Can the Islamic Past Teach Us about Secular Modernity?" *Political Theory* 43, no. 6 (2015).
105 Neguin Yavari, *Advice for the Sultan, Prophetic Voices and Secular Politics in Medieval Islam* (Oxford: Oxford University Press, 2014); Neguin Yavari, *The Future of Iran's Past* (Cambridge: Cambridge University Press, 2017).
106 See, for example, Sherman A. Jackson, "The Islamic Secular," *American Journal of Islamic Social Sciences* 34, no. 2 (2017); Yavari, *Advice for the Sultan*; an early example is Ira M. Lapidus, "The Separation of State and Religion in the Development of Early Islamic Society," *International Journal of Middle East Studies* 6, no. 4 (1975).
107 Armando Salvatore, "The Islamicate Adab Tradition vs. the Islamic Shari'a, from Pre-Colonial to Colonial," *Working Paper Series of the HCAS "Multiple Secularities—Beyond the West, Beyond Modernities,"* no. 3 (Leipzig, March 2018).
108 Charles Taylor argues differently. He assumes that in archaic societies religion was "everywhere." Taylor, *A Secular Age*, 15.
109 The relation to reference problems and guiding ideas was first developed in Monika Wohlrab-Sahr and Marian Burchardt, "Multiple Secularities: Towards a Cultural Sociology of Secular Modernities," *Comparative Sociology* 11, no. 6 (2012).

Bibliography

Introduction

Anidjar, Gil. "Secularism." *Critical Inquiry* 33, no. 1 (2006): 52–77.

Asad, Talal. *Formations of the Secular: Christianity, Islam, Modernity*. Stanford: Stanford University Press, 2003.

Asprem, Egil. *The Language of Disenchantment: Scientific Naturalism and Esoteric Discourse, 1900–1939*. Leiden: Brill, 2014.

Blumenberg, Hans. *The Legitimacy of the Modern Age*. Translated by Robert M. Wallace. Cambridge, MA: MIT Press, 1985 [1976].

Casanova, José. *Public Religions in the Modern World*. Chicago: University of Chicago Press, 1994.

Graf, Friedrich Wilhelm. "Max Weber und die protestantische Theologie seiner Zeit." *Zeitschrift für Religions- und Geistesgeschichte* 39, no. 2 (1987): 122–47.

Griffioen, Sjoerd. "Modernity and the Problem of Its Christian Past: The *Geistesgeschichten* of Blumenberg, Berger, and Gauchet." *History and Theory* 55, no. 2 (2016): 185–209.

Hanegraaff, Wouter J. *New Age Religion and Western Culture: Esotericism in the Mirror of Secular Thought*. Leiden: Brill, 1996.

Hanegraaff, Wouter J. "How Magic Survived the Disenchantment of the World." *Religion* 33, no. 4 (2003): 357–80.

Harrison, Peter. "Introduction: Narratives of Secularization." *Intellectual History Review* 27, no. 1 (2017): 1–6.

Israel, Jonathan I. *Radical Enlightenment: Philosophy and the Making of Modernity 1650–1750*. New York: Oxford University Press, 2001.

Jellinek, Georg. *Die Erklärung der Menschen- und Bürgerrechte: Ein Beitrag zur modernen Verfassungsgeschichte*. Leipzig: Duncker & Humblot, 1895.

Josephson-Storm, Jason Ā. *The Myth of Disenchantment: Magic, Modernity, and the Birth of the Human Sciences*. Chicago: University of Chicago Press, 2017.

Kippenberg, Hans. *Die Entdeckung der Religionsgeschichte: Religionswissenschaft und Moderne*. Munich: Beck, 1997.

Kippenberg, Hans. "Dialektik der Entzauberung: Säkularisierung aus der Perspektive von Webers Religionssystematik." In *Alte Begriffe—Neue Probleme: Max Webers Soziologie im Lichte aktueller Problemstellungen*, edited by Thomas Schwinn and Gert Albert, 81–116. Tübingen: Mohr Siebeck, 2016.

Koselleck, Reinhart. "Zeitverkürzung und Beschleunigung: Eine Studie zur Säkularisation." In Reinhart Koselleck, *Zeitschichten: Studien zur Historik*, 177–202. Frankfurt am Main: Suhrkamp, 2013.

Kroll, Thomas. "Max Webers Idealtypus der charismatischen Herrschaft und die zeitgenössische Charisma-Debatte." In *Max Webers Herrschaftssoziologie: Studien zu Entstehung und Wirkung*, edited by Edith Hanke and Wolfgang J. Mommsen, 47–72. Tübingen: Mohr Siebeck, 2001.

Landy, Joshua, and Michael Saler, eds. *The Re-Enchantment of the World: Secular Magic in a Rational Age*. Stanford: Stanford University Press, 2009.

Löwith, Karl. *Meaning in History: The Theological Implications of the Philosophy of History*. 2nd ed. Chicago: University of Chicago Press, 1950.

Nietzsche, Friedrich. *The Genealogy of Morals*. Translated by Horace B. Samuel. New York: Boni and Liveright, 1918 [1887].

Saler, Michael. "Modernity and Enchantment: A Historiographic Review." *The American Historical Review* 111, no. 3 (2006): 692–716.

Sheehan, Jonathan. "When Was Disenchantment? History and the Secular Age." In *Varieties of Secularism in a Secular Age*, edited by Michael Warner, Jonathan VanAntwerpen, and Craig Calhoun, 217–42. Cambridge, MA: Harvard University Press, 2010.

Taylor, Charles. *A Secular Age*. Cambridge, MA: Belknap Press of Harvard University Press, 2007.

Weber, Max. "Science as a Vocation." In *From Max Weber: Essays in Sociology*, edited and translated by Hans H. Geerth and C. Wright Mills, 129–56. New York: Oxford University Press, 1946.

Weber, Max. *The Protestant Ethic and the Spirit of Capitalism*. Translated by Talcott Parsons with an Introduction by Anthony Giddens. New York: Charles Scribner's Sons, 1958 [1920].

Weber, Max. *Gesammelte Aufsätze zur Religionssoziologie*. Volume 1. Tübingen: J. C. B. Mohr, 1972 [1920].

White, Andrew Dickson. *A History of the Warfare of Science with Theology in Christendom*. 2 volumes. London: Macmillan and Co., 1896.

Chapter 1

Asprem, Egil. *The Problem of Disenchantment: Scientific Naturalism and Esoteric Discourse, 1900–1939*. Leiden: Brill, 2014.

Asprem, Egil. "The Disenchantment of Problems: Musings on a Cognitive Turn in Intellectual History." *Journal of Religion in Europe* 8, no. 3–4 (2015): 304–19.

Berman, Morris. *The Reenchantment of the World*. Ithaca, NY: Cornell University Press, 1981.

Blumenberg, Hans. *Die Legitimität der Neuzeit*. Frankfurt: Suhrkamp, 1966.

Breuer, Stefan. "Magie, Zauber, Entzauberung." In *Max Webers 'Religionssystematik,'* edited by Hans G. Kippenberg and Martin Riesebrodt, 119–30. Tübingen: Mohr Siebeck, 2001.

Bücher, Karl, Joseph Schumpeter, and Fr. Freiherr von Wiese. *Wirtschaft und Wirtschaftswissenschaft: Grundriß der Sozialökonomik*. Part 1. Tübingen: J.C.B. Mohr (Paul Siebeck), 1914.

Bull, Malcolm, ed. *Apocalypse Theory and the Ends of the World*. Oxford: Oxford University Press, 1995.

Burger, Thomas. "Deutsche Geschichtstheorie und Webersche Soziologie." In *Max Webers Wissenschaftslehre: Interpretation und Kritik*, edited by Gerhard Wagner and Heinz Zipprian, 29–104. Frankfurt: Suhrkamp, 1994.

Calhoun, Craig, Mark Juergensmeyer, and Jonathan VanAntwerpen, eds. *Rethinking Secularism*. Oxford: Oxford University Press, 2011.

Casanova, José. *Public Religions in the Modern World*. Chicago: University of Chicago Press, 1994.

Daston, Lorraine. *Wunder, Beweise, Tatsachen*. Frankfurt: Fischer, 2001.

Faivre, Antoine. *Access to Western Esotericism*. Albany: SUNY Press, 1994.

Gauchet, Marcel. *The Disenchantment of the World: A Political History of Religion*. Princeton, NJ: Princeton University Press, 1999.

Gerth, Hans H., and C. Wright Mills, eds. *From Max Weber: Essays in Sociology*. Oxford: Oxford University Press, 1958.

Ghosh, Peter. *Max Weber and "The Protestant Ethic": Twin Histories*. Oxford: Oxford University Press, 2014.

Habermas, Jürgen, and Joseph Ratzinger. *Dialectics of Secularization: On Reason and Religion*. Translated by Brian McNeil. San Francisco: Ignatius Press, 2006.

Hanegraaff, Wouter J. *Esotericism and the Academy: Rejected Knowledge in Western Culture*. Cambridge: Cambridge University Press, 2012.

Hidas, Zoltan. *Entzauberte Geschichte: Max Weber und die Krise des Historismus*. Frankfurt am Main: Lang, 2004.

Hölscher, Lucian. *Weltgericht oder Revolution: Protestantische und sozialistische Zukunftsvorstellungen im deutschen Kaiserreich*. Stuttgart: Klett, 1989.

Hölscher, Lucian. *Die Entdeckung der Zukunft*. Frankfurt am Main: Fischer, 1999.

Joas, Hans. "Gefährliche Prozessbegriffe: Eine Warnung vor der Rede von Differenzierung, Rationalisierung und Modernisierung." In *Umstrittene Säkularisierung: Soziologische und Historische Analysen zur Differenzierung von Religion und Politik*, edited by Karl Gabriel, Christel Gärtner and Detlef Pollack, 603–22. Berlin: Berlin University Press, 2012.

Joas, Hans. *Die Macht des Heiligen: Eine Alternative zur Geschichte von der Entzauberung*. Berlin: Suhrkamp, 2017.

Josephson-Storm, Jason Ā. *The Myth of Disenchantment. Magic, Modernity, and the Birth of the Human Sciences*. Chicago: University of Chicago Press, 2017.

Käsler, Dirk. "Max Weber." In *Klassiker der Soziologie*, volume 1, edited by Dirk Käsler, 191–214. Munich: C.H. Beck, 2006.

Katz, David S., and Richard H. Popkin. *Messianic Revolution: Radical Religious Politics to the End of the Second Millennium*. New York: Hill and Wang, 1998.

Kern, Thomas. *Zeichen und Wunder: Enthusiastische Glaubensformen in der modernen Gesellschaft*. Frankfurt: Lang, 1997.

Kippenberg, Hans G. "The Study of Religions in the Twentieth Century." In *The Future of the Study of Religion: Proceedings of Congress 2000*, edited by Slavica Jakelić and Lori Pearson, 47–64. Brill: Leiden, 2004.

Kippenberg, Hans G. "Religionswissenschaft." In *Handbuch Moderneforschung*, edited by Friedrich Jäger, Wolfgang Knöbl, and Ute Schneider, 231–43. Stuttgart: Metzler, 2015.

Kippenberg, Hans G. "Tracing Modern Roots of Esotericism: Discussing Limits of Disenchantment." *Journal of Religion in Europe* 8, no. 3–4 (2015): 281–87.

Kippenberg, Hans G., and Martin Riesebrodt, eds. *Max Webers "Religionssystematik."* Tübingen: Mohr Siebeck, 2001.

Krech, Volkhard. "Secularization, Re-Enchantment, or Something in between?: Methodological Considerations and Empirical Observations Concerning a Controversial Historical Idea." In *Religion and Secularity: Transformations and Transfers of Religious Discourses in Europe and Asia*, edited by Marion Eggert and Lucian Hölscher, 77–108. Leiden: Brill, 2013.

Krech, Volkhard. "Magischer Orient und rationaler Okzident? Eine metaphorologische Notiz zum 'Zaubergarten,' 'stahlharten Gehäuse,' und zur 'Welt als Text.'" *Bochumer Jahrbuch zur Ostasienforschung* 38 (2015): 371–81.

Lawrence, Bruce B. *Defenders of God: The Fundamentalist Revolt against the Modern Age*. San Francisco: Harper & Row, 1989.

Lehmann, Edvard. "Erscheinungswelt der Religion: Phänomenologie der Religion." *Religion in Geschichte und Gegenwart*, volume 2 (1910), 497–577.

Lehmann, Hartmut. *Die Entzauberung der Welt: Studien zu Themen von Max Weber*. Göttingen: Vandenhoeck & Ruprecht, 2009.

Lepsius, Rainer M. "Eigenart und Potenzial des Weber-Paradigmas." In *Das Weber-Paradigma: Studien zur Weiterentwicklung von Max Webers Forschungsprogramm*, edited by Gert Albert, Agathe Bienfait, Steffen Sigmund, and Claus Wendt, 32–41. Tübingen: Mohr Siebeck, 2002.

Löwith, Karl. *Weltgeschichte und Heilsgeschehen: Die theologischen Voraussetzungen der Geschichtsphilosophie*. Stuttgart and Heidelberg: Metzler, 1953.

Marty, Martin E. "Fundamentalism as a Social Phenomenon." *Bulletin of the American Academy of Arts and Sciences* 42, no. 2 (1988): 15–29.

Marty, Martin E., and R. Scott Appleby, eds. *The Fundamentalism Project*. 5 volumes. Chicago: University of Chicago Press, 1991–1995.

Miller, Donald E., and Tetsunao Yamamori. *Global Pentecostalism: The New Face of Christian Social Engagement*. Berkeley: University of California Press, 2007.

Oldenberg, Hermann. "Die indische Religion." In *Die orientalischen Religionen*, part 1.3.1 of *Die Kultur der Gegenwart: Ihre Entwicklung und ihre Ziele*, edited by Paul Hinneberg, 51–73. Berlin and Leipzig: B.G. Teubner, 1906.

Riesebrodt, Martin. *Fundamentalismus als patriarchalische Protestbewegung*. Tübingen: Mohr Siebeck, 1990. English translation, *Pious Passion: The Emergence of Modern Fundamentalism in the United States and Iran*. Translated by Don Reneau. Berkeley: University of California Press, 1993.

Rohde, Erwin. *Psyche: Seelencult und Unsterblichkeitsglaube der Griechen*. Freiburg im Breisgau: Mohr, 1894.

Said, Edward W. *Orientalism*. New York: Vintage, 1979.

Sandeen, Ernest R. *The Roots of Fundamentalism: British and American Millenarianism 1800–1930*. Chicago: University of Chicago Press, 2008 [1970].

Schluchter, Wolfgang. "Max Webers Religionssoziologie: Eine werkgeschichtliche Rekonstruktion." In *Max Webers Sicht des antiken Christentums: Interpretation und Kritik*, edited by Wolfgang Schluchter, 525–56. Frankfurt: Suhrkamp, 1985.

Schluchter, Wolfgang. *Religion und Lebensführung*, volume 1, *Studien zu Max Webers Kultur- und Werttheorie*. Frankfurt: Suhrkamp, 1988.

Schluchter, Wolfgang. "'Wirtschaft und Gesellschaft': Das Ende eines Mythos." In Wolfgang Schluchter, *Religion und Lebensführung*, vol. 2, 597–634. Frankfurt: Suhrkamp, 1988.

Schluchter, Wolfgang. *Die Entzauberung der Welt: Sechs Studien zu Max Weber*. Tübingen: Mohr Siebeck, 2009.

Siebeck, Hermann. *Lehrbuch der Religionsphilosophie*. Freiburg and Leipzig: Mohr Siebeck, 1893.

Stauth, Georg. *Islam und westlicher Rationalismus: Der Beitrag des Orientalismus zur Entstehung der Soziologie*. Frankfurt: Campus, 1993.

Stuckrad, Kocku von. *Western Esotericism: A Brief History of Secret Knowledge*. London and Oakville: Equinox, 2005.

Stuckrad, Kocku von. *The Scientification of Religion: An Historical Study of Discursive Change, 1800–2000*. Berlin: De Gruyter, 2014.

Swedberg, Richard. *Max Weber Dictionary: Key Words and Central Concepts*. Stanford: Stanford University Press, 2005.

Tenbruck, Friedrich H. "Abschied von Wirtschaft und Gesellschaft." *Zeitschrift für die gesamte Staatswissenschaft* 133, no. 4 (1977): 703–36.

Tyrell, Hartmann. "Das Narrativ von der Entzauberung der Welt." *Soziopolis* (February 15, 2018): https://www.soziopolis.de/lesen/buecher/artikel/das-narrativ-von-der-entzauberung-der-welt/ (accessed December 16, 2019).

Weber, Marianne. *Max Weber: Ein Lebensbild*. Tübingen: Mohr Siebeck, 1926.

Weber, Marianne. *Max Weber: A Biography*. Edited and translated by Harry Zohn, with a new introduction by Guenther Roth. New Brunswick and Oxford: Transaction Books, 1988.

Weber, Max. "Antikritisches zum 'Geist' des Kapitalismus." *Archiv für Sozialwissenschaft und Sozialpolitik* 30 (1910): 176–202.

Weber, Max. *Gesammelte Aufsätze zur Religionssoziologie*. Volume 1. Tübingen: J.C.B. Mohr, 1972 [1920].
Weber, Max. *Critique of Stammler*. Translated by Guy Oakes. New York: Free Press, 1977.
Weber, Max. "Anticritical Last Word on *The Spirit of Capitalism*." Translated with an introduction by Wallace M. Davis. *American Journal of Sociology* 83, no. 5 (1978): 1105–31.
Weber, Max. *Economy and Society: An Outline of Interpretive Sociology*. Edited and translated by Guenther Roth and Claus Wittich. Berkeley: University of California Press, 1978 [1921–1922].
Weber, Max. "Categories of Interpretive Sociology" [1913]. Translated by Edith Graber. *The Sociological Quarterly* 22, no. 2 (1981): 151–80.
Weber, Max. "R. Stammlers 'Überwindung' der materialistischen Geschichtsauffassung" [1907]. In *Gesammelte Aufsätze zur Wissenschaftslehre*, edited by Johannes Winckelmann, 291–359. Tübingen: Mohr Siebeck, 1988.
Weber, Max. "Über einige Kategorien der verstehenden Soziologie" [1913]. In Max Weber: *Gesammelte Aufsätze zur Wissenschaftslehre*, edited by Johannes Winckelmann, 427–74. Tübingen: Mohr Siebeck, 1988.
Weber, Max. *Die Wirtschaftsethik der Weltreligionen. Konfuzianismus und Taoismus* [1915–1920]. Edited by Helwig Schmidt-Glintzer. *Max Weber Gesamtausgabe* (*MWG*) I/19. Tübingen: Mohr Siebeck, 1989.
Weber, Max. *The Protestant Ethic and the Spirit of Capitalism*. Translated by Talcott Parsons with a new Introduction by Anthony Giddens. London and New York: Routledge, 1992 [1920].
Weber, Max. *Wissenschaft als Beruf & Politik als Beruf* [1917/1919]. Edited by Wolfgang J. Mommsen and Wolfgang Schluchter. *MWG* I/17. Tübingen: Mohr Siebeck, 1992.
Weber, Max. *Wirtschaft und Gesellschaft*. Volume 2. *Religiöse Gemeinschaften*. *MWG* I/22-2. Edited by Hans G. Kippenberg in cooperation with Petra Schilm with the help of Jutta Niemeier. Tübingen: J.C.B. Mohr Siebeck, 2001.
Weber, Max. *The Protestant Ethic and the "Spirit" of Capitalism (1905) and Other Writings*. Edited, translated, and with an introduction by Peter Baehr and Gordon Wells. Harmondsworth: Penguin, 2002.
Weber, Max. *Die protestantische Ethik und der Geist des Kapitalismus*. Edited by Dirk Käsler. Vollständige Ausgabe. Munich: C.H. Beck, 2013.
Winckelmann, Johannes. *Max Webers Hauptwerk*. Tübingen: Mohr Siebeck, 1986.
Yelle, Robert A. *The Language of Disenchantment: Protestant Literalism and Colonial Discourse in British India*. New York: Oxford University Press, 2013.
Yelle, Robert A. *Sovereignty and the Sacred: Secularism and the Political Economy of Religion*. Chicago: University of Chicago Press, 2019.

Chapter 2

Asprem, Egil. *The Problem of Disenchantment: Scientific Naturalism and Esoteric Discourse, 1900–1939*. Boston: Brill, 2014.

BBC News. "U.S. Faces Growing Problems in Regulating Fortune Tellers." September 28, 2010.

Beck, Julie. "The New Age of Astrology." *The Atlantic*, January 16, 2018.

Breuer, Stefan. "Magie, Zauber, Entzauberung." In *Max Webers "Religionssystematik,"* edited by Hans G. Kippenberg and Martin Riesebrodt, 119–30. Tübingen: Mohr Siebeck, 2001.

Cullen, Christopher. *Heavenly Numbers: Astronomy and Authority in Early Imperial China*. New York: Oxford University Press, 2017.

De Blécourt, Willem, and Cornelie Usborne. "Women's Medicine, Women's Culture: Abortion and Fortune-Telling in Early Twentieth-Century Germany and the Netherlands." *Medical History* 43 (1999): 376–92.

Freytag, Gustav Willibald. "Rainer Maria Rilkes Briefe an Alfred Schuler." *Jahrbuch der deutschen Schillergesellschaft* 4 (1960): 425–33.

Furness, Raymond. *Zarathustra's Children: A Study of a Lost Generation of German Writers*. Rochester, NY: Camden House, 2000.

Ghosh, Peter. *Max Weber and "The Protestant Ethic": Twin Histories*. Oxford: Oxford University Press, 2014: 174–202.

Green, Martin. *The Von Richthofen Sisters*. New York: Basic Books, 1974.

Jenkins, Richard. "Disenchantment, Enchantment and Re-Enchantment: Max Weber at the Millennium." *Max Weber Studies* 1, no.1 (2000): 11–32.

Josephson-Storm, Jason Ā. *The Myth of Disenchantment: Magic, Modernity and the Birth of the Human Sciences*. Chicago: University of Chicago Press, 2017.

Kalberg, Stephen. "Max Weber's Types of Rationality: Cornerstones for the Analysis of Rationalization Processes in History." *American Journal of Sociology* 85, no. 5 (1980): 1145–79.

Karlauf, Thomas. *Stefan George: Die Entdeckung des Charisma*. Munich: Blessing, 2007.

Klages, Ludwig. *Rhythmen und Runen*. Leipzig: Barth, 1944.

Klages, Ludwig. *Sämtliche Werke*. Edited by Ernst Frauchiger. Bonn: H. Bouvier, 1964–1992.

Klages, Ludwig. *The Biocentric Worldview: Selected Essays and Poems of Ludwig Klages*. Translated by Joseph Pryce. London: Arktos Media, 2013.

Kroll, Thomas. "Max Webers Idealtypus der charismatischen Herrschaft und die zeitgenössische Charisma-Debatte." In *Max Webers Herrschaftssoziologie: Studien zu Entstehung und Wirkung*, edited by Edith Hanke and Wolfgang Mommsen, 47–72. Tübingen: Mohr Siebeck, 2001.

Little, William. "Britain's Psychic Turn." *The Guardian*, May 19, 2009.

McCrary, Charles. "Fortune Telling and American Religious Freedom." *Religion and American Culture* 28, no. 2 (2018): 269–306.

Reventlow, Franziska. *Herrn Dames Aufzeichnungen, oder, Begebenheiten aus einem merkwürdigen Stadtteil*. Munich: Langen, 1913.

Schmied-Knittel, Ina. "Außergewöhnliche Erfahrungen: Repräsentative Studien und aktuelle Befunde." *Zeitschrift für Anomalistik* 8, no. 1–3 (2008): 98–117.

Schmied-Knittel, Ina, and Michael T. Schetsche. "Psi-Report Deutschland: Eine repräsentative Bevölkerungsumfrage zu außergewöhnlichen Erfahrungen." In *Alltägliche Wunder: Erfahrungen mit dem Übersinnlichen. Wissenschaftliche Befunde*, edited by Eberhard Bauer and Michael Schetsche, 13–38. Würzburg: Ergon, 2003.

Schmied-Knittel, Ina, and Michael T. Schetsche. "Everyday Miracles: Results of a Representative Survey in Germany." *European Journal of Parapsychology* 20, no. 1 (2005): 3–21.

Schuler, Alfred. *Alfred Schuler: Fragmente und Vorträge aus dem Nachlass*. Edited by Ludwig Klages. Leipzig: Barth, 1940.

Squires, Nick. "Boom Time for Fortune-Tellers and Tarot Card Readers in Italy as Economic Crisis Bites." *Telegraph*, October 2, 2017.

Voit, Friedrich. *Karl Wolfskehl: Leben und Werk im Exil*. Göttingen: Wallstein-Verlag, 2005.

Weber, Max. *Gesammelte Aufsätze zur Religionssoziologie*. Tübingen: Mohr, 1922.

Weber, Max. *Wirtschaft und Gesellschaft*. Tübingen: Mohr, 1922.

Weber, Max. *The Theory of Social and Economic Organizations*. New York: Oxford University Press, 1947.

Weber, Max. *General Economic History*. New York: Collier Books, 1961.

Weber, Max. *Gesamtausgabe*. Tübingen: Mohr Siebeck, 1984–2012.

Weber, Max. *The Protestant Ethic and the Spirit of Capitalism*. Translated by Talcott Parsons. New York: Routledge, 1992.

Winckelmann, Johannes. "Die Herkunft von Max Webers Entzauberungs-Konzeption." *Kölner Zeitschrift für Soziologie und Sozialpsychologie* 32, no. 1 (1980): 12–53.

Wigzell, Faith. *Reading Russian Fortunes: Print Culture, Gender and Divination in Russia from 1765*. Cambridge: Cambridge University Press, 2015.

Yelle, Robert A. *Sovereignty and the Sacred: Secularism and the Political Economy of Religion*. Chicago: University of Chicago Press, 2019.

Chapter 3

Aad, George et al. "Combined Measurement of the Higgs Boson Mass in *pp* Collisions at $s\sqrt{}$=7 and 8 TeV with the ATLAS and CMS Experiments." *Physics Review Letters* 114 (2015): http://inspirehep.net/record/1356276 (accessed March 26, 2020).

Akin, William E. *Technocracy and the American Dream: The Technocrat Movement, 1900–1941*. Berkeley: University of California Press, 1977.

Alexander, Eben. *Proof of Heaven: A Neurosurgeon's Journey into the Afterlife*. London: Piaktus, 2012.

Anon. *SCIO: Ancient Healing Meets Modern Technology*: https://www.scio.co.za/how-does-it-work (accessed February 7, 2018).

Asprem, Egil. *The Problem of Disenchantment: Scientific Naturalism and Esoteric Discourse 1900–1939*. Leiden and Boston: Brill, 2014.

Asprem, Egil. "The Disenchantment of Problems: Musings on a Cognitive Turn in Intellectual History." *Journal of Religion in Europe* 8, no. 3–4 (2015): 305–20.

Asprem, Egil. "How Schrödinger's Cat Became a Zombie: On the Epidemiology of Science-Based Representations in Popular and Religious Contexts." *Method & Theory in the Study of Religion* 28, no. 2 (2016): 113–40.

Asprem, Egil. "Dialectics of Darkness." *Inference: Review of Science* 4, no. 2 (2018): https://inference-review.com/article/dialectics-of-darkness (accessed March 26, 2020).

Barrett, Stephen. "Some Notes on the Quantum Xrroid (QXCI) and William C. Nelson." *Quackwatch*, July 12, 2009: http://www.quackwatch.org/01QuackeryRelatedTopics/Tests/xrroid.html (accessed February 7, 2018).

Bohr, Niels. *Atomic Physics and Human Knowledge*. New York: John Wiley and Sons, 1958.

Bourdieu, Pierre. *Distinction: A Social Critique of the Judgment of Taste*. Cambridge, MA: Harvard University Press, 1984 [1979].

Bourdieu, Pierre. "The Forms of Capital." In *Handbook of Theory and Research for the Sociology of Education*, edited by John G. Richardson, 241–58. New York: Greenwood Press, 1986.

Bowler, Peter J. *Reconciling Science and Religion: The Debate in Early Twentieth-Century Britain*. Chicago: University of Chicago Press, 2001.

Bowler, Peter J. *Science for All: The Popularization of Science in Early Twentieth-Century Britain*. Chicago: University of Chicago Press, 2009.

Boyer, Pascal. *Religion Explained: The Evolutionary Origins of Religious Thought*. New York: Basic Books, 2001.

Daum, Andreas W. *Wissenschaftspopularisierung im 19. Jahrhundert: Bürgerliche Kultur, naturwissenschaftliche Bildung und die deutsche Öffentlichkeit 1848–1914*. 2nd ed. Munich: Oldenburg Wissenschaftsverlag, 2002.

Dawkins, Richard. *The Selfish Gene*. 30th Anniversary edition. Oxford: Oxford University Press, 2006.

Diggins, John Patrick. *Thorstein Veblen: Theorist of the Leisure Class*. Princeton, NJ: Princeton University Press, 1999.

Dyrendal, Asbjørn. "Devillish Consumption: Popular Culture in Satanic Socialization." *Numen* 55, no. 1 (2008): 68–98.

Forman, Paul. "Weimar Culture, Causality, and Quantum Theory: Adaptation by German Physicists and Mathematicians to a Hostile Environment." *Historical Studies in the Physical Sciences* 3 (1971): 1–115.

Frank, Thomas. *The Conquest of Cool: Business Culture, Counterculture, and the Rise of Hip Consumerism*. Chicago: University of Chicago Press, 1997.

Hallonsten, Olof. *Big Science Transformed: Science, Politics, and Organization in Europe and the United States*. London: Palgrave Macmillan, 2016.
Hammer, Olav. *Claiming Knowledge: Strategies of Epistemology from Theosophy to the New Age*. Leiden and Boston: Brill, 2001.
Hanegraaff, Wouter J. *New Age Religion and Western Culture: Esotericism in the Mirror of Secular Thought*. Albany, NY: SUNY Press, 1998.
Heisenberg, Werner. "The Physical Content of Quantum Kinematics and Mechanics" [1927]. In *Quantum Theory and Measurement*, edited and translated by John Archibald Wheeler and Wojchiech Hubert Zurek, 62–84. Princeton, NJ: Princeton University Press, 1983.
Jaki, Stanley L. *Lord Gifford and His Lectures: A Centenary Retrospect*. Edinburgh: Scottish Academic Press, 1987.
Jeans, James Hopwood. *The Mysterious Universe*. Cambridge: Cambridge University Press, 1930.
Jordan, Pascual. *Die Physik und das Geheimnis des organischen Lebens*. Braunschweig: Friedr. Vieweg, 1941.
Josephson-Storm, Jason Ā. *The Myth of Disenchantment: Magic, Modernity, and the Birth of the Human Sciences*. Chicago and London: University of Chicago Press, 2017.
Kaiser, David. *How the Hippies Saved Physics: Science, Counterculture, and the Quantum Revival*. New York and London: W.W. Norton & Co., 2011.
Kincaid, Harold, John Dupré, and Alison Wylie, eds. *Value-Free Science? Ideals and Illusions*. Oxford: Oxford University Press, 2007.
Lederman, Leon M., with Dick Teresi. *The God Particle: If the Universe Is the Answer, What Is the Question?* Boston and New York: Houghton Mifflin Harcourt, 1993.
Marx, Karl. *Capital*. Volume 1. London: J. M. Dent and Sons, 1930.
Pauli, Wolfgang. "Der Einfluss archetypischer Vorstellungen auf die Bildung naturwissenschaftlicher Theorien bei Kepler." In *Naturerklärung und Psyche*, edited by Carl Gustav Jung and Wolfgang Pauli, 109–94. Zürich: Rascher Verlag, 1952.
Putnam, Hilary. *The Collapse of the Fact/Value Dichotomy and Other Essays*. Cambridge, MA: Harvard University Press, 2002.
Schlieter, Jens. *What Is It Like to Be Dead? Near-Death Experiences, Christianity, and the Occult*. Oxford: Oxford University Press, 2018.
Sussman, Sarah Gail. *Pragmatic Enchantment: William James, Psychical Research, and the Humanities in the American Research University, 1890–1910*. PhD dissertation, Faculty of the Graduate School, University of Texas at Austin, 2017.
Taves, Ann. "Non-Ordinary Powers: Charisma, Special Affordances and the Study of Religion." In *Mental Culture: Classical Social Theory and the Cognitive Science of Religion*, edited by Dimitris Xygalatas and William W. McCorkle, Jr., 80–97. Chesham: Acumen, 2013.
Veblen, Thorstein. *The Theory of the Leisure Class*. New York: Macmillan, 1899.

Veblen, Thorstein. *The Higher Learning in America: A Memorandum on the Conduct of Universities by Business Men*. New York: B.W. Huebsch, 1918.

Veblen, Thorstein. *The Engineers and the Price System*. New York: B.W. Huebsch, 1921.

Veblen, Thorstein. *Absentee Ownership and Business Enterprise in Recent Times: The Case of America*. New York: B.W. Huebsch, 1923.

Weber, Max. "Science as a Vocation." In *From Max Weber: Essays in Sociology*, edited by Hans H. Gerth and C. Wright Mills, 129–56. London: Routledge and Kegan Paul, 1948.

Weber, Max. *The Protestant Ethic and the Spirit of Capitalism*. Translated by Talcott Parsons with an Introduction by Anthony Giddens. New York: Charles Scribner's Sons, 1958.

Weber, Max. "Some Categories of Interpretive Sociology." *The Sociological Quarterly* 22, no. 2 (1981): 179.

Chapter 4

Assmann, Aleida. *Zeit und Tradition: Kulturelle Strategien der Dauer*. Köln: Böhlau, 1999.

Blumenberg, Hans. *The Legitimacy of the Modern Age*. Translated by Robert M. Wallace. Cambridge, MA: MIT Press, 1985 [1976].

Borutta, Manuel. "Genealogie der Säkularisierungstheorie: Zur Historisierung einer großen Erzählung der Moderne." *Geschichte und Gesellschaft* 36, no. 3 (2010): 347–76.

Conrad, Sebastian. "A Cultural History of Global Transformation." In *An Emerging Modern World 1750–1870*, edited by Sebastian Conrad and Jürgen Osterhammel, chapter translation by Peter Lewis, 413–659. Cambridge, MA: The Belknap Press of Harvard University Press, 2018.

Davis, Kathleen. *Periodization and Sovereignty: How Ideas of Feudalism and Secularization Govern the Politics of Time*. Philadelphia: University of Pennsylvania Press, 2008.

Dunkhase, Jan Eike. *Absurde Geschichte: Reinhart Kosellecks historischer Existentialismus*. Marbach am Neckar: Deutsche Schillergesellschaft, 2015.

Eßbach, Wolfgang. *Religionssoziologie 1: Glaubenskrieg und Revolution als Wiege neuer Religionen*. Paderborn: Wilhelm Fink, 2014.

Haley, Peter. "Rudolph Sohm on Charisma." *Journal of Religion* 60, no. 2 (1980): 185–97.

Harnack, Adolf. *Die Mission und Ausbreitung des Christentums in den ersten drei Jahrhunderten*. Volume 1. *Die Mission in Wort und Tat*. 2nd ed. Leipzig: J.C. Hinrichs Buchhandlung, 1906.

Harnack, Adolf. "Art. Verfassung, kirchliche, und kirchliches Recht im 1. und 2. Jahrhundert." In *Realencyclopädie für protestantische Theologie und Kirche*, volume 20, edited by Albert Hauck, 508–46. 3rd ed. Leipzig: J.C. Hinrichs Buchhandlung, 1908.

Harnack, Adolf. *The Mission and Expansion of Christianity in the First Three Centuries.* Volume 1. 2nd ed. Edited and translated by James Moffatt. London: Williams and Norgate, 1908.

Hegel, Georg Wilhelm Friedrich. *Lectures on the Philosophy of World History: Introduction: Reason in History.* Translated by H.B. Nisbet. Cambridge: Cambridge University Press, 1984.

Heppe, Heinrich. *Dogmatik des deutschen Protestantismus im sechzehnten Jahrhundert.* Volume 3. Gotha: Friedrich Andreas Perthes, 1857.

Hirschkind, Charles. "Is There a Secular Body?" *Cultural Anthropology* 26, no. 4 (2011): 633–47.

Hölscher, Lucian. *Die Entdeckung der Zukunft.* Frankfurt am Main: Fischer, 1999.

Joas, Hans. "Die Kontingenz der Säkularisierung: Überlegungen zum Problem der Säkularisierung im Werk Reinhart Kosellecks." In *Begriffene Geschichte: Beiträge zum Werk Reinhart Kosellecks,* edited by Hans Joas and Peter Vogt, 319–38. Berlin: Suhrkamp, 2011.

Jordheim, Helge. "Against Periodization: Koselleck's Theory of Multiple Temporalities." *History and Theory* 51, no. 2 (2012): 151–71.

Jordheim, Helge. "Introduction: Multiple Times and the Work of Synchronization." *History and Theory* 53, no. 4 (2014): 498–518.

Josephson-Storm, Jason Ā. *The Myth of Disenchantment. Magic, Modernity, and the Birth of the Human Sciences.* Chicago: University of Chicago Press, 2017.

Joskowicz, Ari, and Ethan B. Katz. "Introduction: Rethinking Jews and Secularism." In *Secularism in Question: Jews and Judaism in Modern Times,* edited by Ari Joskowicz and Ethan B. Katz, 1–21. Philadelphia: University of Pennsylvania Press, 2015.

Jülicher, Adolf. "Die Religion Jesu und die Anfänge des Christentums bis zum Nicaenum." In J. Wellhausen, et al., *Die christliche Religion mit Einschluss der Israelitisch-Jüdischen Religion (=Die Kultur der Gegenwart, ihre Entwicklung und Ziele I/IV,* edited by Paul Hinneberg), 41–128. Berlin: B.G. Teubner, 1906.

Kippenberg, Hans. "Religious History, Displaced by Modernity." *Numen* 47, no. 3 (2000): 221–43.

Koselleck, Reinhart, ed. *Historische Semantik und Begriffsgeschichte.* Stuttgart: Klett-Cotta, 1978.

Koselleck, Reinhart. "Modernity and the Planes of Historicity" [1968]. In Reinhart Koselleck, *Futures Past: On the Semantics of Historical Time,* translated by Keith Tribe, 3–20. Cambridge, MA: MIT Press, 1985.

Koselleck, Reinhart. "Perspective and Temporality: A Contribution to the Historiographical Exposure of the Historical World" [1977]. In *Futures Past: On the Semantics of Historical Time,* translated by Keith Tribe, 130–55. Cambridge, MA: MIT Press, 1985.

Koselleck, Reinhart. *Critique and Crisis: Enlightenment and the Pathogenesis of Modern Society.* Cambridge, MA: MIT Press, 1988 [1959].

Koselleck, Reinhart. "Concepts of Historical Time and Social History" [1982]. In Reinhart Koselleck, *The Practice of Conceptual History: Timing History, Spacing Concepts*, translated by Todd Samuel Presner et al., 115–30. Stanford: Stanford University Press, 2002.

Koselleck, Reinhart. "Formen der Bürgerlichkeit: Reinhart Koselleck im Gespräch mit Manfred Hettling und Bernd Ulrich." *Mittelweg 36: Zeitschrift des Hamburger Instituts für Sozialforschung* 12, no. 2 (2003): 62–82.

Koselleck, Reinhart. *Kritik und Krise: Eine Studie zur Pathogenese der bürgerlichen Welt.* Frankfurt am Main: Suhrkamp, 2013 [1959].

Koselleck, Reinhart. "Zeitverkürzung und Beschleunigung: Eine Studie zur Säkularisation." In Reinhart Koselleck, *Zeitschichten: Studien zur Historik*, 177–202. 3rd ed. Frankfurt am Main: Suhrkamp, 2013.

Kroll, Thomas. "Max Webers Idealtypus der charismatischen Herrschaft und die zeitgenössische Charisma-Debatte." In *Max Webers Herrschaftssoziologie: Studien zu Entstehung und Wirkung*, edited by Edith Hanke and Wolfgang J. Mommsen, 47–72. Tübingen: Mohr Siebeck, 2001.

Lomler, F.W. et al., eds. *Geist aus Luthers Schriften oder Concordanz der Ansichten und Urtheile des großen Reformators über die wichtigsten Gegenstände des Glaubens, der Wissenschaft und des Lebens.* Volume 4. Darmstadt: Karl Wilhelm Leske, 1831.

Löwith, Karl. *Meaning in History: The Theological Implications of the Philosophy of History.* 2nd ed. Chicago: University of Chicago Press, 1950.

Löwith, Karl. "Die Entzauberung der Welt durch Wissenschaft: Zu Max Webers 100. Geburtstag." *Merkur: Deutsche Zeitschrift für europäisches Denken* 18, no. 6 (=issue 196) (1964): 501–19.

Löwith, Karl. "Das Verhängnis des Fortschritts" [1963]. In *Vorträge und Abhandlungen: Zur Kritik der christlichen Überlieferung*, 139–55. Stuttgart: W. Kohlhammer, 1966.

Löwith, Karl. "Hegels Aufhebung der christlichen Religion" [1962]. In Karl Löwith, *Vorträge und Abhandlungen: Zur Kritik der christlichen Überlieferung*, 54–96. Stuttgart: W. Kohlhammer, 1966.

Löwith, Karl. "Max Webers Stellung zur Wissenschaft" [1965]. In *Vorträge und Abhandlungen: Zur Kritik der christlichen Überlieferung*, 228–52. Stuttgart: W. Kohlhammer, 1966.

Löwith, Karl. "Max Weber's Position on Science" [1965]. In *Max Weber's "Science as a Vocation,"* edited by Peter Lassman, Irving Velody, Herminio Martins, translated by Erica Carter and Christopher Turner, 138–56. London: Unwin Hyman, 1989.

Luther, Martin. *Werke: Kritische Gesamtausgabe.* Volume 41. Weimar: Hermann Böhlaus Nachfolger, 1910.

Müller, Jan Werner. *A Dangerous Mind: Carl Schmitt in Post-War European Thought.* New Haven, CT: Yale University Press, 2003.

Neudecker, Gotthold. *Dr. Wilhelm Münschers Lehrbuch der christlichen Dogmengeschichte.* Volume 2/2. Kassel: Joh. Chr. Krieger, 1838.

Olsen, Niklas. *History in the Plural: An Introduction to the Work of Reinhart Koselleck.* New York: Berghahn Books, 2012.

Rae, Gavin. "The Theology of Carl Schmitt's Political Theology." *Political Theology* 17, no. 6 (2016): 555–72.

Sheehan, Jonathan. "When Was Disenchantment? History and the Secular Age." In *Varieties of Secularism in a Secular Age*, edited by Michael Warner, Jonathan VanAntwerpen, and Craig Calhoun, 217–42. Cambridge, MA: Harvard University Press, 2010.

Sohm, Rudolph. *Kirchenrecht*. Volume 1. *Die geschichtlichen Grundlagen.* Munich: Duncker & Humblot, 1923 [1892].

Steinmetz, Willibald. "Nachruf auf Reinhart Koselleck (1923–2006)" [2006]. In *Begriffene Geschichte: Beiträge zum Werk Reinhart Kosellecks*, 57–83. Berlin: Suhrkamp, 2011.

Tal, Uriel. *Christians and Jews in Germany: Religion, Politics, and Ideology in the Second Reich, 1870–1914.* Translated by Noah Jonathan Jacobs. Ithaca, NY: Cornell University Press, 1975 [1969].

Trein, Lorenz. "'Weil das Christentum nie eine Geschichte hat haben wollen': Theologische Voraussetzungen und eschatologische Ambiguität der Säkularisierung in religionswissenschaftlicher Sicht." *Theologische Zeitschrift* 76, no. 1 (2020): 56–77.

Vahland, Joachim. *Max Webers entzauberte Welt.* Würzburg: Königshausen & Neumann, 2001.

Warner, Michael, Jonathan VanAntwerpen, and Craig Calhoun, eds. "Introduction." In *Varieties of Secularism in a Secular Age*, 1–31. Cambridge, MA: Harvard University Press, 2010.

Weber, Max. "Science as a Vocation." In *From Max Weber: Essays in Sociology*, edited and translated by H.H. Geerth and C. Wright Mills, 129–56. New York: Oxford University Press, 1946.

Weber, Max. *Ancient Judaism.* Edited and translated by Hans H. Gerth and Don Martindale. New York: Free Press, 1967 [1921].

Weber, Max. *Economy and Society: An Outline of Interpretive Sociology.* Volume 1. Edited by Guenther Roth and Claus Wittich. Translated by Ephraim Fischoff et al. Berkeley: University of California Press, 1978 [1956].

Weizsäcker, Carl. *Das Apostolische Zeitalter der christlichen Kirche.* 3rd ed. Tübingen: J.C.B. Mohr, 1902.

Wellhausen, Julius. *Briefe.* Edited by Rudolf Smend, Peter Porzig, and Reinhard Müller. Tübingen: Mohr Siebeck, 2013.

Westphal, K. "Aufhebung." In *A Dictionary of Continental Philosophy*, edited by John Protevi, 42–3. New Haven, CT: Yale University Press, 2006.

Yelle, Robert. "Secularism Reconsidered: Three Approaches." *Politics, Religion & Ideology* 17, no. 4 (2016): 429–32.

Zammito, John. "Koselleck's Philosophy of Historical Time(s) and the Practice of History." *History and Theory* 43, no. 1 (2004): 124–35.

Chapter 5

Arnold, Matthew. "Dover Beach": https://www.poetryfoundation.org/poems/43588/dover-beach (accessed July 19, 2019).

Asprem, Egil. *The Problem of Disenchantment: Scientific Naturalism and Esoteric Discourse, 1900–1939*. Leiden: Brill, 2014.

Baer, Marc. *Mere Believers: How Eight Faithful Lives Changed the Course of History*. Eugene, OR: Cascade Books, 2013.

Barnum, Phineas Taylor. *The Life of P.T. Barnum, Written by Himself*. New York: Redfield, 1855.

Becker, Carl. "Everyman His Own Historian." *The American Historical Review* 37, no. 2 (1932): 221–36.

Benjamin, Walter. *The Arcades Project*. Translated by Howard Eiland and Kevin McLaughlin. Cambridge, MA: Harvard University Press, 1999.

Benjamin, Walter. *The Origin of the German Trauerspiel*. Translated by Howard Eiland. Cambridge, MA: Harvard University Press, 2019.

Berger, Peter, Brigitte Berger, and Hansfried Kellner. *The Homeless Mind: Modernization and Consciousness*. New York: Vintage Books, 1974.

Brabazon, James. *Dorothy L. Sayers: A Biography*. New York: Scribner, 1981.

Brann, Eva. *The World of the Imagination: Sum and Substance*. Lanham, MD: Rowman and Littlefield, 1992.

Chesterton, G.K. *Orthodoxy*: https://www.pagebypagebooks.com/Gilbert_K_Chesterton/Orthodoxy/The_Paradoxes_of_Christianity_p13.html (accessed July 23, 2019).

Coleridge, Samuel Taylor. *Biographia Literaria*. Edited by James Engell and W. Jackson Bate. 2 vols. Princeton, NJ: Princeton University Press, 1983-84.

Conan Doyle, Arthur. *The Hound of the Baskervilles*. Edited by W.W. Robson. Oxford: Oxford University Press, 1998.

Coomes, David. *Dorothy L. Sayers: A Careless Rage for Life*. New York: Lion Books, 1992.

Cusack, Carole M. *Invented Religions: Imagination, Fiction and Faith*. New York: Routledge, 2016.

Daston, Lorraine. "Fear and Loathing of the Imagination in Science." *Daedalus* 127, no. 1 (1998): 73–95.

Daston, Lorraine, and Peter Galison. *Objectivity*. Cambridge, MA: Zone Books, 2007.

Davidson, Markus Altena, ed. *Religion* 46, no. 5. Thematic Issue on *Religion and Fiction* (2016).

Davis, Erik. *High Weirdness: Drugs, Esoterica, and Visionary Experience in the Seventies.* Cambridge, MA: MIT Press, 2019.

Dawkins, Richard. *Unweaving the Rainbow: Science, Delusion and the Appetite for Wonder.* New York: Houghton Mifflin, 1998.

Dibua, Jeremiah. *Modernization and the Crisis of Development in Africa: The Nigerian Experience.* London: Ashgate, 2006.

Dickinson, Edward. *Dancing in the Blood: Modern Dance and European Culture on the Eve of the First World War.* Cambridge: Cambridge University Press, 2017.

Fernández-Armesto, Felipe. *Out of Our Minds: What We Think and How We Came to Think It.* Berkeley: University of California Press, 2019.

Fisher, Walter R. *Human Communication as Narration: Toward a Philosophy of Reason, Value and Action.* Columbia, SC: University of South Carolina Press, 1989.

Gallagher, Catherine. "The Rise of Fictionality." In *The Novel*, volume 1, *History, Geography and Culture*, edited by Franco Moretti, 337–63. Princeton, NJ: Princeton University Press, 2006.

Habermas, Jürgen. *The Structural Transformation of the Public Sphere: An Inquiry into a Category of Bourgeois Society.* Translated by Thomas Burger with Frederick Lawrence. Cambridge, MA: MIT Press, 1991.

Hughes, H. Stuart. *Consciousness and Society.* New York: Alfred A. Knopf, 1958.

Jenkins, Richard. "Disenchantment, Enchantment and Re-Enchantment: Max Weber at the Millennium." *Max Weber Studies* 1, no. 1 (2000): 11–32.

Johnson, Kirsten. "Tolkien's Mythopoesis." In *Tree of Tales: Tolkien, Literature and Theology*, edited by Trevor A. Hart and Ivan Khovacs, 25–38. Waco, TX: Baylor University Press, 2007.

Kearney, Richard. *The Wake of Imagination.* New York: Routledge, 2003.

Landy, Joshua, and Michael Saler, eds. *The Re-Enchantment of the World: Secular Magic in a Rational Age.* Stanford: Stanford University Press, 2009.

Lepenies, Wolf. *Between Literature and Science: The Rise of Sociology.* Cambridge: Cambridge University Press, 1988.

Lewis, C.S. *Surprised by Joy: The Shape of My Early Life.* New York: Harcourt Brace & Company, 1955.

Luhrmann, Tanya M. *When God Talks Back: Understanding the American Evangelical Relationship with God.* Kindle edition. New York: Alfred A. Knopf, 2012.

McKenna, Grainne, David Hevey, and Elaine Martin. *Patients' and Providers' Perspectives on Bibliotherapy in Primary Care*: https://www.hse.ie/eng/services/list/4/mental-health-services/powerofwords/patientsbibliotherapy.pdf (accessed July 16, 2019).

McNeill, William H. "Mythistory, or Truth, Myth, History, and Historians." *The American Historical Review* 91, no. 1 (1986): 1–10.

Nietzsche, Friedrich. *The Birth of Tragedy & The Genealogy of Morals.* Edited by Francis Golffing. New York: Anchor Books, 1956.

Nietzsche, Friedrich. *Beyond Good and Evil.* Translated by Walter Kaufmann. New York: Vintage Books, 1989.

Nietzsche, Friedrich. *Human, All-Too Human*. Translated by Helen Zimmern and Paul V. Cohn. New York: Dover, 2006.

Radkau, Joachim. *Max Weber: A Biography*. Cambridge: Polity Press, 2009.

Rae, Patricia. *The Practical Muse: Pragmatist Poetics in Hulme, Pound, and Stevens*. Lewisburg, PA: Bucknell University Press, 1997.

Reynolds, Barbara. *Dorothy L. Sayers: Her Life and Soul*. New York: St. Martin's Press, 1997.

Robert-Houdin, Jean-Eugène. *Secrets of Conjuring and Magic*. Edited and translated by Louis Hoffman. Cambridge: Cambridge University Press, 2011.

Rousseau, Jean-Jacques. *Emile, or On Education*. Translated by Christopher Kelly and Allan Bloom. Hanover, NH: Dartmouth College Press, 2010.

Saler, Michael. "Modernity and Enchantment: A Historiographic Review." *The American Historical Review* 111 no. 3 (2006): 692–716.

Saler, Michael. *As If: Modern Enchantment and the Literary Prehistory of Virtual Reality*. New York: Oxford University Press, 2012.

Saler, Michael. "Enchantment." *Oxford Research Encyclopedia of Literature*. New York: Oxford University Press, forthcoming.

Saunders, Max. *Self-Impression: Life-Writing, Autobiografiction, and the Forms of Modern Literature*. New York: Oxford University Press, 2010.

Sayer, Derek. *Surrealism and the Human Sciences*. Chicago: Prickly Paradigm Press, 2015.

Sayers, Dorothy L. *Christian Letters to a Post-Christian World: A Selection of Essays*. Grand Rapids, MI: Eerdmans, 1969.

Sayers, Dorothy L. "Gaudy Night." In *The Art of the Mystery Story*, edited by Howard Haycraft, 208–21. New York: Carroll & Graf, 1974.

Scaff, Lawrence A. *Fleeing the Iron Cage: Culture, Politics, and Modernity in the Thought of Max Weber*. Berkeley: University of California Press, 1989.

Sheehan, Jonathan. *The Enlightenment Bible: Translation, Scholarship, Culture*. Princeton, NJ: Princeton University Press, 2005.

Stevens, Wallace. *Opus Posthumous*. Edited by M.J. Bates. New York: Alfred A. Knopf, 1989.

Tolkien, J.R.R. *The Letters of J.R.R. Tolkien*. Edited by Humphrey Carpenter. Boston, MA: Houghton Mifflin Company, 2000.

Toulmin, Stephen. *Cosmopolis: The Hidden Agenda of Modernity*. Chicago: University of Chicago Press, 1990.

Weber, Max. "'Objectivity' in Social Science and Social Policy." In *The Methodology of the Social Sciences*, edited and translated by E.A. Shils and H.A. Finch, 49–112. New York: Free Press, 1949.

Weber, Max. *From Max Weber: Essays in Sociology*. Edited and translated by Hans H. Gerth and C. Wright Mills. London: Routledge, 1991.

Weber, Max. *The Protestant Ethic and the Spirit of Capitalism*. Translated by Gordon C. Wells. New York: Penguin, 2002.

Weber, Max. "Science as a Vocation": https://trialectics.net/projects/political-theory/max-weber/science-as-vocation/ (accessed July 14, 2019).
Wilde, Oscar. "Phrases and Philosophies for the Uses of the Young." *The Chameleon* 1, no. 1 (1894): 1–3.
Williamson, Jack. "Scientifiction, Searchlight of Science." *Amazing Stories Quarterly* 1, no. 4 (1928): 435.
Yelle, Robert A. "Bentham's Fictions: Canon and Idolatry in the Genealogy of Law." *Yale Journal of Law & the Humanities* 17, no. 2 (2005): 151–79.

Chapter 6

Bates, David. "Rousseau and Schmitt: Sovereigns and Dictators." In *Thinking with Rousseau: From Machiavelli to Schmitt*, edited by Helena Rosenblatt and P. Schweigert, 276–94. Cambridge: Cambridge University Press, 2017.
Burrow, J.W. *The Crisis of Reason: European Thought, 1848–1914*. New Haven, CT: Yale University Press, 2000.
Dubos, Nicolas. "Hobbes et les Lumières radicales." *Lumières* (Publication du Centre interdisciplinaire bordelais d'étude des Lumières) 13 (2010): 35–63.
Einhorn, Ignaz. *Spinoza's Staatslehre, Zum ersten Male dargestellt*. Dessau: Gebrüder Katz, 1851.
Gaddo, Irene, and Edoardo Tortarolo. *Secolarizzione e modernità*. Rome: Carocci, 2017.
García-Alonso, Marta. "Jonathan Israel et Carl Schmitt: Révolution philosophique versus contre-révolution théologique." In *Les Lumières radicales et le politique: Études critiques sur les travaux de Jonathan Israel*, edited by M. García-Alonso, 355–86. Paris: Honoré Champion, 2017.
Goldberg, Chad Alan. *Modernity and the Jews in Western Social Thought*. Chicago: University of Chicago Press, 2017.
Horkheimer, Max, and Theodor Adorno. *Dialectic of Enlightenment*. New York: Continuum, 2000.
Hunter, Ian. *The Secularisation of the Confessional State: The Political Thought of Christian Thomasius*. Cambridge: Cambridge University Press, 2007.
Israel, Jonathan. *Enlightenment Contested: Philosophy, Modernity, and the Emancipation of Man 1670–1752*. Oxford: Oxford University Press, 2006.
Israel, Jonathan. "Leo Strauss and the Radical Enlightenment." In *Reading Between the Lines: Leo Strauss and the History of Early Modern Philosophy*, edited by Winfried Schröder, 9–28. Berlin: De Gruyter, 2015.
Israel, Jonathan. *The Expanding Blaze: How the American Revolution Ignited the World, 1775–1848*. Princeton, NJ: Princeton University Press, 2017.
Israel, Jonathan. "'Radical Enlightenment': A Game-Changing Concept." In *Reassessing the Radical Enlightenment*, edited by Steffen Ducheyne, 15–47. London: Routledge, 2017.

Israel, Jonathan. "Rousseau and d'Holbach: The Revolutionary Implications of *la philosophie anti-Thérésienne*." In *Thinking with Rousseau: From Machiavelli to Schmitt*, edited by Helena Rosenblatt and Paul Schweigert, 149–74. Cambridge: Cambridge University Press, 2017.

Kiesel, Helmuth. "Aufklärung und neuer Irrationalismus in der Weimarer Republik." In *Aufklärung und Gegenaufklärung in der europäischen Literatur, Philosophie und Politik von der Antike bis zur Gegenwart*, edited by Jochen Schmidt, 497–521. Darmstadt: Wgb Academic, 1989.

Kloppenberg, James T. *Toward Democracy: The Struggle for Self-Rule in European and American Thought*. New York: Oxford University Press, 2016.

McCormick, John P. *Carl Schmitt's Critique of Liberalism: Against Politics as Technology*. Cambridge: Cambridge University Press, 1997.

McCormick, John P. "Legal Theory and the Weimar Crisis of Law and Social Change." In *Weimar Thought: A Contested Legacy*, edited by P.E. Gordon and J.P. McCormick, 55–71. Princeton, NJ: Princeton University Press, 2013.

Moreau, Pierre-François. "Adorno und Horkheimer als Spinoza-Leser." In *Aufklärungs-Kritik und Aufklärungs-Mythen: Horkheimer und Adorno in philosophiehistorischer Perspektive*, edited by Sonja Lavaert and Winfried Schröder, 113–21. Berlin: De Gruyter, 2018.

Mulsow, Martin. *Enlightenment Underground: Radical Germany, 1680–1720*. Translated by H.C. Erik Midelfort. Charlottesville, VA: University of Virginia Press, 2015.

Nuovo, Victor. *Christianity, Antiquity and Enlightenment: Interpretations of Locke*. Dordrecht: Springer, 2011.

Pelluchon, Corine. *Leo Strauss and the Crisis of Rationalism*. Albany, NY: SUNY Press, 2014.

Ringer, Fritz. *Max Weber: An Intellectual Biography*. Chicago: University of Chicago Press, 2004.

Schmitt, Carl. *Political Theology: Four Chapters on the Concept of Sovereignty*. Translated by George Schwab. Chicago: University of Chicago Press, 2007.

Smith, Steven B. *Spinoza's Book of Life*. New Haven, CT: Yale University Press, 2003.

Smith, Steven B. *Reading Leo Strauss: Politics, Philosophy, Judaism*. Chicago: University of Chicago Press, 2006.

Spinoza, Benedict de. *Theological-Political Treatise*. Edited by Jonathan Israel. Cambridge: Cambridge University Press, 2007.

Stjernfelt, Frederik. "'Radical Enlightenment': Aspects of the History of a Term." In *Reassessing the Radical Enlightenment*, edited by Steffen Ducheyne, 80–103. London: Routledge, 2017.

Strauss, Leo. *Spinoza's Critique of Religion*. Translated by E.M. Sinclair. 2nd ed. Chicago: University of Chicago Press, 1997.

Tanguay, Daniel. *Leo Strauss: An Intellectual Biography*. Translated by Christopher Nadon. New Haven, CT: Yale University Press, 2007.

van Sluis, Jacob. *Bekkeriana: Balthasar Bekker biografisch en bibliografisch*. Leeuwarden: Fryske Akademy, 1994.
Vatter, Miguel. "Strauss and Schmitt as Readers of Hobbes and Spinoza: On the Relation between Political Theology and Liberalism." *The New Centennial Review* 4, no. 3 (2004): 161–214.
Walther, Manfred. "Carl Schmitt contra Baruch Spinoza oder Vom Ende der politischen Theologie." In *Spinoza in der europäischen Geistesgeschichte*, edited by Hanna Delf, Julius H. Schoeps, and Manfred Walther, 422–42. Berlin: Edition Hentrich, 1994.
Watson, Peter. *The German Genius: Europe's Third Renaissance, the Second Scientific Revolution, and the Twentieth Century*. New York: HarperCollins, 2010.
Wertheim, David. *Salvation through Spinoza: A Study of Jewish Culture in Weimar Germany*. Leiden: Brill, 2011.
Wolin, Richard. *The Seduction of Unreason: The Intellectual Romance with Fascism from Nietzsche to Postmodernism*. Princeton, NJ: Princeton University Press, 2004.
Yelle, Robert A. "The Trouble with Transcendence: Carl Schmitt's 'Exception' as a Challenge for Religious Studies." *Method & Theory in the Study of Religion* 22, no. 2–3 (2010): 189–206.

Chapter 7

Abraham, Gary A. *Max Weber and the Jewish Question: A Study of the Social Outlook of His Sociology*. Urbana and Chicago: University of Illinois Press, 1992.
Adair-Toteff, Christopher. "Max Weber's Charismatic Prophets." *History of the Human Sciences* 27 (2014): 3–20.
Anter, Andreas. "Entzauberung der Welt und okzidentale Rationalisierung (Weber)." In *Religion und Säkularisierung: Ein interdisziplinäres Handbuch*, edited by Thomas M. Schmidt and Annette Pitschmann, 14–20. Stuttgart: J.B. Metzler, 2014.
Asad, Talal. *Formations of the Secular: Christianity, Islam, Modernity*. Stanford: Stanford University Press, 2003.
Asprem, Egil. *The Problem of Disenchantment: Scientific Naturalism and Esoteric Discourse 1900–1939*. Leiden: Brill, 2014.
Berger, Peter L. "Charisma and Religious Innovation: The Social Location of Israelite Prophecy." *American Sociological Review* 28 (1963): 940–50.
Bloch, Marc. *Les rois thaumaturges*. Paris: Armand Colin, 1961.
Blumenberg, Hans. *Arbeit am Mythos*. 2nd ed. Frankfurt am Main: Suhrkamp, 1981.
Blumenberg, Hans. *The Legitimacy of the Modern Age*. Translated by Robert M. Wallace. Cambridge, MA: MIT Press, 1983.
Bourgeaud, Philippe. "The Death of the Great Pan: The Problem of Interpretation." *History of Religions* 22, no. 3 (1983): 254–83.

Cameron, Euan. *Enchanted Europe: Superstition, Reason, and Religion, 1250–1750.* Oxford: Oxford University Press, 2010.

Carroll, Anthony. *Protestant Modernity: Weber, Secularisation, and Protestantism.* Scranton, PA: University of Scranton Press, 2007.

Casanova, José. *Public Religions in the Modern World.* Chicago: University of Chicago Press, 1994.

Clark, J.C.D. "The Re-Enchantment of the World?: Religion and Monarchy in Eighteenth-Century Europe." In *Monarchy and Religion: The Transformation of Royal Culture in Eighteenth-Century Europe,* edited by Michael Schaich, 41–75. Oxford: Oxford University Press, 2007.

Daston, Lorraine and Katharine Park. *Wonders and the Order of Nature 1150–1750.* New York: Zone Books, 1998.

Derman, Joshua. "Max Weber and Charisma: A Transatlantic Affair." *New German Critique* 113 (2011); 51–88.

Dörrfuß, Ernst Michael. *Mose in den Chronikbüchern: Garant theokratischer Zukunftserwartung.* Berlin: De Gruyter, 1994.

Ellenson, David. "Max Weber on Judaism and the Jews." In *After Emancipation: Jewish Religious Responses to Modernity,* 80–95. Cincinnati: Hebrew Union College Press, 2004.

Funkenstein, Amos. *Theology and the Scientific Imagination: From the Middle Ages to the Seventeenth Century.* Princeton, NJ: Princeton University Press, 1986.

Geertz, Clifford. "Religion as a Cultural System." In *Anthropological Approaches to the Study of Religion,* edited by Michael Banton, 1–46. New York: Tavistock, 1985.

Geertz, Hildred. "An Anthropology of Religion and Magic, I." *Journal of Interdisciplinary History* 6 (1975): 71–89.

Ghosh, Peter. *A Historian Reads Max Weber: Essays on the Protestant Ethic.* Wiesbaden: Harrassowitz, 2008.

Ghosh, Peter. *Max Weber and "The Protestant Ethic": Twin Histories.* Oxford: Oxford University Press, 2014.

Gibbon, Edward. *The Decline and Fall of the Roman Empire.* London, 1776.

Gorski, Philip S. "Historicizing the Secularization Debate: Church, State, and Society in Late Medieval and Early Modern Europe, ca. 1300 to 1700." *American Sociological Review* 65 (2000): 138–67.

Gorski, Philip S., and Ateş Altınordu, "After Secularization?," *Annual Review of Sociology* 34 (2008): 55–85.

Graf, Friedrich Wilhelm. "Max Weber und die protestantische Theologie seiner Zeit." *Zeitschrift für Religions- und Geistesgeschichte* 39, no. 2 (1987): 122–47.

Graf, Friedrich Wilhelm. "The German Theological Sources and Protestant Church Politics." In *Weber's Protestant Ethic: Origins, Evidence, Contexts,* edited by Hartmut Lehmann and Guenther Roth, 27–49. Cambridge: Cambridge University Press, 1993.

Haley, Peter. "Rudolph Sohm on Charisma." *Journal of Religion* 60 (1980): 185–97.

Harnack, Adolf. *What Is Christianity?* Translated by Thomas Bailey Saunders. New York: Harper Torchbooks, 1957.

Hobbes, Thomas. *Leviathan*. Edited by Edwin Curley. Indianapolis: Hackett Publishing Co., 1994 [1651].

Israel, Jonathan. *Radical Enlightenment: Philosophy and the Making of Modernity, 1650–1750*. Oxford: Oxford University Press, 2001.

Joas, Hans. *Die Macht des Heiligen: Eine Alternative zur Geschichte von der Entzauberung*. Berlin: Suhrkamp, 2017.

Josephson-Storm, Jason Ā. *The Myth of Disenchantment: Magic, Modernity, and the Birth of the Human Sciences*. Chicago: University of Chicago Press, 2017.

Kippenberg, Hans. *Die Entdeckung der Religionsgeschichte: Religionswissenschaft und Moderne*. Munich: C.H. Beck, 1997.

Kippenberg, Hans. "Dialektik der Entzauberung: Säkularisierung aus der Perspektive von Webers Religionssystematik." In *Alte Begriffe–Neue Probleme: Max Webers Soziologie im Lichte aktueller Problemstellungen*, edited by Thomas Schwinn and Gert Albert, 81–116. Tübingen: Mohr Siebeck, 2016.

Kroll, Thomas. "Max Webers Idealtypus der charismatischen Herrschaft und die zeitgenössische Charisma-Debatte." In *Max Webers Herrschaftssoziologie: Studien zu Entstehung und Wirkung*, edited by Edith Hanke and Wolfgang J. Mommsen, 47–72. Tübigen: Mohr Siebeck, 2001.

Laum, Bernhard. *Heiliges Geld: Eine historische Untersuchung über den sakralen Ursprung des Geldes*. Tübingen: Mohr, 1924.

Lehmann, Hartmut. *Die Entzauberung der Welt: Studien zu Themen von Max Weber*. Göttingen: Wallstein, 2009.

Liebeschutz, Hans. "Max Weber's Historical Interpretation of Judaism." *The Leo Baeck Institute Year Book* 9, no. 1 (1964).

Lowrie, Walter. *The Church and Its Organization in Primitive and Catholic Times: An Interpretation of Rudolph Sohm's Kirchenrecht*. London and Bombay: Longmans, Green, and Co., 1904.

Middleton, Conyers. *A Free Inquiry into the Miraculous Powers, Which Are Supposed to Have Subsisted in the Christian Church*. London, 1749.

Milbank, John. *Theology and Social Theory: Beyond Secular Reason*. Oxford: Blackwell, 1990.

Monod, Paul Kléber. *The Power of Kings: Monarchy and Religion in Europe, 1589–1715*. New Haven, CT: Yale University Press, 1999.

Mosheim, Johann Lorenz von. *Institutes of Ecclesiastical History*. Translated by James Murdock. London: William Tegg, 1867 [1755].

Otto, Eckart. *Max Webers Studien des Antiken Judentums: Historische Grundlegung einer Theorie der Moderne*. Tübingen: Mohr Siebeck, 2002.

Otto, Rudolf. *Gottheit und Gottheiten der Arier*. Gießen: Alfred Töpelmann, 1932.

Pocock, J.G.A. *Barbarism and Religion*. Volume 1. *The Enlightenments of Edward Gibbon, 1737–1764*. Cambridge: Cambridge University Press, 1999.

Pocock, J.G.A. "Perceptions of Modernity in Early Modern Historical Thinking." *Intellectual History Review* 17 (2007): 55–63.

Potts, John. *A History of Charisma*. New York: Palgrave Macmillan, 2009.

Preus, J. Samuel. *Explaining Religion: Criticism and Theory from Bodin to Freud*. Atlanta: Scholars Press, 1996.

Riesebrodt, Martin. "Charisma in Max Weber's Sociology of Religion." *Religion* 29, no. 1 (1999): 1–14.

Riesebrodt, Martin. "Dimensions of the *Protestant Ethic*." In *The Protestant Ethic Turns 100: Essays on the Centenary of the Weber Thesis*, edited by William H. Swatos, Jr. and Lutz Kaelber, 23–52. Boulder, CO: Paradigm Publishers, 2005.

Rousseau, Jean-Jacques. *The Basic Political Writings*. Translated by Donald A. Cress. 2nd ed. Indianapolis: Hackett Publishing, 2011.

Saler, Michael. "Modernity and Enchantment: A Historiographic Review." *The American Historical Review* 111, no. 3 (2006): 692–716.

Schaich, Michael, ed. *Monarchy and Religion: The Transformation of Royal Culture in Eighteenth-Century Europe*. Oxford: Oxford University Press, 2007.

Schluchter, Wolfgang, ed. *Max Webers Studie über das antike Judentum*. Frankfurt am Main: Suhrkamp, 1981.

Schmitt, Carl. *Roman Catholicism and Political Form*. Translated by G.L. Ulmen. Westport, CT: Greenwood Press, 1996.

Schmitt, Carl. *Political Theology: Four Chapters on the Concept of Sovereignty*. Translated by George Schwab. Chicago: University of Chicago Press, 2005.

Schmitt, Carl. *The Leviathan in the State Theory of Thomas Hobbes*. Translated by George Schwab. Chicago: University of Chicago Press, 2008.

Scribner, Robert. "The Reformation, Popular Magic, and the 'Disenchantment of the World.'" *Journal of Interdisciplinary History* 23, no. 3 (1993): 475–94.

Shaw, Jane. *Miracles in Enlightenment England*. New Haven, CT: Yale University Press, 2006.

Sheehan, Jonathan. "Enlightenment, Religion, and the Enigma of Secularization: A Review Essay." *The American Historical Review* 108 (2003): 1061–80.

Sheehan, Jonathan. "When Was Disenchantment?: History and the Secular Age." In *Varieties of Secularism in a Secular Age*, edited by Michael Warner, Jonathan VanAntwerpen, and Craig Calhoun, 217–42. Cambridge, MA: Harvard University Press, 2010.

Smith, David Norman. "Faith, Reason, and Charisma: Rudolph Sohm, Max Weber, and the Theology of Grace." *Sociological Inquiry* 68 (1998): 32–60.

Sohm, Rudolph. *Kirchenrecht*. Volume 1. *Die geschichtlichen Grundlagen*. Leipzig: Duncker & Humblot, 1892.

Sohm, Rudolph. *Kirchenrecht*. Volume 2. *Katholisches Kirchenrecht*. Munich and Leipzig: Duncker & Humblot, 1923.

Spencer, John. *A Discourse concerning Prodigies*. Cambridge, 1663.

Sprat, Thomas. *History of the Royal Society*. London, 1667.

Strake, Gerald. "The Final Phase of Divine Right Theory in England, 1688–1702." *English Historical Review* 77 (1962): 638–58.
Styers, Randall. *Making Magic: Religion, Magic, and Science in the Modern World*. New York: Oxford University Press, 2004.
Swatos, William H., Jr. "The Disenchantment of Charisma: A Weberian Assessment of Revolution in a Rationalized World." *Sociological Analysis* 42 (1981): 119–36.
Thomas, Keith. *Religion and the Decline of Magic*. New York: Charles Scribner's Sons, 1971.
Treiber, Hubert. "Anmerkungen zu Max Webers Charismakonzept." *Zeitschrift für Altorientalische und Biblische Rechtsgeschichte* 11 (2005): 195–213.
Troeltsch, Ernst. *The Social Teaching of the Christian Churches*. Translated by Olive Wyon. Chicago: University of Chicago Press, 1981 [1911].
van Bunge, Wiep. "Balthasar Bekker." In *Encyclopedia of the Enlightenment*, edited by Alan Kors, 1: 132–33. 4 vols. Oxford: Oxford University Press, 2003.
Vickers, Brian. "Analogy versus Identity: The Rejection of Occult Symbolism, 1580–1680." In *Occult and Scientific Mentalities in the Renaissance*, edited by Brian Vickers, 95–163. Cambridge: Cambridge University Press, 1984.
Voigt, Friedemann. "Das protestantische Erbe in Max Webers Vorträgen über 'Wissenschaft als Beruf' und 'Politik als Beruf.'" *Zeitschrift für Neuere Theologiegeschichte* 9, no. 2 (2002): 245–67.
Walker, D.P. "The Cessation of Miracles." In *Hermeticism and the Renaissance: Intellectual History and the Occult in Early Modern Europe*, edited by Ingrid Merkel and Allen G. Debus, 111–24. Washington, DC: Folger Books, 1988.
Walsham, Alexandra. "Miracles in Post-Reformation England." In *Signs, Wonders, Miracles: Representations of Divine Power in the Life of the Church*, edited by Kate Cooper and Jeremy Gregory, 273–306. Woodbridge: Boydell Press, 2005.
Walsham, Alexandra. "The Reformation and 'The Disenchantment of the World' Reassessed." *Historical Journal* 51, no. 2 (2008): 497–528.
Weber, Marianne. *Max Weber: Ein Lebensbild*. Tübingen: J.C.B. Mohr (Paul Siebeck), 1926.
Weber, Max. "Über einige Kategorien der verstehenden Soziologie" [1913]. In *Gesammelte Aufsätze zur Wissenschaftslehre*, edited by Johannes Winckelmann, 427–74. Tübingen: Mohr Siebeck, 1988.
Weber, Max. *Wissenschaft als Beruf*. Munich and Leipzig: Duncker & Humblot, 1919.
Weber, Max. *The Religion of India: The Sociology of Hinduism and Buddhism*. Translated by Hans H. Gerth and Don Martindale. New York: Free Press, 1958.
Weber, Max. *The Sociology of Religion*. Translated by Ephraim Fischoff. Boston: Beacon Press, 1964.
Weber, Max. *Ancient Judaism*. Translated by Hans H. Gerth and Don Martindale. New York: Free Press, 1967.
Weber, Max. *Economy and Society*. Edited by Guenther Roth and Claus Wittich. 2 volumes. Berkeley: University of California Press, 1978.

Weber, Max. "Science as a Vocation." In *From Max Weber: Essays in Sociology*, edited by Hans H. Gerth and C. Wright Mills, 129–56. London: Routledge, 1991.

Weber, Max. *The Protestant Ethic and the Spirit of Capitalism, with Other Writings on the Rise of the West*. 4th ed. Translated by Stephen Kalberg. New York: Oxford University Press, 2009.

Wellhausen, Julius. *Prolegomena to the History of Ancient Israel*. Cleveland: Meridian Books, 1957 [1878].

Winckelmann, Johannes. "Die Herkunft von Max Webers 'Entzauberungs'-Konzeption." *Kölner Zeitschrift für Soziologie und Sozialpsychologie* 32 (1980): 12–53.

Yelle, Robert A. "The Hindu Moses: Christian Polemics against Jewish Ritual and the Secularization of Hindu Law under Colonialism." *History of Religions* 49 (2009): 141–71.

Yelle, Robert A. "The Trouble with Transcendence: Carl Schmitt's 'Exception' as a Challenge for Religious Studies." *Method & Theory in the Study of Religion* 22 (2010): 189–206.

Yelle, Robert A. "Moses' Veil: Secularization as Christian Myth." In *After Secular Law*, edited by Winnifred F. Sullivan, Robert A. Yelle, and Mateo Taussig-Rubbo, 23–42. Stanford: Stanford University Press, 2011.

Yelle, Robert A. *The Language of Disenchantment: Protestant Literalism and Colonial Discourse in British India*. New York: Oxford University Press, 2013.

Yelle, Robert A. *Semiotics of Religion: Signs of the Sacred in History*. London: Bloomsbury, 2013.

Yelle, Robert A. "Imagining the Hebrew Republic: Christian Genealogies of Religious Freedom." In *Politics of Religious Freedom*, edited by Winnifred Fallers Sullivan, Elizabeth Shakman Hurd, Saba Mahmood, and Peter Danchin, 17–28. Chicago: University of Chicago Press, 2015.

Yelle, Robert A. "Protestant (An)aesthetics." In *Bloomsbury Handbook for the Cultural and Cognitive Aesthetics of Religion*, edited by Anne Koch and Katharina Wilkens, 241–51. London: Bloomsbury, 2019.

Yelle, Robert A. *Sovereignty and the Sacred: Secularism and the Political Economy of Religion*. Chicago: University of Chicago Press, 2019.

Yelle, Robert A. "From Sovereignty to Solidarity: Some Transformations in the Politics of Sacrifice from the Reformation to Robertson Smith." *History of Religions* 58 (2019): 319–46.

Chapter 8

Anidjar, Gil. "Secularism." *Critical Inquiry* 33 (2006): 52–77.

Asad, Talal. *Genealogies of Religion: Discipline and Reasons of Power in Christianity and Islam*. Baltimore: Johns Hopkins University Press, 1993.

Asad, Talal. "Religion, Nation-State, Secularism." In *Nation and Religion: Perspectives on Europe and Asia*, edited by Peter van der Veer and Hartmut Lehmann, 178–96. Princeton, NJ: Princeton University Press, 1999.

Asad, Talal. *Formations of the Secular: Christianity, Islam, Modernity*. Stanford: Stanford University Press, 2003.

Asad, Talal. "Reflections on Violence, Law, and Humanitarianism." *Critical Inquiry* 41, no. 2 (2015): 390–427.

Asad, Talal, Judith Butler, and Saba Mahmood. *Is Critique Secular?: Blasphemy, Injury, and Free Speech*. Berkeley: Townsend Center, 2009.

Bangstad, Sindre. "Contesting Secularism/s. Secularism and Islam in the Work of Talal Asad." *Anthropological Theory* 9, no. 2 (2009): 188–208.

Bergunder, Michael. "Comparison in the Maelstrom of Historicity: A Postcolonial Perspective on Comparative Religion." In *Interreligious Comparisons in Religious Studies and Theology: Comparison Revisited*, edited by P. Schmidt-Leukel and A. Nehring, 34–52. London: Bloomsbury, 2016.

Bowen, John R. "Secularism: Conceptual Genealogy or Political Dilemma?" *Comparative Studies in Society and History* 52, no. 3 (2010): 680–94.

Casanova, José. *Public Religions in the Modern World*. Chicago: University of Chicago Press, 1994.

Casanova, José. "Global Religious Trends at the Turn of the Millennium." Unpublished lecture at Max-Weber-Kolleg, University of Erfurt, Germany, July 7, 2003.

Casanova, José. "Rethinking Secularization: A Global Comparative Perspective." *The Hedgehog Review* 8, no. 1–2 (2006): 7–22.

Casanova, José. "Secularization Revisited: A Reply to Talal Asad." In *Powers of the Secular Modern: Talal Asad and His Interlocutors*, edited by David Scott and Charles Hirschkind, 12–30. Stanford: Stanford University Press, 2006.

Casanova, José. "Public Religions Revisited." In *Religion: Beyond a Concept*, edited by Hent de Vries, 101–20. New York: Fordham University Press, 2008.

Conze, Werner, Hans-Wolfgang Strätz, and Hermann Zabel. "Säkularisation, Säkularisierung." In *Geschichtliche Grundbegriffe: Historisches Lexikon zur politisch-sozialen Sprache in Deutschland*, edited by Otto Brunner, Werner Conze and Reinhart Koselleck, volume 5, 792–829. Stuttgart: Klett-Cotta, 1984.

Durkheim, Émile. *The Elementary Forms of Religious Life*. Translated by Karen E. Fields. New York: Free Press, 1995.

Eichendorff, Joseph von. "Über die Folgen von der Aufhebung der Landeshoheit der Bischöfe und der Klöster in Deutschland" [1818]. In Joseph von Eichendorff, *Historische und politische Schriften*. Historisch-kritische Ausgabe, volume 10.1, edited by Antonie Magen, 1–87. Tübingen: Max Niemeyer Verlag, 2007.

Elmessiri, Abdelwahab. "Secularism, Immanence, and Deconstruction." In *Islam and Secularism in the Middle East*, edited by John Esposito and Azzam Tamimi, 52–80. New York: New York University Press, 2000.

Enayat, Hadi. *Islam and Secularism in Post-Colonial Thought: A Cartography of Asadian Genealogies*. Cham: Springer International Publishing, 2017.

Esposito, John L. "Introduction: Islam and Secularism in the 21st Century." In *Islam and Secularism in the Middle East*, edited by John Esposito and Azzam Tamimi, 1–12. London: Hurst & Company, 2000.

Esposito, John L., and Azzam Tamimi, eds. *Islam and Secularism in the Middle East*. London: Hurst & Company, 2000.

Eßbach, Wolfgang. *Religionssoziologie 1: Glaubenskrieg und Revolution als Wiege neuer Religionen*. Munich: Wilhelm Fink, 2014.

Fester, Richard. "Die Säkularisation der Historie." *Historische Vierteljahrschrift* 11 (1908): 441–59.

Fitzgerald, Timothy. "A Critique of 'Religion' as a Cross-cultural Category." *Method & Theory in the Study of Religion* 9, no. 2 (1997): 91–110.

Foucault, Michel. "What Are the Iranians Dreaming About?" [1978]. In *Foucault and the Iranian Revolution: Gender and the Seductions of Islamism*, edited by Janet Afary and Kevin B. Anderson, 203–5. Chicago: University of Chicago Press, 2005.

Gorski, Philip. "Historicizing the Secularization Debate: Church, State, and Society in Late Medieval and Early Modern Europe, ca. 1300 to 1700." *American Sociological Review* 65, no. 1 (2000): 138–67.

Harrison, Peter. "Introduction: Narratives of Secularization." *Intellectual History Review* 27, no. 1 (2017): 1–6.

Hölscher, Lucian, ed. *Datenatlas zur religiösen Geographie im protestantischen Deutschland: Von der Mitte des 19. Jahrhunderts bis zum Zweiten Weltkrieg*. 4 volumes. Berlin and New York: De Gruyter, 2003.

Hunter, Ian. "Charles Taylor's *A Secular Age* and Secularization in Early Modern Germany." *Modern Intellectual History* 8, no. 3 (2011): 621–46.

Hunter, Ian. "Secularization: The Birth of a Modern Combat Concept." *Modern Intellectual History* 12, no. 1 (2015): 1–32.

Hurd, Elizabeth Shakman. *The Politics of Secularism in International Relations*. Princeton, NJ: Princeton University Press, 2008.

Hutten, Kurt. *Kulturbolschewismus: Eine deutsche Schicksalsfrage*. Stuttgart: Kohlhammer, 1932.

Jackson, Sherman A. "The Islamic Secular." *American Journal of Islamic Social Sciences* 34, no. 2 (2017): 1–38.

Jakobsen, Janet R., and Ann Pellegrini. "Introduction: Times Like These." In *Secularisms*, edited by Janet R. Jakobsen and Ann Pellegrini, 1–35. Durham and London: Duke University Press, 2008.

Joas, Hans. *Die Macht des Heiligen: Eine Alternative zur Geschichte von der Entzauberung*. Frankfurt am Main: Suhrkamp, 2017.

Josephson-Storm, Jason Ā. *The Myth of Disenchantment: Magic, Modernity, and the Birth of the Human Sciences*. Chicago: University of Chicago Press, 2017.

Kaiser, Jochen-Christoph. "Organisierter Atheismus im 19. Jahrhundert." In *Atheismus und religiöse Indifferenz*, edited by Christel Gärtner, Detlef Pollack, and Monika Wohlrab-Sahr, 99–127. Opladen: Leske+Budrich, 2003.

Kleine, Christoph. "Zur Universalität der Unterscheidung religiös/säkular: Eine systemtheoretische Betrachtung." In *Religionswissenschaft: Ein Studienbuch*, edited by Michael Stausberg, 65–80. Berlin: De Gruyter, 2012.

Kleine, Christoph. "Religion and the Secular in Premodern Japan from the Viewpoint of Systems Theory." *Journal of Religion in Japan* 2, no. 1 (2013): 1–34.

Knöbl, Wolfgang. *Die Kontingenz der Moderne: Wege in Europa, Asien und Amerika*. Frankfurt and New York: Campus, 2007.

Knoblauch, Hubert. *Populäre Religion: Auf dem Weg in eine spirituelle Gesellschaft*. Frankfurt am Main: Campus, 2009.

Koenig, Matthias. "How Nation-States Respond to Religious Diversity." In *International Migration and the Governance of Religious Diversity* (Queen's Policy Studies series), edited by Paul Bramadat and Matthias Koenig, 293–322. Montreal: McGill-Queen's University Press, 2009.

Kuru, Ahmet T. *Secularism and State Policies toward Religion: The United States, France, and Turkey*. Cambridge: Cambridge University Press, 2009.

Lapidus, Ira M. "The Separation of State and Religion in the Development of Early Islamic Society." *International Journal of Middle East Studies* 6 (1975): 363–85.

Lübbe, Hermann. *Säkularisierung: Geschichte eines ideenpolitischen Begriffs*. Freiburg and Munich: Alber, 1975.

Luckmann, Thomas. "Säkularisierung—ein moderner Mythos." In *Lebenswelt und Gesellschaft: Grundstrukturen und gesellschaftliche Wandlungen*, edited by Thomas Luckmann, 161–72. Paderborn: utb, 1980.

Luckmann, Thomas. "Schrumpfende Transzendenzen, expandierende Religion?" In *Wissen und Gesellschaft: Ausgewählte Aufsätze 1981–2002*, edited by Thomas Luckmann, 139–54. Konstanz: UVK, 2002.

Mahmood, Saba. "Religious Reason and Secular Affect: An Incommensurable Divide?" *Critical Inquiry* 35 (2009): 836–62.

Mahmood, Saba. *Religious Difference in the Secular Age: A Minority Report*. Princeton, NJ: Princeton University Press, 2015.

Manzoor, Parvez. "Desacralising Secularism." In *Islam and Secularism in the Middle East*, edited by John Esposito and Azzam Tamimi, 81–96. New York: New York University Press, 2000.

March, Andrew F. "Speaking about Muhammad, Speaking for Muslims." *Critical Inquiry* 37 (2011): 806–21.

March, Andrew F. "Is Critique Secular?: Poppies and Prophets." *The Immanent Frame*, March 2011: http://blogs.ssrc.org/tif/2011/03/17/poppies-and-prophets/?disp=print (last access: December 8, 2019).

March, Andrew F. "What Can the Islamic Past Teach Us about Secular Modernity?" *Political Theory* 43 (2015): 838–49.

Martin, David. "What I Really Said about Secularization." *Dialog* 46, no. 2 (2007): 139–52.

Mas, Ruth. "Why Critique?" *Method & Theory in the Study of Religion* 24 (2012): 389–407.

McLennan, Gregor. "The Postsecular Turn." *Theory, Culture, and Society* 27, no. 4 (2010): 3–20.

McLeod, Hugh. "Secular Cities?: Berlin, London and New York in the Later Nineteenth and Early Twentieth Centuries." In *Religion and Modernization: Sociologists and Historians Debate the Secularization Thesis*, edited by Steve Bruce, 59–89. Oxford: Oxford University Press, 1992.

Mufti, Aamir. "The Aura of Authenticity." *Social Text* 18, no. 3 (2000): 87–103.

Nandy, Ashis. "An Anti-Secularist Manifesto." *India International Centre Quarterly* 22, no. 1 (1995): 35–64.

Nandy, Ashis. "The Politics of Secularism and the Recovery of Religious Tolerance." In *Secularism and Its Critics*, edited by Rajeev Bhargava, 321–44. New Delhi: Oxford University Press, 1998.

Nowak, Kurt. "Staat ohne Kirche?: Überlegungen zur Entkirchlichung der evangelischen Bevölkerung im Staatsgebiet der DDR." In *Christen, Staat und Gesellschaft in der DDR*, edited by Gert Kaiser and Ewald Frie, 23–43. Frankfurt am Main: Wallstein, 1996.

Pollack, Detlef. *Säkularisierung—ein moderner Mythos? Studien zum religiösen Wandel in Deutschland*. Tübingen: Mohr Siebeck, 2003.

Rox, Barbara. *Schutz religiöser Gefühle im freiheitlichen Verfassungsstaat?* Tübingen: Mohr Siebeck, 2012.

Saar, Martin. "Genealogy and Subjectivity." *European Journal of Philosophy* 10, no. 2 (2002): 231–45.

Salvatore, Armando. "The Islamicate Adab Tradition vs. the Islamic Shari'a, from Pre-Colonial to Colonial." *Working Paper Series of the HCAS "Multiple Secularities—Beyond the West, Beyond Modernities,"* no. 3. Leipzig, March 2018.

Schulze, Reinhard. "Die Dritte Unterscheidung: Islam, Religion und Säkularität." In *Religionen—Wahrheitsansprüche—Konflikte: Theologische Perspektiven*, edited by Walter Dietrich and Wolfgang Lienemann, 147–206. Zürich: TVZ, 2000.

Scott, David and Charles Hirschkind, eds. *Powers of the Secular Modern: Talal Asad and His Interlocutors*. Stanford: Stanford University Press, 2006.

Sheehan, Jonathan. "When Was Disenchantment? History and the Secular Age." In *Varieties of Secularism in a Secular Age*, edited by Michael Warner, Jonathan VanAntwerpen, and Craig Calhoun, 217–42. Cambridge, MA: Harvard University Press, 2013.

Smith, Christian. "Introduction: Rethinking the Secularization of American Public Life." In *The Secular Revolution: Power, Interests, and Conflict in the Secularization of American Public Life*, edited by Christian Smith, 1–96. Berkeley and Los Angeles: University of California Press, 2003.

Stark, Rodney. "Secularization, R.I.P." *Sociology of Religion* 60, no. 3 (1999): 249–73.

Tamimi, Azzam. "The Origins of Arab Secularism." In *Islam and Secularism in the Middle East*, edited by John Esposito and Azzam Tamimi, 13–28. New York: New York University Press, 2000.

Tamimi, Azzam. "Admiro a los talibán: son unos valientes." *La Vanguardia*, November 8 (2001): 88.

Taylor, Charles. *A Secular Age*. Cambridge, MA: Harvard University Press, 2007.

van der Veer, Peter. *Imperial Encounters: Religion and Modernity in India and Britain*. Princeton, NJ: Princeton University Press, 2001.

Weber, Max. "Über einige Kategorien der Verstehenden Soziologie" [1913]. In *Gesammelte Aufsätze zur Wissenschaftslehre*, 403–50. Tübingen: Mohr Siebeck, 1922.

Weber, Max. *Wirtschaft und Gesellschaft*. Tübingen: Mohr Siebeck, 1985 [1922].

Weber, Max. "Die protestantische Ethik und der Geist des Kapitalismus." In *Gesammelte Aufsätze zur Religionssoziologie* I, 17–206. Tübingen: Mohr Siebeck, 1988.

Weber, Max. "Zwischenbetrachtung." In *Gesammelte Aufsätze zur Religionssoziologie* I, 536–73. Tübingen: Mohr Siebeck, 1988.

Weber, Max. *Wissenschaft als Beruf*. Nachwort von Friedrich Tenbruck. Stuttgart: Reclam, 2002.

Weidner, Daniel. "Zur Rhetorik der Säkularisierung." *Deutsche Vierteljahresschrift für Literaturwissenschaft und Geistesgeschichte* 78, no. 1 (2004): 95–132.

Weir, Todd. "Germany and the New Global History of Secularism: Questioning the Postcolonial Genealogy." *The Germanic Review: Literature, Culture, Theory* 90, no. 1 (2015): 6–20.

Wohlrab-Sahr, Monika, and Marian Burchardt. "Multiple Secularities: Towards a Cultural Sociology of Secular Modernities." *Comparative Sociology* 11, no. 6 (2012): 875–909.

Wohlrab-Sahr, Monika, and Thomas Schmidt-Lux. "Science versus Religion: The Process of Secularization in the GDR as a Specific Response to the Challenges of Modernity." In *Religion and Politics in Europe and the United States: Transnational Historical Approaches*, edited by Volker Depkat and Jürgen Martschukat, 187–218. Washington, DC and Baltimore: Johns Hopkins University Press, 2013.

Yavari, Neguin. *Advice for the Sultan: Prophetic Voices and Secular Politics in Medieval Islam*. Oxford: Oxford University Press, 2014.

Yavari, Neguin. *The Future of Iran's Past*. Cambridge: Cambridge University Press, 2017.

Yelle, Robert A. "The Hindu Moses: Christian Polemics against Jewish Ritual and the Secularization of Hindu Law under Colonialism." *History of Religions* 49 (2009): 141–71.

Yelle, Robert A. *The Language of Disenchantment: Protestant Literalism and Colonial Discourse in British India*. Oxford: Oxford University Press, 2013.

Zabel, Hermann. "Verweltlichung/Säkularisierung: Zur Geschichte einer Interpretationskategorie." PhD diss., Westphalian Wilhelms University, Münster, 1968.

Index

Abraham (biblical figure) 29, 78
absolutism 74, 75
Adorno, Theodor 87, 89, 93, 117, 123
aesthetics 44, 46, 88, 100, 185 n.64
Afro-Caribbean traditions 37
agency 44, 103, 148, 150
Ahmad, Al-e 168
alchemy 23, 25, 61
alcoholism 27
Alexander, Eben 66–7
Alice in Wonderland (Carroll) 97
alienation 19, 33, 35, 36, 42, 64, 65, 67, 83, 117
allegory 62
alternative medicine 66
alternative spirituality 66, 67, 68, 69
Altinordu, Ateş 130
Amazing Stories Quarterly 98
American Historical Association 101
analytic philosophy 91, 197 n.36
Ancient Judaism (Weber) 143
ancient theology *(prisca theologia)* 127. *See also* natural theology
angels 36, 41, 134
Angels Fear (Bateson) 24
Anidjar, Gil 3, 162–3
animism 38, 39, 45, 65, 98, 106
anthropology 55, 65, 72, 134, 155, 185 n.2
antimodernism 60
antisemitism 123. *See also* Nazism
apocalypse 15
Apostolic Age 81, 82, 136, 137, 142, 145
Apple products 65
Arnold, Matthew 102
Asad, Talal 1, 3, 8, 141, 150, 159, 160, 162–4, 170 n.3
Ascent of Man, The (TV series) 99
asceticism 10, 16, 17, 18, 19, 117, 145, 146, 149, 162
Asia 20
Asian religions 20

Asprem, Egil 1, 5–6, 23, 24, 51–69, 134
assimilation 105, 126
astrology 23, 25, 45, 47, 48
astronomy 23, 45, 53
atheism 103, 115, 125, 127
Atman (soul) 14
Atterbury, Francis 206 n.51
aura/auratisation 54, 151
authoritarianism 68, 112, 121, 123, 128, 157, 165, 166, 218 n.90
autobiografiction 100
autonomy 11, 15, 18, 20, 21, 26, 27, 28, 44, 45, 125, 161
avant-garde 89, 99
avatars 100

Barnum, Phineas Taylor 96
Bateson, Gregory 24
Bateson, Mary Catherine 24
Bauer, Bruno 120
Bayle, Pierre 127
BBC 98–9, 108
Becker, Carl 101
becoming, ontology of 35
Behrangi, Samad 168
Bekker, Balthasar 114, 133
Benjamin, Walter 91
Bentham, Jeremy 100, 197 n.37
Berger, Peter 147
Bergson, Henri 103
Bergunder, Michael 171
Beth, David 37
Betoverde Weereld, De (The World Bewitched) (Bekker) 114, 133
Beyond Good and Evil (Nietzsche) 96
Bible. *See also* New Testament
    divine authority of 115–16
    infallibility of 27
    translation of 136
bibliotherapy 100
Big Science 67–8

Bloch, Marc 136
Blumenberg, Hans 2, 26, 76-7, 101, 130, 139
Bohr, Niels 61
Bolshevism 166
Bonald, Louis 116
"Book of Mormon, The" (musical) 101
Bourdieu, Pierre 56
Bowen, John R. 161, 162
Boyer, Pascal 64
Brahman 14, 41
Breton, André 99
Breuer, Stefan 17
Bronowski, Jacob 98
brotherliness 15, 80
    ethic of 27-30
Buber, Martin 128
Buddhism 13, 14, 169, 214 n.24
Bull, Malcolm 180 n.93
bureaucracy 30
bureaucratization 26, 40, 44, 46, 47, 51, 64, 68, 88, 90, 98, 132, 141, 142
Burke, Kenneth 101

Cabbala/Cabbalism 25, 61
Calhoun, Craig 21
Calvin/Calvinism 114, 115, 117, 133, 137, 206 n.52, 207 n.58. *See also* Puritanism
Cameron, Euan 134-5
Cancellation (*Aufhebung*) 79, 84
canon law 3
capitalism 12, 26, 28, 43, 48, 55, 57, 59, 88, 111, 113, 116, 117, 130, 162
Capra, Fritjof 66
Carroll, Lewis 96-7
Carroll, Sean 101
Casanova, José 5, 8, 11, 157, 159, 160, 161
Catholicism/Catholic
    confessions 156, 158, 159, 164
    diminishing power of 153, 157-8
    legalism 141-2, 145, 153
    rise of 141-2
    ritualism 57, 83, 142, 145
    unity under 17, 35, 76, 107, 142, 153-4, 158, 165, 168
causality 35, 39, 55, 61
CERN 68
Cervantes, Miguel de 100

cessationism 7, 82. *See also* miracles, cessation of; oracles, pagan, silencing of; supersessionism, Christian
Chaos magic 102
charisma
    in ancient Israelite religion 141-6
    bearers of (charismatics) 10, 16, 21, 32, 54, 60, 66, 81, 92, 94, 135-7, 142, 144-5, 147, 156
    concept of 143, 210 n.89
    Harnack on 81-2
    and law/legal authority 143, 145, 148, 209 n.81
    rationalization of 141
    routinization of 7, 129, 132, 137, 141, 146-7
    Sohm on 2, 7, 81, 137, 142-5, 209-10 n.83, 210 n.89
    Weber's notion 34, 39-41, 52, 81, 112, 119, 132, 141-8, 184 n.45, 184 n.47, 202 n.3, 208 n.77, 210 n.89, 211 n.100
charismata 81-2, 177 n.48, 184 n.45
charismatic movements 5, 208 n.77
Charles II of England 136
Chesterton, G.K. 103, 105
China 12, 17, 38, 40-1, 45-6, 47, 49, 65, 161, 184 n.39
Christian apologetics 104, 107
Christianity
    and Christian values 123, 125
    comparative studies of 13, 152
    as myth/fiction 103-8
    primitive/early 2, 7, 12, 81-3, 137, 140-5, 207 n.67, 210 n.83, 209 n.88
Church Fathers 82, 137
Church of All Worlds 102
CIA 68
circumcision 138
Civil War, English 136
clairvoyance 32, 47
class
    leisure 5, 55-8, 60
    middle 61, 94
    petit bourgeoisie 58
    ruling 59
    structures 157
    warfare 117

Cold War 68
Coleridge, Samuel Taylor 89, 96, 102–3
colonialism 13, 135, 159–60, 163, 164, 165, 170 n.3
commodity fetishism 64–6
Communist Manifesto (Marx and Engels) 26
comparative religious studies 11, 12–13, 14, 152, 160–1
complementarity 61, 88, 91–2, 99
complementary medicine 66
Confucianism 13, 17
conscience 93, 115, 124
consciousness 15, 61, 65, 67, 79, 100
conservatism 60, 128, 130
conspicuous consumption 5–6, 55–8, 66, 68, 69
constellations 20, 91
contemplation 12, 15, 17
Cortés, Donoso 122
Cosmic Circle 33–5
cosmology 14, 61, 67, 134
Cosmos (TV series) 99
cosmotheism 24
costly signaling 56
counterculture 61, 68
counter-narratives 8, 149–71
creation 89, 104
Critique of Stammler (Weber) 25
Crucifixion 137, 139
cults 10, 15, 16, 128, 147
Cultural Bolshevism 166

Darwinism 61, 157
Daston, Lorraine 136
Davis, Erik 102
Davis, Kathleen 75
Dawkins, Richard 63, 99
decisionism 122
Decline and Fall of the Roman Empire, The (Gibbon) 140–1
deconstruction 4, 131
degeneration 142, 143, 145
de Groot, Jan Jakob Maria 185 n.62
deism 114, 119, 134, 138–9
De legibus hebraeorum (Spencer) 136
democracy, principle of 111, 119, 121–2, 124, 125, 160
demonic possession 144

demonic powers 114
demonology 41
demons 35, 36, 41, 42, 133, 134, 135, 139
De oraculis veterum ethnicorum dissertatione (Van Dale) 114
Descartes, René 121
desire 93, 95, 109
despotism 113, 128
destiny, human 112
devil 126
Dialectical Imagination, The (Jay) 99
Dialectic of Enlightenment (Horkheimer and Adorno) 87, 89
dialectics 23, 27, 29–30, 79–80, 83
Dick, Philip K. 100
Die Macht des Heiligen (Joas) 10
differentiation 5, 8, 40, 72, 75, 77, 80, 149–54, 157–9, 161, 163, 165, 168, 169–71, 203 n.10, 214 n.24, 216 n.49
Dilthey, Wilhelm 15
disbelief 95, 96
disenchanting world 6, 32, 37–49, 79, 80, 84
disenchantment
  conceptions/interpretations 5, 10, 15–21, 84, 92, 111, 129–48, 152, 174 n.8, 175 n.10
  and enchantment 6, 32–7, 87–99, 102, 109, 152
  influence of Protestantism on 2, 41, 129–48
  and re-enchantment 6, 43, 87–8
  scholarship on 1–6
  and secularization, distinction between 30, 31, 43–4, 84–5
divination 40, 45, 47, 48, 132
divine right kingship 132, 136
dogma/dogmatism 82, 104, 107, 126
double consciousness 95–6, 102, 103, 105
Doyle, Arthur Conan 97, 98
Dramatism 101
dualism 75, 125, 127, 145
Durkheim, Émile 10
Dutch society 112, 114, 133, 139

ecclesia 81, 142
Economic Ethic of the World Religions (Weber) 13

economic theory 55–6
Economy and Society (Weber) 11–15, 16, 18, 39, 132
ecstasy 16, 21, 29, 143, 144
Eichendorff, Joseph von 153, 168
Einhorn, Ignać 120
Ellenson, David 146
Elmessiri, Abdelwahab 166
embeddedness 65, 113, 119, 151, 152, 155
empiricism 12, 45, 95, 131, 155, 197 n.37
Enayat, Hadi 160
enchantment
    and disenchantment 87–8, 91–2, 102, 108–9
    fictionalism and 99–108
    and intellectual integrity 89, 90, 105–8, 109, 123
    meaning of 88
    negative 92
    positive 92
energy healing 48
Enlightenment
    Counter- 116, 117, 127
    German 153, 157–8
    and imagination 93, 100
    moderate 115–16, 125, 126
    narratives 3, 87–9, 93, 153, 158
    radical 7, 111–28, 139, 141, 201 n.45
    Reformation and 130, 138–9
    and religion 132–3, 138, 166
eons 32
epistemic overconfidence 43
equality 90, 112, 115, 124, 125
equity 125
Esalen Institute 68
Eßbach, Wolfgang 153
eschatology 15, 26, 74, 77, 79, 130, 146
esotericism 1, 5, 6, 10, 15, 24, 25, 30, 33, 37, 61, 68, 93, 127, 132
Esposito, John 165–6
essentialism 89, 160
ethic(s)
    alternative principles 178 n.51
    of brotherliness 27–30
    and capitalism 111
    of commitment 16
    of compliance/conviction 18, 20
    of conviction 178 nn.51–2
    Protestant 116–17. *See also Protestant Ethic and the Spirit of Capitalism, The* (Weber)
    of reciprocity 28, 125
    of responsibility 18, 20, 178 nn.51–2
    of ultimate ends 18, 28, 178 n.51, 181 n.106
    and values 56, 178 n.52
ethical predeterminism 43
Eucharist 134
European Court of Human Rights 167
Eusebius 82, 137, 139
evangelicalism 10, 101, 102, 106
evolution theory 63, 112
existentialism 102, 106, 107, 192 n.52
exorcism 135

faith healing 48
Faivre, Antoine 25
Fanon, Frantz 168
fantasy/*Phantasie* 91, 94, 97, 99, 101, 103, 104, 106
Fascism 112, 119, 122, 128
Feuerbach, Ludwig 120
Fichte, Johann Gottlieb 120
fictionalism 6, 87–109
    vs. fictionality 100
    and reality 107
    and religion 101–8
final judgment 25, 26, 27. *See also* eschatology
fin de siècle 33, 88, 109, 195 n.7
Fisher, Walter 101
Fontenelle, Bernard 139
force fields 91
Forman, Paul 60
form and structure 118
fortune-telling 47–8, 49
Foucault, Michel 87, 93, 160, 163, 168
Frank, Thomas 68
freedom 30, 37, 91, 101, 111, 115, 119, 121, 124, 128, 145, 162
freedom of the press 127
Free German Youth Movement 36
French National Assembly 121
French Revolution 25, 74, 128, 136, 153
frenzy 94
Freud, Sigmund 91
Freytag, Gustav Willibald 32–3
Fundamental Fysiks Group 68
fundamentalism 10, 15, 26–9, 67, 165, 166
Fundamentalism Project 26
future, conceptions of 25–7, 78, 79, 84, 92

Gallagher, Catherine 100
Game of Thrones 97
García-Alonso, Marta 124
Gaudy Night (Sayers) 106–7
Geertz, Clifford 148
Geertz, Hildred 133–4
Geist (mind) 35, 36
genealogy
 continuity/discontinuity 1, 3, 4, 8, 26, 65, 71, 72, 75–7, 84, 118, 124, 146, 154
 as critique 150–2, 163–4
 narratives/counter-narratives 146–7, 163
 origin 79, 84, 118, 129, 137–41
 retrospective construction 2, 17, 153
 theological underpinning 80–3, 129–30, 139, 148
General Will (*volonté générale*) 121–2
George, Stefan 33, 34
George I of England 206 n.52
German idealism 120
Germany 25, 37, 51, 60, 61, 74, 116–21, 124, 128, 130, 132–3, 152–3, 156–8, 161
 secularization and religious decline 157–8
Gernsback, Hugo 98
Ghosh, Peter 31, 38
ghosts 36, 64
ghouls 64
Gibbon, Edward 140–1
Gifford Lectures 53, 67
"gifts of grace" (*Gnadengaben*) 132, 137, 141, 142, 143. *See also* charisma; charismata
globalization 29
global warming 112
Glorious Revolution 136
Gnosticism 25
Gnostic Voudon 37
God. *See also* Trinity, Holy
 as Creator 107
 divine intervention 126
 divine providence 26
 immanence 17, 22
 ruach (breath/wind) of 144
 transcendence 16
God Particle, The (Lederman and Teresi) 62

Goethe, Johann Wolfgang von 120
Goldziher, Ignaz 13
Gorski, Philip S. 130
Gospel 7, 82, 129, 137–9, 142, 145, 146
Gottheit und Gottheiten der Arier (Otto) 133
"Greatest Drama Ever Staged, The" (Sayers) 107
Great Mother Goddess (Magna Mater) 33
Great War 67
Gunkel, Hermann 144

Habermas, Jürgen 11, 29–30
habitus 151, 167, 168
Hammer, Olav 65–6
Hanegraaff, Wouter 1
Harnack, Adolf 81–3
Harrison, Peter 4
healing 29, 66, 100, 135–6, 140
Hegel, Georg Wilhelm Friedrich 77, 83, 84, 103, 115, 120, 156
Heidegger, Martin 160
Heinlein, Robert 102
Heisenberg, Werner 6, 61, 91
Hemel, Ernst van den 112
Heppe, Heinrich 82
Herder, Johann Gottfried von 120
heresy/heretics 105, 115, 124, 140
hermeneutics 15
Hermeticism 25
heteronyms 100
Higgs boson 62, 68
Higher Education in America, The (Veblen) 56
Hinduism 13–14, 145
Hinneberg, Paul 13, 14
hip consumerism 68
history/historicity
 "historical concept-formation" 19, 71, 76, 77, 80, 84, 85, 156
 modernity and 74–5
 as myth 101
 periodization models 75–7
 philosophy of 1, 26, 74, 83–4, 189 n.1
 and progress 10, 15, 25–7, 71, 73–6, 78–80, 83–4, 141, 180 n.89
 time and 71–85
History of the Royal Society (Sprat) 138
Hobbes, Thomas 118, 120, 121, 122, 123, 129, 133, 136

holism 24
Holmes, Sherlock 97–8, 106
Hölscher, Lucian 25, 26, 157
Holy Alliance 116, 127
Holy Spirit 82, 105, 108, 137. *See also* gifts
    of grace; Trinity, Holy
"Homo Islamicus" 168
Homo sapiens 101
Hopkins, Anthony 101
Horkheimer, Max 87, 89, 93, 117, 123
Houdin, Robert 96
How the Hippies Saved Physics (Kaiser) 68
Hubble 68
Huet, Pierre-Daniel 127
Human, All-Too-Human (Nietzsche) 95
human potential movement 68
human rights 160, 167
Hume, David 93, 100, 115
Hunter, Ian 156–8, 159
Hurd, Elizabeth Shakman 163
Huxley, Thomas Henry 61

ideal type 87, 92
idolatry 33, 132
illiberalism 7, 111–28
imaginary world 95, 96–8, 102, 105
imagination
    in children's literature 96–7
    conceptions of 94–5, 96
    creative 89, 94, 96–8
    evolutionary perspective 196 n.21
    and fantasy 97, 99
    and fictionalism 89–90, 93, 96–8, 99–109
    historical 6, 72, 74, 75, 77, 80, 83
    legitimation of 94, 99, 102
    modernity and 94
    as a "mysterious, incalculable force"
        89, 94
    and new media 97–9, 109
    reason and 87–90, 93–6, 106
    Romanticism and 87, 88, 89, 91, 93–5,
        104–5
    traditional Western view of 94
imagined communities 99
immanence 10, 17, 22, 28, 144, 160, 166
immortality 22, 126
indeterminacy 2, 63–4
India, magic in 12, 14, 17, 21, 40–1, 145,
    151, 161, 164, 165
individualism 5, 124

industrialization 25, 27, 57, 67, 157
information technology 109
information theory 68
intellectual integrity 90, 105–8
"interactional perspective" 164, 165
Interpretation of Dreams, The (Freud) 91
interpretive sociology 17
intuition 62–4, 93, 94, 96, 97–8, 107
iPhone apps 48
iPod 65
Iranian Revolution 168
"iron cage" (*stahlhartes Gehäuse*) 6, 43, 88,
    92, 98, 109
irreducibility 61
Islam
    adab 170
    blasphemy/defamation laws 167–8
    forms of distinction and differentiation
        169–71
    fundamentalism 165–6
    Muhammad 151, 167–8
    Organization of Islamic Cooperation
        167–8
    and secularism 163, 165–71
    sharia law 170
    as a "way of life" 151
Islam and Secularism in the Middle East
    (Esposito and Tamimi) 165, 166
Islamic studies 12, 13, 150
Israel, Jonathan 2, 7, 13, 111–28, 139

Jainism 14
Jakobsen, Janet R. 161
James I of England 136, 206 n.52
Jay, Martin 99
Jeans, James 61–2
Jediism 102
Jellinek, Dora 34
Jellinek, Georg 2, 130
*Jerusalem, oder über religiöse Macht und
    Judentum* (Mendelssohn) 124
Jesus Christ 27, 83, 92, 102, 103, 104, 106,
    107, 138, 139
Jews 41, 113, 115, 123, 126, 145
Jews and Economic Life, The (Sombart) 113
Joas, Hans 10
Jordan, Pascual 61
Jordheim, Helge 76–7
Josephson-Storm, Jason 1, 5, 31–49, 54,
    134

Journal of Religion in Europe 24
Judaism 12, 13, 29, 41, 80, 83, 90, 124, 137, 143–9
Judges *(shofetim)* 143
Juergensmeyer, Mark 21
Jülicher, Adolf 82
justice 90, 101, 128

Kabbalah. *See* Cabbala/Cabbalism
Kaiser, David 68
Kant, Immanuel 93, 115, 118, 122, 156
karma 14
Kierkegaard, Søren 61
kingdom of God 26
Kippenberg, Hans 3, 5, 9–30, 132
Kirchenrecht (The Law of the Church) (Sohm) 142
Kircher, Athanasius 127
Kirlian photography 65–6
Klages, Ludwig 5, 33–7
Kleine, Christoph 169
Kloppenberg, James 124–5
Korzybski, Alfred 91
Koselleck, Reinhart 3, 6, 73–6, 85
kosher dietary prohibitions 138
Kosmic Gnosis 37
Kuenen, Abraham 144

Language of Disenchantment, The (Yelle) 129
Laum, Bernhard 130
Lawrence, Bruce 26
Lederman, Leon 62
Lehmann, Edvard 14
Lehmann, Hartmut 133
leisure class 5, 55–8, 60
Lessing, Gotthold Ephraim 120, 124
Lewis, C.S. 102–4, 108
Liberal Imagination, The (Trilling) 99
liberalism 121, 166
L'Imagination (Sartre) 99
literary genres 98, 191 n.38
Literature and Dogma (Arnold) 102
Locke, John 115–16, 125–6
logic 27, 29, 77, 85, 91, 96, 98, 119, 127, 161, 197 n.36
Lord of the Rings (Tolkien) 102
Lovecraft, H.P. 102
Löwith, Karl 3, 26, 73, 74, 76–9, 84–5

Luckács, Georg 118
Luckmann, Thomas 154–5, 159
Luhrmann, Tanya M. 102, 106
Lutheranism 114–15
Luther, Martin 2, 137, 207 n.58

MacDonald, George 103
magic
 amateur practitioners 48
 belief in 5, 36–7, 41
 and charisma 39–41
 Cosmic Circle and 33–4, 35
 decline of 133–6
 demonization of 41, 42
 and disenchantment 37–43
 early/primitive 38–40, 134
 and enchantment 32–7
 Klages and 34–6
 magical arts 40
 magic sphere 43–8
 monarchy and/Royal Touch 115, 132, 135–6
 music and 46
 and popular concepts 15
 rationality and 5, 19–20, 21, 31, 32, 36, 38, 42–8
 and religion 6, 10, 14, 15–16, 41
 Schuler and 32–4
 sorcery 64, 96, 114
 spells 35, 38, 40, 42, 92
 standardization/systematization of 46–8
 and technology 47–8
 and value spheres 44–5, 48
magicians 10, 16, 21, 40, 96
"magic if" (Stanislavski method) 101
Mahmood, Saba 167, 168
Maistre, Joseph de 116
Manhattan Project 68
March, Andrew 167, 169
Martin, David 151
Marx, Karl 43, 65, 117
Marxism 36, 118, 156, 157
materialism 90, 103, 117, 125
McLeod, Hugh 157
McNeil, William H. 101
meaning 53, 60, 73, 103
Meaning in History (Löwith) 74, 78
meaninglessness 23, 78–9, 83, 84

Meiners, Christoph 115
Mendelssohn, Moses 120, 124, 126
Mennonite Church 114
Metahistory 101
Metaphorology 101
metaphors 62, 63, 64, 72, 99, 101, 149, 160, 163
metaphysics 17, 22, 24, 43, 53–4, 61, 89, 102, 103, 104, 115, 119–21, 147, 166
method acting 101
Michelson, Albert 91
Middle Ages 123, 133, 135
Middleton, Conyers 140
Milbank, John 145
millenarianism 15, 27
Mills, C. Wright 99
Miłosz, Czesław 22
mind and matter 24
Mind of the Maker, The (Sayers) 104–5, 108
miracles
 belief in 134–5
 cessation of 7, 81–2, 120, 134–48, 177 n.48, 205–6 n.47, 207 n.58
 signs and wonders 82, 137, 179 n.68
Mirror Funnel model 6, 63
modernity/modernization
 emergence of 26, 87, 149
 and historicity 74–5
 new definition 87–8
 Protestantism and 2, 26–7, 130–2, 134, 138–9, 145–6, 149
 secularization and 151, 159
modern state 20, 29, 43, 67, 113, 115, 118–27, 153, 154, 159–61, 163, 171
monism 119
monotheism 2, 83, 90, 132, 146
Montaigne, Michel de 100, 128
moral purity 112
Morhof, Daniel Georg 127
Mosaic law (Torah) 138, 143, 212 n.124
 abrogation of 145–6
Mosheim, Johann Lorenz von 209 n.88
Mufti, Aamir 151
Mulsow, Martin 126, 127
Murder Must Advertise (Sayers) 106
music 46–7, 58, 69, 185 n.64, 212 n.124
Mysterious Universe, The (Jean) 61–2
mysticism 10, 15–21, 25, 32–4, 38, 40, 54, 61, 67, 68, 80, 128, 145

myth/mythology 3, 4, 8, 32, 54, 75, 92, 93, 101, 103, 111–18, 120, 124, 126–8, 139–41, 148, 152, 154–5, 158–9
Myth of Disenchantment, The (Josephson-Storm) 5, 32, 33, 34, 36, 42

Napoleon 116
Narrative Paradigm 101
Narratives. *See also* counter-narratives
 as concealment 154–8, 159
 as discourse 158–64
 function of 1
 romanticizing 4
 sensemaking 152–4
 sense of time 3
Narratives of Secularization (Harrison) 4
National Socialism 74
naturalism 23, 67, 127
natural philosophy 95
natural sciences 24, 57, 58, 67, 100. *See also* science
natural theology 24, 53, 55, 67. *See also* deism
natura naturans/natura naturata 121
nature, disenchantment of 22–5
Nazism 112, 121, 124
"Near Death Experience" discourse 66–7
neo-paganism 34
Neo-Platonism 93
New Age 5, 10, 15, 25, 48, 61, 66, 69, 102, 130, 155
New Age movements 10, 61
new mysticism 15
New Physics 60, 61, 91
new religious movements 18, 66, 83, 102
New Testament 137, 138, 146
Nietzsche, Friedrich 2, 33, 35, 92–6, 116–18, 125, 130, 160, 163
Ninety-Five Theses (Luther) 2
non-contradiction 91
non-simultaneity 77

occultism 32, 33, 36, 37, 39, 102, 103, 132
Oldenberg, Hermann 13, 14
Old Testament 138, 145
Olsen, Niklas 74
omen 45
online astrology portals 48
ontological homogeneity 43

oracles
  Israelite 132, 143
  pagan, silencing of 7, 114, 129, 136–9, 204 n.22, 205–6 n.47, 206 n.51, 207 n.67
orgy 16, 21
Orientalism 12–13, 40, 43, 46, 145, 162–4
Origen 82, 137
Original Sin 122
Otherkins 102
Otto, Rudolf 15, 133
Outline of Social Economics (Weber) 13

pacifism 18
paganism 32–4, 36, 114, 129, 134, 135, 137, 139, 146, 147
palm reading 47, 48
panentheism 24
pantheism 127
paranormal phenomena 37, 61. *See also* magic
parapsychology 53, 61, 67, 68
paratechnology 69
Park, Katherine 136
Parsons, Talcott 92
Passion of Christ 137, 139
Pauli, Wolfgang 61
Peace of Westphalia 153
Pellegrini, Ann 161
Pentagon 68
Pentecostalism 29
periodization 2, 71, 75–6
"perpetual world-time" 79
Pessoa, Fernando 100
phenomenology 14, 89, 97
Philosophy of "As If" (Vaihinger) 101
Plutarch 129, 137, 139
pneuma 80–3, 142, 144
Pocock, J.G.A. 138
Poetic Naturalism 101
political theology *(theologia politica)* 116, 119–28
  as subterfuge 128
Political Theology (Schmitt) 7, 118–20, 126–7
political theory 116–22, 126
Politics as a Vocation (Weber) 33
Portuguese Inquisition 111
positivism 97, 101

postcolonialism 150, 151, 213 n.7
  auratisation of the past 151
postmillenarianism/premillenarianism 27
postmodernism 131, 135, 183 n.31
power struggle 118, 143, 168
pragmatism 23, 38, 53, 57–8, 60, 76
priests/priestly ministry 10, 16, 21, 40, 41, 81, 83, 139, 143, 144–7
Problem of Disenchantment, The (Asprem) 5–6, 23, 24, 54–5, 68
progress, notions of 10, 15, 25–7, 71, 73–6, 78–80, 83–4, 141, 180 n.89
promiscuity 27
prophecy/prophets 10, 16–17, 21, 28, 41, 75, 80–3, 140–5, 147, 183 n.38
  cessation of 81–3, 129, 136–7, 140–1, 143–5, 147, 207 n.60, 209 n.88
  Muhammad 151, 167–8
prosperity gospel 29
prostitution 27
Protestant Ethic and the Spirit of Capitalism, The (Weber) 12, 13, 41, 130, 132, 162
Protestantism 2, 7, 12–14, 19, 26, 27, 41, 80, 82–4, 90, 95, 104, 111, 113, 116–17, 119, 130–51, 161–2, 166, 167. *See also* Luther, Martin; Lutheranism; Calvin/Calvinism; Puritanism; Reformation
psychedelics 68
psychics 36, 47–8, 53, 144
psychometry 32, 182 n.6
Puritanism 12, 17, 37, 41, 42, 113, 132, 134, 136, 146, 148, 212 n.124. *See also* Calvin/Calvinism

qi energy 45
quantum healing 66
quantum mechanics 55, 60, 61, 91, 196 n.14
quantum mysticism 61
quantum physics 6, 60–4, 91
quantum probability 88
Queen Anne of England 136, 206 n.52

race
  racial hierarchy 115
  and religion 168
Radical Enlightenment (Israel) 2
rapture 27

Rational and Social Foundations of Music, The (Weber) 46
rationality/rationalization
　abstract 118
　Cartesian 121
　causal 21
　formalized 44, 47
　and imagination 87–109
　instrumental reason 41, 44, 46, 48, 87, 88, 90, 98, 109, 117
　intellectual rationality/ intellectualization 9, 10, 22, 44, 46
　of magic 43–8, 84
　of modernity 89
　theory(ies) of 44, 64
　types of 44
　value spheres 44, 45
realism 43, 94
realm of the dead *(Totenreich)* 33
re-enchantment 7, 18, 42, 43, 55, 59–64, 87–8
Reformation 2, 7, 20, 41, 84, 117, 129, 132, 134–9
religion
　blasphemy/defamation laws 167–8
　and capitalism 162
　and culture 26
　decline of 151, 154–5, 162
　and democracy 125
　de-ritualization of 47, 149
　distinction and differentiation 151, 159, 165, 169–71, 203 n.10, 214 n.24
　and Enlightenment 139
　and fiction 101–5, 198 n.48
　historical concepts 191 n.37
　and monarchy 203 n.19, 206 n.52, 207 n.60
　moral 14
　natural 14
　organized 111, 113, 209 n.83
　popular concepts 14–15, 151
　post-Enlightenment beliefs 166
　and salvation 14, 29, 181 n.106
　and spirituality 155
　and tolerance 218 n.91
　Weber on 10–18, 24, 27–8, 47
Religion and the Decline of Magic (Thomas) 133
Religion in Geschichte und Gegenwart (Schiele and Zscharnack) 14–15

religious studies 3, 11, 14, 134, 150
Renaissance 53, 93, 99, 168
Restoration 116, 136
resurrection 27
Rethinking Secularism (Calhoun, et. al.) 21
revelation 7, 32, 114, 126, 127, 129, 137–41, 143, 146
Reventlow, Franziska zu 34, 36
Rickert, Heinrich 12
Rilke, Rainer Maria 32, 33
ritualism 35, 46, 48, 57, 65, 66, 83–4, 101, 129–30, 134–5, 138, 143–8, 148, 164
ritualization 65–6
Robespierre, Maximilien 112, 127, 128
robots 101
Rolfe, Frederic 100
Romanticism 2, 3, 87–95, 139, 141, 204 n.22
Rousseau, Jean-Jacques 95, 96, 121–2, 127–8
Rox, Barbara 167, 168
Royal Touch. *See under* magic
Rukeyser, Muriel 101
rule of law 121, 122

Saar, Martin 163
sacrifice 14, 27, 138, 145
Sagan, Carl 99
Said, Edward 13, 162–3
Saler, Michael 1–2, 6, 87–109, 141
salvation 10, 12, 14, 16–19, 25–30, 41–2, 66, 74, 75, 79, 82, 112, 117, 121, 124, 134, 138, 181 n.106
Salvatore, Armando 170
Sartre, Jean-Paul 99
Sayers, Dorothy L. 90, 102, 104–9
Schelling, Friedrich Wilhelm Joseph 120
Schiele, Friedrich Michael 14
Schiller, Friedrich 133
Schluchter, Wolfgang 20–1
Schmitt, Carl 7, 74–5, 116–28, 130, 136
Schrödinger, Erwin 63
Schrödinger's cat 63, 91
Schuler, Alfred 32–4, 182 n.6
science
　and art 92–3, 101
　commodification and consumerism 51–69
　and enchantment 66–9, 99

fetishization of 64–6
literature 52, 61–4, 69
nepotistic hiring practices 51–2
popularization process 61–4
prestige hierarchies 67
professionalization of 95
prospective disciplines 53
and re-enchantment 59–64, 99
and spirituality 68–9
and technological supremacy 57–8, 64–6
value-free 52
value sphere of 53–5, 185–6 n.2
Veblen's theories and 55–8
Science as a Vocation (Weber) 1, 5, 6, 9–10, 31, 37, 51–2, 77–8, 80, 88, 90, 93, 101, 131, 141
science fiction 91, 98, 101
scientific naturalism 23
Scientifiction 98
scientific world view *(wissenschaftliche Weltanschauung)* 157
Scientology 65–6
SCIO machine 66
Scribner, Robert 134, 135
scripture. *See* Bible; New Testament
Second Coming 27
Second World War 68, 104
sect 15, 127
Secular Age, A (Taylor) 4, 21–2, 141
secularism, notion 3, 21–2, 150, 160–1
secularization
    Casanova on 8, 157, 159, 161
    as combat concept 156, 157–8
    Enlightenment and 111–28
    Hunter on 156–8
    Jordheim on 76–7
    Jülicher on 82
    as myth 154–5
    narratives/counter-narratives 152–69, 189–90 n.5
    as political-theological construct 111–15
    Taylor on 214 n.15
    Weber on 9–10, 79, 149, 174 n.2
    Weir on 160
secular time. *See* temporality
SED (Socialist Union Party of Germany) 157
self-help literature 68
selfish gene 63

sexuality, Weber on 18
Shakespeare, William 100
Shamanism 25
Shariati, Ali 168
Sheehan, Jonathan 4, 139, 141
Sheldrake, Rupert 66
Shihuangdi, Emperor 45
Siebeck, Paul 12
Sieyès, Emmanuel Joseph 121
simultaneity 25, 77, 78, 139
Smith, Adam 93, 100
Social Contract (Rousseau) 122
Social Democrats 157
Social Gospel 27
social imaginaries 99
social media 51, 69
social sciences 99, 150
socio-cognitive alienation 65
Sociological Imagination, The (Mills) 99
Sohm, Rudolph 2, 7, 81, 137, 142–5, 209–10 n.83, 210 n.89
solidarity 27–30, 102
Sombart, Werner 113, 116
Sommerfeld, Arnold 61
sorcery. *See under* magic
Sorel, Georges 96
soteriology 43, 66, 131
soul 14, 22, 33, 66, 117, 126, 154
Sovereignty and the Sacred (Yelle) 129
Spanish Inquisition 111
Spencer, John 136, 138
Spinoza, Baruch 7, 112, 113, 118–27, 139
"spirit of the age" 115
spirituality 53, 61, 66–9, 99, 155, 168
spirit-world 32, 33, 41
Sprat, Thomas 138
standardization of magic 44, 46–8
Stanislavski, Konstantin 101
Star Wars 102
Stefan George Circle 5
Stevens, Wallace 89, 90
Stranger in a Strange Land (Heinlein) 102
Strauss, Leo 115–28
Stuckrad, Kocku von 23–4, 25
subcultures 58
'subtraction stories' 4
supernatural powers 24, 34, 42, 102, 108, 112, 114, 125, 126, 135, 136, 140
supersessionism, Christian 7, 80, 131, 136, 138, 139, 145–8, 212 n.124

superstition 24, 37, 41, 113–14, 125, 128, 133, 136
Surrealism 99
Swedberg, Richard 9
Swedenborg, Emanuel 33
synchrony/synchronization 72, 75, 76–7, 139, 191 n.38

Tamimi, Azzam 166
Taoism 13
Taylor, Charles 4, 21–2, 141, 152
technofetishism 65
technology
    fetishization of 64–6
    and production 67
    science and 58
teleology 44, 63, 87, 151, 191 n.38
'telesmatic' energies 4
temporality, historical time/s 71–85
Teresi, Dick 62
Terror of 1793–94 127
thaumaturgy 135–6
Theion Publishing 37
theism 103
theoretical rationality 43, 44, 47
"theory of everything" 91
Theory of the Leisure Class, The (Veblen) 56
Theosophy 25
"thing-ification" 36
Third Reich 119
Thomas, Keith 133
Thomasius, Christian 115, 125–6
thought experiment 32, 43–8, 63–4
Thousand Years' Reign 27
Three Musketeers, The (Sayers) 105
Toland, John 127
toleration 115, 125, 128, 151, 156, 165
Tolkien, Christopher 104
Tolkien, J.R.R. 102–4
Tolstoi, Leo 78
totalitarianism 119, 166
Tractatus Theologico-Politicus (Spinoza) 7, 112, 113
traditionalism, notion of 17
"tragedy of the theologian" 64
transcendence 10, 16, 19, 29, 65, 80, 101–2, 146, 153–5
translation 62, 64, 92, 136
transubstantiation 105, 134
Trein, Lorenz 6, 71–85

Trilling, Lionel 99
Trinity, Holy 105, 108
Troeltsch, Ernst 12, 181 n.105
Twin Peaks (Lynch) 97
Two Cultures (Snow) 98
Tylor, E.B. 65
Tyndall, John 61

uncertainty principle 6, 61, 91
United Nations Human Rights Council 167
United States 47, 59, 74, 128, 161–3
universalism 124, 126, 145
urbanization 67
user interfaces 65

Vaihinger, Hans 6, 101, 197 n.36
value nihilism 43
value rationality 44, 46, 47
value spheres 44–5, 48, 53–5, 88, 90, 149
VanAntwerpen, Jonathan 21
van Dale, Anthonie 114
van der Veer, Peter 164
Vane, Harriet 106–7
van Vogt, A.E. 91
Veblen, Thorstein 5, 55–60, 64, 67
virgin birth 27
virtual reality 94
volonté générale (General Will) 121–2
Voltaire 126

Wachter, Johann Georg 127
Walker, D.P. 137
Walsham, Alexandra 134, 135
wealth 55–7
Weber, Alfred 36
Weber, Marianne 11
Weber, Max. *See also specific topics*
    on art 18
    on charisma 34, 39–41, 52, 81, 112, 119, 132, 141–8, 184 n.45, 184 n.47, 202 n.3, 208 n.77, 210 n.89, 211 n.100
    on religion 10–18, 24, 27–8, 47
    on secularization 9–10, 79, 149, 174 n.2
    on sexuality 18
    and Stefan George Circle 5
Weidner, Daniel 155
Weimar period 61, 117–19, 121, 124, 128, 133

Weir, Todd 158, 160
Weizsäcker, Carl 82
Wellhausen, Julius 13, 83, 143–5, 147
Wertheim, David 124
Westoxification 168
Westworld (TV series) 101
White, Hayden 101
Wilde, Oscar 100
William III of England 136, 206 n.52
Wimsey, Lord Peter 106
witchcraft 114, 132, 135
witches 36, 41, 135
witch trials 37, 41, 42
Wittenberg 2
Wohlrab-Sahr, Monika 7–8, 130, 149–71
Wolfskehl, Karl 33, 34

"world-denial" 14, 18–19
"world-mastery" 38
World of Null-A, The (van Vogt) 91
world religions 12–13, 19
worldview 14, 17, 20, 24, 25, 61, 65, 67, 84, 90, 104, 157, 158, 165–6

Yavari, Neguin 170
Yeats, William Butler 103
Yelle, Robert 1–8, 21, 129–48, 152, 171

Zammito, John 76
zombies 64
Zoroastrianism 13
Zscharnack, Leopold 14
Zwingli, Huldrych 134

www.ingramcontent.com/pod-product-compliance
Lightning Source LLC
Chambersburg PA
CBHW072135290426
44111CB00012B/1880